Imagery

The notion of mental imagery has always had a fundamental role in the discipline of psychology. It is a function that lies at the meeting point of mind, brain, and behaviour; it also mediates and integrates perception, cognition, action and affect. In this collection of original papers by some of the leading figures in the field the intention has been to show many of the exciting and innovative developments that have been taking place in imagery research.

Peter J. Hampson is Lecturer in Psychology, in the Department of Applied Psychology, University College, Cork, Ireland.

David F. Marks is Professor of Psychology at the School of Psychology, Middlesex Polytechnic, Middlesex.

John T.E. Richardson is Reader in Psychology and Head of the Department of Human Sciences at Brunel University, Uxbridge, Middlesex.

International Library of Psychology

Imagery
Current developments

Edited by
Peter J. Hampson,
David F. Marks,
and
John T. E. Richardson

Routledge
London and New York

First published 1990 by Routledge
11 New Fetter Lane, London EC4P 4EE
29 West 35th Street, New York, NY 10001

© 1990 Peter J. Hampson, David F. Marks, and John T. E. Richardson

Typeset by LaserScript Ltd, Mitcham, Surrey
Printed and bound in Great Britain by
Biddles Ltd, Guildford and King's Lynn

British Library Cataloguing in Publication Data

Imagery: current developments. – (International library of psychology)
1. Mental images
I. Hampson, Peter J. II. Marks, David F. III. Richardson,
John T. E. (John Thomas Edwin), *1948–* IIII. Series
153.3′2

Library of Congress Cataloging in Publication Data

Imagery : current developments / edited by Peter J. Hampson,
David F. Marks, and John T. E. Richardson.
p.   cm. – (International library of psychology)
Includes bibliographical references.
1. Imagery (Psychology) I. Hampson, Peter J. II. Marks,
David F., 1945–   . III. Richardson, John T. E. IV. Series.
BF367.I4615 1990
153.3′2–dc20   89–39162
                                                          CIP

ISBN 0–415–00788–7

Contents

Contents

Figures and plates

Figures

Plates

Tables

Contributors

Susan Aylwin, Department of Applied Psychology, University College, Cork, Ireland

Alan D. Baddeley, MRC Applied Psychology Unit, 15 Chaucer Road, Cambridge CB2 2EF, United Kingdom

Maryvonne Carfantan, Centre d'Études de Psychologie Cognitive, Université de Paris-Sud, Centre Scientifique d'Orsay, 91405 Orsay Cedex, France

Michel Denis, Centre d'Études de Psychologie Cognitive, Université de Paris-Sud, Centre Scientifique d'Orsay, 91405 Orsay Cedex, France

Johannes Engelkamp, Fachrichtung Psychologie, Universität des Saarlandes, D-6600 Saarbrücken, Federal Republic of Germany

Georg Goldenberg, Neurologische Universitätsklinik, Lazarettgasse 14, A-1090 Wien, Austria

Peter J. Hampson, Department of Applied Psychology, University College, Cork, Ireland

Liam Hudson, Department of Human Sciences, Brunel University, Uxbridge, Middlesex UB8 3PH, United Kingdom

Geir Kaufmann, Department of Cognitive Psychology, University of Bergen, N-5000 Bergen-Univ., Norway

Kris N. Kirby, Department of Psychology and Social Relations, Harvard University, Cambridge, Massachusetts 02138, USA

Stephen M. Kosslyn, Department of Psychology and Social Relations, Harvard University, Cambridge, Massachusetts 02138, USA

Robert H. Logie, Department of Psychology, University of Aberdeen, Aberdeen AB9 2UB, United Kingdom

David F. Marks, School of Psychology, Middlesex Polytechnic, Queensway, Enfield, Middlesex EN3 4SF; and Department of Psychology, University College London, Gower Street, London WC1H 0AP, United Kingdom

Maryanne Martin, Department of Experimental Psychology, University of Oxford, South Parks Road, Oxford OX1 3UD, United Kingdom

Susanna Millar, Department of Experimental Psychology, University of Oxford, South Parks Road, Oxford OX1 3UD, United Kingdom

Peter E. Morris, Department of Psychology, University of Lancaster, Lancaster LA1 4YF, United Kingdom

Ivo Podreka, Neurologische Universitätsklinik, Lazarettgasse 14, A-1090 Wien, Austria

John T. E. Richardson, Department of Human Sciences, Brunel University, Uxbridge, Middlesex UB8 3PH, United Kingdom

Margarete Steiner, Neurologische Universitätsklinik, Lazarettgasse 14, A-1090 Wien, Austria

Alan Sunderland, Avon Stroke Unit, Frenchay Hospital, Bristol BS16 1LE, United Kingdom

Michael H. Van Kleeck, Department of Psychology and Social Relations, Harvard University, Cambridge, Massachusetts 02138, USA

Rachel Williams, Department of Experimental Psychology, University of Oxford, South Parks Road, Oxford OX1 3UD, United Kingdom

Hubert D. Zimmer, Fachrichtung Psychologie, Universität des Saarlandes, D-6600 Saarbrücken, Federal Republic of Germany

Preface

In assembling this collection of original papers, our intention is to provide a showcase of the many exciting and innovative developments that are currently taking place in imagery research.

The notion of mental imagery has always had a fundamental role in the discipline of psychology: as David Marks explains in his opening chapter, it is a function that lies at the meeting-point of the study of mind, brain, and behaviour. It also mediates and integrates perception, cognition, action, and affect and it is these faculties which provide the focus for many of the subsequent chapters. Stephen Kosslyn, Michael Van Kleeck, and Kris Kirby provide an account of the hypothetical mechanisms responsible for individual differences in visual imagery and visual perception which is directly motivated by our current knowledge of the neuroanatomical structures involved. Peter Hampson and Peter Morris assess the role of conscious control mechanisms in imagery and perception, while Robert Logie and Alan Baddeley consider the notion of a hypothetical 'visuo-spatial sketch-pad' within their more elaborated theory of working memory. Susanna Millar proposes that shape imagery and representation in the blind are based upon experience of using movement and feedback from active touch as symbols for shapes and spatial relations, and Johannes Engelkamp and Hubert Zimmer argue for a distinction between sensory and motor encoding based upon the differential processing of concrete nouns and action verbs. There then follow two chapters, by Geir Kaufmann and by Michel Denis and Maryvonne Carfantan, on the theoretical question of the role of mental imagery in thinking and reasoning and on the educational question as to whether more flexible forms of 'metacognition' would be promoted by formal instruction on the efficacy of imaginal strategies.

The second half of the collection considers the wider ramifications of imagery research beyond the specific domain of experimental cognitive psychology, and in particular its relevance to social, developmental, clinical, and physiological psychology. Mental imagery is often regarded as being inherently private and evanescent, but Liam Hudson takes as his object of study the patently concrete and shareable images of photography, raising fundamental issues concerning the social transaction of meaning and representation. His chapter is followed by two complementary chapters on the relationship between imagery and emotion: Susan Aylwin considers the more theoretical and experiential aspects of the study of affect and cognition, while Maryanne Martin and Rachel Williams examine its clinical and experimental aspects. Finally, we have included three contributions which are concerned in different ways with the brain mechanisms which are responsible for mental imagery. In the first of these, Georg Goldenberg, Ivo Podreka, and Margarete Steiner describe their work using computerized tomography of regional cerebral blood-flow to study the neuroanatomical localization of mental imagery in healthy volunteers. In the second, Alan Sunderland provides a critical evaluation of theories concerning the intriguing phenomenon of unilateral visual neglect in patients who have suffered damage to the right cerebral hemisphere. In the third, John Richardson considers the theoretical implications of research on imagery and memory in brain-damaged individuals.

Three points are worth making about the nature of the psychological research described in this book. First, the reader will find many profound theoretical questions discussed in the following chapters, and these go far beyond the rather narrow concern with the status of imagery as a mental representation which characterized research during the 1970s. Second, imagery is *par excellence* a topic for multidisciplinary and hence interdisciplinary research. Nearly all of the contributions to this volume are grounded in one way or another in contemporary cognitive psychology, but together they draw upon the wider conceptual and methodological perspectives of cognitive science, social science, and neuroscience. Third, imagery is equally a topic that is fostered by a multinational research effort, and roughly one-half of our contributors are based in countries outside the United Kingdom. In our choice of contributors, we have tried both to reflect and to stimulate further the growth of international collaboration in this field.

Peter J. Hampson
David F. Marks
John T. E. Richardson

July 1989

Abbreviations

ARC	Adjusted ratio of clustering
BDI	The Beck Depression Inventory
DSM-III	*Diagnostic and Statistical Manual of Mental Disorders* (3rd edn)
EEG	Electroencephalogram
EMG	Electromyogram
GAD	Generalized Anxiety Disorder
HMPAO	Tc-99-Hexamethylpropylenamineoxime
IMP	123-I-isopropylamphetamine
LTP	Long-term potentiation
MOTQ	Modes of Thought Questionnaire
PDP	Parallel distributed processing
PGO	Ponto-geniculate-occipital
rCBF	Regional cerebral blood-flow
REM	Rapid eye-movement
SPECT	Single photon emission computer tomography
SSA	Smallest space analysis
VVIQ	Vividness of Visual Imagery Questionnaire
VSSP	Visuo-spatial sketch-pad

Chapter one

On the relationship between imagery, body, and mind

David F. Marks

On the time scale of the life history, the classic topics of the psychology of thinking – problem solving, concept formation, and imagery – are not only processes to be explained: beyond that they take their places in a longer process of growth, the formation of a point of view. (Howard E. Gruber 1981)

We do not introspect; we internally reconstruct – at least in outline or in edited or dramatized or surmised version – overt intelligent performances. (William Lyons 1986)

It is obvious that a main function of the brain is to provide higher vertebrates with such mental images derived from the surrounding world. And it is customary to say that when one evokes these images, one has the picture in one's mind. Why we are unable to put all of this together is that our methods of research are apt for analysis but very poor at synthesis. (Peter W. Nathan 1987)

The microcosm of an individual mind is animated by the same principles as the macrocosm of the universe. (Keith Oatley 1985)

Imagery's renaissance in psychology has been associated with the rebirth of the study of mental processes in addition to the study of brain and behaviour. Cognitive psychology has provided a home for the study of imagery, and a number of theoretical approaches to imagery have emerged: for instance, Paivio's (1971) dual-coding theory, Shepard's (1975) internal representation concept, and Kosslyn's (1980) computer analogue model. Yet none of the current cognitive systems for handling

1

imagery has succeeded in coping with *both* the physical *and* the mental requirements of a general theory. Thus, for example, what is the function of imagery in mental and physical development? How do we explain the ability to improve physical skill using imagery rehearsal? What neurological processes and structures participate in image generation? And how do we account for the observed relationships between image content and emotional state? This chapter outlines a new approach to image theory which attempts to answer these and other questions that require analysis of images as both physiological and mental entities.

Theories of image formation have been formulated within a variety of psychological systems: psychoanalytical, behaviourist, neuropsychological, developmental, and cognitive. Each of these approaches has made significant contributions, yet substantial gaps in our understanding of imagery remain. Indeed, the fundamental question concerning the *function* of imagery remains almost completely unanswered. Some even wonder if it has a function. To be sure it has been established that imagery is useful in memory tasks of various kinds (J.T.E. Richardson 1980) and may participate in cognitive problem solving, at least in the early stages (Kaufmann 1984, Chapter 7 in this volume), and in other tasks such as mental rotation (Shepard 1975) and mental comparisons (Paivio 1978). However, imagery clearly did not evolve so that college students could demonstrate significant 'imagery effects' in psychological laboratories: something else a little more fundamental must be involved.

The reasons our understanding of that 'something else' is not more advanced are, no doubt, diverse and complex. One suspects that psychology's adoption of pure science as a model has had a lot to do with it. The latter has led to two cleavages which have had some undesirable results: first, between psychology and the humanities, where interest in the laboratory experiment has replaced an interest in the human condition; second, between cognitive psychology and other important areas such as clinical, social, and personality psychology. Experimentalists have generally been quite unwilling to accept introspective reports, and therefore an understanding of how the *subject* views an experimental task often remains a complete mystery. Yet this information can have major implications for understanding the performance one observes (Orne 1969). It is therefore unlikely that we will succeed in the task of understanding imagery's functions unless methods are developed for the analysis of image *content* in addition to the usual kind of performance variables. A further problem with many existing paradigms is that there are important components to imagery other than the purely cognitive, two of these being the affective and the somatic. In Ahsen's (1984) statement the affective component is equated with the somatic response. However, it may be more helpful to consider the somatic component separately from the affective since enactive imagery typically produces a variety of muscular effects which can be measured using electromyographical techniques (for example, Jacobsen 1931) even though the affect associated with the activity, which may be as mundane as imagining throwing a ball, is fairly slight or strong when imagining throwing a grenade.

It is not my intention here to rehearse the well-known arguments and counterarguments of the body-mind problem. I would simply like to place in full focus the fact that there is what Honderich (1987) calls an *intimate relationship* between mind and body and, more specifically, between mind and brain. Talking at the most general level, it can be readily agreed that there is a co-occurrence of mental episodes and physical events and that '*there is a certain sort of explanation* of the co-occurrence . . . *in terms of the related events themselves*' (ibid.: 448, original emphasis). The closest form of intimacy is union or identity and the current approach leans in that direction. As far as imagery is concerned there can be no question of a very intimate relationship to neural and bodily events, as we shall see later.

It will be helpful to begin with a set of observations which an adequate theory of imagery should be able to explain. In order to achieve this I will describe an experience which, somewhat conveniently, occurred during the period when this chapter was being written. I awoke one morning at about the usual time from a restful sleep. Immediately upon opening my eyes I 'saw' an after-image of a paragraph of printed text. The image was quite assuredly text because the shape of the letters and their grouping into words, spread across a dozen or so lines, were quite distinct. Somewhat curiously, though, I could not actually read the text because it appeared to be inverted from left to right as though one was looking through a transparent screen with fairly small lettering on it. The letters were also blurred or 'rounded off' at the edges making them even more difficult to read. Also, as I moved my eyes the paragraph of text moved with my eye movements and as I looked at the wall and the ceiling the size of the image altered, apparently following Emmert's Law. The image was completely absorbing and although it was in one way exciting and joyful, paradoxically it somehow seemed 'natural' and almost 'ordinary'. Yet I had never experienced such an after-image before. Presumably the inducing image must have been a dream or hypnopompic image. It was probably the latter because I could not recall a dream and the image was quite stable. It seemed to last about 60–90 seconds, but I could not be certain of its duration. It lacked vivid colour, the letters appearing to be almost black against a pale reddish-orange ground. Logically, if this were an after-image, there had to be an inducing image, and therefore the example implies an interesting double-image. Although quite rare, after-images of images are not unknown in the literature. Barber (1959), for example, reported that some subjects could produce such after-images to imagined colours. Other reports have been published by Weiskrantz (1950) and Oswald (1957).

This example can be used as a benchmark for the following proposals for an adequate theory of imagery:

(1) Mental imagery is generated by top–down processes. In most cases imagery occurs in the absence of changing sensory input and so bottom–up processes are irrelevant because they have nothing to operate on. In some instances, perceptual images may be combined with mental images and in these cases bottom–up and top–down perceptual processes operate in coalition with top–down imaging processes.

(2) Mental imagery is produced by a computational system which allows the 'point of view' and/or the image to be shifted or rotated. In such transformations the image structure remains unaffected. In the example, the text had apparently been rotated 180 degrees. This characteristic provides structural invariance.

(3) Mental imagery is capable of producing and preserving fine detail through 'high-resolution graphics'.

(4) Mental imagery *may* be associated with perceptual activity such as eye movements or other search behaviours, both overt and covert.

(5) Mental imagery produces physical effects in the body which can include the sensory systems, such as the ocular effects of the example. The formation of an after-image requires photochemical changes in the retinae.

(6) Mental imagery is often associated with various kinds of affect.

Other goals for an adequate theory are:

(7) Ideally the theory should form part of a general, systematic approach to mental theory.
(8) The theory should, if possible, aid understanding of practical applications in clinical, health, sports, and other applied settings.
(9) An account should be provided of imagery's role in creativity and altered states of consciousness.
(10) The theory should attempt to provide an account of image content.

This introductory chapter makes some tentative stabs at a general theory of imagery. First, I examine the function of imagery in relation to schemata, perceptual theory, affect, and action. I then consider the role of mental models in image generation. The third section outlines proposals for the neurological basis of imagery and its somatic components and suggests some of the implications of individual differences.

Imagery and the activity cycle: perception, action, and affect

New perceptual theory

Imagery is usually understood to be a quasi-perceptual experience which shares at least some of its generating processes with perception (Shepard 1975; Finke 1980; Kosslyn 1987; see also Chapters 2 and 3 in this volume). Before we can be sure of such equivalences, however, we need to consider possible perceptual mechanisms and only then decide which of them, if any, imagery shares. There are several illustrious competitors for a theory of perception ranging from the Helmholzian theory of unconscious inference, Gregory's (1966) hypothesis-testing approach, Bartlett-type schemata (Bartlett 1932), Piaget-type schemata (Piaget 1952), and Gibson's (1966) ecological optics. Neisser (1976), Turvey (1977), and Weimer (1977) suggest a coalitional style of organization in which perceptual processes are inextricably mixed with the action system so that perceiving something either leads to, or affords, some corresponding activity. Neisser's 'perceptual cycle' consists of a schema, exploration, and information interlinked by perceptual activity and sensory feedback to the schema. Neisser adapted perceptual cycle theory to provide an account of imagery in which the schema is activated in the absence of the object to be seen, leading to an unfulfilled expectancy. This theory is problematic on a number of grounds (Hampson and Morris 1978): one can certainly anticipate objects without imagery and image without any sense of surprise. It also fails as a theory of perception because it ignores a crucial property in which perceptual schemata and action schemata (other than purely perceptual activity) are interrelated:

> Suppose I am making a stroke in a quick game, such as tennis or cricket. How I make the stroke depends on the relating of certain new experiences, most of them visual experiences, and to my posture, or balance of posture, at the moment. The latter, the balance of postures, is the result of a whole series of earlier movements, in which the last movement before the stroke is played has a predominant function. When I make the stroke I do not, as a matter of fact, produce something absolutely new, and I never really repeat something old. The stroke is literally manufactured out of the living visual and postural 'schemata' of the moment and their interrelations.
>
> (Bartlett 1932: 201–2)

Perceiving and imaging are not merely processes of identification brought about by looking and listening but active performances in which specific intentions, purposes, and actions need to be fulfilled. In part, this is the distinction between 'seeing what' and 'seeing as' (Wittgenstein 1953). What something is seen *as* has implications for immediate and longer-term action. This is problematic for theories in which perception and action are not functionally linked. If I am feeling thirsty in the desert and I see a reflection as a lake I will move as rapidly as possible towards it feeling hopeful and encouraged. If I see it as a mirage I will try to ignore it and continue slowly on my way feeling discouraged. *Note that this example includes an affective component which is absent from all of the above-mentioned theories of perception.* Affect is in fact a characteristic of all types of activity and not just that of a carefully selected example. We therefore have arrived at what might be termed an 'activity cycle' (see Figure 1.1).

Imagery occurs when the schema of the cycle is activated by a top-down process in the absence of both a real-world object and overt activity. In this case a quasi-perceptual experience occurs within the appropriate but covertly excited activity cycle. The image will therefore

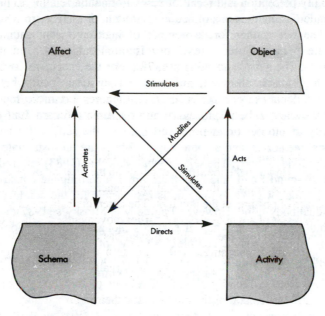

Figure 1.1 The activity cycle

contain affective and somatic elements associated with quasi-perceptual experience. The experimental and clinical evidence for the affective and somatic components of imagery is very strong (Aylwin 1985; Martin 1986; see Chapters 10 and 11 in this volume) and I shall outline further evidence of these components later in this chapter. When the schema and activity occur in the absence of the object, we are playing, pretending, or miming (see Chapter 6 in this volume). Imagery thus provides a crucible for the understanding of body-mind relationships both within and between individuals. Its basic function appears to be that of *mental simulation*: the capacity to rehearse actions and activities, and to explore the possible outcomes of these in the real world. Imagery therefore functions in all areas of mental and physical life where adaptation and change are necessary or where there is a need better to understand existing states of affairs.

Schemata can reach high levels of complexity and perhaps one of the most significant is the 'self-schema' which contains unconscious mental knowledge about the self from which one can construct various personal memories in the form of images: 'This self-schema then comes to modify perception and recall of new information relating to the self and underlies many forms of action relating to the self' (Brewer 1986: 31). The self is therefore a number of high-level schemata which activate personal memories, autobiographical facts, and action schemata. The activity cycle is usually under the executive control of such high-level schemata, although dissociations occur between different domains of experience and action so that more than one activity cycle can be in process at any one time (Hilgard 1986). The integrity of the person is preserved because the self, self-schemata, personal memories, and autobiographical facts are all instantiated in a single individual body. The self, or what McKellar (1983) referred to as 'the body-mind I call "me"', is therefore a superordinate construct or agency which we like to imagine is responsible for the conduct of an individual body-mind. However, I agree with Minsky's (1987) 'society of mind' approach in which a person's thought, will, decisions, and actions emerge from a complex 'society' of processes. This latter concept is related to the 'BOSS' model of consciousness reviewed in Chapter 3 of this volume by Hampson and Morris.

The schema concept and its transformations

The schema concept can be traced back in one form or another to Kant. Its first appearance in the twentieth century was Head's (1920) concept of a postural model of the body against which perceptual inputs could be referred. Bartlett's (1932) definition of the 'schema' was similar to Head's except that the schema was now seen as primarily an organization of responses rather than sensory impressions (see Oldfield and Zangwill 1942) and Bartlett elaborated the schema concept by applying it to a general theory of memory: 'an active organization of past reactions, or of past experiences, which must always be supposed to be operating in any well-adapted organic response' (Bartlett 1932: 201). Already suffering from vagueness, Bartlett's ideas on schemata become quite difficult to comprehend when we learn how an organism must acquire a capacity to 'turn round upon its own "schemata" and to construct them afresh' (ibid.: 206). This mysterious process apparently occurs as consciousness's most prominent function. Piaget's (1952) use of 'schema' has also been problematic and difficult to understand in a clear and consistent manner.

The concept resurfaced in the 1970s (for example, Bobrow and Norman 1975; Rumelhart 1975) together with a number of related ideas such as Minsky's (1975) 'frames' and Schank and Abelson's (1977) 'scripts', and it has recently been translated by Rumelhart *et al.* (1986) into the theoretical framework of parallel distributed processing (PDP). As McClelland *et al.* (1986) point out, many events do not easily fit into a particular schema or script but require a special intersection or connectivity between two or more different schemata sometimes of a quite diverse nature. If images really are the excitation of schemata in the activity cycle, as suggested above, then we must find a mechanism for generating the kind of novel and bizarre imagery which so often occurs in dreams, the hypnagogic state, and in the successful use of mnemonic techniques. Clearly, existing schemata must be combined in new and interesting ways and how this happens is never clear in traditional schema theory. PDP models assume that psychological processes are instantiated in large networks of interconnected units in which the strength of the connections varies in systematic and lawful ways. The neurological substrate is readily visualized as large systems of neuronal networks of the kind described originally by McCulloch and Pitts (1943) and Hebb (1949). I shall return to the neurological basis for the PDP approach in a later section, but it should be noted immediately that PDP uses a brain metaphor instead of a computer metaphor for its models of mental processes.

It would be an easy but mistaken inference that PDP and schema approaches to mental theory are incompatible. While schema theory is essentially symbolist and top–down, PDP theory is connectionist and bottom–up. However, it is clearly the case that top–down and bottom–up procedures must actually meet somewhere in the middle, assuming, that is, that both kinds of procedures are necessary. Schemata can be viewed as organizations of large networks of interconnected units which interpret the input from the environment and generate appropriate outputs. A detailed discussion of the PDP approach to schemata can be found in Rumelhart *et al.* (1986).

A schema theory of emotion has been described by Mandler (1984) in which the intensity of emotion depends upon the degree of incongruity between external events and what is expected (see Figure 1.2). I would extend Mandler's approach to allow for the possibility of high positive affect in certain skilful productions when there is a perfect match between the performer's schema and his/her performance, as in figure skating, football, or playing the piano. In these activities aesthetic appreciation depends upon the 'right' mix of surprise and expectation on the perceiver's part but of perfectly activated schemata in the performer.

9

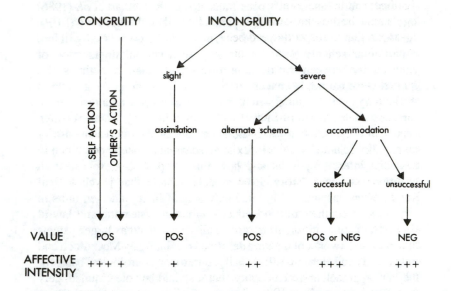

Figure 1.2 A modification of Mandler's (1984) schema theory of emotion. The degree of affective intensity and its positive or negative tone depends upon the level of incongruity between events and the current schema and how the discrepancy is dealt with using 'assimilation' or 'accommodation'. In contrast with Mandler's theory, *congruity* between action schemata and events can also produce positive affect (for example, in producing successful performances of a skill).

A parallel, distributed approach seems necessary for such performances because purely serial computations would be too slow.

Imagery and mental models

The problem defined

Mental models are constructed, dynamic representations of systems or aspects of the physical and social worlds. They include the schemata which participate in the activity cycle described above. The processes by which such high-level representations are generated have been discussed in several areas of psychology: cognitive, developmental, social, and psychoanalytical. One of the most challenging features of psychological research – and a characteristic of any science – is that the significant structures are hidden from direct experience. In psychology's case the most important processes are unconscious. Not only does this mean that introspective and behavioural techniques, necessary and informative though they are, can only give direct information on mental products, but our theoretical constructs can only ever be examined by the most indirect means. No matter how 'hard' the data may appear on methodological grounds, whether physiological, behavioural, or cognitive, a large leap of faith is necessary in relating the data to the hypothetical operations which underlie them. As a consequence it is not easy to find a single, universally agreed paradigm for psychological research. At present we have a variety of research programmes with supporters and antagonists in the vein of Lakatos (1974) rather than Kuhn (1970).

Clearly, mental imagery of all kinds must be the product of more abstract, higher-level structures which provide the top–down computations to generate particular images. How imagery can best be conceptualized in relation to such higher-level processes has been the subject of fairly heated but unproductive debate (Pylyshyn 1973; Anderson 1978; Kosslyn 1981). Broadly speaking the world seems to be divided into 'iconophiles' and 'iconophobes' (Dennett 1978), the former of which are certainly overrepresented in the present volume. My prediction is that iconophiles will typically have scores on the Vividness of Visual Imagery Questionnaire (VVIQ) in the range 32–95, indicating relatively vivid visual imagery, while iconophobes occupy the region 97–160 with unvivid or non-existent waking imagery. A further division into camps occurs in relation to cognitivists vs. clinicians. This division corresponds to 'pure' vs. applied research and to theory vs. practice. In the next two sections illustrative approaches of each kind are outlined. What emerges from an examination of both areas is a surprisingly consistent interpretation of psychologically significant events in terms of 'mental models'.

The term 'mental model' appears to have been coined by Peter McKellar in his classic text *Imagination and Thinking* (1957). The glossary of this work defines 'mental model' as:

> A more explicit or implicit analogy (simile or metaphor) applied to other subject matter for the purposes of thought or communication. (For example, simile type: the mind is like an iceberg – the major part of it beneath the surface, i.e. unconscious).

It is difficult to think of a significant question in theoretical psychology which does not depend in one way or another on the existence (or not) of mental models. The investigation of mental imagery is certainly no exception.

Cognitive approaches

In his short but insightful book *The Nature of Explanation*, Craik (1943) defined a 'model' thus:

> By a model we thus mean any physical or chemical system which has a similar relation-structure to that of the processes it imitates. By 'relation-structure' I do not mean some obscure non-physical entity that attends the model, but the fact that it is a physical working model which works in the same way as the processes it parallels.

Craik's definition leads quite naturally to the functionalist doctrine that one can understand mind without bothering with the physiological 'hardware' or 'wetware' that instantiates it, one of the fundamental precepts of the computer metaphor in cognitive science (see, for example, Neisser 1967; Johnson-Laird 1983). On the other hand, why not consider the known properties of neuronal networks as necessary constraints on the computational procedures?

In discussing the problem of understanding text, George Miller (1979) differentiates between 'images' and 'semantic models'. Describing his introspections upon reading a passage by Thoreau, Miller (ibid.: 203) notes the gradual generation of 'a sort of mental picture to which I added details as I encountered successive phrases and sentences'. In addition to the construction of images, Miller proposed a second, selective procedure which generates 'a collection of possible states of affairs that correspond to the written passage only with respect to their shared features, but which differ from one another in all other respects' (ibid.: 206). The latter Miller calls 'semantic models'. Semantic models are clearly more abstract than memory images because they are a set of all possible, but as yet unimagined, images. Miller suggests that an author uses a semantic model to select true descriptive sentences while the reader reverses this and uses the true descriptive sentence to select a model. Miller proposes that image generation and model building both take place while reading descriptive text.

Johnson-Laird (1983) suggests three kinds of representations: propositions, mental models, and images. As we are assuming in the current chapter: 'images correspond to *views* of models: as a result either of perception or imagination, they represent the perceptible features of the corresponding real-world objects' (ibid.: 157). Consequently, while propositions are more abstract or indeterminate than models, models are more abstract or indeterminate than images. This can be illustrated by these three cases:

(A) Proposition: 'There are two objects, one beside the other, one smaller than the other.'

(B) Mental Model: Smaller   Larger
                      object   object

(C) Image:

B is more determinate than A because it specifies that the smaller object is on the left, while C is more determinate than B because it specifies that the objects are cubes. However it should be noted that

(D) Image:

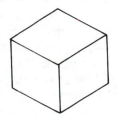

is also consistent with B, allowing for a 180–degree alteration in the point of view. The point of view can be altered in two ways: first, by using a mental transformation of the object which includes three kinds of rigid motion and three kinds of translation (Shepard and Cooper 1982); and second, by the direct regeneration of the image from another viewpoint.

While propositions clearly have the advantage of economy, models have the advantage of operationalizing what Craik termed the *relation-structure*. Images enable mental exploration of that relation-structure from as many different points of view as are necessary *to understand what it is that is being represented*. Understanding is the perception of the relation-structure within models – a process which can be greatly facilitated with the production of images.

Clinical approaches

Mental models within clinical psychology and psychiatry are rarely referred to explicitly. The closest to this is Bowlby's attachment theory. Bowlby (1969) uses the term 'internal working model' to describe how individuals build mental models of themselves and significant others within the social world in which events are perceived and interpreted. A key feature is the knowledge of one's attachment figures or primary care-givers, when and where they are found, and how they may be expected to respond when called upon for help or nurturance. Primary models of oneself, one's care-givers, and the reciprocity between the two, appear to be formed quite automatically early in life rather in the manner of the imprinting process described by ethologists. Attachment patterns established in infancy play a potent role in social interactions throughout life, operating as a kind of 'blueprint' for the patterning of one's personality, especially in relation to care-giving, intimacy, separation, and loss.

Infants seem to develop their capacity to regard a person as a persisting if not permanent object by around the age of six months. At sixteen months infants seem genuinely to mourn the loss of a parent when she or he is absent for the first time over a period of days. Bowlby's (ibid.) evidence, and also Piaget's (1954), suggests that by this age the infant can recall images of the missing parent. Bowlby (1980) cites a case reported by Furman (1974) of how a two-year-old boy, Clive, recalled an absent father and mourned his loss:

Clive's mother helped him it was thought successfully, to understand that his father would not return. Thereafter for several weeks Clive spent much time repeating the daily play activities which he had enjoyed with his father; and he also insisted, over and over, on taking the walks he had taken with his father, stopping at the stores where his father had shopped and recalling specific items.

Attachment theory assumes that independent models are formed of each significant relationship and also that multiple models may be formed of the same parent which tend to vary in dominance and in their image clarity. Images are the conscious products of internal working models. It is possible to elicit parental images for both research and clinical purposes using Ahsen's (1972) Eidetic Parents Test. The subject is asked to compare and contrast various qualities of his or her parental images projected in a number of standard situations (for example, subjects try to visualize their two parents standing in front of them). Subjects who report parental images which are vague, distant, mutilated, or unstable are more likely to show signs of psychopathology in their interpersonal and family relationships (ibid.).

In the formation of a self-concept or image there is the complementary concept of 'other' and the necessary formation of an adequate theory of mind. A theory of mind provides a mental model of another's beliefs, hopes, and desires so that the other's behaviour can be sensibly understood. The ability to empathize rests upon a mental model of what it would be like 'to be in another's shoes', to experience the world from the other's point of view. Similar positions, with reference to consciousness and introspection respectively, have been argued by Humphrey (1983) and Lyons (1986). It has been suggested that a child's theory of mind normally develops between the ages of three and four, but that in the case of autistic children, who have particular problems with pretend play, the ability to model or theorize other minds is problematic (Leslie 1987). It should be noted that the concept of empathy has also been applied to the theory of aesthetics in which 'Aesthetic pleasure is an enjoyment of *our own* activity *in* an object' (Gregory 1987: 221, original emphasis).

To summarize the argument thus far, mental models are an important category of schemata for representing activities, events, objects, persons, the self, states of affairs in general, and their various diverse interrelationships. Images allow conscious exploration of modelled relation-structures from various points of view. The cognitive scientist tends to view imagery as a potentially useful strategy for remembering or problem solving, while the clinician tends to view imagery as a diagnostically and therapeutically valuable procedure. In both cases, images are seen as aids to understanding through the concrete representation of models. Mental models and imagery have many significant applications in education, literature, science, art, and design, and it is in these areas, as in the clinical applications, that the affective and multimodal nature of imagery becomes most evident.

Anthropomorphic epistemology

Sayeki (1987) proposes that anthropomorphism, often derided as a 'primitive' or 'unscientific' way of thinking, is an important heuristic technique for adults and scientists:

> We consider that the development of scientific knowledge is not the replacement of primitive thought like anthropomorphism by the more 'rationalistic' thought such as formal reasoning, but, instead, the sophistication of the anthropomorphic understandings which are underlying our tacit knowledge of the world.
>
> (ibid.: 52)

'Anthropomorphism' is defined by Sayeki as a way of 'seeing' other beings or objects and interpreting their behaviour in terms of *kobitos* ('little people' in Japanese). Kobitos are imaginary beings who are dispatched by the self to examine or mimic a particular object or person.

Kobitos have bodies who see, touch, smell, and feel emotion, perceiving and experiencing the world as a whole rather than as a composite stimulus. Kobitos can conduct active examinations of the world by observing an object from different points of view and by performing intentional activities on the environment to 'see what happens'. The basic activities of kobitos are assumed by Sayeki to consist of mimicking, acting, and monitoring. 'Big' kobitos integrate and co-ordinate the activities of 'little' kobitos whose activities are constrained by the current mental model of the phenomena being explored. Sayeki's kobitos provide a beautiful model of the process of mental modelling itself and Sayeki has successfully applied the kobito procedure in helping children to understand and solve mathematical and other kinds of problems.

The role of affect in kobito exploration has been discussed by Miyazaki (1987) in relation to traditional Japanese poetry. The principle of 'Kibtu–Chinsi' in which the poet expresses feelings by depicting things can be traced back to the eighth century with the Manyoushu:

> With her
> No night of love is mine tonight
> On the field of withered pampas grass
> The moon is sinking behind Urano.

The poem communicates the poet's feelings indirectly via the description of the scenery from a particular point of view. The reader is also inclined to imagine the scene from the poet's point of view and in so doing experiences similar feelings:

> It seems that the knowledge about the feeling is closely connected to the knowledge about the appearance of the things in the readers' knowledge structure, and the relation makes it possible for them to grasp the feeling by generating the appearance.
>
> (ibid.: 65)

Miyazaki's theory is supported by T. S. Eliot's suggestion that 'The only way of expressing emotion in the form of art is by finding an "objective correlative"; in other words, a set of objects, a situation, a chain of events which shall be the formula of that particular emotion' (Eliot 1966). Conway and Bekerian (1987) have demonstrated experimentally the existence of emotional networks in which particular emotions are strongly associated with situations in the manner suggested by Miyazaki and Eliot.

The cultural origins of behaviours and experiences which correlate socially with particular situations and contexts were described by Vygotsky (1978). Private events are interpreted in particular ways according to cultural models. The private events become public property when they are verbally reported and these in turn shape public models. Harré (1983) refers to this process as 'Vygotsky's cycle' (see Figure 1.3). Oatley (1985) uses a programming metaphor for the processes through which cultural theories of 'self' are socially constructed in the individual.

Models in science

Kuhn's (1970) analysis of paradigms in science sees science as an accretion of accepted facts explained within a single theoretical

17

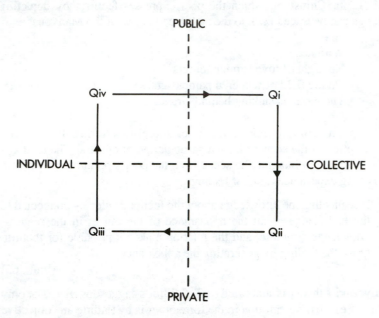

Figure 1.3 'Vygotsky's cycle' (adapted from Harré 1983)

framework agreed upon by the majority. The paradigm changes following the discovery of anomalous or difficult phenomena. A paradigm is, therefore, a shared point of view or mental model which is only given up when serious difficulties place excessive strain on the plausibility of the particular point of view. Within creative scientists mental models change more easily, perhaps even intentionally.

Gruber's (1981) study of Charles Darwin provides an analysis of the changing points of view which finally led to Darwin's theory of evolution. Darwin's image of the 'Tree of Nature' appeared in 1837 one year after the five year voyage of the Beagle (1831–6) and was a clear representation of the principle of divergence between species. The principle of selection, however, was associated with a quite different mental model and a different associated image. Darwin saw the local natural forces producing a selection as a kind of wedging process in which 'the struggle for existence' is likened to 'ten thousand sharp wedges packed close together, splitting the surface of nature' (ibid.: 118). Although Darwin himself attributed his idea of natural selection to his reading of Malthus' *Essay on Population* in 1838, Gruber points out that the idea was already present in his notebooks before he read Malthus. It took several further years before Darwin published *On the Origin of Species* (1859). 'Eureka' experiences seemingly require considerable preparation and incubation before the final illumination (Wallas 1926).

Scientific models and discoveries are highly analogous to the revelations of self-models which occur in therapy. In both science and therapy discoveries are made when new links are forged between previously separate or dissociated areas of knowledge: the unvivid becomes vivid (Ahsen 1985). Many investigators of the creative process have talked about discovery and invention in terms of the often sudden availability to consciousness of material which was hitherto 'hidden' or missing from overall awareness. Henri Poincaré (1924) assumed that the unconscious selects among various combinations of ideas and chooses the conclusion which is the most beautiful. Galton (1883) described the ante-chamber to consciousness and Freud (1917/1963) the pre-conscious and unconscious, and William James (1890) and then Wallas (1926) spoke of 'fringe consciousness'. Albert Einstein (1921/1979) noted that full consciousness is a limiting case which can never be fully accomplished while the usual case consists of a certain 'narrowness of consciousness'. Many of these authors have used the visual system as a mental model for their analysis of consciousness showing a characteristic bias towards a visual and/or spatial frame of reference in talking about a multi-modal experiential world. Einstein, Faraday, and Rutherford all emphasized that the most significant part of their thinking was non-verbal. In a letter to Jacques Hadamard (1945) Einstein wrote:

> The physical entities which seem to serve as elements in thought are certain signs and more or less clear images which can be voluntarily reproduced and combined .... The ... elements are, in my case, of visual and some muscular type. Conventional words or other signs have to be sought for laboriously only in a secondary stage.

Using his imagery, Einstein conducted several brilliant *Gedanken-experiments*. It was Einstein's strongly held view that imagistic thinking can liberate one from slavish habits and routines which tend to reify constructs when they are really matters of only temporary convenience.

The 'Eureka' experiences of the scientist and self-discovery in therapy are parallel experiences as they are based upon similar mechanisms. In both cases it is necessary to take a so-called 'detached' view of the

19

social or physical worlds and to revise one's mental models in some kind of 'dissociated' way. This is the explanation for the observation of the greatest scientists that although newly discovered laws are invariably expressed abstractly, their genesis is imagistic. The role of imagery in artistic and literary endeavours is well documented (see, for example, Lindauer 1983). In the final analysis, art, literature, music, science, and life are all products of human consciousness within which creative mental models and their associated imagery form essential building-blocks.

'Imago' : the perfect idea

Davies and Talbot (1987) report their data on how Royal Designers for Industry (RDI) experience their most creative ideas. In-depth interviews were conducted with 35 RDI in the UK with particular reference to their experience of *the* idea, the idea that is 'known' to be perfect or completely 'right'. A number of phenomena, similar to those in mystical experience, were reported: (1) oneness (people and things coming together with a sense of wholeness or unity); (2) transcendence of self; (3) experience of paradox; (4) certainty; (5) deeply positive, pleasant, ecstatic feelings; (6) beyond analysis; (7) a sense of something ultimate or universal; (8) a sense of something sacred; (9) synthesis and harmony; (10) effortlessness; (11) suddenness; (12) obviousness; (13) originality; and finally (14) ineffability (*sic*). Davies and Talbot summarize their data on the creative experience with the term 'imago', a state of consciousness in which there is an experience of a final, perfect form.

The PDP approach to mental models

The flow diagram in Figure 1.1 representing the activity cycle can be readily translated into the concepts of PDP. To do this we need to explain what actually goes on inside the schema and affect boxes. These two mental boxes are actually combined into one 'schema-affective' system of interconnected units which provides an interpretation network. The interpretation network deals with events and activities in the real world. However, it also contains models of the real world which take as an input possible but, as yet, imaginary activities, and produces an interpretation of what would happen if these activities were actually carried out. Thus, we have a system for generating the imaginary outcomes of imaginary activities in a model of the world. Such a system has some extremely useful functions: it can carry out mental simulations, learn through mental practice, hold imaginary conversations, reason, and think (Rumelhart *et al.* 1986).

To consider the example of mental practice in more detail, if a gymnast mentally repeats a perfect performance of a skill over and over, the schema for the movement pattern will become better tuned to the particular kinaesthetic and temporal patterning required by the successful performance. Enactive imagery of an excellent performance can therefore have a better effect on the skill schema than that achieved by actual performance. This follows from the fact that actual performance is imperfect and therefore the schema is never able to become perfectly tuned. This is associated with a demotivating emotion of failure and disappointment. An imagined perfect performance actually improves the schema in the desired direction and it is strongly reinforced by the motivating emotions of success and joy. This theory therefore explains the excellent results which are obtained with imagery practice (Feltz and Landers 1983), especially among subjects who can produce vivid imagery. Some possible *disadvantages* of vivid imagery will be described later in this chapter.

Imagery, brain, and body

Neurological mechanisms

Neuropsychological research supports the view that imagery provides a fundamental system for representing the external world, or what we fondly term 'reality'. The neuropsychological theory of Hebb (1949, 1980) is a useful starting-point for reviewing much of the relevant research. Hebb suggested that imagery and thought are the activity of a neural holding mechanism which he termed the 'cell-assembly'. Hebb developed this idea after seeing Lorente de Nó's (1938) description of neural networks which contained closed loops or re-entrant paths.

Figure 1.4 gives an example of how these reverberatory circuits might operate. A single fibre from outside the system excites four neurons, A, B, C, and D. A excites B, which re-excites A, as well as exciting E. E re-excites B directly and also indirectly via E', and so on. Two of the four neurons send their axons out of the system so that the internal activity will have effects elsewhere. When an input enters the system, instead of being transmitted immediately on to a motor path, or

21

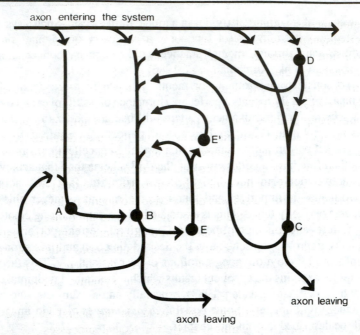

axon entering the system

D

E'

A B

E C

axon leaving

axon leaving

Figure 1.4 A simple Hebbian reverberatory circuit (adapted from Hebb 1980). A fibre from outside the system excites four neurons, A, B, C, and D. A excites B, which re-excites A as well as exciting E. E re-excites B directly and also indirectly via E'. Two neurons send axons to produce effects outside the system.

extinguishing itself, the signal can be held long after the original sensory stimulation has ceased. Such cortical holding activity can be set off centrally and so a cell-assembly originally activated by perceptual activity can later be re-activated through its connection with other cortical assemblies. No sensory inputs are necessary for the central 'perceptual' cell-assemblies to set off a train of thought. Thus, we have a neural mechanism for a simple kind of schema. Of course, such reverberatory circuits could be massive in size as any neurone can be connected to as many as 10,000 others and so schemata could easily entail the activity of millions, or perhaps billions of units.

A major postulate in Hebb's theory was the assumption that the interconnectivity of neurons can be strengthened. This strengthening was assumed by Hebb to occur whenever a synapse was active at the time the postsynaptic neuron discharges. Synaptic strengthening provides a neural basis for association. If several inputs to a cell occur simultaneously, they will be sufficient to activate the cell and all the active synapses will be strengthened. Later on, each of those input cells will find it easier to fire the target cell and may do so without the existence of the other associated inputs. When Hebb's theory was proposed in 1949, it was impossible to test for technical reasons. Eventually, in the 1970s, Bliss and Lomo (1973) were able to show that long-lasting changes could be produced in the strength of synapses in the brain of adult mammals. The technique they used delivered a pulse of electricity to a neural pathway and the magnitude of the response in the area where the pathway projects was recorded. Once a baseline had been established for the evoked response due to the test pulse, a high frequency train of pulses was delivered to the neural pathway. The test pulses were then repeated at some later time and the evoked response was again recorded. Bliss and Lomo discovered that long-lasting increases in excitability occurred in the hippocampus following pulse trains in the perforant path, and they termed this phenomenon 'long-term potentiation' (LTP). It provided the synaptic strengthening mechanism postulated by Hebb.

A fundamental similarity surely exists in the neural mechanisms underlying imagery, learning, and other mental processes. Learning represents the associating together of sensory inputs with one another, with schemata, activities, and affect, while imagery represents the activity of neural networks when excited by associated sensory processes or schemata. LTP provides the neural mechanism for all processes which rely on increased connectivity of large numbers of units.

Memory, imagination, hypnagogic imagery and even eidetic imagery all result from the triggering of the relevant associative schemata. Even dream imagery must result from associations formed in everyday waking reality, but precisely how this happens has never been clear. Crick and Mitchison (1983) have proposed a new theory of dream sleep which does away with much of the mystery:

> The cortical system ... can be regarded as a network of inter-connected cells which can support a great variety of modes of mutual excitation. Such a system is likely to be subject to unwanted or 'parasitic' modes of behaviour, which arise as it is disturbed either by the growth of the brain or by modifications produced by experience. We propose that such modes are detected and suppressed by a special mechanism which operates during REM sleep and has

the character of an active process which is, loosely speaking, the opposite of learning.

(ibid.: 111)

Crick and Mitchison call this process 'reverse learning' or 'unlearning'. During cortical growth and alteration as a result of experience, Crick and Mitchison have predicted that a number of undesirable or 'parasitic' modes of activity would be expected to occur in complex neural networks which are being 'wired' together. As associations are acquired in various cell-assemblies, the information is not necessarily stored in a highly specific location for each particular item. Information is distributed over many synapses and is therefore robust in that it won't be lost if a small number of synapses are deleted or added. Information is also superimposed as a given synapse may be involved in several different schemata-networks.

A well-formed cell-assembly can be trained so that a given input will produce an appropriate output. Certain properties of a well-formed cell-assembly are described by Crick and Mitchison (1983) as follows: first, *completion*: the memory is content addressable; given part of the input, it can produce the whole of the output; and second, *classification*: given an input which is related to several of a cell-assembly's associations, an output can be produced which combines the common features of its input.

One problem with such neural networks, Crick and Mitchison argue, is their ability to become overloaded when an attempt is made to store too many different patterns or if there is too much overlap. Such overloading leads to poor performance which can take any of the following forms:

(1) the network may produce too many far-fetched or bizarre associations or fantasies;
(2) the network may tend to produce the same perseverative state regardless of the specific input – it becomes 'obsessed';
(3) networks which contain feedback loops may respond to inappropriate signal levels which normally should elicit no response. The system as a whole 'hallucinates'.

How has evolution coped with these apparently inevitable dysfunctions of growing, complex neural networks? How are bizarre fantasy, obsession, and hallucination successfully avoided in the normal waking state? Crick and Mitchison suggest that the system would require the following actions: first, major inputs and outputs should be switched off so the system is largely cut off from outside influence; and second, random activation from inside should then be switched on to weaken the synapses which are becoming falsely strengthened purely because of this overloading. REM (rapid eye-movement) sleep has these very characteristics. The cortex is periodically but widely stimulated by the brain stem by PGO (ponto-geniculate-occipital) spikes. Hobson and McCarley (1977), following Jouvet (1962), suggest that PGO waves cause the REMs themselves and also dreams.

In Crick and Mitchison's theory, PGO spikes are assumed to weaken the synapses that tend to be involved in the temporary effects of growth and new experience, the causes of the undesired modes of activity. Hence, dreams have the opposite effect to learning: we dream in order to forget. Hopfield *et al.* (1983) report evidence from neural modelling that false memories produced in growing neural networks can indeed be successfully suppressed by an unlearning mechanism such as that described by Crick and Mitchison. Although Crick and Mitchison's unlearning theory is highly speculative, it is compatible with a large amount of empirical data:

(1) it explains the observation of the large amount of REM-sleep found in young, developing animals;
(2) it explains the hallucinatory nature of dreams;
(3) it explains why we seldom remember dreams; and
(4) it explains the relationship which exists between brain size and REM time: the larger and neuronally more complex the neocortex, the greater the amount of REM sleep.

Crick and Mitchison suggest that without REMs and the dreams that are generated by PGO spikes, evolution could not have produced such a highly successful neocortex. A breakdown of the reverse learning mechanism would produce the phenomena of hallucinations, delusions, and obsessions, which happen to be some of the major symptoms of schizophrenia.

Localization and individual differences revisited

In the light of recent investigations employing brain-imaging pro-cedures, the brain appears to consist of a large set of intercon-nected networks which become co-activated in various combinations according to task demands and the subject's (or brain's) strategy for meeting them. As Roland (1984) has pointed out, 'the brain organises its own activity'. As an illustration of this principle consider the observation from measures of regional blood flow during visual processing of a total of nineteen different activated areas in the left hemisphere and another nineteen areas in the right hemisphere (Roland 1982, 1984). Several regions occur in the pre-frontal areas, particularly on the right side. These results are consistent with the activity cycle of Figure 1.1 in which perception entails not only sensory processing, but a readiness to act. According to our theory, imagery and imagination also entail implicit activity.

The starting-point for the experiment to be reported was a series of reports on EEG (electroencephalogram) topographical analysis of higher cortical functions. In this technique EEG activity is recorded from a large number of electrodes distributed across the scalp. Spectral analysis is performed using the fast Fourier transform on the digitized waveforms after removal of all artifact-containing epochs. The resulting power spectra are averaged within specific frequency bands and values at many thousands of points across the scalp between the electrodes are estimated by mathematical interpolation. The resulting maps provide a picture of brain electrical activity which can be studied as a function of alterations in the subject's mental activity. Non-invasiveness, speed of operation, and the ability to investigate the normal brain are three major advantages of this brain-imaging technique. Low resolution in the resulting maps is the major disadvantage. The EEG alpha rhythm (8–13Hz) is of particular interest in studies with awake subjects. By subtracting the activity pattern for an imagery task from that obtained for a resting baseline, the effect of uncontrolled variables such as arousal level can be eliminated. In a recent study, Marks et al. (1988) obtained EEG maps from four vivid imagers and four non-vivid imagers. Subjects were selected from a sample of 100 students who had completed the VVIQ (Marks 1973). Needle electrodes were attached to twelve locations: Fp1, Fp2, F7, F8, C3, C4, T5, T6, O1, O2, Fz, and Pz. Subjects lay in a supine position with their eyes closed and blindfolded. EEGs were recorded in two main conditions which were alternated with periods of rest: first, visual imagery: the sixteen items from the VVIQ, imaged in groups of four; and second, calculation: continuous serial subtraction of sevens. Each trial lasted one minute, with four trials of imagery and four of calculation. As no motor responses were required, and all artefact-containing epochs were eliminated, any intergroup or intertask differences cannot be attributed to differing efferent activity (cf. Gevins et al. 1979).

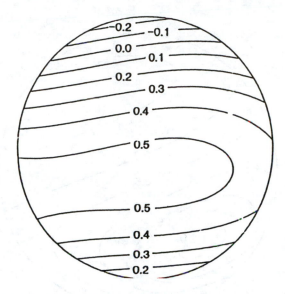

Figure 1.5 Alpha attenuation map for vivid imagers. The upper part of the map represents the frontal region. The isopotential contours represent average imagery attenuation values, relative to baseline, in microvolts.

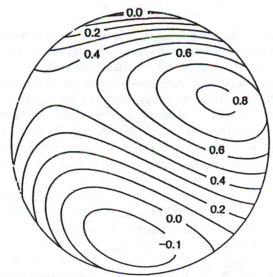

Figure 1.6 Alpha attenuation map for non-vivid imagers.

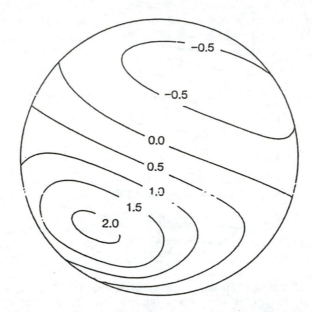

Figure 1.7 *t*-value map for differences between vivid and non-vivid imagers.

Figure 1.5 displays the imagery map for vivid imagers, which is almost perfectly symmetrical and shows widespread cortical activation in frontal, temporal, and parietal cortex. These data provide clear disconfirmation of the hypothesis which makes imagery a specialization of the right hemisphere. Among non-vivid imagers (Figure 1.6) there is a right-hemisphere focus, and this appears in the prefrontal area, an area which until recently has been poorly understood. Figure 1.7 shows the *t*-value map in which statistically significant differences in brain activation occur in the left parieto-occipital cortex. Vivid images produce more activation in the posterior portion of the left hemisphere. This finding is supported by the data obtained by Goldenberg and his colleagues (see Chapter 12 of this volume) using the SPECT imaging technique, and by the results of clinical investigations (Farah 1984; see Chapter 14 by Richardson in this volume).

Our EEG findings are further supported by a more direct brain-imaging technique, PET. Mazziotta *et al.* (1982) observed the brain's response to the Seashore tonal memory test. This test consists of tone sequence pairs, each containing between three and five tones differing only in frequency. A post-test interview revealed that three of the eight subjects had used visual imagery to accomplish the task (for instance, by visualizing a frequency histogram or an image of the notes on the musical scale), while others reported no particular strategy (three subjects) or stated that they had mentally 'resung' the tone sequence (two subjects). Activation maps for the visualizing and non-visualizing subjects were quite different, showing left temporal and right frontal asymmetries, respectively, although the cortical activation for the visualizing subjects was essentially symmetrical, as we found in our EEG study.

One of the most interesting findings is the observed activation of an area of prefrontal cortex during visual imagery. This finding is consistent with recent investigations of metabolic measurements of the working frontal cortex in humans (Roland 1984). It is supported by anatomical investigation of the frontal association cortex in primates (Goldman-Rakic and Schwartz 1982). Roland (1984: 435) concluded that 'one or more prefrontal areas participate in any structured treatment of information by the brain in the awake state'.

Our EEG mapping in subjects with vivid and non-vivid imagery and the relevant PET data suggest that visual images are generated and accessed in a system consisting of three 'modules' or large 'insulated' networks which can participate in both serial and parallel processing:

(1) An image-compiling network (IC) in the right frontal lobe which computes and composes the image from elements retrieved in memory. This module has the same function with respect to image production as Broca's area has for speech, and it is indicated by significant alpha-attenuation in the right frontal region in both imagery groups.

(2) A long-term memory file (IF) containing elements of the visual appearance of objects. This network is located in the occipital and parietal regions, and is indicated by alpha-attenuation in these regions among both groups.

(3) An image read-out network (IR) in the left temporo-parietal area which enables conscious monitoring of the image, sets the initial formulation, provides checks and comparisons, and allows inspection of the final product. This is indicated by the significantly higher amount of alpha-attenuation which occurs in this region in the group of vivid imagers (see Figure 1.7).

This brain model is obviously only a preliminary sketch. Almost certainly there are other important sub-cortical structures which remain invisible to the EEG topographic technique, such as the thalamus, amygdala, and limbic system (LeDoux 1984; Nelson-Burford 1987). Also, the modules described will ultimately require subdivision into more compact and specific sub-modular units which remain undetected in the coarse grain of co-activating structures detectable by the EEG. Kosslyn (1987) has suggested what functions some of these subsystems may perform (see also Chapter 2 by Kosslyn *et al.* in this volume). However, this brain model provides a first tentative step towards specifying some of the cortical structures involved in image generation in the normal brain. It takes us beyond the simplistic notion of considering the brain functionally as consisting of a left hemisphere and a right hemisphere. Different regions of both hemispheres contribute in different ways to the production of mental performances including sensory, motor, and association pathways. Such a brain model is incompatible with theories of imagery which define images as the epiphenomenal products of a propositional system (Pylyshyn 1973) or as copies of sensory events (Haber 1979).

There appear to be large individual differences in the access of the read-out module (IR) in the left temporoparietal region to the image-compiling module (IC) in the right frontal region. These differences are apparent in the subjects' image vividness reports and their EEG maps. It seems probable that interhemispheric transfer involves the thalamus and limbic system in addition to the corpus callosum and anterior commissure. LeDoux (1984) suggests that the participation of such sub-cortical systems should provide a 'neurologically inherited gap' in the image generating system, *shielding consciousness from certain affective processes.* The access of the IR module to the IC module, whether by cortical or sub-cortical routes, seems to be greater in vivid imagers, at least in the waking state. Variations in such access are apparent in different biological states such as lowered arousal, relaxation, drowsiness, or sleep, or the higher arousal of emotional and drug-induced states, or as a function of image structure or content. The fact that patients with left-hemisphere damage tend to lose their ability to image (Farah 1984) could result from the destruction of the IR module, or from a 'disconnection syndrome' in which the IR or IF modules are disconnected from the module in the right prefrontal area.

Conscious inspection of images accessed in the IR system is associated with a variety of somatic responses. These are similar in kind to, but of lesser intensity than, responses produced during perception of the corresponding events. These somatic responses are theoretically and practically significant. A. Richardson (1984) provides an account of how the theoretical links between imaged stimuli and physiological responses can be strengthened. The EEG study previously described provides evidence of the first kind of link, an isomorphic relationship between the attribute of image vividness and a corresponding change in activity of the neurological substrate. Kunzendorf (1984) provides experimental confirmation of a second kind of link, between currently experienced imagery and the physiological activity that accompanies it. Vivid imagers' electroretinograms appear to be altered as a function of imaginally induced colour-specific responses, an ability which is correlated with voluntary control of local skin temperature, and autonomic control of heart rate. Research by Molteno (1982) on heart-rate changes during emotional imagery supports the studies presented by A. Richardson and Kunzendorf. The heart-rate increases of vivid imagers show a U-shaped function of increased affect, whether positive (happiness) or negative (fear). Non-vivid imagers' cardiac responses were significantly lower, especially for the negative emotions. This leads to the hypothesis that non-vivid imagery may serve an adaptive function by providing immunity (or what LeDoux calls 'shielding') against the deleterious physical effects of stress.

Some support for this hypothesis was obtained by Baird (1984) in an investigation of distress and suffering in cancer patients. A significant correlation was obtained between the patients' scores on the Creative Imagination Scale (Wilson and Barber 1978) and their level of distress. Those who suffered the most symptoms had the higher imagination scores. Vivid imagery appears to be a two-edged sword, with benefits in some domains and costs in others. There is now a huge quantity of research on the physiological and psychosomatic consequences of individual differences in imagery (see Sheikh and Kunzendorf 1984 for a review). The intimate relationship between body and mind has many consequences for individual health and imagery appears to be a significant mediator of many health-related body-mind events. The implications of the relationship between imagery, body, and mind for the health of the individual have yet to be fully explored, but there seem to be many exciting possibilities. The potential role of imagery in the mediation of the immune response, frequently cited as being sensitive to stress, depression, and anxiety, is of particular current interest and might well have implications for the psychological management of AIDS-related diseases and other viral conditions. The literature reviewed by Sheikh and Kunzendorf (ibid.) has shown imagery effects in the following somatic variables: heart rate, electrodermal activity, voluntary muscles, blood flow, blood chemistry, and ocular effects. It is also the case that imagery participates in many kinds of therapeutic procedures (for example, behaviour therapy, cognitive therapy, psychotherapy, hypnosis, meditation, and yoga; see Chapter 11 by Martin and Williams in this volume).

Image content and affect are often associated in a simple and direct fashion. In Ahsen's (1972) Eidetic Parents Test a wide range of affective responses are evoked simply by imagining one's parents performing various activities, and in a manner reminiscent of reports of Gassner and Mesmer, physical symptoms can be produced or eliminated using so-called 'mental' imagery. In a case reported by Marks and McKellar (1982) a female client was able to relax what she experienced as her 'angry red' muscles of her shoulder and neck regions by imagining that they had changed from red into blue, a colour associated with the other, more relaxed parts of her body. Such direct links between image content and psychosomatic processes warrants controlled investigation. The inability to form images and express emotion, or alexythymia (Kruck and Sheikh 1986), has been shown to correlate with a variety of psycho-somatic symptoms, and imagery training procedures such as those investigated by A. Richardson and Patterson (1986) may well prove helpful in such cases. In cases where dysfunctional images are too vivid, as suggested by Baird's (1984) study of cancer patients, techniques should be developed for channelling the imagery into more positive and health-promoting directions.

Schema-affective networks are strengthened through activity cycles in which performances are tried and succeed or fail. Mental models are the schemata which enable interpretations and predictions to be made about the external world and other minds. Images provide concrete quasi-perceptual representations of models from various points of view. Because of their intimate relationship, the physical and mental components of imagery manifest many simple and direct relationships. Individual differences in conscious availability of images depend upon the connectivity between units for production and read-out. Imagery enables a person to rehearse potential activities in the environment and to explore the world mentally from different points of view. Ultimately the value of the image depends upon the quality of the underlying model and the point of view which prevails.

Conclusions

Since the work of Rosenblatt (1962) on perceptrons there has been a growing realization that symbolic representation requires both serial and parallel processes. It is difficult to see, given what is known about brain organization, how a brain model can be constructed without both modules and networks: there are networks of modules and networks within modules. Minsky (1987) describes this as 'The Society of Mind' in which a large number of components operate on problems of relatively small scale. One of the well-known implications is that higher-level systems which control the smaller distributed subsystems provide inputs and receive outputs without knowing how either are actually produced.

Mental models and schemata are the essential building-blocks of physical and mental activity. Both kinds of activity are generated in a cycle of performance which includes the initiating schema, action, objects, affects, and feedback of various kinds. Imagery is schematic activation in the absence of overt actions and physical objects.

References

Ahsen, A. (1972) *Eidetic Parents Test and Analysis*, New York: Brandon House.
   (1984) 'ISM: the triple code model for imagery and psychophysiology', *Journal of Mental Imagery* 8: 1–41.
   (1985) 'Unvividness paradox', *Journal of Mental Imagery* 9(3): 1–18.
Anderson, J. R. (1978) 'Arguments concerning representations for mental imagery', *Psychological Review* 85: 249–77.
Aylwin, S. (1985) *Structure in Thought and Feeling*, London: Methuen.
Baird, J. (1984) *'Imagination, Disease, and Distress'*, unpublished MA dissertation, University of Otago, Dunedin.
Barber, T. X. (1959) 'The after-images of "hallucinated" and "imagined" colors', *Journal of Abnormal and Social Psychology* 59: 136–9.
Bartlett, F. C. (1932) *Remembering*, London: Cambridge University Press.
Bliss, T. V. P., and Lomo, T. (1973) 'Long-lasting potentiation of synaptic transmission in the dentate area of the anaesthetized rabbit following stimulation of the perforant path', *Journal of Physiology* 232: 331–56.
Bobrow, D. G., and Norman, D. A. (1975) 'Some principles of memory schemata', in D. G. Bobrow and A. Collins (eds) *Representation and Understanding*, New York: Academic Press.
Bowlby, J. (1969) *Attachment and Loss*, vol. 1, *Attachment*, London: Hogarth Press.
   (1980) *Attachment and Loss*, vol. 3, *Loss, Sadness and Depression*, London: Hogarth Press.

Brewer, W. F. (1986) 'What is autobiographical memory?' in D. C. Rubin (ed.) *Autobiographical Memory*, London: Cambridge University Press.

Conway, M. A., and Bekerian, D. A. (1987) 'Situational knowledge and emotions', *Cognition and Emotion* 1: 145–91.

Craik, K. (1943) *The Nature of Explanation*, London: Cambridge University Press.

Crick, F., and Mitchison, G. (1983) 'The function of dream sleep', *Nature* 304: 111–14.

Davies, R., and Talbot, R. J. (1987) 'Experiencing ideas: identity, insight and the imago', *Design Studies* 8: 17–25.

Dennett, D. C. (1978) *Brainstorms*, Hassocks: Harvester Press.

Einstein, A. (1921/1979) 'Geometry and experience', lecture delivered to the Prussian Academy of Sciences, reprinted in A. P. French (ed.), *Einstein: A Centenary Volume*, London: Heinemann.

Eliot, T. S. (1966) *Selected Essays*, London: Faber.

Farah, M. J. (1984) 'The neurological basis of mental imagery: a componential analysis', *Cognition* 18: 245–72.

Feltz, D. L., and Landers, D. M. (1983) 'The effects of mental practice on motor skill learning and performance: a meta-analysis', *Journal of Sports Psychology* 5: 25–57.

Finke, R. A. (1980) 'Levels of equivalence in imagery and perception', *Psychological Review* 87: 113–32.

Freud, S. (1917/1963) 'Introductory lectures on psychoanalysis, Part III', in J. Strachey (ed.) *Standard Edition of the Complete Psychological Works of Sigmund Freud*, vol. 15, London: Hogarth Press.

Furman, E. (1974) *A Child's Parent Dies: Studies in Childhood Bereavement*, New Haven, CT: Yale University Press.

Galton, F. (1883) *Inquiries in Human Faculty and its Development*, London: Macmillan.

Gevins, A. S., Zeitlin, G. M., Doyle, J. C., Yingling, C. D., Schaffer, R. E., Callaway, E., and Yeager, C. L. (1979) 'Electroencephalogram correlates of higher cortical functions', *Science* 203: 665–8.

Gibson, J. J. (1966) *The Senses Considered as Perceptual Systems*, Boston, MA: Houghton Mifflin.

Goldman-Rakic, P. S., and Schwartz, M. L. (1982) 'Interdigitation of contralateral and ipsilateral columnar projections to frontal association cortex in primates', *Science* 216: 755–7.

Gregory, R. L. (1966) *Eye and Brain*, London: Duckworth.
—— (ed.) (1987) *The Oxford Companion to the Mind*, London: Oxford University Press.

Gruber, H. E. (1981) *Darwin on Man*, Chicago, IL: University of Chicago Press.

Haber, R. N. (1979) 'Twenty years of haunting eidetic imagery: where's the ghost?', *The Behavioral and Brain Sciences* 2: 583–630.

Hadamard, J. (1945) *The Psychology of Invention in the Mathematical Field*, Princeton, NJ: Princeton University Press.

Hampson, P. J., and Morris, P. E. (1978) 'Unfulfilled expectations: a criticism of Neisser's theory of imagery', *Cognition* 6: 79–85.

Harré, R. (1983) *Personal Being*, Oxford: Blackwell.

Head, H. (1920) *Studies in Neurology*, vol. II, London: Hodder and Stoughton.

Hebb, D. O. (1949) *The Organization of Behavior*, New York: Wiley. (1980) *Essay on Mind*, Hillsdale, NJ: Erlbaum.

Hilgard, E. R. (1986) *Divided Consciousness: Multiple Controls in Human Thought and Action*, New York: Wiley.

Hobson, J. A., and McCarley, R. W. (1977) 'The brain as a dream state generator: an activator synthesis hypothesis of the dream process', *American Journal of Psychiatry* 134: 1335–48.

Honderich, T. (1987) 'Mind, brain and self-conscious mind', in C. Blakemore and S. Greenfield (eds) *Mindwaves*, Oxford: Blackwell.

Hopfield, J. J., Feinstein, D. I., and Palmer, R. G. (1983) '"Unlearning" has a stabilizing effect in collective memories', *Nature* 304: 158–9.

Humphrey, N. (1983) *Consciousness Regained*, Oxford, Pergamon.

Jacobsen, E. (1931) 'Variation of specific muscles contracting during imagination', *American Journal of Physiology* 96: 115–21.

James, W. (1890) *Principles of Psychology*, New York: Holt, Rinehart & Winston.

Johnson-Laird, P. N. (1983) *Mental Models*, London: Cambridge University Press.

Jouvet, M. (1962) 'Recherches sur les structures nerveuses et les mecanisms responsables des differentes phases du sommeil physiologique', *Archives of Italian Biology* 100: 125–206.

Kaufmann, G. (1984) 'Mental imagery and problem solving', in A. Sheikh (ed.) *International Review of Mental Imagery*, vol. 1, New York: Human Sciences Press.

Kosslyn, S. M. (1980) *Image and Mind*, Cambridge, MA: Harvard University Press.

(1981) 'The medium and the message in mental imagery', *Psychological Review* 88: 46–66.

(1987) 'Seeing and imagining in the cerebral hemispheres: a computational approach', *Psychological Review* 94: 148–75.

Kruck, J. S., and Sheikh, A. A. (1986) 'Alexithymia: a critical review', in A. A. Sheikh (ed.) *International Review of Mental Imagery*, vol. 2, New York: Human Sciences Press.

Kuhn, T. S. (1970) *The Structure of Scientific Revolutions*, Chicago, IL: University of Chicago Press.

Kunzendorf, R. G. (1984) 'Centrifugal effects of eidetic imaging on flash electroretinograms and autonomic responses', *Journal of Mental Imagery* 8: 67–76.

Lakatos, I. (1974) 'Falsification and the methodology of scientific research programmes', in I. Lakatos and A. Musgrave (eds) *Criticism and the Growth of Knowledge*, London: Cambridge University Press.

LeDoux, J. E. (1984) 'Cognition and emotion: processing functions and brain systems', in M. S. Gazzaniga (ed.) *Handbook of Cognitive Neuroscience*, New York: Plenum Press.

Leslie, A. M. (1987) 'Pretence and representation in infancy: the origins of "theory of mind"', *Psychological Review* 94: 412–26.

Lindauer, M. S. (1983) 'Imagery and the arts', in A. A. Sheikh (ed.) *Imagery: Current Theory, Research, and Application*, New York: Academic Press.

Lorente de Nó, R. (1938) 'Analysis of the activity of the chains of internuncial neurons', *Journal of Neurophysiology* 1: 207–44.

Lyons, W. (1986) *The Disappearance of Introspection*, Cambridge, MA: MIT Press.

McClelland, J. L., Rumelhard, D. E., and Hinton, G. E. (1986) 'The appeal of parallel distributed processing', in D. E. Rumelhart, J. L. McClelland, and the PDP Research Group (eds), *Parallel Distributed Processing*, vol. 1, *Foundations*, Cambridge, MA: MIT Press.

McCulloch, W. G., and Pitts, W. (1943) 'A logical calculus of the ideas immanent in neural nets', *Bulletin of Mathematical Biophysics* 5: 115–37.

McKellar, P. (1957) *Imagination and Thinking*, London: Cohen & West.

—— (1983) 'The body-mind I call "me"', paper presented to the First International Imagery Conference, Queenstown, New Zealand.

Mandler, G. (1984) *Mind and Body*, New York: Norton.

Marks, D. F. (1972) 'Individual differences in the vividness of visual imagery and their effect on function', in P. W. Sheehan (ed.) *The Function and Nature of Imagery*, New York: Academic Press.

—— (1973) 'Visual imagery differences in the recall of pictures', *British Journal of Psychology* 64: 17–24.

—— and McKellar, P. (1982) 'The nature and function of eidetic imagery', *Journal of Mental Imagery* 6: 1–124.

Marks, D. F., Tatsuno, J., Uemura, K., Ashida, H., and Imamura, Y. (1988) 'EEG topographical analysis of imagery and calculation in vivid and non-vivid imagers', in preparation.

Martin, M. (1986) 'Imagery and emotion in episodic memory', in D. G. Russell, D. F. Marks, and J. T. E. Richardson (eds) *Imagery 2*, Dunedin: Human Performance Associates.

Mazziotta, J. C., Phelps, M. E., Carson, R. E., and Kuhl, D. E. (1982) 'Tomographic mapping of human cerebral metabolism: auditory stimulation', *Neurology* 32: 921–37.

Miller, G. A. (1979) 'Images, models, similes, and metaphors', in A. Ortony (ed.) *Metaphor and Thought*, London: Cambridge University Press.

Minsky, M. (1975) 'A framework for representing knowledge', in P. Winston (ed.) *The Psychology of Computer Vision*, New York: McGraw-Hill.

—— (1987) *The Society of Mind*, London: Heinemann.

Miyazaki, K. (1987) 'Mental imagery and the traditional Japanese poetry', in G. Naruse (ed.) *3rd International Imagery Conference*, Kyushu University, Japan.

Molteno, T. E. S. (1982) '*Imagery: Heart Rate Responses to Pleasant and Unpleasant Scenes*', unpublished Postgraduate Diploma of Science thesis, University of Otago, Dunedin.

Morris, P. E., and Hampson, P. J. (1983) *Imagery and Consciousness*, London: Academic Press.

Nathan, P. W. (1987) 'Nervous system', in R. L. Gregory (ed.) *The Oxford Companion to the Mind*, London: Oxford University Press.

Neisser, U. (1967) *Cognitive Psychology*, New York: Appleton-Century-Crofts.

—— (1976) *Cognition and Reality*, San Francisco: Freeman.

Nelson-Burford, A. (1987) 'Imagery's physiological base: the limbic system', paper presented at the Third International Imagery Conference, Fukuoka, Japan.

Oatley, K. (1985) 'Representations of the physical and social world', in D. A. Oakley (ed.) *Brain and Mind*, London: Methuen.

Oldfield, R. C., and Zangwill, O. L. (1942) 'Head's concept of the schema and its application in contemporary British psychology, Part III: Bartlett's theory of memory', *British Journal of Psychology* 33: 113–29.

Orne, M. T. (1969) 'Demand characteristics and the concept of quasi-controls', in R. Rosenthal and R. Rosnow (eds) *Artifact in Behavioral Research*, New York: Academic Press.

Oswald, I. (1957) 'After-images from retina and brain', *Quarterly Journal of Experimental Psychology* 9: 88–100.

Paivio, A. (1971) *Imagery and Verbal Processes*, New York: Holt, Rinehart & Winston.

—— (1978) 'Comparisons of mental clocks', *Journal of Experimental Psychology: Human Perception and Performance* 4: 61–71.

Piaget, J. (1952) *The Origins of Intelligence in Children*, New York: International Universities Press.

—— (1954) *The Construction of Reality in the Child*, New York: Basic Books.

Poincaré, H. (1924) *The Foundations of Science*, New York: Science Press.

Pylyshyn, Z. W. (1973) 'What the mind's eye tells the mind's brain: a critique of mental imagery', *Psychological Bulletin* 80: 1–24.

Richardson, A. (1984) 'Strengthening the theoretical links between imaged stimuli and physiological responses', *Journal of Mental Imagery* 8: 113–26.

—— and Patterson, Y. (1986) 'An evaluation of three procedures for increasing imagery vividness', in A. A. Sheikh (ed.) *International Review of Mental Imagery*, vol. 2, New York: Human Sciences Press.

Richardson, J. T. E. (1980) *Mental Imagery and Human Memory*, London: Macmillan.

Roland P. E. (1982) 'Cortical regulation of selective attention in main: a regional cerebral blood flow study', *Journal of Neurophysiology* 48: 1059–78.

—— (1984) 'Metabolic measurements of working frontal cortex in man', *Trends in Neuroscience*, November: 430–5.

Rosenblatt, F. (1962) *Principles of Neurodynamics*, New York: Spartan Books.

Rumelhart, D. E. (1975) 'Notes on a schema for stories', in D. G. Bobrow and A. Collins (eds) *Representation and Understanding*, New York: Academic Press.

Smolensky, P., McClelland, J. L., and Hinton, G. E. (1986) 'Schemata and sequential thought processes in PDP models', in J. L. McClelland, D. E. Rumelhart, and the PDP Research Group (eds), *Parallel Distributed Processing*, vol. 2, *Psychological and Biological Models*, Cambridge, MA: MIT Press.

Sayeki, Y. (1987) 'Anthropomorphic epistemology', in G. Naruse (ed.) *3rd International Imagery Conference*, Kyushu University, Japan.

Schank, R., and Abelson, R. (1977) *Scripts, Plans, Goals and Understanding: An Inquiry into Human Knowledge Structures*, Hillsdale, NJ: Erlbaum.

Sheikh, A. A., and Kunzendorf, R. G. (1984) 'Imagery, physiology, and psychosomatic illness', in A. A. Sheikh (ed.) *International Review of Mental Imagery*, vol. 1, New York: Human Sciences Press.

Shepard, R. N. (1975) 'Form, formation, and transformation of internal representations', in R. Solso (ed.) *Information Processing and Cognition: The Loyola Symposium*, Hillsdale, NJ: Erlbaum.

—— (1978) 'Externalization of mental images and the act of creation', in B. S. Randhawa and W. E. Coffman (eds) *Visual Learning, Thinking, and Communication*, New York: Academic Press.

—— and Cooper, L. A. (1982) *Mental Images and Their Transformations*, Cambridge, MA: MIT Press.

Turvey, M.T. (1977) 'Preliminaries to a theory of action with reference to vision', in R. Shaw and J. Bransford (eds) *Perceiving, Acting, and Knowing*, Hillsdale, NJ: Erlbaum.

Vygotsky, L. S. (1978) *Mind in Society*, Cambridge, MA: Harvard University Press.

Wallas, G. (1926) *The Art of Thought*, New York: Harcourt Brace.

Weimer, W. B. (1977) 'A conceptual framework for cognitive psychology: motor theories of the mind', in R. Shaw and J. Bransford (eds) *Perceiving, Acting, and Knowing*, Hillsdale, NJ: Erlbaum.

Weiskrantz, L. (1950) 'An unusual case of after-imagery following fixation of an "imaginary" visual pattern', *Quarterly Journal of Experimental Psychology* 2: 170–5.

Wilson, S. C., and Barber, T. X. (1978) 'The Creative Imagination Scale as a measure of hypnotic responsiveness: applications to experimental and clinical hypnosis', *Journal of Clinical Hypnosis* 20: 235–49.

Wittgenstein, L. (1953) *Philosophical Investigations*, Oxford: Blackwell.

Chapter two

A neurologically plausible model of individual differences in visual mental imagery

Stephen M. Kosslyn, Michael H. Van Kleeck, and Kris N. Kirby

Interest in mental imagery has been intertwined with interest in individual differences in imagery at least since the time of Galton, and arguably since the time of Plato. To the extent that imagery is an important aspect of mental function, then individual differences in imagery will have important ramifications for performance. It is difficult to believe, for example, that a person with no imagery whatsoever would ever be a successful architect, or would be superb at navigating through Rome. Although these intuitions would be unlikely to brook argument, it is worth pausing and wondering why not. Why are most people likely to accept these statements? Apparently, we have implicit concepts of how imagery functions and when it is used. It is the purpose of this chapter to begin to make these notions explicit and to specify the ways in which people can differ in their imagery abilities.

One question that has been asked about individual differences in imagery centres on the generality of such differences: that is, a person could simply be relatively good or bad at all imagery tasks, with imagery ability assuming the status of a trait. Alternatively, at another extreme, each imagery task could be a separate skill, and how well a person performs one task might have no bearing whatsoever on how well he or she would perform another. A third possibility is that imagery involves a fixed number of underlying processing components, and the similarity of performance between two tasks depends on the extent to which the tasks recruit the same component processes.

Kosslyn *et al.* (1984) present evidence that the third possibility is correct. They tested fifty people on a variety of imagery tasks, and simply correlated the ranked performance on each task. If imagery were a trait and generalized across tasks, uniformly high correlations would have been expected; if imagery were a set of task-specific independent skills, correlations of essentially zero would have been expected; and if imagery were carried out by a set of underlying processing components, which were shared to greater or lesser degrees by each pair of tasks, then a wide range of correlations would be expected. In fact, the correlations ranged from –0.44 to 0.79, with more than twice as many being significant than would be expected merely due to chance.

Kosslyn *et al.* (ibid.) then proceeded to try to characterize the nature of the underlying processing components. They used the Kosslyn and Shwartz (1977) theory (see Kosslyn 1980) to generate a model for each task, and essentially compared how many processing subsystems were shared by each pair of models. (The procedure was more complicated than this, however, because some subsystems were more important than others, as will be discussed shortly when we describe weighting rules.) Although the model did quite well – its predicted similarities correlating (r = 0.56) with the observed pattern of correlations – we are uncomfortable with leaving matters where they lay.

The Kosslyn and Shwartz model was based primarily on a combination of intuition, fitting behavioural data, and convenience for implementation as a computer simulation model. This is hardly the most satisfactory set of motivations. In particular, there was no attempt whatsoever to consider properties of the brain, nor was there an awareness that computers might not provide the best foundations for a theory of human information-processing. Clearly, the predominance of the computer metaphor and the corresponding neglect of brain properties were unwarranted, for descriptions of mental activity are in fact descriptions of brain functions.

The earlier theory has since been revised in accordance with neuroanatomical and neurophysiological considerations, and has been conceptualized in terms of an articulated (i.e. multi-component) parallel processing system like the brain. Some very basic observations about the brain had a large impact on the theory. In this chapter we consider whether the revised theory lends insight into the nature of individual differences. If this theory is truly an improvement over the earlier one, we expect it to do at least as well as the earlier one in accounting for the underlying structure of imagery differences in a more plausible way.

The present theory is a theory of the 'processing subsystems' used to perform a task. A processing subsystem corresponds to a group of neurons that work together to carry out some aspect of information-processing. Subsystems are 'black boxes' that receive input and transform it in some way to produce output, which is used in turn as input by other subsystems. However, not all aspects of processing are equally important in performing a given task. Thus, when we describe the hypothesized subsystems we will indicate the circumstances in which each subsystem is used, and the conditions in which each subsystem plays a disproportionately important role in processing (and hence should be 'weighted' in analyses). It is useful to begin by considering the rules for determining when a subsystem should be weighted.

Weighting rules

The results of the Kosslyn *et al.* (1984) study indicate that individual differences in performance will primarily be due to differences in the efficacy of the subsystems required by a task. At first glance, the sheer number of components shared by those tasks might be expected to predict the similarity in performance by a given individual. However, the situation is not so simple: depending on the dependent measure and precise nature of the task, some subsystems will be more important than others. The efficacy of these subsystems must be 'weighted' when comparing tasks: great dissimilarity in the most important subsystems could overwhelm great similarity among many more relatively unimportant subsystems. Thus, we are faced with two requirements: determining which subsystems are likely to be recruited in each task, and determining the subsystems whose operation contributes most highly to the score on the dependent measure; these subsystems will be weighted in subsequent analyses.

To determine which subsystems should be weighted for a given task, one must (1) identify the dependent measure of interest; (2) establish which subsystems are used if the task is to be performed; and (3) determine for which of these subsystems improved performance would improve the score on the dependent measure. This last idea is at the heart of our weighting scheme. For some subsystems, increased speed, capacity, sensitivity, or accuracy will directly affect the assessed performance. These are the subsystems that should be weighted. Other subsystems need only perform at a bare minimum for the task to be accomplished near maximum performance: that is, provided that they operate at all, further efficacy of some subsystems will have only a slight influence on the assessed performance. Individual differences in these subsystems would not be expected to contribute significantly to the individual differences in performance on a given task.

41

Another way of conceptualizing the weighting criterion is as follows: as a task becomes more difficult (according to the dependent measure of interest), some subsystems will be stressed more than others. It is these subsystems that have to 'work harder' as the task becomes more difficult that should be weighted. Performance on the task will be better as the task becomes more difficult if the stressed subsystems are more effective.

Neurological constraints on theories of visual imagery

The theory described by Kosslyn et al. (in press) addresses more than visual mental imagery. Rather, the theory specifies component processes used in 'high-level' vision in general – that is, visual processing can be divided into two general levels: *low-level* processes are driven purely by the stimulus input and are concerned with locating edges, establishing depth, and so on; *high-level* processes, in contrast, involve the use of stored information. In perception high-level processes are concerned with accessing information pertaining to a visible object, and in imagery they are concerned with using stored information to reconstruct the appearance of, reinterpret, and possibly anticipate the consequences of transforming an object. Given the considerable amount of evidence indicating that visual imagery and visual perception share mechanisms (for example, Shepard and Cooper 1982; Kosslyn 1983; Finke and Shepard 1986; and Farah, 1988), it seems reasonable to attempt to specify the nature of those shared subsystems.

The Kosslyn et al. (in press) theory was shaped by a number of neuroanatomical and neurophysiological observations, the most important of which will be summarized here. These observations pertain to the visual system proper. Given the assumption of shared mechanisms between imagery and like-modality perception, we gain considerable leverage by considering how these constraints apply to a system that performs both imagery and perception.

Retinotopic maps

There are now approximately thirty distinct areas in the brain that are known to be concerned with processing visual information (Van Essen 1985, personal communication). There are several features of these areas that are particularly pertinent to the present concerns. Perhaps the most fundamental is the fact that some ten of these areas preserve the local geometry of the retina (with magnification factors and other slight distortions – see Van Essen 1985): that is, the image projected on the back of the retina is physically laid out on the back of the brain in multiple places. Tootell *et al.* (1982) provided a particularly dramatic demonstration of this by having a monkey stare at a pattern after being injected with 2–deoxyglucose, a radioactive metabolic marker. The marker allowed them to see which groups of cells were most active when the animal was seeing the pattern. And indeed, a picture of the pattern was literally projected on to the back of the brain, and could be 'developed' and easily seen in the largest visual area (V1).

Reciprocal connections

To date, it has been found that every visual area that sends information to another area also receives information from that area. Furthermore, the efferent and afferent pathways are of comparable size. Thus, a considerable amount of information flows upstream as well as downstream.

Two cortical visual systems

Perhaps the most striking neurological constraint is the evidence that shape and location information are processed in separate systems (for a summary, see Ungerleider and Mishkin 1982). The shape pathway leads from the occipital lobe down to the inferior temporal lobe. If this pathway is cut or if the inferior temporal lobe is removed (on both sides), the animal will fail to recognize shapes (Mishkin and Ungerleider 1982). In addition, single-cell recordings have revealed that cells in this area are sensitive to higher-order shape properties (e.g. Gross *et al.* 1981, 1984). The animal is not very impaired in learning location information when this area has been ablated. In contrast, the location pathway leads from the occipital lobe up to the parietal lobe. If this area is ablated, location learning is disrupted but shape learning is relatively spared (Ungerleider and Mishkin 1982). And single-cell recordings in nonhuman primates have revealed that cells in this area are sensitive to location (as gated by eye position; see Andersen *et al.* 1985).

Thus, the 'ventral' system in the inferior temporal lobe appears to process shape independently of location, whereas the 'dorsal' system in the parietal lobe appears to process location independently of shape.

Connections to the frontal lobes

There are direct and precise connections between the regions of the parietal lobe concerned with representing location and the frontal lobe (Goldman-Rakic 1987). Indeed, the projections are relatively close to Area 8, the 'frontal eye fields'; this area has a role in directing eye movements. In addition, there is a major connection, the arcuate fasciculus, between the posterior superior temporal lobe and the posterior inferior frontal lobe. These connections could allow information about shape and location to be used to guide eye movements.

Although there are many other aspects of the neuroanatomy and neurophysiology that are relevant (for example, projections from the pulvinar, the nature of chandelier cells, and so on), the ones summarized here will prove most important for present purposes.

Subsystems of high-level vision

The findings about neuroanatomy and neurophysiology summarized above have particular power when combined with an analysis of the information-processing that must underlie the observed behavioural abilities of humans. Kosslyn *et al.* (in press) used both sorts of considerations to develop a theory of the 'processing subsystems' used in high-level vision. We briefly summarize the subsystems they posit without delving deeply into the information-processing analyses. Nor do we summarize the results of the many experiments conducted to investigate the assumptions and local predictions of the theory. Our goal here is to describe the subsystems clearly enough to be able to use them in analyses of individual differences; for a detailed motivation for each subsystem, see Kosslyn *et al.* (ibid.).

We will begin by describing the role of the various subsystems in perception. After the system is described, we will summarize how these subsystems function in imagery proper. The same subsystems are used in both domains, and the weighting rules as described here apply in both modes of operation.

Input to the system

The theory posits a representational structure that receives the output from low-level visual processes in perception; selected contents of this structure are then sent on for further processing.

Visual buffer

High-level visual recognition processes take as input the patterns of activation in a series of retinotopic maps (cf. Allman and Kaas 1976; Van Essen and Maunsell 1983; Cowey 1985; Van Essen 1985). Taken together, the maps provide a topographic representation at different levels of resolution. We conceptualize the multiple patterns of activation in this representation as forming a single functional structure, which we call the 'visual buffer'. The visual buffer corresponds roughly to the structure supporting Marr's (1982) '2½ D sketch'.

One strong claim we make is that a visual mental image is a pattern of activity in this structure, which is evoked by activating stored information: this pattern can then be processed in the same way as a pattern originating from low-level visual processing during perception.

Attention window

Because the visual buffer at any given moment contains more information than can be processed, some information must be ignored and some must be selected for further processing. The 'attention window' accomplishes this selection by targeting a region within the visual buffer for further processing. The size of the window, as well as its location, can be varied (cf. Larsen and Bundesen 1978; Treisman and Gelade 1980).

The attention window is critical for co-ordinating the separate processing of shape and location information. The contents of the attention window are routed to the ventral system, which encodes shapes, whereas the location of the window is sent to the dorsal system, which tracks locations. Evidence consistent with the hypothesis that an attention window gates input to the ventral system has been provided by studies of the effects of attention on the response properties of shape-sensitive cells in the inferior temporal lobe of primate cortex (Moran and Desimone 1985). These cells are inhibited from responding to stimuli at unattended locations, even when those locations fall within the cell's receptive field. Thus the cells apparently display greatest sensitivity to the current contents of the attention window.

Subsystems of the ventral system

The ventral system can be decomposed into a number of sub-systems, as described here. Following each description, we indicate the circumstances in which the subsystem will be weighted. In determining which subsystems should be weighted, we have found it useful to begin by distinguishing between dependent measures involving response times and those that do not. To improve one's speed on a given task, it is likely that one or more subsystems would need to perform their duties faster; if speeding up a subsystem would improve the score on the dependent measure, that subsystem should be weighted. However, when the dependent measure on a task is not speed-dependent (for example, is the accuracy with which it is performed, the distance an image is transformed, or the sensitivity of detection), increasing the speed with which a subsystem performs will not improve performance as assessed by the dependent measure. Instead, in these cases, performance scores will be improved by increasing not the speed but rather the accuracy, sensitivity, or capacity of the critical subsystems.

Preprocessing

Description   Any workable vision system must be able to derive the same perceptual representation for an object under three classes of varying observational conditions:

(1) different locations of the object in the visual field;
(2) different viewing distances (which result in changes in visual angle); and
(3) different viewpoints, resulting in different planar projections of the shape.

The attention window helps solve the first two problems, those of visual field position and viewing distance, in the following ways. First, because the attention window is movable, it can encode patterns irrespective of their location within the visual buffer. Second, because the size of the attention window can be adjusted, it can envelop shapes that occupy different areas in the buffer (that is, that subtend different visual angles). The third and most difficult problem, however – namely, the variations in perceptual input caused by changing viewpoints – cannot be solved even in part by the attention window. Instead, a preprocessing subsystem must be used. (Note that various sorts of preprocessing are likely to be used throughout the system, especially in low-level vision: we refer here only to the specific kind of preprocessing discussed in the remainder of this section.)

This preprocessing subsystem selects stable features of the stimulus that do not change when viewpoint or visual angle change. Thus, for example, such properties as parallel lines (usually indicating edges) and line intersections are likely to remain invariant under translation, rotation, and scale changes (cf. Biederman 1987; Lowe 1987a, b). The preprocessing subsystem extracts these useful invariants for subsequent matching against stored information.

Weighting Which subsystems are weighted depends on what measure of performance is being assessed. Thus, when discussing the weighting rules, we consider separate tasks in which different measures are taken. (For convenience, the weighting rules for each processing subsystem are summarized in Appendix 1.)

When the dependent measure is response time: because the preprocessing subsystem plays a crucial role in overcoming input variability due to viewpoint changes, it will be weighted whenever objects must be recognized from unusual viewpoints. In addition, even when objects are seen from ordinary viewpoints, figure/ground segregation relies on the invariant properties extracted by the preprocessing subsystem. Consequently, the preprocessing subsystem is also weighted whenever a task involves figure/ground segregation.

When the dependent measure is accuracy: when a figure is camouflaged, or otherwise partially occluded, it will be more difficult for the preprocessing subsystem to extract invariants. The better it is at doing so under adverse conditions, the better will be the information provided to the pattern activation subsystem, and thus the more accurate the matching process will be. Therefore, when the dependent measure is accuracy, the preprocessing subsystem is weighted whenever a figure is camouflaged or partially occluded.

Pattern activation

Description Another type of problem that must be solved in object recognition involves ignoring the irrelevant shape variations of objects that occur in diverse shapes and sizes, such as tables, knives, and hands. The pattern activation subsystem provides part of the solution to some of these 'generalization' problems by mapping a range of similar inputs onto a single output. The features (in specific positions) extracted by the preprocessing subsystem are used to index a pattern stored in the pattern activation subsystem. If the match is less than optimal, this pattern is then projected back into the visual buffer and matched against the original input there. If the pattern matches, the object has been identified (cf. Lowe 1987a, b). This top–down projection of patterns into the visual buffer is exactly equivalent to generating an image; the reciprocal connections in the visual system are consistent with this notion.

When shapes are viewed with sufficiently high resolution for the parts to be clearly visible, the shapes are parsed into separate parts (for example, Reed and Johnsen 1975; Bower and Glass 1976; Biederman 1987). The present theory posits that separate parts are encoded in the same way that entire shapes can be encoded. Because the attention window operates at the boundary between low-level and high-level vision, it is insulated from knowledge of whether a parsed unit selected for further processing corresponds to a part or to a whole object. Depending on the level of resolution that has been selected, a stimulus can be encoded as one lower-resolution whole or as several distinct higher-resolution parts. Thus, patterns of individual parts can later be activated into an image as well as a pattern representing the overall shape of an object.

Weighting When the dependent measure is response time: as described above, the pattern activation subsystem is used both in object recognition and in image generation. In tasks that require either of those processes, the pattern activation subsystem is weighted when the dependent measure is response time.

When the dependent measure is accuracy: in tasks that require one to maintain in an image more than about four perceptual units, or that require one to maintain a single perceptual unit for more than its fade time (about one second), the pattern activation subsystem must be used repeatedly to 'recycle' a pattern, repeatedly pumping it into the visual buffer. This repeated use offers greater opportunity for error; consequently, if the dependent measure is accuracy in such tasks, the pattern activation subsystem is weighted.

Feature detection

Description Because each eye fixation can encode only a limited amount of high-acuity information, the visual system must solve the problem of where to look next in order to obtain further information. In determining the pattern of eye fixations, stimulus properties play an important role (Yarbus 1967). Such properties must be available for encoding even when they fall outside the current focus of attention, for otherwise one's knowledge of the stimulus would be limited to already-attended properties. Substantial evidence supports the inference that not all visual properties require attention in order to be encoded (Neisser 1967; Treisman and Gelade 1980). We therefore posit a feature detection subsystem that can access visual properties that do not require focal attention (defined by the location of the attention window). Examples of such properties are texture variation, colour, location, and simple shape features (see Treisman and Gelade 1980). The feature-detection subsystem can bypass the attention window and detect features and visual properties distributed throughout the visual buffer.

Weighting When the dependent measure is response time: the faster one is at assessing visual properties such as those described above, the faster one will make decisions in tasks requiring such assessments. Consequently, the feature detection subsystem is weighted in all such assessment tasks when the dependent measure is response time.

When the dependent measure is accuracy: in tasks in which a property of a representation in the visual buffer (for example, the colour of the represented object) is used to guide processing, or in which the property judgement itself (for example, acuity) is the accuracy measure, the accuracy of the feature-detection subsystem will affect accuracy on the task. In these cases, the feature-detection subsystem is weighted.

Subsystems of the dorsal system

The dorsal, location-encoding system can also be decomposed into a number of subsystems.

Spatiotopic mapping

Description In the visual buffer, location information is retinotopic; in other words, it is represented relative to the retina, not to physical space. Because a retinotopic representation fluctuates wildly according to the position of the eyes and head, it has only limited usefulness for such tasks as recognition, navigation, and tracking, and it is virtually useless for helping one to integrate inputs from separate eye fixations. In order to co-ordinate separate objects or parts in a single, unified frame of reference, one needs a representation of the location of objects in physical space rather than relative to the retina. We therefore posit a subsystem that uses retinotopic position and the position of the head, body, and eyes to compute where an object or part thereof is located in space.

The locations computed by the spatiotopic mapping subsystem must of course be specified relative to some reference point. Different reference systems may be more or less useful for different problems. In distinguishing two similar faces, for example, good cues are provided by subtle differences in distances between parts, so a location specified relative to a central facial feature such as the nose might be appropriate. In contrast, the location of an object that one wants to reach for and grasp should be represented relative to one's body. Although some evidence suggests that separate allocentric and egocentric position-mapping subsystems exist (for example, see Rizzolatti *et al.* 1985), we have not explicitly developed this distinction in our current theory.

Weighting When the dependent measure is response time or accuracy: the position information computed by the spatiotopic mapping subsystem serves as input to the categorical and co-ordinate encoding subsystems (see below). Therefore if either the categorical or co-ordinate encoding subsystems or both are weighted in a given task, the spatiotopic mapping subsystem is also weighted.

Categorical relations encoding

Description Flexible objects, such as human bodies, can assume so many positions that it is impossible to store a pattern for each configuration. Instead, such objects are more usefully encoded in terms of their parts and the relations among the parts. For maximum usefulness in recognizing flexible objects in their myriad configurations, one's representation of interpart relations should be invariant under a large range of spatial transformations of the parts. A type of representation that fulfils this criterion is an abstract, 'categorical' representation, such as 'connected to', 'left of', 'under', or 'above'. These categorical relations capture what is stable across instances that may differ in terms of precise metric relationships. The categorical relations encoding subsystem computes categorical relations between locations of objects or parts.

This subsystem is used whenever there is more than one perceptual unit in an image. It encodes relations between items within the attention window, and it also encodes relations between shifts in the position of the attention window. The categorical representations encode general properties of a relationship while leaving the details unspecified (for example, the relation 'above' is represented without specifying the exact distance between the relevant parts or locations). Subsequently, in associative memory, the representations of these relations are combined with representations of the associated parts to construct a 'structural description' of a complete object (cf. Palmer 1977; Marr 1982).

Weighting   When the dependent measure is response time: this subsystem is weighted whenever

(1) an image is parsed into parts, and
(2) the parts of image must be positioned (as in image generation or in repositioning of parts during image transformations) and approximate positioning (via a nameable spatial relation such as 'left of' or 'above') is adequate for the task; or
(3) a categorical relationship between parts of an object is to be reported.

When the dependent measure is accuracy: the categorical relations encoding subsystem is not weighted. If the subsystem operates efficiently enough for one to be able to do the task at all, further efficiency in this subsystem will not significantly improve task performance.

Co-ordinate relations encoding

Description   The virtues of categorical relations for encoding flexible objects are matched by disadvantages in the encoding of relatively rigid objects that have important but subtle metric spatial relations among their parts. In face recognition, for example, simply knowing that a particular face has a nose that is 'above' the mouth is useless, because that relationship is true of all faces. For faces and other objects that are distinguished by subtle spatial relations among their parts, metric position information must be represented. The co-ordinate relations encoding subsystem computes this information. In general, whenever precise metric locations must be encoded, or when precise metric positioning of objects or parts is required (including repositioning of parts during image transformations), the co-ordinate relations encoding subsystem will be used instead of the categorical relations encoding subsystem.

Weighting   When the dependent measure is response time or accuracy: when precise metric locations or precise positioning of objects or parts is required, the co-ordinate relations encoding subsystem is used instead of the categorical relations encoding subsystem. The faster and more accurately it operates, the faster and more accurate will be decisions based on precise encoding. Consequently, the co-ordinate relations encoding subsystem is weighted whenever precise metric information is necessary for the task.

Subsystems of the hypothesis-testing system

An object will be encoded with multiple eye-movements when it subtends a large visual angle or is in an unusual configuration and hence does not match a single stored pattern. In such cases, knowledge is used to guide the sequence of encodings and the path of eye movements necessary for that sequence. We assume that the connections between the frontal lobe and the parietal lobe are involved in these processes. At least four subsystems are used in this process.

Co-ordinate lookup

Description In order to test an hypothesis about whether a pattern of visual input represents a particular object, we must first be able to look up in associative memory the properties that the object should have. The co-ordinate lookup subsystem accesses representations (stored in associative memory) of object parts whose locations are encoded in terms of co-ordinate relations. As discussed above, co-ordinate relations are particularly useful for encoding rigid objects that are distinguished by subtle metric differences in spatial relations among their parts. Once the properties that have locations specified as co-ordinate relations have been accessed in associative memory, the attention shifting subsystem can use this information to move attention to the given co-ordinates, and then a test for the property can begin.

Weighting When the dependent measure is response time: if precise metric positioning or locating of parts is necessary in a task such as image generation or transformation, the speed of the task will partially be a function of the speed of co-ordinate lookup. In these cases, the co-ordinate lookup subsystem is weighted. In addition, when the object is viewed at a large visual angle or is degraded, requiring hypothesis-generation and testing, then this subsystem will be weighted during inspection tasks.

When the dependent measure is accuracy: the co-ordinate lookup subsystem is not weighted when the dependent measure is accuracy. If the subsystem operates efficiently enough for one to be able to do the task at all, performance will not be significantly improved by further efficiency in this subsystem.

Categorical lookup

Description The categorical lookup subsystem accesses stored representations of object parts whose locations are encoded in terms of categorical relations. This subsystem, distinct from the co-ordinate lookup system, is posited because different problems must be solved in accessing parts encoded by categorical relations than in accessing parts encoded by co-ordinate relations. In the latter case, one simply looks in the location specified by the co-ordinates. In using a categorical relation, however, one must first locate the reference part specified in the relation. If, for example, the location of a thumbnail is encoded as 'connected at the top end of the thumb', then in accessing the head from the thumbnail one must first locate the thumb, which is part of the hand, which in turn is connected to the wrist, and so on. Compared with the straightforward access possible with co-ordinate relations, this added complication suggests positing a categorical lookup system distinct from the co-ordinate lookup system (see Kosslyn *et al.*, in press).

Weighting When the dependent measure is response time: 'what' and 'where' information is brought together explicitly only in associative memory. Sometimes the relations between parts of a representation in associative memory will be stored categorically, rather than with precise metric relations. In such cases, parts can be located only with reference to other parts. As a result, when (1) a multi-part object is imaged, inspected, or transformed, and (2) a nameable spatial relation is adequate for locating or positioning the parts, the speed with which the task is accomplished will be partially a function of the speed of the categorical lookup subsystem. In such cases, this subsystem is weighted.

When the dependent measure is accuracy: the categorical lookup subsystem is not weighted when the dependent measure is accuracy, for the same reason that the co-ordinate lookup subsystem is not weighted in that case.

Categorical-co-ordinate conversion

Description Because categorical relations abstract over particular locations, they are necessarily imprecise. As a result, when categorical relations are used by the attention shifting subsystem (described below) to direct attention in the visual buffer, they must be converted to a range of co-ordinates. The categorical-co-ordinate conversion subsystem accomplishes this conversion.

Weighting   When the dependent measure is response time: whenever the categorical lookup subsystem is weighted, the categorical-co-ordinate conversion subsystem is also weighted.

When the dependent measure is accuracy: the categorical-co-ordinate conversion subsystem is not weighted when the dependent measure is accuracy, for the same reason that the two lookup subsystems are not weighted.

Attention shifting

Description   The human visual system probably includes at least three subsystems for shifting attention: one to shift attention to a location in space, a second to engage attention at that location, and a third to disengage attention when appropriate (Posner *et al*. 1985). In our simulation model, we have chosen a coarser level of modelling and included all attentional control mechanisms in a single attention shifting subsystem. This subsystem moves the attention window and also initiates eye, head, and body movements when necessary. During hypothesis testing, when the attention window has been shifted to a new location, the new perceptual unit found at that location is sent to the ventral system, and the new location is sent to the dorsal system. The new dorsal and ventral inputs (whose arrival provides feedback about whether the attention window was moved appropriately) are processed by the relevant subsystems and yield a new input to associative memory. If this input to associative memory is consistent with the properties of the object implicated by the current hypothesis, then one has evidence in favour of that hypothesis.

Weighting   When the dependent measure is response time: the speed of the attention shifting subsystem will affect the speed of performing a task whenever the task requires (1) shifting attention across or between objects or parts, or (2) changing the resolution of the image (that is, shifting levels within the visual buffer). This will occur when constructing images of multipart objects, comparing arbitrarily defined segments, or performing part searches using one of the lookup subsystems. In these cases, if the dependent measure is response time, the attention shifting subsystem is weighted.

When the dependent measure is accuracy: the attention shifting subsystem is not weighted when the dependent measure is accuracy, because beyond the basic level of functioning required to perform a task at all, an improvement in the efficiency of the subsystem will not significantly improve the accuracy of performance.

Transformation shift

Description   Imagery tasks such as rotation, translation, scaling, and scanning require shifting the locations of patterns in the visual buffer. This shifting is performed by the transformation shift subsystem, which fixes parts in the attention window and then shifts them in the visual buffer. The progress of the transformation subsystem is monitored by various other subsystems, depending on the nature of the task. When an image must be shifted to a precise metric location, for example, the spatiotopic mapping and co-ordinate encoding subsystems must be used to determine when the image has arrived at the desired location. Furthermore, if the image represents a multipart object, one of the lookup subsystems will be used to access previously stored information about the arrangement of the parts, in order to align parts properly in the transformed image.

Weighting   When the dependent measure is response time or accuracy: the transformation subsystem is weighted in response time tasks when the task requires that an object be rotated, translated, scaled, or scanned more than about four degrees (and hence the image itself will be translated, in addition to shifting the attention window); it is weighted in accuracy tasks when precise metric relations are required for performing one of the operations just mentioned.

Using the subsystems during imagery

Before continuing, it will be useful to summarize how the subsystems operate during imagery (see also Appendix 2). Consider a typical imagery task, loading suitcases into a car's trunk in the most efficient manner. One would encode the appearance of the suitcases, turn and *generate* an image of each one in the trunk. One would then mentally *transform* the image by imagining how the cases would look in different positions. One would *inspect* the image while transforming it. Finally, one would *maintain* the image all the while. These four imagery abilities are realized by the subsystems as follows.

Image generation

Individual shapes are imaged by activating the corresponding stored pattern in the pattern-activation subsystem, which evokes an image in the visual buffer. If a multipart object or scene is to be imaged, an initial part is generated into the visual buffer. Following this, the spatial relation between that and another part is looked up, either by the categorical lookup or co-ordinate lookup subsystems. The location of the reference part is computed (which is relative to the part initially generated in the image). If a categorical relation is accessed, it is converted to a range of co-ordinates by the categorical-co-ordinate conversion subsystem. The co-ordinates are then provided to the attention shifting subsystem, and the attention window is moved to the appropriate location in the visual buffer at which the reference part should be located. If, for example, one were generating an image of a hand, and wanted to image the thumbnail, the location might be specified relative to the tip of the thumb. Once that part was in view, the attention window could be shifted to the appropriate relative location for the new part. (Thus, image inspection is an integral part of image generation.) Once the attention window is in place, the new part is imaged using the pattern activation subsystem. This procedure is repeated until the object is fully imaged.

Image inspection

Interpreting a pattern in the visual buffer is done in exactly the same way in perception and imagery: shapes, textures, and colours are processed in the ventral system and locations are processed in the dorsal system.

Image transformation

The to-be-transformed object is manipulated a part at a time, in relatively small shifts. One part is fixed in the attention window, via the operation of the transformation shift subsystem. The attention window is then moved, via the attention shift subsystem. The relation between the shifted part and its reference part in the image is then encoded, via the categorical and co-ordinate encoding subsystems. The correct relation is accessed from associative memory, via the categorical or co-ordinate property lookup subsystems. The reference part is then shifted into proper alignment. This process is performed iteratively until the entire shape is transformed.

Image maintenance

As an image is built up a part at a time, the emergent form is encoded into the pattern-activation subsystem as a new pattern. In order to retain the image, this new encoding is activated, which evokes a pattern of activity in the visual buffer. Patterns can only be so complicated before they cannot be encoded.

The task battery

The data collected by Kosslyn *et al.* (1984) were reanalyzed using the new theory. In order to explain how the theory accounts for task performance, then, we must first briefly review the tasks. Following the description of each task is a description of which subsystems are hypothesized to be used to perform it, indicating which ones were weighted.

Acuity

The subjects first were shown a projected image of a 'standard' striped grating, which was blurred to the point where the dark and white bars were barely distinguishable. The subjects were asked to practise adjusting a projector to produce just this amount of blurring in similar gratings. The subjects then received training in estimating distances, and practised until they became skilled at this task as well.

In the task proper, each of three different sized gratings were presented separately on a rear-projection screen. The subjects studied each grating, closed their eyes, and then imaged the grating moving away from them. At the point at which the subjects detected the same amount of blurring in the imaged grating as had been evident in the standard, they were to stop the image and estimate its distance: that is, they were asked to decide how far away the grating would have been if it were being seen as it appeared in the image. The dependent measure was this estimate of the apparent distance at which the image matched the blur criterion. This task was very similar to one used by Pennington and Kosslyn (1981), who found that the distance at the point of blur increased when the stripes were broader, and who found similar results in imagery and in a perceptual condition, when the gratings were physically present during the task. For purposes of the individual differences analyses, a mean distance estimate over all trials was computed for each subject. Larger means – that is, the greater the average apparent distances at which the gratings could be moved before the stripes were no longer distinguishable – were taken to indicate better performance.

The model

The grating is initially encoded by extracting its nonaccidental features via the preprocessing subsystem (the black and white bars) and loading them into the pattern-activation subsystem, which then projects an image of the pattern back into the visual buffer. The apparent distance is manipulated via the transformation shift subsystem, which alters the angle subtended by the pattern in the visual buffer. The spatiotopic mapping and co-ordinate encoding subsystems are used to encode the apparent size of the pattern as it is being transformed, which is used to infer distance. The image is transformed until the pattern has blurred, which is registered by the feature-detection subsystem, at which point the apparent distance is reported (based on the visual angle subtended by the stimulus field).

Consulting the weighting rules described above, we see that when the dependent measure is accuracy, the feature detection subsystem should be weighted when a property of a representation in the visual buffer (in this case, blur) is used to guide processing. No other subsystems are implicated by the weighting rules here, and hence only the feature-detection subsystem is weighted. Given that the subject can perform the task at all, only improvement in the sensitivity of the feature-detection subsystem will improve performance, and hence this subsystem is the only one weighted.

Oblique effect

After estimating each distance in the acuity task, subjects were asked to imagine rotating the grating 45 degrees clockwise, so that it now consisted of oblique stripes. The subjects were then asked whether the grating still matched the blur criterion, and if did not, whether it would need to be moved closer or farther away in order to match. Pennington and Kosslyn (ibid.) found that subjects in this situation show an 'oblique effect': that is, oblique gratings seem closer when they blur than do vertical ones. Because this phenomenon normally occurs in perception (for example, Appelle 1972), we shall assume that it occurs in imagery and that the task measures the subjects' ability to detect it. Therefore, more frequent reports of the oblique effect were taken as evidence of better performance.

The model

The image of the grating is maintained by projecting the pattern from the pattern-activation subsystem back into the visual buffer. The orientation is manipulated via the transformation-shift subsystem, which alters the pattern in the visual buffer. The spatiotopic mapping and categorical relations encoding subsystems are used to register when the pattern has been rotated 45 degrees. The feature detection subsystem registers whether the sharpness of the pattern has changed; if so, the transformation subsystem is used to 'move' it in depth (as in the acuity task) until the blur criterion is reached, and the direction (closer/farther) of movement is registered. Again, given that the subject can perform the task at all, only improvement in the sensitivity of the feature-detection subsystem will improve performance, and hence according to the weighting rules this subsystem is weighted.

Extent task

Two identical black-and-white striped gratings were presented side by side: the subjects were asked to image them moving apart at the same rate, and to stop this movement when the gratings matched the blur criterion. By moving their index fingers apart to indicate the positions of the gratings at the point of blur, the horizontal extent of each subject's 'imagery field' could be estimated (cf. Finke and Kosslyn 1980). The gratings were small circles 24 mm in diameter, with vertical stripes within. The same three widths were used as were used in the acuity task. A larger mean distance between the gratings at the point where the stripes merged together was taken as better performance, indicating an enhanced ability to detect fine distinctions in intensity between light and dark stripes at a location in the visual buffer where the resolution is coarse.

The model

This model is almost identical to that for the acuity task; the only difference is that the transformation-shift-subsystem is used to move the patterns apart, and the co-ordinate encoding subsystem registers the distance between them at the point of blur. As before, the feature-detection subsystem is weighted.

Mental rotation

Subjects were shown a series of alphanumeric characters presented at six different orientations about the circle (spaced at 60–degree increments). Half of the time the characters faced normally and half the time they were mirror-reversed. Subjects imaged the character rotating in a clockwise direction until it was upright, and were asked to classify the direction in which it faced. Such rotation requires a constant monitoring to ensure that the relations among parts in the stimuli are preserved. The speed with which subjects rotated the images was computed, and it was found that more time was required to classify characters that were rotated greater amounts, replicating Cooper (1975). Faster rates of rotation – that is, shallower slopes in the function relating response times to angle of rotation – were taken as evidence of better performance.

The model

The transformation-shift subsystem moves a part of the object in the visual buffer, pivoting around the centre of the object. The categorical property lookup subsystem accesses the spatial relation between that part and another one, the categorical-co-ordinate conversion subsystem converts the relation to co-ordinates, and the attention shifting subsystem moves the attention window to the to-be-moved part. The part is then moved via the transformation-shift subsystem to the proper location, as registered by the categorical encoding subsystem (via the spatiotopic mapping subsystem). When the figure is upright, as registered by the categorical encoding subsystem, its direction is also classified by that subsystem.

Because the speed of all these subsystems affects the slope, they are all weighted. In other words, when the dependent measure is response time, the weighting rules tell us that the transformation-shift subsystem should be weighted whenever the task requires rotation. The categorical lookup subsystem is to be weighted when a transformation is performed and a nameable spatial relation is adequate for positioning parts. The categorical encoding subsystem is weighted whenever the parts of an image must be repositioned during image transformation. The categorical-co-ordinate conversion subsystem is weighted whenever categorical lookup is weighted. Finally, the attention shifting subsystem is weighted whenever attention is shifted between parts, as is done here. Thus, all of the subsystems used in this task should be weighted.

Line drawings probe times

In this task subjects heard a tape-recorded sequence of directions (such as North, North-west, West . . .) and constructed an image of a pathway by connecting one-inch line segments end-to-end. Each line segment was connected to the previous one according to the direction given. The number of segments was varied from 2 to 10. After the last direction was presented the word 'end' was read on the tape, at which point the subjects were to make a speeded judgement about whether the endpoint of the configuration was above or below the starting-point. This task encouraged the use of imagery and provided a measure of how well the images were maintained. The time to decide whether the end-point was above the starting-point was recorded, with faster times taken as better performance.

The model

When the 'end' cue is presented, the pattern activation subsystem is used to pick out the terminal segments, at which point the categorical encoding subsystem encodes the relation, above/below, of the endpoint to the start point (via the spatiotopic mapping subsystem). The pattern activation subsystem is used to maintain the image (see below): as the quality of the image degrades, the task becomes more difficult and responses will be slower. Hence, this subsystem is weighted. Furthermore, because the speed of each of the other relevant subsystems directly affects the dependent measure, all of these subsystems are weighted: according to the weighting rules, categorical encoding is weighted whenever categorical properties are to be extracted, and spatiotopic mapping is weighted whenever categorical encoding is weighted.

Line–drawings memory

After judging the relative locations of the endpoints of the imaged pathway, the subjects drew the configuration. This task was based on one devised by Bower (1972), who found that the inclusion of more segments impaired memory for the configuration. The dependent measure, then, was the mean number of segments correctly drawn, with a larger number taken as better performance.

The model

The first segment is generated via the pattern-activation subsystem. When the direction of the second segment is encoded, the categorical lookup subsystem is used to access the relation 'connected to end of previous segment', and the categorical-co-ordinate conversion subsystem is used to instruct the attention-shifting subsystem on where to attend; when the attention window is properly positioned, as registered by the categorical encoding subsystem (via the spatiotopic mapping subsystem), the pattern activation subsystem generates an image of the new segment. The combined pattern is now encoded into the pattern-activation subsystem, which 'pumps' it back into the visual buffer to maintain the image. The sequence is repeated for each new segment. Given that a person can perform the task with two segments, the only subsystem that is strained increasingly as more segments are added is the pattern-activation subsystem – which must encode and regenerate increasingly complex patterns. According to the weighting rules, the pattern-activation subsystem is weighted in accuracy tasks whenever more than about four perceptual units are to be maintained. Thus, the pattern-activation subsystem is the only one weighted in this task.

Described scenes

In this task, subjects heard the names of four objects and their spatial relations and were asked to form an image of the described scene. Thus, for example, they might hear 'Briefcase; 4 inches up place a horse; 1 inch left place a beaver; 1 inch down place an onion.' The subjects were given practice in drawing such configurations, using labelled dots for the objects, until they reached an accuracy criterion of ¼" on all relations. The scenes were described on a tape. After the final object, the subjects were asked to 'focus' on one of the objects, and then were to scan to a target object, and press one button if they had scanned left and another if they had scanned right. Eight different distances were scanned across, and the dependent measure was the increase in time to scan with increasing distance in the image: Kosslyn *et al.* (1978) had previously demonstrated such scanning effects.

The model

The name of the first object results in the pattern-activation subsystem's forming an image of the general form of the object (details are not needed for the task, so we assume they are not included). When the relation of the next object is heard, the categorical-co-ordinate conversion subsystem is used to provide input to the attention-shifting subsystem. The next object is then imaged in this position, and so on until the entire image is formed. The co-ordinate encoding subsystem encodes the location of each object in the image (via the spatiotopic mapping subsystem). When the target object is named, the object's location is accessed in memory via the co-ordinate lookup subsystem, and the co-ordinates are passed to the attention-shifting subsystem. Attention is shifted to the object, and the categorical encoding subsystem is used to encode the direction of scan. When the attention window is focused on the target object (as indicated by the pattern activation subsystem, via the preprocessing subsystem), the response is made. Because slopes were used as the dependent measure, only one subsystem was weighted: the speed of the attention-shifting subsystem clearly affects scan rate. Training in placing the objects prior to the task presumably resulted in uniformly high accuracy of the categorical-co-ordinate conversion subsystem, which determines how accurately the objects will be placed in the image (which also affects the slope): if not for such training, this subsystem would also have been weighted.

Image generation

In this task the subjects saw a series of ambiguous geometrical figures, with each one being presented after a description of how it should be composed. Thus, the description indicated the components used to construct the figure. The figures were described as being composed of either relatively few large overlapping shapes, or relatively many small adjacent shapes. Thus, for example, a subject might be presented with the description 'two triangles' and then see the Star of David, which would be seen as composed of the two overlapping shapes. Alternatively, the Star would be described as a hexagon and six triangles. After the figure was removed, the subjects were to form an image of it and press a button when the image was completed. Kosslyn (1980) summarizes much data indicating that image formation times increase with the number of units predicated in the descriptions. Indeed, the same shape requires different amounts of time to image, depending on the way it is encoded.

The dependent measure of interest here is the increase in time taken to form images as each additional part is added. Therefore, the slope of the function relating image formation time to the number of parts was measured, with shallower slopes taken as evidence of better performance.

The model

The model is identical to that for the line-drawing memory task: in both cases images are generated a part at a time. In this case, however, the name of the part is also looked up in associative memory as well as the location. The nature of the parts and their relations is determined in part by the description, which results in different parses (via a different way of positioning the attention window during encoding). Because the speed of each subsystem directly contributes to the dependent measure, all of the subsystems that are used are weighted.

Reorganization task

After forming the image in the previous task, on half of the trials the subjects were asked to reverse the organization of the imaged figure – that is, contiguous figures were to be reorganized as overlapping forms, and vice versa. This operation requires locating a configuration of lines corresponding to each 'new part', parsing the overall figure, and re-encoding it into visual memory accordingly. A button was pressed when the reorganization was complete. The dependent measure was the time taken to reorganize the figure, with shorter times taken as evidence of better performance.

The model

The description of the new pattern is accessed in associative memory via the categorical lookup subsystem, which is used to direct the attention-shifting subsystem to the location of one part of the new pattern (via the categorical-co-ordinate conversion subsystem). Once the attention window is positioned at the location of a part in the image, the new part is imaged via the pattern-activation subsystem and is imposed on the existing pattern in the visual buffer. The new pattern is encoded via the preprocessing and pattern-activation subsystems. The pattern-activation subsystem is used to maintain the image as it is being reorganized (exactly as it maintains pathways in the line-drawing task). This process is performed repeatedly until the new pattern has been fully imposed over the old one. Because overall speed is the dependent measure, the speed of each subsystem is important – and hence all of the subsystems used in the task are weighted.

Image inspection

After generating and reorganizing the figures in the above tasks (if reorganization was required), the subjects were asked to determine whether the figure contained a specified geometric shape (for example, triangle, square) embedded within it. The mean time to 'see' a new part for non-reorganized and reorganized images was computed for each subject, and faster times were taken as evidence of better performance.

The model

The categorical lookup subsystem accesses the location of the named part, the categorical-co-ordinate conversion subsystem directs the attention-shifting subsystem to move the attention window to the location where the part should be, and the pattern in that region is encoded via the preprocessing and pattern-activation subsystems. The part encoded is noted and a response is made. Because the dependent measure is overall speed, all of the subsystems used in the task are weighted.

Form board

Five two-dimensional shape fragments were presented together with a standard pattern. The subject was asked to decide which fragments can be put together to form the pattern. The task was performed for a fixed amount of time, and the number of correct patterns was the dependent measure. Due to time constraints, we used only the twenty-four trials contained in part 1 of the test.

The model

A fragment is encoded via the preprocessing and pattern-activation subsystems. The attention window is shifted to the pattern itself, and an image of the fragment projected on to it via the pattern-activation subsystem. The location and orientation of the imaged fragment are altered via the transformation-shift subsystem until it matches part of the pattern or fails to match, as indicated by the preprocessing and pattern-activation subsystems. When a match is found, the location of the fragment is encoded via the co-ordinate encoding subsystem (the precise position is critical), which also requires the spatiotopic mapping subsystem. Another fragment is encoded, but now an image of the first one – in the proper location – is imposed on the pattern before the image of the second fragment is manipulated. (In order to image the first fragment, the co-ordinate lookup subsystem is used to access its location, the attention-shifting subsystem moves the attention window to the location, and the part is imaged via the pattern-activation subsystem.) If a match is found for the second fragment, its location is encoded, and the process is repeated for the other fragments. Once the pattern is completely matched, the subject moves on to the next pattern. Because the speed and accuracy of each subsystem are critical for the dependent measure, all subsystems used in the task are weighted.

Vividness of visual imagery questionnaire (VVIQ)

This questionnaire requires subjects to visualize described scenes and to rate the subjective vividness of each scene on a five-point scale (Marks 1973). The scale ranged from 'perfectly clear and vivid as normal vision' to 'no image at all, you only "know" that you are thinking of the object'. The questionnaire included thirty-two items; each subject rated each item twice, once with eyes open and once with eyes closed.

The model

All of the subsystems used in the image generation and inspection tasks are used here. Vividness is assessed by the feature detection subsystem. The vividness depends on how well the pattern-activation subsystem projects the image plus the sensitivity of the feature-detection subsystem, which are the only subsystems weighted, according to the weighting rules.

Table 2.1 summarizes the models and weighting subsystems for each task.

Predicting processing similarity

If the new theory is to be satisfactory, it must predict the structure of individual differences at least as well as did the previous theory. Thus, we derived predictions about which tasks should have been performed to a similar degree of effectiveness, if they in fact share many weighted subsystems. The predicted similarity in processing was computed for each pair of tasks by forming a ratio in the following way. First, we

Table 2.1 Use of visual processing subsystems in imagery tasks

Task	PREPR	PATAC	FEATD	CATLK	COOLK	CCCON	ATTNS	SMAP	CATENC	COORENC	TRANS
Acuity	1	1	2	0	0	0	0	1	0	1	1
Oblique	0	1	2	0	0	0	0	1	1	0	1
Extent	1	1	2	0	0	0	0	1	0	1	1
Rot.slope	0	0	0	2	0	2	2	2	2	0	2
Line time	0	2	0	0	0	0	0	2	2	0	0
Line mem.	0	2	0	1	0	1	1	1	1	0	0
Des. scenes	1	1	0	0	1	1	2	1	1	1	0
Gen. slope	2	2	0	2	0	2	2	2	2	0	0
Reorg. time	2	2	0	2	0	2	2	0	0	0	0
Reorg. probe	2	2	0	2	0	2	2	0	0	0	0
Nonreorg. pr.	2	2	0	2	0	2	2	0	0	0	0
Form board	2	2	0	0	2	0	2	2	0	2	2
VVIQ	1	2	2	1	0	1	1	1	1	0	0

Note: For each subsystem, a 0 in the row corresponding to a particular task indicates that the subsystem is not used in that task. A 1 indicates that the subsystem is used in the task but not weighted in computing the predicted similarity between performance on that task and performance on the other tasks (see text for explanation of weighting rules and similarity computations). A 2 indicates that the subsystem is used in the task and weighted in similarity computations.

Key:

PREPR	Preprocessing	CCCON	Categorical-co-ordinate conversion
PATAC	Pattern activation	ATTNS	Attention shifting
FEATD	Feature detection	SMAP	Spatiotopic mapping
CATLK	Categorical lookup	CATENC	Categorical relations encoding
COOLK	Co-ordinate lookup	COORENC	Co-ordinate relations encoding
		TRANS	Transformation shift

Table 2.2 Correlations among performance scores for the different tasks

Tasks	1	2	3	4	5	6	7	8	9	10	11	12	13
1. Acuity	X												
2. Oblique	0.43	X											
3. Extent	0.55	0.59	X										
4. Rot. slope	-0.09	0.06	-0.12	X									
5. Line time	0.11	-0.22	0.16	-0.23	X								
6. Line mem.	-0.19	-0.10	0.13	-0.09	0.39	X							
7. Des. scenes	-0.08	-0.13	-0.17	-0.02	-0.25	0.05	X						
8. Gen. slope	0.02	0.26	0.04	0.02	0.21	0.05	-0.10	X					
9. Reorg. time	0.02	0.10	-0.04	0.11	-0.04	0.00	-0.18	0.26	X				
10. Reorg. probe	0.00	0.09	-0.04	0.21	0.23	0.28	-0.27	0.30	0.64	X			
11. Nonreorg. pr.	-0.08	0.19	0.10	0.16	0.01	0.18	-0.25	0.28	0.63	0.79	X		
12. Form board	-0.31	0.01	0.02	-0.01	0.01	0.51	0.06	-0.04	-0.01	0.26	0.32	X	
13. VVIQ	-0.06	-0.44	-0.26	-0.19	0.08	0.04	-0.14	-0.19	0.29	0.07	0.06	0.07	X

counted the number of times that both tasks weighted the same subsystem (that is, the number of shared weighted subsystems). This quantity served as the numerator of the similarity ratio. Second, to compute a denominator for the similarity ratio, we added together the number of times that either (1) both tasks weighted a given subsystem, or (2) only one task weighted a given subsystem. Hence, the denominator consisted of the numerator (the number of shared weighted subsystems) plus the number of subsystems that were weighted by only one of the two tasks. Defined in this way, the similarity ratio can vary between 0 and 1 but can never be less than 0.

Thus, rather than predicting the actual correlation coefficients between pairs of tasks we computed an alternative measure of similarity. Next, we tested the predictive power of our analysis of the imagery tasks described above. This was done by computing the correlation between (1) the predicted similarities between tasks, as measured by the similarity ratios described above, and (2) the observed similarities between tasks, as measured by the data-derived matrix of intercorrelations between the tasks, shown in Table 2.2. This correlation between the predicted and observed similarities was $r = 0.63$. This correlation is higher than that obtained by Kosslyn *et al.* (1984) using the Kosslyn and Shwartz (1977) model, which was $r = 0.56$, while at the same time using fewer parameters (eleven here, versus thirteen as before).

In addition, we examined the degree to which the new analyses provided insight into the structure underlying the observed correlations. Figure 2.1 provides the result of cluster analysis (HICLUS), with weighted subsystems for each task noted on the right. As is evident, tasks with similar models did indeed cluster together.

The models suggest another interpretation for results of clustering analysis – that is, the models appear to provide some insight into underlying 'psychological complexity'. The models with more weighted subsystems presumably have more junctures at which individual differences can make themselves known: if any of the weighted subsystems is particularly ineffective, it will result in poor task performance. Thus, among the more weighted subsystems, the more likely it is that one of the subsystems is ineffective and that a given person will perform the task poorly. It is not obvious that simply pushing a button when an image has been formed involves more complex processing (in this sense) than does imagining a grating moving away until it blurs, and so forth.

Conclusions

We have demonstrated how a theory that is motivated by neurological facts and computational considerations can be used to understand individual differences. The present use of the theory is particularly interesting because even though it was not designed with individual

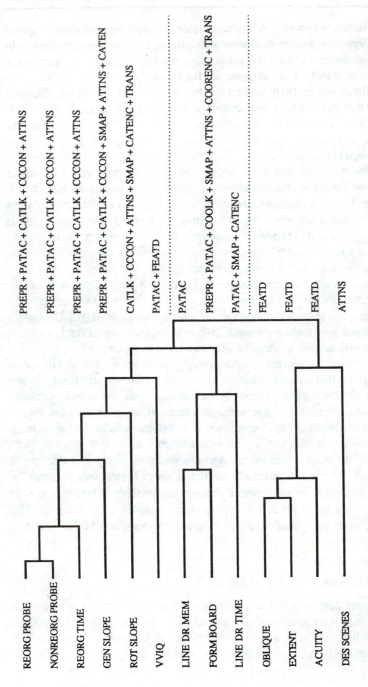

Figure 2.1 The results of hierarchical clustering of the correlations presented in Table 2.2. The weighted subsystems for each task are indicated at the right.

differences in mind, it yielded at least as powerful predictions of those differences than did the previous theory. If the task analyses and weighting rules turn out to be reliably applied by independent users, they will provide a valuable tool for predicting task performance. And to the extent that applications can be derived from the theory, the theory itself thereby gains added credence.

Acknowledgements

This work was supported by AFOSR contract 88–0012. We wish to thank Jonathan Amsterdam, Rex Flynn, and Michael Sokolov for their role in developing the theory on which this work is based.

Appendix 1

Weighting Rules

Preprocessing

Response time: (1) objects or parts must be recognized from unusual viewpoints; (2) a task involves figure/ground segregation.

Accuracy: (1) a figure is camouflaged or partially occluded.

Pattern activation

Response time: (1) objects or parts are recognized by their shape; (2) images of shapes are generated.

Accuracy: (1) one must maintain in an image more than about four perceptual units; (2) one must maintain in an image a single perceptual unit for more than its fade time (about 1 second).

Feature detection

Response time: (1) one assesses texture or colour.

Accuracy: (1) texture or colour is used to guide processing; (2) a texture or colour judgement itself is the accuracy measure.

Spatiotopic mapping

Response time: (1) the categorical or co-ordinate encoding subsystem is weighted.

Accuracy: (1) the categorical or co-ordinate encoding system is weighted.

Categorical relations encoding

Response time: (1) a categorical relation between parts or objects is to be reported or evaluated; (2) the parts of an image must be positioned (as in image generation or in the repositioning of parts during image transformations) or located, and approximate locations (via a nameable spatial relationship such as 'to the left of' or 'above') are adequate for the task.

Accuracy: the categorical-relations encoding subsystem is not weighted.

Co-ordinate relations encoding

Response time: (1) a precise metric location between parts or objects is to be reported or evaluated; (2) the parts of an image must be positioned or located precisely in order to perform the task.

Accuracy: (1) precise metric positioning or locating of objects or parts is required.

Categorical lookup

Response time: (1) an image of a multi-part object is generated, inspected or transformed, and recall of nameable spatial relations is adequate for positioning or locating the parts.

Accuracy: the categorical lookup subsystem is not weighted.

Co-ordinate lookup

Response time: (1) an image of a multi-part object is generated, inspected, or transformed, and recall of precise metric locations of parts is necessary for positioning or locating the parts.

Accuracy: the co-ordinate lookup subsystem is not weighted.

Categorical-co-ordinate conversion

Response time: (1) the categorical property lookup subsystem is weighted.

Accuracy: the categorical-co-ordinate subsystem is not weighted.

Attention shifting

Response time: (1) the task requires shifting attention across or between objects or parts; (2) the task requires changing the resolution of the image (that is, shifting levels within the visual buffer).

Accuracy: the attention-shifting subsystem is not weighted.

Transformation shift

Response time: (1) an object in an image must be rotated, translated, scaled or scanned more than about 4 degrees (and hence the image itself will be translated, in addition to shifting the attention window).

Accuracy: (1) precise metric relations are required in order to rotate, translate, scale, or scan more than about 4 degrees.

Appendix 2

Subsystem assignment rules

Image generation
Used whenever images are formed from memory.

Single unit patterns: associative memory, pattern activation, visual buffer.

Multi-unit patterns: (1) for mutable objects or when named spatial relations among parts are adequate for positioning or locating them: associative memory, pattern activation, visual buffer, categorical lookup, categorical-co-ordinate conversion, attention shifting, categorical relations encoding; (2) for specific exemplars where precise metric positioning or location is required: associative memory, pattern activation, visual buffer, co-ordinate lookup, attention shifting, co-ordinate relations encoding.

Image inspection
Used whenever imagery is used.

Shape identification: (1) normal viewpoint, small visual angle (4 degrees or less), highly familiar shape configuration: preprocessing, pattern activation, associative memory; (2) not highly familiar shape configuration or viewed at a large visual angle, mutable object: pre-processing, pattern activation, associative memory, spatiotopic mapping, categorical relations encoding, categorical lookup, categorical-co-ordinate conversion, attention shifting; (3) unusual viewpoint or viewed at a large visual angle, specific exemplar: preprocessing, pattern activation, associative memory, spatiotopic mapping, co-ordinate relations encoding, co-ordinate lookup, attention shifting.

Colour or texture identification: feature detection, associative memory.

Spatial relations identification: (1) categorical: spatiotopic mapping, categorical relations encoding, associative memory; (2) co-ordinate: spatiotopic mapping, co-ordinate relations encoding, associative memory.

Image retention

Used whenever an image (generated or perceived) is retained for more than 1 second after being formed.

Single-unit patterns: preprocessing, pattern activation.

Multi-unit patterns: (1) for mutable objects: associative memory, pattern activation, visual buffer, categorical lookup, categorical-co-ordinate conversion, attention shifting, categorical relations encoding; (2) for specific exemplars: associative memory, pattern activation, visual buffer, co-ordinate lookup, attention shifting, co-ordinate relations encoding.

Image transformation

Used whenever imaged size, orientation or perceived position is altered.

Single unit patterns: transformation, attention shifting.

Multi-unit patterns: (1) for mutable objects: transformation, attention shifting, categorical relations encoding, co-ordinate relations encoding, associative memory, categorical lookup; (2) for specific exemplars: transformation, attention shifting, co-ordinate relations encoding, associative memory, co-ordinate lookup.

References

Allman, J. M., and Kaas, J. H. (1976) 'Representation of the visual field on the medial wall of the occipital lobe of the owl monkey', *Science* 191: 572–6.

Andersen, R. A., Essick, G. K., and Siegel, R.M. (1985) 'Encoding of spatial location by posterior parietal neurons', *Science* 230: 456–8.

Appelle, S. (1972) 'Perception and discrimination as a function of stimulus orientation: the "oblique effect" in man and animals', *Psychological Bulletin* 89: 266–73.

Biederman, I. (1987) 'Recognition-by-components: a theory of human image understanding', *Psychological Review* 94: 115–47

Bower, G. H. (1972) 'Mental imagery and associative learning', in L.W. Gregg (ed.) *Cognition in Learning and Memory*, New York: Wiley.
  and Glass, A. L. (1976) 'Structural units and the redintegrative power of picture fragments', *Journal of Experimental Psychology: Human Learning and Memory* 2: 456–66.

Cooper, L. A. (1975) 'Mental rotation of random two-dimensional shapes', *Cognitive Psychology* 7: 20–43.

Cowey, A. (1985) 'Aspects of cortical organization related to selective attention and selective impairments of visual perception: a tutorial review', in M. I. Posner and O. S. M. Marin (eds) *Attention and Performance XI*, Hillsdale, NJ: Erlbaum.

Farah, M. J. (1984) 'The neurological basis of mental imagery: a componential analysis', *Cognition* 18: 245–72.
  (1988) 'Is visual imagery really visual? Overlooked evidence from neuropsychology', *Psychological Review* 95: 307–17.

Feldman, J. A. (1984) 'Four frames suffice: a provisional model of vision and space', *The Behavioral and Brain Sciences* 8: 265–89.

Finke, R., and Kosslyn, S. M. (1980) 'Mental imagery acuity in the peripheral visual field', *Journal of Experimental Psychology: Human Perception and Performance* 6: 126–39.

Finke, R., and Shepard, R. N. (1986) 'Visual functions of mental imagery', in K. R. Boff, L. Kaufman, and J. P. Thomas (eds) *Handbook of Perception and Human Performance*, New York: Wiley.

Goldman-Rakic, P. S. (1987) 'Circuitry of primate prefrontal cortex and regulation of behaviour by representational memory', in F. Plum (ed.) *Handbook of Physiology: The Nervous System V*, Bethesda, MD: American Physiological Society.

Gross, C. G., Bruce, C. J., Desimone, R., Fleming, J., and Gattass, R. (1981) 'Cortical visual areas of the temporal lobe', in C. N. Woolsey (ed.) *Cortical Sensory Organization II: Multiple Visual Areas*, Clinton, NJ: Humana Press.
  Desimone, R., Albright, T. D., and Schwartz, E. L. (1984) 'Inferior temporal cortex as a visual integration area', in F. Reinoso-Suarez and C. Ajmone-Marsan (eds), *Cortical Integration*, New York: Raven Press.

Kosslyn, S. M. (1980) *Image and Mind*, Cambridge, MA: Harvard University Press.

(1983) *Ghosts in the Mind's Machine: Creating and Using Images in the Brain*, New York: Norton.

(1987) 'Seeing and imagining in the cerebral hemispheres: a computational approach', *Psychological Review* 94: 148–75.

and Shwartz, S. P. (1977) 'A simulation of visual imagery', *Cognitive Science* 1: 265–95.

Ball, T. M., and Reiser, B. J. (1978) 'Visual images preserve metric spatial information: evidence from studies of image scanning', *Journal of Experimental Psychology: Human Perception and Performance* 4: 47–60.

Brunn, J. L., Cave, K. R., and Wallach, R. W. (1984) 'Individual differences in mental imagery ability: a computational analysis', *Cognition* 18: 195–243.

Cave, C. B., Provost, D. A., and von Gierke, S. M. (1988) 'Sequential processes in image generation', *Cognitive Psychology* 20: 319–43.

Flynn, R. A., Amsterdam, J. B., and Wang, G. (in press) 'Components of high-level vision: a cognitive neuroscience analysis and accounts of neurological syndromes', *Cognition*.

Larsen, A., and Bundesen, C. (1978) 'Size scaling in visual pattern recognition', *Journal of Experimental Psychology: Human Perception and Performance* 4: 1–20.

Lowe, D. G. (1987a) 'Three-dimensional object recognition from single two-dimensional images', *Artificial Intelligence* 31: 355–95.

(1987b) 'The viewpoint consistency constraint', *International Journal of Computer Vision* 1: 57–72.

Marks, D. F. (1973) 'Visual imagery differences and eye movements in the recall of pictures', *Perception and Psychophysics* 14: 407–12.

Marr, D. (1982) *Vision*, San Francisco: Freeman.

Mishkin, M., and Ungerleider, L. G. (1982) 'Contribution of striate inputs to the visuospatial functions of parieto-preoccipital cortex in monkeys', *Behavioural Brain Research* 6: 57–77.

Moran, J., and Desimone, R. (1985) 'Selective attention gates visual processing in the extrastriate cortex', *Science* 229: 782–4.

Neisser, U. (1967) *Cognitive Psychology*, New York: Appleton-Century-Crofts.

Palmer, S. E. (1977) 'Hierarchical structure in perceptual representations', *Cognitive Psychology* 9: 441–74.

Pennington, N., and Kosslyn, S. M. (1981) 'The "oblique effect" in mental imagery', unpublished manuscript, Harvard University.

Posner, M. I., Inhoff, A. W., Friedrich, F. J., and Cohen, A. (1985) 'Isolating attentional systems: a cognitive-anatomical analysis', paper presented at the meetings of the Psychonomic Society, Boston, MA.

Reed, S. K. and Johnsen, J. A. (1975) 'Detection of parts in patterns and images', *Memory and Cognition* 3: 569–75.

Rizzolatti, G., Gentilucci, M., and Matelli, M. (1985) 'Selective spatial attention: one center, one circuit, or many circuits?' in M. I. Posner and O. S. M. Marin (eds) *Attention and Performance XI*, Hillsdale, NJ: Erlbaum.

Shepard, R. N., and Cooper, L. A. (1982) *Mental Images and Their Transformations*, Cambridge, MA: MIT Press.

Tootell, R. B. H., Silverman, M. S., Switkes, E., and De Valois, R. L. (1982) 'Deoxyglucose analysis of retinotopic organization in primate striate cortex', *Science* 218: 902–4.

Treisman, A. M., and Gelade, G. (1980) 'A feature integration theory of attention', *Cognitive Psychology* 12: 97–136.

Ungerleider, L. G. and Mishkin, M. (1982) 'Two cortical visual systems', in D. J. Ingle, M. A. Goodale, and R. J. W. Mansfield (eds) *Analysis of Visual Behavior*, Cambridge, MA: MIT Press.

Van Essen, D. C. (1985) 'Functional organization of primate visual cortex', in A. Peters and E. G. Jones (eds) *Cerebral Cortex*, Vol 3, New York: Plenum Press.

and Maunsell, J. H. R. (1983) 'Hierarchical organization and functional streams in visual cortex', *Trends in Neuroscience*, September: 370–5.

Yarbus, A. L. (1967) *Eye Movements and Vision*, New York: Plenum Press.

Chapter three

Imagery, consciousness, and cognitive control

the BOSS model reviewed

Peter J. Hampson and Peter E. Morris

There is by now considerable evidence that imagery shares many of its properties with perception. Several perceptual operations such as scanning, rotation, or size comparisons can be recapitulated using imagery (for example, Kosslyn 1980; Shepard and Cooper 1982); imagery and perception can interfere in certain circumstances, suggesting competition for similar processes (for example, Brooks 1968; Logie and Baddeley, Chapter 4 in this volume); and damage to neuronal mechanisms known to affect perception often results in impairment of imagery too (Sunderland, Chapter 13 in this volume). During the past fifteen years a large amount of work has been done to try to establish the limits of this functional equivalence (for example, Finke 1980) and progress has been encouraging. Until recently, however, there has been a tendency simply to leave the nature of the parent perceptual theory rather vague or unspecified (though see Neisser 1976; Kosslyn *et al.* 1985; Marks, Chapter 1 in this volume; Kosslyn *et al.*, Chapter 2 in this volume).

What would a parent perceptual theory capable of generating a theory of imagery look like? We suggest that any theory of perception from which an imagery theory could be deduced would need to account for at least the following:

(1) how basic sensory information is analysed, combined, and stored;
(2) what information is processed (as well as how);
(3) how objects are recognized;
(4) how perception and action are interrelated; and
(5) how non-conscious information-processing mechanisms yield consciously reportable perceptions.

Certain workers have examined aspects of these. Kosslyn's research group, for example, has considered aspects of (1) and (3) (Kosslyn *et al.* 1985; Kosslyn *et al.*, Chapter 2 in this volume), while Neisser's (1976) cyclical theory of perception and now Marks' theory (see Chapter 1 in this volume) address (2) and (4). On the other hand the way in which aspects of non-conscious processing afford consciousness in both imagery and perception has received less attention to date. The issue is important since it is generally assumed that while the majority of perceptual operations are non-conscious they can nevertheless result in a conscious percept or at least in a mental experience which the perceiver can describe. If imagery does recapitulate perception it seems reasonable to ask whether a similar relationship between non-conscious and conscious processing also arises when imaging.

A second, and closely related theme is that imagery is known to have subjective as well as information-processing dimensions but that there has generally been a tendency for these to be studied separately from information processing. These dimensions include: qualitative aspects such as vividness and clarity; the intentionality and significance of the image for the imager; the integration and cross-sensory transfer of information (for example, synaesthesia); and the fact that one can be aware of imaging. All of these have been described at various times at the phenomenological level but we do not have at our disposal an adequate process description. How, in information-processing terms, do conscious images emerge or arise from non-conscious mental activity?

Third, images are known to be used in quite demanding or effortful cognitive activities such as problem solving, reasoning, and planning, especially when the task is novel – just the sort of activities, in fact, in which the organism must deploy its cognitive functions most flexibly and consciously. Many of these activities require the co-ordination of several aspects of the cognitive system: no one single process is involved. Such co-ordination is likely to require high levels of control over mental activity. Typical examples here would be the imagery which often accompanies the mental models used in syllogistic reasoning (Johnson-Laird 1983), or the imagery used when novices deal with problems involving the mental manipulation of complex spatial arrangements, as in chess (see Kaufmann, Chapter 7 in this volume).

From three different starting-points the same point is reached: to ground imagery more adequately in perceptual theory, to account for its experiential character more satisfactorily, and to describe its wider function in thinking and problem solving we need a theory which links information processing, subjective mental experience, and cognitive control. The resulting theory of consciousness must be sufficiently powerful to cover both imagery and perception and to allow extension to other cognitive functions.

The aim of this chapter is to discuss the progress that has been made towards such a goal. First we review a number of wider philosophical and psychological reasons why a theory of consciousness is required. Next, some recent accounts are discussed, and one, the BOSS model, first described by Morris (1981) and subsequently applied to imagery by Morris and Hampson (1983), is considered in some detail. When first proposed, the BOSS model was reasonably successful in accounting for a wide variety of imagery phenomena, but it has since become apparent that a number of its key characteristics were inadequately specified, such as the nature of the programs and information used by BOSS, the central controller, and the links between BOSS and other control systems. Here we attempt to rectify this by indicating ways in which the model can be elaborated and, at the same time, be made more precise. Recent work in perception on the relation between conscious and non-conscious processing is then discussed and extrapolated to clarify an important feature of the BOSS model. Finally the revised BOSS account is reapplied to imagery.

General reasons why we need a theory of consciousness

The place that consciousness should occupy in psychological research has been the subject of much stormy debate. When Wundt first defined the new science of psychology, conscious experience was the central subject matter to be studied and explained (for example, Wundt 1896). Later, attacks by behaviourist psychologists, led by Watson (1913), and by philosophers (for example, Ryle 1949; Wittgenstein 1953) relegated consciousness and, with it, imagery to the status of unscientific constructs. Only recently has the need for an adequate theory of consciousness become accepted and have serious attempts been made to provide one. There are a number of reasons why we need such a theory.

To begin with there are several classic philosophical issues in which notions of consciousness figure. For the sake of brevity these can be reduced to three: the mind-body problem and the private-language argument, problems of self-awareness, and issues of intentionality. Any comprehensive account of consciousness would illuminate these problems.

Next, there are three main psychological reasons why we need a theory of consciousness. First, there is the fact that subjective mental experience needs to be explained. Second, there are new data which require an account of the relation between conscious and non-conscious mental activity. Third, there are a number of gaps to be filled and inconsistencies and contradictions in our current cognitive theories which might be resolved by an appropriate theory of consciousness. We will examine these in turn.

For most people, they and their world are constituted by their conscious experiences. These are more than mere self-reports, though self-reports depend on them. What we have in mind is broader than this. It includes the vast number of phenomena which people experience and sometimes report that are not yet fully captured by our current theories. As Morris and Hampson (1983) have listed many of these elsewhere, only a brief indication of what we have in mind will be given here. People frequently claim, for instance, that they are aware of perceiving objects and events, that they are conscious of thoughts and memories, and that they experience emotions and fears. Moreover, most adult humans of normal intelligence are aware of their own special mental state or consciousness: people know that they are conscious. Indeed, for most people, they are their conscious experiences. These subjective dimensions or correlates of mental activity are the prima facie bricks and mortar of life. Such phenomena and their associated reports require explanation. It may, of course, turn out that some self-reports are inaccurate and misleading. The reasons why psychology treats the introspective method with caution are well known. Nevertheless, the fact that introspection does occur is not seriously disputed and some account of its operation is needed. Nor is the claim doubted that many cognitive processes appear to carry with them an experiential dimension, even though the functional role of such experiences may be doubted. Whether they have a role or not, their very existence needs to be considered. Curiously, psychologists often need to be convinced that conscious experience itself is worth studying while the layperson often believes that only conscious experience is really important.

While subjective experiences and their reports are, as far as we are concerned, the primary data to be explained, these may be less obvious and thought-provoking for psychologists than demonstrations that the normal relation between processing and experience can be disassociated in various ways. There are now a number of such demonstrations though perhaps those reported by Marcel (1983a) on processing without awareness are among the best known (though see also Dixon 1971). Weiskrantz *et al.* (1974) have also discussed some interesting experiments in which certain neurological patients who are effectively blind, in that they lack conscious visual experience, can nevertheless perform on perceptual tests at levels which indicate that they are perceiving stimuli without realizing that they are doing so. The conclusions which Marcel draws from his work, which though performed on normal subjects is similar in spirit to that reported by Weiskrantz *et al.*, will be discussed more fully later. In both cases the question is raised as to what consciousness adds to processes that are otherwise closed to introspection.

A good theory of consciousness is also needed because of certain gaps and inadequacies in otherwise uncontroversial cognitive theories used to explain quite conventional data. There are in fact many such gaps. To begin with, many of our cognitive models are designed to account for quite restricted domains or sets of phenomena. There are obviously good reasons for this. Psychologists have learned from long experience that problems of behaviour and mental life are often only made tractable by reduction and simplification. Unfortunately, a by-product of this strategy is that many interesting problems situated at the interstices of neighbouring research areas tend to be ignored. One such interesting problem is the co-ordination of different cognitive activities, cognitive subsystems, and the management of the system as a whole. Take the case of activities within the memory system, for example, where a useful distinction has been made between episodic and semantic remembering (for example, Tulving 1983). Researchers have taken great pains to establish in isolation the properties of the different subsystems thought to support these two forms of remembering, but have rarely addressed how, in the normal course of events, the memory system as a whole switches from one type of remembering to another. This argument is not vitiated by recent claims (for example, Tulving 1985) that the semantic and episodic subsystems may be hierarchically embedded rather than parallel and independent (for example, Tulving 1983) since the issue of how activities are switched still remains. However, if the reader prefers a different example, how does the cognitive system change, say, from listening to speech to remembering a view seen on holiday? Whenever a mechanism of cognitive control or switching is clearly required, its role is typically delegated to the unexplained and unanalysed 'subject'. Other gaps include the links between major cognitive systems (how are perception and action really related?), the links between activities calling on two or more systems (how do reasoning and remembering interact?), and links between cognition and emotion (how does feeling affect thought and vice versa?). The reader will protest at this point that there is considerable activity in many of these very research areas, citing their favourite references as support. It is true that work is ongoing on many of these problems and some theorists have made good progress in this regard. Thus, for example, the central executive in the working-memory model could well perform the switching functions discussed above (Baddeley 1986; Logie and Baddeley, Chapter 4 in this volume), but it is also true that we are still a long way from a theory of how the cognitive system is managed that is at once sufficiently general to explain more than a limited range of these phenomena without being so general as to make no predictions.

Another problem with cognitive theory is that some of our familiar categories are themselves looking rather tired and suspect. Take as an example the idea that cognitive processes are broadly of two types, controlled and automatic. A variety of evidence can be adduced to support this, and there is some consensus that the former are generally slow, conscious, effortful or attention-demanding, and avoidable while the latter are fast, non-conscious, effortless, attention-free, and unavoidable (for example, Schneider and Shiffrin 1977; Shiffrin and Schneider 1977). The distinction has crept into our introductory textbooks and has affected areas of cognitive psychology further afield than its birthplace in the attention literature. Yet all is not well. To begin with, there is currently some disagreement concerning the precise criteria used to underwrite these labels. Despite some broad agreement and consistency among attention theorists as to the acceptable yardsticks for automatic processes, workers in other areas such as memory have used the term 'automatic' in a much looser way to mean simply non-conscious or not open to introspection. This seems to be the sense in which Tulving (1983), for example, talks about automatic retrieval processes. Second, if we do restrict ourselves to one commonly accepted criterion, namely that automatic processes demand zero attention, other problems arise. Careful experimentation has shown that automatic processes may not only require attention, as indexed by their effect on concurrent, secondary, attention-demanding tasks, but may also interfere with other apparently automatic processes. Also, the idea that automatic processes are unavoidable has been undermined. Automatic processes seem to be easily suppressed if their initiating stimuli are outside the attentional field. Conversely they are harder to avoid when they fall within the spotlight of attention. It is as if central, attentional, controlled processes are needed to initiate and run automatic ones. The boundary between automatic and controlled processes is now less clear-cut than was previously thought. It can no longer be confidently asserted that non-conscious, automatic processes demand zero attention or run without some controlled process assistance (see Kahneman and Treisman, 1984, for a full discussion of all these issues).

At this point the reader may be forgiven for wondering what all this has to do with the need for a theory of consciousness. The problem is this: the previous neat theoretical separation between controlled and automatic processes went hand in hand with that between conscious and non-conscious mental activities. It was often tacitly assumed that consciousness was strictly and solely associated with controlled or non-automatic mental activity. Processes were either controlled or automatic, those that were controlled were conscious and those that were automatic were non-conscious. The real issues, it was implied, concerned the characteristics of automatic versus controlled processes. The problem of consciousness, it was further implied, would be dealt with by default.

Recently, because of the blurring of the boundary between automatic and controlled processes, this simple equation of cognitive control with consciousness has started to break down. Many non-conscious cognitive processes, previously thought of as fully automatic, seem only able to run with the help of some co-ordination or management or attentional input, but this form of attention or control does not seem to be associated with consciousness at all. We must now distinguish between two classes of cognitive control: one involved in the planning and management of conscious processes, the other in the more routine regulation of non-conscious mental activity. Attention, or controlled processing, and consciousness are not equivalent. The relation of attention and consciousness thus needs to be re-evaluated (see Norman and Shallice 1980, for a similar view), as does the problem of how consciousness 'fades out' as processing becomes more automatic.

A third difficulty is that there is general uncertainty in the discipline regarding the relation between information processing and phenomenology. Marcel (1986: 40) has alluded to this problem:

A peculiar state of affairs exists in cognitive psychology. Most current accounts of perception, cognition and task execution have no place for consciousness. Phenomenal experience and subjectivity are apparently unnecessary in models of cognition and there is certainly no evidence of them in the behaviour of artificial intelligence programs and automata. Yet information processing theorists react with scepticism when models and data are offered that explore the idea that phenomenal experience is dissociable from or not a prerequisite for the processing of sensory data.

Marcel (1983b) suggests that consciousness and information processing are dissociable and in turn indicates that phenomenal experience may not be isomorphic with or reducible to underlying information processing. Simple information processing accounts of mind appear necessary but not sufficient to explain all mental phenomena.

The tension between information processing and phenomenology is also evident in work on imagery. There have for quite some time been two traditions in imagery research. One, the older of the two, dating back to Galton (1883), has been concerned with issues such as the vividness, clarity, and other experiential dimensions of imagery. The other, more recent tradition has investigated imagery as an internal representation or cognitive code (for example, Paivio 1971, 1986; Kosslyn 1980). The two traditions ran in parallel with comparatively little cross-fertilization until the status of the experiential dimensions of imagery was debated in the last decade as part of the wider discussion on the function and nature of imagery as a whole (Pylyshyn 1973, 1981; Kosslyn and Pomerantz 1977; Kosslyn 1980). The debate raised the issue of whether the conscious or surface image was functional or epiphenomenal.

Another reason to be interested in consciousness is that we are aware of emotions as well as information or sensations. It tends to be assumed without further analysis that emotions and feelings are conscious, except perhaps the putative repressed feelings discussed by the psychoanalytic tradition. Also, only recently have psychologists really started to examine the links between cognition and emotion, but it is reasonable to assume that an examination of the way in which thinking and feeling combine will also involve an examination of the conscious forum in which the two interact.

Finally, there are models in existence which do incorporate a system whose functions appear to be equivalent to consciousness. These models, some of which we discuss below, should map onto or at least complement each other, but, formed as they are in different research areas, they often deal only with restricted applications or functions of consciousness. A sufficiently general theory of consciousness is needed to accommodate the wide range of cognitive phenomena.

We would not like to convey at this point the impression that an adequate theory of consciousness will, like a fairy godmother, solve all our problems! Substantive issues would surely still remain even if one were available right now. Nor do we believe that any of the points we have raised, taken singly, are likely to motivate many psychologists to study consciousness. Thus, the subliminal data are interesting but the history of science is replete with examples where data which fit uncomfortably into contemporary explanatory frameworks are often ignored for years. Nor do we think that pressure for a theory of consciousness will arise solely from the need to make sense of the basic lived experiences of people, the raw stuff of everyday mental life. Even though we believe this to be sufficient justification in its own right for the expenditure of research time and resources and ultimately to be the focal point of any complete theory of consciousness, we are not convinced that all our colleagues would agree. Taken together, however, the gaps in our models, the subliminal processing data, the problems of subjective experience, and the difficulties of linking thought and feeling provide converging pressure for a theory. Many of these problems, which are currently somewhat poorly specified, would be thrown into sharper relief if a more complete theory of consciousness were to be found.

In the next section we discuss some general characteristics of existing approaches to consciousness as well as examining our own model in some detail, before reapplying it to imagery.

Contemporary accounts of consciousness and the BOSS model

Contemporary accounts of consciousness can be grouped as follows. First, there are models which concentrate on the mechanism or system believed to support consciousness. The names given to this vary widely and range from the 'Supervisory Attentional System' (Norman and Shallice 1980), the 'Central Executive' in working memory (Baddeley 1986), the 'Limited Capacity Central Processor' (Craik and Lockhart 1972), and 'BOSS-consciousness' (Morris and Hampson 1983). These accounts differ in various ways, such as the range of phenomena they are meant to explain and their primary function as models of attention, memory, or cognitive control, but they do share the notion that consciousness is in some sense involved with the operations of a central control or co-ordinating system. Second, there are other accounts which put more emphasis on the way in which the representations or processes which form the content of consciousness differ from those of non-conscious information processing (for example, Marcel 1983b; Reason 1984). (As for the wider evolutionary function of consciousness, this has not been addressed in much detail by psychologists until recently; see however Humphrey 1983, 1986.)

The two major psychological approaches to consciousness, which we can label 'system' accounts and 'information' accounts, are not necessarily mutually exclusive. It is quite possible that consciousness depends on the operations of a specific component of the cognitive system while also making use of different representational forms from the rest of the system. If this is so, a more comprehensive model is needed which marries both approaches. A few years ago the BOSS model was proposed in an attempt to do precisely this (for a more recent account with a similar flavour, see Minsky 1987).

The original BOSS model was designed to do justice to the managerial function of consciousness and to accommodate the qualitative aspects of conscious representations. The model started from the assumption that many tasks undertaken by the cognitive system are carried out by specialist EMPLOYEE or slave systems whose operations are non-conscious. Thus, for instance, several basic perceptual processes such as feature detection, object segmentation, and visual analysis operate smoothly and in a non-conscious fashion, as do many of the preparatory phases of action or, say, the component processes involved in rapid retrieval of information from memory. However, it was also suggested that a superordinate system is needed to oversee, plan, and make decisions on behalf of the system as a whole. We called this system BOSS-consciousness. BOSS, it was argued, has two main jobs: to accept specially prepared information from the EMPLOYEES or specialist processors and to direct and co-ordinate the operations of the same by running its own high-level programs. The EMPLOYEES can be thought of as quasi-autonomous processing systems or modules (cf. Fodor 1983).

Because the main task of BOSS is to guide the system as a whole, the information fed to it by the EMPLOYEES has to be in such a form that decisions about the future of the entire organism can be made. To this end, it was suggested that BOSS is supplied with 'high-level' information and in turn issues high-level directives or commands to the EMPLOYEES. The organizational metaphor implicit in the BOSS model makes this clearer. The controller or manager of a large factory or organization is fed with information by his or her subordinates. This information is prepackaged in a form that the manager can easily digest and use to make decisions. Often the information will represent a summary of a department's activities rather than an account of the exact details of each and every job its members have performed. The manager may wish to know, for instance, how many new customers have been won by the sales team rather than the precise number of business lunches consumed in the process. At times, however, a real manager can enquire more closely into the workings of individual departments and order that details of their operation be supplied. Then, though, the 'story' the manager receives from the employees may not be the whole truth. To extend the above example: if the entertainment expenditure of a firm is too high, the manager may enquire more closely into the number and necessity of the business lunches partaken, though a wily set of sales employees might then provide a plausible justification, perhaps with some connivance from the department of creative accounting! Alternatively, to take another analogy, just as a sophisticated civil service can easily dupe its political masters, so the EMPLOYEES can 'mislead' BOSS. We think of this as the Principle of Executive Ignorance or the 'Yes, Prime Minister' syndrome!

On other occasions, BOSS may be required to describe the activities of the EMPLOYEES while being ignorant of their actual operations. The attempt by BOSS to do this will then reflect the concepts and explanations within which BOSS works rather than the EMPLOYEE processes. Many (erroneous) subjective reports of lower-level cognitive processes may come about in this way (cf. Nisbett and Wilson 1977; Morris 1981).

Thus, BOSS-consciousness is assumed to be at the mercy of the EMPLOYEES which it ostensibly controls. All information received by BOSS is already heavily processed, and BOSS has to take a lot of it at face value. The information fed to BOSS by the perceptual system, for example, will describe the position and appearance of putative objects-in-the-world: it will not be a description of lines, points, and angles. Similarly, BOSS outputs take the form of high-level directives, the details of their execution being left to subordinates. An order to the response system, for example, is more likely to be in the form of a command to perform such-and-such an action rather than to request that certain types of neural impulses be sent to such-and-such an effector.

To summarize, the essential elements of the model were:

(1) An overall control or management system, BOSS, together with a set of subordinate, EMPLOYEE systems.
(2) A distinction between high-level information and the information used by the rest of the system.
(3) The proposition that BOSS runs programs for the benefit of the system as a whole.
(4) The proposition that we are conscious of the information made available to the BOSS system, which includes summaries of its own output instructions. We are not conscious of the BOSS processes themselves.

Morris and Hampson (1983) applied the basic BOSS model to imagery in some detail. They pointed out that the surface or conscious image would be written in a form that BOSS could use, namely one analogous to the objects or events that the image represented. On the other hand, the information from which imagery was constructed was assumed to be retained in a more abstract form, with the construction process itself handled by dedicated EMPLOYEES. Once the image was constructed, certain high-level operations such as image scanning and inspection could then be carried out on the image itself by BOSS; others, such as the replacement of one image by another or a request for more detail, could only be effected with the help of the EMPLOYEES. This model was used to account for a large amount of the data on imagery existing at the time.

Problems, elaborations and extensions of model

While the original BOSS model captured a number of interesting facets of cognition, particularly the need for a central system for novel decision-making, planning, and control, it is as it stands weak in certain respects. We identify below some of the more serious problems with the model and suggest some possible remedies.

First, more detail is needed on BOSS programs. What basic types exist? What 'language' do they use? Is there one language of the executive or several?

Given that BOSS is the system which is used whenever a flexible, novel response with consequences for the system as a whole is required, it is possible to list in more detail the general sorts of programs for which BOSS would have to have responsibility.

To begin with, a set of programs for planning is necessary for any system whose function it is to guide the activities of the organism as a whole. Among these will be programs for strategy creation and selection, for organizing goal-directed behaviour, for problem solving and for the selection and implementation of learning strategies.

Next, programs for the organization and classification of fresh information, the reorganization of old, and the creation of new mental structures are needed. Thus, forming new categories and concepts, decisions about the category membership of ambiguous instances and the formation of organizational and logical structures would be included here.

Plan debugging, 'trouble shooting', and monitoring when things go wrong are activities traditionally associated with consciousness. BOSS must therefore be able to switch in more powerful programs, or adopt suitable heuristics, when the need arises, to deal with errors or hitches. As an example, consider the retrieval of information from long-term memory. This often occurs without the need for too much supervision. According to one popular account, retrieval is controlled largely by the interaction between trace information and that provided by retrieval cues (Tulving 1983). At times, however, direct access to the required information fails and the system has to engage in a more effortful, problem-solving mode of retrieval which Baddeley (1982) has referred to as 'recollection'. The decision to initiate recollection and take control over its progress will be undertaken by BOSS. Another example is the situation which arises when problem solving with a familiar algorithm which normally works fails to deliver an appropriate solution. Once again, more flexible and powerful programs will be called up by BOSS.

Decision-making is another BOSS role. All non-trivial decisions will involve BOSS activity, as will situations in which some evaluation is required. A task for students of decision-making is to identify clearly which aspects of their models are associated with conscious and which with non-conscious mental activity. Reasoning processes are also likely to require BOSS programs. These need not necessarily use logical rules but may work analogically, as Johnson-Laird (1983) has indicated.

The starting and stopping of processes and output monitoring will also require special BOSS programs. A function of consciousness stressed by Shallice (1972) and Norman and Shallice (1980) is its role in initiating activity. An equally vital function is to terminate behaviours that are no longer functional or to suppress unwanted behaviours. A third is to oversee and monitor activity at the highest and most significant level.

A further role for BOSS is in planning future actions. Where the schemata that control our habitual daily routines have to be modified temporarily, as when we have to break our drive home to call in to collect something from a shop, then the modification of the plan is made via a consciously experienced forming of an intention to act in this way. In general, the planning of our future actions seems always to involve conscious processes, presumably because it involves elements of novelty and decision-making.

Finally, as we noted earlier, an important aspect of consciousness is its ability to engage in self-monitoring and introspection. Self-awareness appears to demand skills of BOSS that were not foreseen in the original model. One important aspect of self-awareness seems to be the ability of the system to represent its own workings. In other words, it is as if BOSS must develop a theory of management as well as being an effective manager.

Having sketched the general sorts of programs which BOSS must deploy, we can also give some indication of the general types of instructions which will be used to run such BOSS programs. As a rule we would expect these to match the highest level of the activity in which the system as a whole is engaged at the time. Some examples might help here. In planning an utterance BOSS will be more heavily involved with the meaning and intention of the message and its impact on the listener than with the niceties of its syntax. Thus, BOSS will deal with highly synthesized representations which are biased towards meaning, though which also contain information about the tone of voice or emphasis to be used when necessary. In these situations BOSS is likely simply to give the go-ahead to the production apparatus if all is well, especially where low-level message elements are concerned, or to order a re-writing of the message if problems are detected. Whether problems are detected will depend on other high-level task demands, but when we do detect errors in speech, or action, we are always conscious that we have done so. Likewise, when BOSS is controlling actions it will issue general descriptions of action at high levels such as 'GO FOR COFFEE' and be concerned with their possible effects such as 'MAY MISS TRAIN IF QUEUE IS LONG' rather than with the niceties of the motor programs needed to walk to the cafeteria and the visual feedback they will use *en route*. In situations such as these, it is the implications and effects of actions and utterances – their instrumentality – with which BOSS will be concerned, not the fine details of their execution.

At other times BOSS programs will more closely match or be analogous to the real-world actions or operations which they, with the help of the EMPLOYEES, are meant to simulate. When imaging, as we pointed out in our initial account, imagery used by BOSS will be synthesized to an ecologically appropriate level. Since, as far as the BOSS system is concerned, the image functions as a surrogate object, it must also afford some of the operations that objects permit such as rotation or scanning or closer inspection. To ask whether or not these operations are cognitively penetrable as some have done (Pylyshyn 1981) is misleading if the goal is to understand the meaning or significance of conscious imagery for the system as a whole. To do so can obscure the point that, since consciousness must deal at the highest, most flexible, and value-laden level of activity, this is the level which must be considered if we wish to understand it; anything lower and we are in the realm of the EMPLOYEE systems (Morris and Hampson 1983).

As for the 'language' used by BOSS, it is probably a mistake to assume that only one is used in all circumstances. A better approach might be to think of there being a suite of BOSS programs, akin perhaps to the operating system of a computer which can run several quite different applications at the same or different times. Thus, when imaging, the language used or switched in by BOSS would be different from that used when directing action. The common component would be the managerial workings of BOSS itself. A similar argument regarding the operation of consciousness has been proposed by Johnson-Laird (1983).

A second problem to be explored is the issue of cognitive control. In the light of the earlier discussion on the nature of automatic processes, is it reasonable to assume that BOSS is the sole control system? Probably not. Although a superficial reading of our original account might lead to this assumption, it is neither inevitable nor necessary. In our account, BOSS is simply the overall, or top, control system. As our earlier discussion indicated, many so-called automatic processes appear to require some control or co-ordination. Routine as well as novel control needs to be exercised in many situations and this may be the province of a separate control system or systems (see, for example, Norman and Shallice 1980). Also, the very fact that BOSS can be fed with integrated representations which have themselves been constructed from the output of several more dedicated processors indicates that some co-ordination of processing at a pre-conscious level is possible.

The final set of problems is perhaps the most serious. The original model fails to specify in sufficient detail the nature of high-level information. In particular, the way in which this might differ from low-level information needs to be explained more clearly. Nor was it made fully explicit how the EMPLOYEES are involved in its production. This lack of specificity meant that while a reasonable account of imagery was provided by Morris and Hampson (1983), some aspects were not fully explored. The phenomenological character of imagery was discussed only briefly and the fact that images often involve blends of information from several sensory modalities was only touched upon.

To clarify all these points in detail would be tantamount to providing a complete account of cognition. A more modest aim is to examine other theories which describe the relation of non-conscious to conscious processes, to see whether these can be used to improve the BOSS model and our understanding of high-level information, and then reapply the elaborated model to imagery.

Conscious and non-conscious processing

From the external standpoint mental activity can be described as a set of information-processing operations involved in the perceiving, integrating, and interpreting of sensory input, retrieval from memory, the control of action, and so on. From the phenomenal perspective, however, some of this processing gives rise to or is correlated, loosely or otherwise, with the experience of consciousness for the system as a whole. How these two aspects are related has not been addressed properly in psychology until quite recently.

Marcel (1983a, b) has recently considered the problem. His approach derives from a series of studies on the effects of pattern masking on the perception of briefly presented visual displays, and before giving details of his theory it is worth describing briefly the nature of his empirical work.

It has been known for some time that when a stimulus is tachistoscopically displayed and quickly followed by another stimulus, the processing of the first can be affected by the second. In a typical iconic memory experiment, if either a brief but intense flash of light, a random arrangement of visual elements (noise mask), or a stimulus comprised of jumbled features of the initial display (pattern mask) is presented shortly after a display of alphanumeric characters, the subject's ability to report the latter is hampered (cf. Neisser 1967). It used to be thought that pattern and noise masks took effect at different stages of information-processing, with the former acting more centrally than the latter, and that pattern masks interrupted processing whereas noise-mask information became integrated with that from the stimulus (Turvey 1973; Baddeley 1976). Both types of mask were believed to curtail processing by hampering reporting or further use of its products. Turvey's distinction between integration and interruption effects in masking accorded well with the subjects' reports in masking studies. Noise masks seem to blend messily with the targets, pattern masks are commonly reported to remove completely any impression of the initial stimulus. Subjective experience in these situations was assumed to reflect, at least partially, aspects of the underlying information processing which masking was believed to disrupt.

Marcel (1983a) has challenged some of these claims. Even when subjects cannot report the presence of a stimulus, they can still sometimes use information from it. Thus, for example, semantic information can be recovered from words presented for as briefly as 10 msec. and pattern-masked to cut out awareness (Experiments 1 and 2). Such words can also affect the processing of subsequently presented stimuli. Masked words can apparently still prime other words despite the subject being unaware of their presence (Experiments 4 and 5), and can create interference in Stroop tasks (Experiment 3). Pattern masking precludes awareness of words without necessarily curtailing processing (see Allport *et al.* 1985, for similar effects with non-verbal stimuli).

Marcel (1983b) accounts for these (and other) results with a new theory of information processing and consciousness. The theory deals with the relation between conscious and non-conscious perceptual processes and rejects the so-called 'Identity Assumption'. This is the notion that 'phenomenal experience is identical to or is a direct reflection of the representations yielded by perceptual processes' (ibid.: 238). Marcel points out that since it is possible to remove awareness of stimuli without completely curtailing information processing, the two, information and experience, cannot be considered to be identical. Instead, the 'phenomenal representations' used in conscious processing are assumed to be separable and qualitatively distinct from those used by non-conscious processes (see also Coltheart 1980). This differs markedly from accounts in which consciousness is thought to emerge chiefly as a result of differences in strength or activation of underlying information-processing systems (for example, Deutsch and Deutsch 1963; Shallice 1972; Reason 1984).

The ways in which the conscious and non-conscious processing differ are explained in some detail by Marcel (1983b). To begin with, he claims that all sensory data picked up by the organism are automatically and non-consciously processed by a series of specialist processors into every representational form which they afford and which their processors permit. Next, he distinguishes between results, records, and perceptual hypotheses. Results are the outputs of non-conscious perceptual processes. They are 'dynamic and impermanent' and provide data which can be used as inputs to other processors. Results are responsible for supporting a great deal of behaviour, and can 'prime' related representations. They can also activate perceptual hypotheses or 'canonical representations of permanently stored perceptual and conceptual categories' (ibid.: 244). Records are the retrievable, temporally extended traces of outputs from specialist processors. They are assumed to have some mnemonic persistence.

Consciousness arises through the interaction of results, records, and perceptual hypotheses. Perceptual hypotheses, activated by results, are best thought of as structural descriptions of objects and events which specify their criterial features and their interrelationships: cf. Minsky's (1975) 'frames' or Neisser's (1976) 'schemata'; see also Marks, Chapter 1 in this volume. These are then tried for fit with the data obtained from records. Marcel suggests that a subset of the activated perceptual hypotheses is tested in parallel against the appropriate records. From this process, one hypothesis will be selected, and competing ones inhibited. The system is conscious neither of records, nor of results, nor of hypotheses, but of the phenomenal representations which result from the fit between records and a perceptual hypothesis.

Pattern masking interferes with the recovery of records and precludes the synthesis of phenomenal representations. It removes awareness of processing without affecting the basic, underlying processing itself. Marcel argues that a similar dissociation can occur in certain neuropathological states and illustrates this with appropriate examples (for example, Weiskrantz et al. 1974).

The theory has several advantages over alternative theories of consciousness. In particular it accounts for several characteristic features of consciousness.

(1) It shows how consciousness has an integrative or synthetic function. 'Consciousness is an attempt to make sense of as much data as possible at the most functionally useful level' (Marcel 1983b: p 238). We are conscious of organized aspects of the world, of objects or properties, rather than simple sensory features. The dominant perceptual hypotheses are used to recover and link together a series of records of underlying processing, perhaps involving information from various modalities, or combinations of emotional and sensory information. This process of recovery parses the information. Subjectively, this also gives the impression of the unity of conscious experience.

(2) A role is found for phenomenology as well as information processing. Recovering a record and integrating it with a perceptual hypothesis accords with the subjective experience of having a percept. The phenomenal level is qualitatively different from the informational. Put another way, the phenomenal level is dependent on and is caused by the underlying (normal) information processing, but cannot be reduced to it. In practice this has important implications for the categories used to describe conscious and non-conscious processes. In visual perception, for example, the most appropriate conscious description may be at the Euclidean level, whereas the non-conscious 'language' of the visual system may involve a non-Euclidean projective geometry.

(3) Consciousness can range over various levels of processing, though it will normally be 'pushed' to higher and higher levels. Perceptual hypotheses can redintegrate information at various levels, though recovery of early, sensory processing may be harder than recovering later stages involving meaning.

(4) Consciousness is selective and intentional. Perceptual hypotheses are directed at subsets of the total records available. Second, hypotheses represent, when instantiated by their records, consciousness of something.

(5) Despite methodological criticisms of Marcel's empirical work (for example, Holender 1986) the theory itself still stands as perhaps the most detailed account of the possible relation between conscious and non-conscious processing available at the moment and as such is worth entertaining.

Imagery and consciousness

Marcel's account was designed as a theory of perception, but it also provides the basis for an explanation of imagery and high-level information. To do this we need only make the assumption that Marcel has given a more exact specification of what we referred to as high-level information in the original BOSS model, and that what we called the perceptual EMPLOYEES are equivalent to Marcel's 'specialist processors'. The first supposition seems reasonable since the phenomenal representations described by Marcel and high-level information appear to have similar qualities. Both are the end-product of the work done by several underlying specialist processors, both are reportable by the system, both are intentional in character, and both could be considered as a story or construction fed to a higher-order system. Also, although high-level information and phenomenal representations are in a sense produced by the action of lower-level systems, the specialist processors or EMPLOYEES, they are not reducible in any simple way to the normal information-processing output of these systems. The production of high-level information or the recovery of perceptual representations introduces qualitative changes in the nature of the raw material of consciousness.

High-level programs use phenomenal representations to control future input and action. Within the framework of the BOSS model, Marcel has specified one possible way in which the perceptual EMPLOYEES could feed high-level information to BOSS for subsequent use. Given this, a number of points of contact between Marcel's work and a new theory of imagery can then be made.

(1) It is commonly accepted that imagery theory should relate to perception. Marcel's theory is particularly attractive since it accounts for the way percepts are constructed, describes the transition from non-conscious processing to conscious percept, and demonstrates the need for different levels of analysis. Percepts are said to be formed by recovering and synthesizing the outputs of several specialist processors; images are likely to require the integration of information from several separate sources too.

(2) As we indicated above, high-level information used by BOSS is equivalent to Marcel's phenomenal representations. Images are therefore the recovered and integrated records of prior

perceptual activity reactivated by the same perceptual hypotheses used in perceiving. They are of course composed of more abstract underlying elements but their high-level qualities cannot be simply reduced to these. Images have phenomenal qualities. They are organized, integrated, and whole. Moreover, they are images of things or events. Images exhibit intentionalilty.

(3) If imagery recapitulates perception, then imaging involves running perceptual programs without any incoming information. The same perceptual hypotheses are used to recover records when imaging as when perceiving. We simply need to assume that records have a certain mnemonic persistence to allow recovery at later dates.

(4) BOSS can be actively involved in image construction by ordering the selection of parent perceptual hypotheses. This is what it means to decide to image X or to follow instructions to image X. The hypothesis is then used to recover the appropriate records. The system is conscious only of the decision to image X, and, if successful, of the image of X itself.

(5) Image construction takes time. More complex images take longer to construct. Images will require several records to be recovered. This will apply particularly to complex images. Not all relevant records may be recoverable simultaneously. Recovering certain records will have the effect of reactivating the corresponding perceptual process. This in turn will set up a weak output to subsequent processes, which in turn will have further records available for recovery. In a complex image these will have to be redintegrated and organized in a cyclical fashion.

(6) When recovery is automatic (or at least less effortful) the system may be fooled into a false feeling of knowing. The ease with which an image is formed can often be a misleading indicator of its veracity. Morris (1986), for example, reported an experiment in which subjects answered questions about a video film they had seen, rating their confidence of their answer and indicating whether or not they had experienced a relevant image while answering the question. The occurrence of such images powerfully influenced confidence ratings, overriding effects due to accuracy of response. Confidence that the answer was correct was significantly higher with an image

but where the answer was incorrect, than it was where no image was experienced but where the answer was correct.

(7) Images will vary in the extent to which they are preconstructed, just as records can be synthesized at various levels. Some images (episodic) will involve a considerable amount of regeneration. This is the equivalent in imagery of Baddeley's (1982) concept of recollection. In other situations image construction occurs automatically with rapidity and efficiency. A word high in imageability, for example, may cue the appropriate perceptual hypothesis without extensive BOSS direction.

(8) Interference effects can occur at the level of the specialist processors (low-level structural interference) or at the recovery stage (high-level interference). The former is likely to be more modality-specific than the latter.

(9) Images need not be modality-pure. A fully integrated image of a scene, for example, could contain recovered visual, verbal, and olfactory information. Nevertheless, it is likely that one information source will predominate, since individuals differ in the preference for and the type of imagery they habitually use.

(10) The process of recovery is assumed to require attention. Processing under conditions of divided attention will restrict the range of records which can be recovered. In this situation, more global aspects of the stimulus will most likely be processed. In the case of visual images the outline of figures will be preserved. Reduction of attentional resource is likely to have other effects. The resulting phenomenal representation is likely to be more schematic, more prototypical, and less context bound. It will have more in common with semantic than episodic memory.

(11) The ability to distinguish memories from percepts (i.e. reality monitoring) is an important skill. It has been suggested that the two are discriminated between using four criteria:

(a) contextual attributes (perception has more);
(b) sensory attributes (ditto);
(c) schematic vs. detailed (memory is more schematic);
(d) effort involved in cognitive operations (memory is more effortful) (Johnson and Raye 1981; Johnson 1985).

Combined with Marcel's account these criteria might explain

how we normally distinguish between images and perception. (a) Contextual: recovery of fewer records, those specifying time and place being likely to be omitted from many images. (b) Sensory attributes: the notion that recovery of lower levels is difficult means that imagery will be less rich in sensory attributes. (c) Schematic: for the same reason, imagery will normally be more schematic than perception. (d) Initiating the process of recovery (imaging) will be more effortful than perceiving.

(12) Recovery of records from peripheral as well as central processors may in special circumstances permit the formation of images which are highly vivid and veridical replicas of the original stimulus (i.e. eidetic images), since peripheral information will preserve the sensory and metrical information from the stimulus in great detail.

(13) Individuals differ in strength and clarity of their imagery. Records will vary in availability and strength. In addition, people may vary in the abstractness of their imagery depending on whether recovery uses predominantly peripheral or central records. A clear but relatively uninterpreted image would result from the recovery of peripheral, sensory information; a more sketchy though more analysed image would result from the recovery of more central information. In certain cases a person may have little or no image at all but just know that he or she is thinking about the object. In this case, recovery of the highest, most categorical information is likely to be taking place.

References

Allport, D. A., Tipper, S. P., and Chmeil, N. R. J. (1985) 'Perceptual integration and postcategorical filtering', in M. I. Posner and O. S. M. Marin (eds) *Attention and Performance XI*, Hillsdale, NJ: Erlbaum.

Baddeley, A. D. (1976) *The Psychology of Memory*, New York: Basic Books.
— (1982) 'Domains of recollection', *Psychological Review* 89: 708–29.
— (1986) *Working Memory*, London: Oxford University Press.

Brooks, L. (1968) 'Spatial and verbal components of the act of recall', *Canadian Journal of Psychology* 22: 349–68.

Coltheart, M. (1980) 'Iconic memory and visible persistence', *Perception and Psychophysics* 27: 183–228.

Craik, F. I. M., and Lockhart, R. S. (1972) 'Levels of processing: a framework for memory research', *Journal of Verbal Learning and Verbal Behaviour* 11: 671–84.

Deutsch, J. A., and Deutsch, D. (1963) 'Attention: some theoretical considerations', *Psychological Review* 87: 272–300.

Dixon, N. F. (1971) *Subliminal Perception: The Nature of a Controversy*, London: McGraw-Hill.

Finke, R. A. (1980) 'Levels of equivalence in imagery and perception', *Psychological Review* 87: 113–32.

Fodor, J. A. (1983) *The Modularity of Mind*, Cambridge, MA: MIT Press.

Galton, F. (1883) *Inquiries into Human Faculty*, London: Dent.

Holender, D. (1986) 'Semantic activation without conscious identification in dichotic listening, parafoveal vision, and visual masking: a survey and appraisal', *The Behavioural and Brain Sciences*, 9: 1–66.

Humphrey, N. (1983) *Consciousness Regained*, Oxford: Pergamon.

(1986) *The Inner Eye*, London: Faber & Faber.

Johnson, M. K. (1985) 'The origin of memories', in P. C. Kendell (ed.) *Advances in Cognitive-Behavioural Research and Therapy*, New York: Academic Press.

and Raye, C. L. (1981) 'Reality monitoring', *Psychological Review* 88: 67–85.

Johnson-Laird, P. N. (1983) *Mental Models*, London: Cambridge University Press.

Kahneman, D., and Treisman, A. M. (1984) 'Changing conceptions of attention and automaticity', in R. Parasuraman and D. R. Davies (eds) *Varieties of Attention*, Orlando, FL: Academic Press.

Kosslyn, S. M. (1980) *Image and Mind*, Cambridge, MA: Harvard University Press.

and Pomerantz, J. R. (1977) 'Imagery, propositions, and the form of internal representations', *Cognitive Psychology* 9: 52–76.

Holtzman, J. D., Farah, M. J., and Gazzaniga, M. S. (1985) 'A computational analysis of mental image generation: evidence from functional dissociations in split brain patients', *Journal of Experimental Psychology: General* 114: 311–41.

Marcel, A. J. (1983a) 'Conscious and unconscious perception: experiments on visual masking and word recognition', *Cognitive Psychology* 15: 197–237.

(1983b) 'Conscious and unconscious perception: an approach to the relation between phenomenal experiences and perceptual processes', *Cognitive Psychology* 15: 238–300.

(1986) 'Consciousness and processing: choosing and testing a null hypothesis', *The Behavioural and Brain Sciences* 9: 40–1.

Minsky, M. (1975) 'A framework for representing knowledge', in P. Winston (ed.) *The Psychology of Computer Vision*, New York: McGraw-Hill.

(1987) *The Society of Mind*, London: Heinemann.

Morris, P. E. (1981) 'The cognitive psychology of self reports', in C. Antaki (ed.) *The Psychology of Ordinary Explanations of Social Behaviour*, London: Academic Press.

(1986) 'Memory images', in D. G. Russell, D. F. Marks, and J. T. E. Richardson (eds) *Imagery 2*, Dunedin: Human Performance Associates.

and Hampson, P. J. (1983) *Imagery and Consciousness*, London: Academic Press.

Neisser, U. (1967) *Cognitive Psychology*, New York: Appleton-Century-Crofts.
— (1976) *Cognition and Reality*, San Francisco: Freeman.
Nisbett, R. E., and Wilson, T. D. (1977) 'Telling more than we know: verbal reports on mental processes', *Psychological Review* 84: 231–59.
Norman, D. A., and Shallice, T. (1980) 'Attention to action: willed and automatic control of behaviour', Report CHIP 99, Centre for Human Information Processing, University of California, San Diego.
Paivio, A. (1971) *Imagery and Verbal Processes*, New York: Holt, Rinehart & Winston.
— (1986) *Mental Representations: A Dual Coding Approach*, New York: Oxford University Press.
Pylyshyn, Z. W. (1973) 'What the mind's eye tells the mind's brain: a critique of mental imagery', *Psychological Bulletin* 80: 1–24.
— (1981) 'The imagery debate: analog media or tact knowledge?', *Psychological Review* 87: 16–45.
Reason, J. (1984) 'Absentmindedness and cognitive control', in J. Harris and P. E. Morris (eds) *Everyday Memory, Actions and Absentmindedness*, London: Academic Press.
Ryle, G. (1949) *The Concept of Mind*, London: Hutchinson.
Schneider, W., and Shiffrin, R. M. (1977) 'Controlled and automatic human information processing: I. Detection, Search, and Attention', *Psychological Review* 84: 1–66.
Shallice, T. (1972) 'Dual functions of consciousness', *Psychological Review* 79: 383–93.
Shepard, R. N., and Cooper, L. A. (1982) *Mental Images and Their Transformations*, Cambridge, MA: MIT Press.
Shiffrin, R. M., and Schneider, W. (1977) 'Controlled and automatic human information processing: II. Perceptual learning, automatic attending, and a general theory', *Psychological Review* 84: 127–90.
Tulving, E. (1983) *Elements of Episodic Memory*, New York: Oxford University Press.
— (1985) 'Memory and consciousness', *Canadian Journal of Psychology* 26: 1–12.
Turvey, M. T. (1973) 'On peripheral and central processes in vision: interference from an information-processing analysis of masking with patterned stimuli', *Psychological Review* 80: 1–52.
Watson, J. B. (1913) 'Psychology as the behaviourist views it', *Psychological Review* 20: 158–77.
Weiskrantz, L., Warrington, E. K., Saunders, M. D., and Marshall, J. (1974) 'Visual capacity in the hemianopic field following a restricted optical ablation', *Brain* 97: 709–28.
Wittgenstein, L. (1953) *Philosophical Investigations*, Oxford: Blackwell.
Wundt, W. (1896) *Grundriss der Psychologie*, Leipzig: Engelmann.

Chapter four

Imagery and working memory

Robert H. Logie and Alan D. Baddeley

Our ability to retain information over short periods of time is fundamental to our ability to carry out an enormous number of everyday tasks. One particular approach which has been particularly fruitful in studying the characteristics of the mechanisms or systems that allow us to perform these tasks is the study of working memory (Baddeley and Hitch 1974). The notion of a working-memory system grew out of a dissatisfaction during the early 1970s with the prevailing 'modal model' of short-term memory (Atkinson and Shiffrin 1968) as a unitary system reliant upon rehearsal for long-term retention.

The term 'working memory' refers to the temporary storage of information. As originally proposed by Baddeley and Hitch, this was thought to consist of a central executive, which was responsible for decision-making and reasoning and the co-ordination of the activities of a number of specialized slave systems. One of these, the articulatory loop, was thought to be involved in the processing and storage of speech-based material and in the translation of visually presented verbal material into a speech-based code. The second system, the visuo-spatial sketch-pad, was thought to perform a similar storage function for visuo-spatial material.

The largest degree of research effort over the last decade or so has been directed towards the development of the concept of the articulatory loop. As a result, there is a considerable body of literature which has clarified the role and characteristics of this system, along with a range of techniques for its investigation (see, for example, see Baddeley 1986). In contrast, the visuo-spatial sketch-pad has received rather less attention, largely due to a lack of elegant and tractable techniques for its investigation. However, over the last few years there has been an increase in the attention paid to the proposed visuo-spatial system, and a number of techniques have been developed that have considerable potential for further exploration. As a result, the body of literature on the topic is growing, with several very recent studies, some as yet unpublished, adding to our understanding of the characteristics of the system.

Much of this review will concentrate on this very recent work, and as such will include material not available in Alan Baddeley's review (ibid.) of the whole area of working memory. However, to set some context for the more recent research, we felt that it would be useful to summarize the main findings on this topic obtained since the original working-memory proposal was published in 1974.

Involvement in imagery

An obvious question to ask of a proposed visuo-spatial sketch-pad (VSSP) would be what sort of purpose such a system might serve. A reasonable approach might be to take a number of established phenomena that we might hypothesize as involving a VSSP, and examine whether there is any evidence for such an involvement.

A very robust finding which might implicate the VSSP is the superior recall of verbal material that is highly imageable and highly concrete in comparison with verbal material that is rather more abstract in nature (for example, Richardson 1980). Paivio (1971) has interpreted this result in terms of his dual-coding theory of memory. This suggests that for highly imageable words subjects tend to create images of the words as well as storing information about the words in a verbal form. It is rather more difficult to generate an image of an abstract word, and therefore subjects store the information in a verbal form only. The advantage for concrete words is assumed to come about because subjects have available two codes, imaginal and verbal, rather than just a verbal code.

The VSSP was assumed to be responsible for generating and maintaining representations of information in the form of visual images. It was also assumed to have some involvement in processing visually presented information (cf. Chapters 2 and 3 in this volume). One prediction from these assumptions is that, where subjects are asked to maintain visual images and at the same time to carry out a task that involves visual input and processing, then the ability to maintain the visual images ought to be impaired. Just such a finding was reported by Atwood (1971).

Atwood required subjects to remember phrases which were either highly imageable such as 'Nudist Devouring Bird' or very abstract phrases such as 'The Intellect of Einstein was a Miracle'. Subjects were then asked to carry out a very simple subsequent task which involved auditory or visual processing of digits. Finally they were asked to recall the phrases. Atwood reported finding a disruption in recall of the imageable phrases when presentation was followed by a visual processing task. Recall of the abstract phrases was disrupted by a subsequent auditory-verbal task.

This seemed to be reasonable evidence for some overlap in the resources required by the task which appeared to mutually interfere, and the VSSP was a good candidate for the system which might underlie this overlap. However, the finding has proved to be very difficult to replicate. An unpublished study by Quinn (personal communication) and a published study by Baddeley *et al.*(1975) both failed to obtain the Atwood result.

Baddeley *et al.* (ibid.: Experiment 3) required subjects to learn paired associates that were either highly imageable such as 'Bullet-Grey' or pairs of associates that were very abstract such as 'idea-original'. This memory task was run concurrently with a perceptuo-motor tracking task. The tracking task involved a pursuit rotor, where subjects had to follow the circular movement of a metal target with the point of a metal-tipped stylus. The speed of movement of the target could be adjusted to give a predefined level of time on target. The prediction was that the requirement to maintain a satisfactory level of performance on the pursuit rotor would interfere with the subject's ability to remember concrete, but not abstract pairs.

Baddeley and his colleagues found the traditional superiority in recall of the concrete material. However, there was no suggestion of selective interference when combined with the tracking task. They concluded that perhaps the superior recall of concrete words is not due to an involvement of imagery, but has more to do with the richness of semantic associations of concrete words in comparison with abstract words – that is, the 'richer' the semantic code, the more readily the word is recalled. This would undermine Paivio's dual-coding hypothesis. More recent evidence for the Baddeley *et al.* interpretation has been provided by Jones (1985; 1988), who has shown that 'ease of predication' (providing definitions or alternative meanings for the word) is at least as good a predictor of recall performance as is imageability. Warren (1977) has also failed to find selective interference of high imagery words with a secondary tracking task.

An alternative conclusion from this is that the VSSP is involved in retention of high-imagery words but is not involved in perceptuo-motor tracking. Thus, even if the memory task does involve visual imagery, it may be carried out quite independently of tracking. However, Baddeley *et al.* provided further evidence to suggest that this was unlikely to be the case.

In two experiments, they examined tasks reported by Brooks (1968) which do appear to involve visualization. The task used most frequently in subsequent experiments involved presenting subjects with a 4x4 square matrix. They were asked to visualize this matrix. Subjects were then presented with a series of auditory instructions which described a path around the squares of the matrix. The path always started in the square on the second row and in the second column, and involved placing consecutive numbers in adjacent squares, for example:

In the starting square put a 1
In the next square to the right put a 2
In the next square down put a 3
In the next square down put a 4
In the next square to the left put a 5
In the next square up put a 6
In the next square to the left put a 7
In the next square up put an 8

Subjects were requested to visualize the path described, and then to recall the sequence of directions, using their visual image to aid recall. Brooks also devised a 'control' version of this task, where the words 'up', 'down', 'left', and 'right' were replaced by the words 'good', 'bad', 'quick', and 'slow'. Brooks found that when the material was presented visually, the performance on the spatial material was impaired relative to the same material being presented aurally. This was not true of the verbal or nonsense material, which appeared to be impaired by auditory presentation. This suggested interference between the visual/ perceptual processes involved in reading stimulus material and the processes involved in maintaining the visual image of the matrix pattern.

Baddeley and his colleagues argued that the Brooks spatial task ought to be sensitive to disruption from a concurrent tracking task. This proved to be the case, with the verbal version of the Brooks task unaffected by concurrent tracking, while the visual version showed marked impairment.

Spatial or visual?

The Brooks matrix task therefore seemed to involve a system with the characteristics of a specialized visuo-spatial short-term memory system. However, the evidence so far appears to confound two different sorts of information: visual and spatial. The Brooks task and the pursuit rotor tasks are both highly spatial in nature, and it may be that the system is specialized for dealing with spatial information rather than visual or both visual and spatial information. This distinction was studied by Baddeley and Lieberman (1980).

One experiment carried out by Baddeley and Lieberman again involved the Brooks spatial matrix task and the verbal equivalent. One of the secondary tasks adopted was again a form of tracking, but it was constructed so as to avoid any visual input. Subjects were blindfolded and were required to track a moving pendulum with a flashlight. Every time the light moved off the pendulum, subjects were given auditory feedback. There was a further secondary task which was designed to involve visual input but to minimize any spatial involvement. This comprised a series of light and dark patches presented to subjects. The task was simply to determine whether the patch was light or dark, and the luminance was adjusted such that subjects did not find the task ridiculously easy.

What Baddeley and Lieberman found was that the non-visual tracking task interfered with the Brooks matrix task, but not with the verbal task. However, the visual, brightness judgement task had no effect on the Brooks matrices, but curiously did interfere with the Brooks verbal task.

Baddeley and Lieberman followed their first experiment by studying the effect on visual and spatial memory of a more traditional visuo-spatial tracking task (pursuit rotor). Subjects were instructed to learn lists of concrete words. For this they were to use rote learning or one of two mnemonic techniques, the method of loci or the peg-word method. The method of loci involves placing items to be remembered at locations on an imaged, familiar route, and this ostensibly involves a strong spatial component. The peg-word method involves the subject first learning a sequence of words, each of which rhymes with a number – for example, 'one-bun', 'two-shoe', and so on. Each of the items on the list of words for recall is then associated in a visual image with one of the rhyming words. In both cases, the images are used to aid recall, and performance using these mnemonic techniques is typically superior to performance with rote rehearsal.

There was a clear effect of tracking on the method of loci. However, the effect on the peg-word mnemonic was very small and there was no effect on rote rehearsal. The contrast in the size of the effect on a spatial mnemonic (method of loci) and that on a visual mnemonic (peg-word) further supported the view that the sketch-pad was a spatially based rather than a visually based system.

One possible confounding in these experiments was the extent to which the interference was task-specific rather than specific to one specialized mechanism: that is, both the method of loci and the Brooks matrix tasks are spatial, but so too is tracking. It may be that tracking did not substantially interfere with the visual, peg-word mnemonic because of the nature of the tasks rather than because of the nature of the mechanism involved. Note that this argument does not necessarily undermine the notion of a specialized VSSP, but it does affect the conclusions as to its characteristics. Baddeley and Lieberman, for example, did not combine the brightness judgement task with the visual, peg-word mnemonic. By this argument, if one were to combine a visually based secondary task with a primary, visual memory task such as the peg-word mnemonic, then interference may well occur. This manipulation was reported by Logie (1986).

In a series of experiments, Logie (1986) contrasted use of the peg-word mnemonic with rote learning of concrete words. In one experiment, the secondary task involved presenting subjects with random matrix patterns. The majority of the patterns were distinct from one another. However, occasionally one pattern was shown twice in succession. When this occurred, the subject was required to press a key. Since only one key was involved, this minimized any spatial component in the response. However, the task required subjects continually to update their memory for the most recently presented pattern in order to perform the task successfully, and because patterns were repeated only occasionally, the physical response demands were minimal. Logie found that this 'running visual memory' task interfered substantially with the use of the peg-word mnemonic. However, there was also a small but significant drop in performance with rote learning. Nonetheless, the differential nature of the interference was sufficient to encourage further exploration.

Logie argued that there may have been a general load due to the requirement to make a decision at each presentation of a new pattern, despite the infrequency with which a physical response was required. This decision component of the task may have been responsible for the drop observed in both memory conditions: a conclusion that is consistent with a role for the 'central executive' component of working memory in this aspect of the task. In the remaining experiments, Logie removed the necessity of making a decision or indeed doing anything with the presented patterns other than simply to watch them passively. Thus, subjects were instructed to keep their eyes open and directed at the position on the screen where the patterns were presented, but to concentrate solely on remembering the auditorily presented words using one or the other of the memory procedures. Under these conditions, there was no effect on rote performance. However, use of the visual imagery mnemonic was significantly disrupted.

These results were open to the criticism that using a visual mnemonic is perhaps more effortful in some sense than is rote learning. Thus, any secondary task is likely to interfere with the more effortful task. This criticism was tackled in a final study in which one group of subjects followed the same procedure as in the experiment described above. A second group were given the same contrasting memory instructions, but with the words for recall presented visually, and secondary material that consisted of unattended speech. Salamé and Baddeley (1982) have shown that unattended speech severely disrupts recall of visually presented digits. From this result, they conclude that unattended speech has 'privileged access' to the mechanism responsible for storing verbal material, namely the articulatory loop.

Logie argued that the Salamé and Baddeley result would predict significant impairment in rote learning performance with unattended speech, as this is presumably analogous to rote learning of digit sequences. If the earlier disruption of the visual mnemonic was due simply to general distraction or general overload of resources, then unattended speech should also have a significant disruptive effect on visual mnemonic performance. However, if the disruption was specific to the nature rather than the amount of processing required, there should be little if any disruption of the visual mnemonic by unattended speech.

In the event, the first group showed a significant impairment in visual mnemonic performance when combined with 'unattended' visual input, but with no effect on rote rehearsal. This replicated the finding in the previous experiment. In contrast, unattended speech impaired rote learning, but had no effect on use of the peg-word mnemonic.

Further evidence for an effect of unattended visual input was reported by Johnson (1982). Johnson's main task involved subjects recalling a linear arm movement of a given length. Subjects can typically do this fairly accurately. However, when a longer movement is interpolated between the original movement and its recall, there is a tendency to recall the original movement as somewhat longer than it actually was. The converse occurs where the interpolated movement is shorter than the original. The interesting finding is that this assimilation effect occurs even when the interpolated movement is imagined rather than actually performed.

The effects of secondary visual input were studied in a second experiment. Here the interpolated movement was imagined as before, but subjects had simultaneously to watch two asymmetric wave forms oscillating on a television monitor. Subjects were not required to respond to the display in any way. Under these conditions, the biasing effect of the imagined movement was removed and subjects were once more able to repeat accurately the original, genuine movement.

There are two major aspects of these studies. The first concerns the characteristics of the postulated VSSP. We have already mentioned the notion of privileged access to the articulatory loop by unattended speech. It appears from these studies that there may also be privileged access by unattended visual material to the system responsible for maintaining (or generating) visual images. This is an important issue in that it is consistent with one of the original assumptions about the VSSP, that it is involved in processing visual input as well as in generating and maintaining visual images. This notion is also consistent with the findings by Brooks (1968) that attempting to generate a visual image from visually presented information is less efficient than generating a visual image from aurally presented information.

The second aspect of Logie's studies concerned the notion as to whether or not the VSSP is a system specialized for spatial but not visual material as suggested by Baddeley and Lieberman (1980). It appears that where both the primary and the secondary tasks emphasize visual rather than spatial processing, analogous interference effects appear. Further evidence for this view is presented by Matthews (1983). Matthews required subjects to remember high- or low-imagery words and demonstrated the traditional superiority effect. He chose a secondary task that involved matching partial outline shapes to previously presented complete shapes. Under these conditions there did appear to be selective interference with recall of high-imagery words.

There are two possible conclusions to be drawn from these studies. One is that the VSSP can deal with both visual and spatial information, but that the degree of interference under dual-task conditions has a task-specific nature. A second conclusion is that there are two separate mechanisms, one responsible for spatial material, the other for visual material.

There is a precedent for a distinction between visual and spatial processing: for example, neuropsychological evidence suggests that different neural structures may be involved. Mishkin (1982) reported that the infero-temporal regions may be concerned with aspects of object recognition, while Hyvarinen (1982) has reported that parietal structures are involved in various aspects of spatial position. Allport (1977) found independence in the reporting of letters in an array and the reporting of their position in the array. Jones (1976) has shown that spatial position in an array appears to be remembered quite independently from object identity. Phillips (1983) has argued, as an analogy to the distinctions in vision proposed by Marr (1982), that the distinction in visual cognition may be taken further in suggesting a distinction between object class and object structure as well as each of these contrasting with object location. Finally, Steiner (1980) has proposed a model of visual cognition which specifically includes a distinction between visual information in the form of the structure of an object and its identity, and spatial information, where he essentially refers to movement of objects or movement of parts of the body in space.

The role of movement

Quinn (1988; Quinn and Ralston 1986) described a number of experiments which have sought to investigate the relationship with movement more directly. In one set of experiments Quinn and Ralston examined the role of arm movement in the disruption of Brooks matrix material. Subjects were required to make unseen arm movements that were either compatible with the directions given for the Brooks matrix, or were incompatible. Quinn and Ralston found that the incompatible movement disrupted memory for the Brooks material even when the movement was passive – that is, the experimenter held the subject's hand and moved it for him or her. There was no disruption associated with compatible movements. This suggests that the effect of movement is unlikely to be due to a general attentional deficit, since even passive movements were disruptive. However, Quinn and Ralston did not include the Brooks verbal material as a control memory task. It would have been nice to demonstrate that the verbal material was insensitive to disruption by movement, since even with passive movement, subjects may covertly monitor and try to process in some way the movement of their hands.

In a further set of studies, Quinn (1988) did contrast the Brooks spatial and nonsense or verbal material, combined with either arm movement or brightness judgement. Quinn found that with the spatial material there was some disruption associated with the brightness judgement. This again contrasts with the finding by Baddeley and Lieberman (1980) discussed earlier. However, there was much more substantial impairment with the movement task. The verbal material was also disrupted but not to the same extent and there was no distinction between the effects of the movement and the brightness judgement tasks.

A further manipulation in the Quinn study was a contrast between the interference effects at initial presentation of the material and during the retention interval. Interference was confined to the presentation phase, suggesting an effect on encoding rather than on the maintenance of visual images. We shall return to the contrast between encoding and maintenance later in the chapter.

The role of eye movements

A possible role for eye movements in imagery was considered in a series of studies by Idzikowski, Baddeley, Dimbleby, and Park (unpublished, cited in Baddeley, 1986). These experiments examined the Brooks matrix and nonsense tasks in conjunction with voluntary or involuntary eye movements. Involuntary eye movements were initiated by rotating the subject in a chair, resulting in post-rotational nystagmus – involuntary reflex movements of the eyes. Voluntary eye movements involved the subject following a moving target on a computer display. There was selective interference with the Brooks spatial, but not verbal material by the voluntary, but not the involuntary eye movements. Nor was there such selective impairment when the background moved while eyes were held stationary.

One possible interpretation of this is that it was the movement of attention across the display screen that was the crucial factor, and not the movement of the eyes. A follow-up study by Baddeley and Logie separated these components such that in one condition, the eyes followed a moving target, but the subjects had to attend and respond to a second target that was stationary on the screen. A second condition involved the converse, where the target requiring a response moved across the display, while the subjects' eyes were fixated on the centre of the screen. It was found that the movement of the eyes, and not the movement of attention was the crucial factor in disrupting the Brooks spatial material.

One further issue is whether any movement and not just eye movements are the cause of this differential disruption. This question has yet to be resolved. However, the studies by Quinn described above suggest that it may indeed by movement *per se* rather than eye movements alone which are crucial.

Recency in visual short-term memory

One of the important findings in the free recall of verbal material is the recency effect – the relative advantage for items towards the end of a serially presented list. The recency effect has traditionally been associated with verbal short-term memory. A series of studies by Phillips and his colleagues investigated memory for serially presented sequences of patterns. In Phillips and Christie (1977a), subjects were presented with a sequence of unique matrix patterns. Their memory for this sequence was tested in a variety of ways. The most frequent method was reverse serial-order testing. This involved presenting the original sequence in reverse serial order with the subject indicating whether a given item had appeared in the previous sequence. The most striking finding was that the serial position curve for correct recognition of the patterns was flat except for the last item in the series (tested first by this method) which was significantly better recognized than patterns from other positions in the list. A similar result was obtained when subjects were required to draw the patterns or fill in squares of a blank matrix (Christie and Phillips 1979).

Phillips argued that the one-item recency effect may reflect the capacity of short-term visual memory, and that other items are retained less efficiently in some longer-term store. However, his experiments go further in examining the effect of secondary tasks interpolated between presentation and memory test. The major finding is that the one-item recency is removed by a variety of interpolated tasks, and in particular by mental arithmetic (for example, Phillips and Christie 1977b). This, he suggests, supports the idea that 'visualization requires general purpose resources' (ibid.: 649). Indeed, on the grounds that mental arithmetic would not appear to be a specifically visual task, it seems a fairly convincing case. However, the situation is not quite so straightforward.

Broadbent and Broadbent (1981) examined recency effects in visual short-term memory using patterns that were rather less regular than those used by Phillips and Christie. In addition, they used a forced-choice recognition procedure, probing items from different positions in the series of patterns. They demonstrated a clear recency effect that was evident over the last *three* list items and not just the final item. They also demonstrated that recency was unaffected by the visual similarity of the patterns in the series or by a secondary task interpolated between presentation and test. However, both similarity and an interpolated task affected overall performance.

They interpreted this last discrepancy between their own results and those of Phillips and Christie as follows. Typically, in the Phillips and Christie procedure, performance is flat and just above chance at all list positions except for the final item. However, in a 4x4 matrix, where half the cells are filled, the probability is quite high of having an identifiable shape such as a vertical line or a T-shape, allowing verbal coding of some patterns. Such intermittent non-visual coding may be sufficient to maintain performance just above chance, but not sufficiently high as to be sensitive to disruption from an interpolated task. Broadbent and Broadbent maintain that where performance is greater than around 70 per cent, this would leave it open to disruption. In the Phillips and Christie study only the last item was above this level and was indeed the only item affected by interpolated arithmetic.

Broadbent and Broadbent describe a final study where their patterns are placed sequentially in different spatial locations, rather than in the same spatial location as previously. Under these conditions, the recency effect disappears. The authors conclude that this provides evidence for a specific visual store that has its contents overwritten by succeeding materials presented in the same spatial location.

One assumption from both the Broadbent and the Phillips studies is that the recency effect obtained reflects some aspect of short-term visual memory in a fashion analogous to the recency effect in verbal free recall. However, there is now a body of evidence to suggest that the recency effect in verbal free recall has little to do specifically with verbal short-term memory. Verbal recency, for example, is unaffected by concurrent articulation (Richardson and Baddeley 1975), and established effects such as phonological similarity are not confined to the recency portion of the serial position curve (Baddeley 1968a). In addition, Watkins and Peynircioglu (1983) have shown three simultaneous recency effects from a single list. There is also evidence of recency occurring over much longer periods of days, weeks, and even months (Baddeley and Hitch 1977; Baddeley 1986). The view taken by Baddeley and Hitch (1977) is that recency may reflect a general strategy for retrieval rather than the contents of some short-term store.

A further difficulty for the Phillips studies is that even if we accept that they may have shown a disruption of memory for pattern sequences, it is not clear whether similar interpolated tasks may interfere as much, if not more so, with memory for verbal sequences. Thus, even if there were a specialized mechanism for short-term visual storage, it may nonetheless involve a certain amount of 'overhead' in general-purpose processing in addition to its specialist role. It may be this use of general-purpose resources which is affected by the interpolated arithmetic rather than the specifically visuo-spatial processing. If, for example, verbal short-term storage were equally affected by a secondary arithmetic task, Phillips would presumably have to argue that it did not involve a specialist mechanism either, and that verbal processing was also carried out by general-purpose resources. However, the evidence for a specialist verbal storage system is now fairly well established, and the concept of an articulatory loop is growing in its influence.

This suggestion was tested directly in a series of experiments by Logie, Zucco, and Baddeley (in press). These experiments adopted a version of the Phillips matrix task that involved a span procedure (Wilson, Scott, and Power 1987). Subjects were presented with a simple matrix pattern, with half of the squares of the matrix randomly filled. After a short blank interval this pattern was replaced by the same pattern, but with one of the previously filled squares now blank. The subjects' task was to point to the square that had been blanked out. The patterns started with just two squares in the matrix, one filled and one blank for the initial presentation. The complexity of the pattern was gradually increased by adding squares, two at a time. This procedure continued until the subject could no longer accurately identify the square that was changed between presentation and test, according to a normal span procedure.

This form of a span procedure has two major advantages. First, it is less prone to problems of differences in abilities among subjects since changes in performance are measured against an individual subject's optimal score. Second, the one-item recency effect reported by Phillips and his colleagues is all-or-none on any one trial. The span procedure gives a wider range of scores and therefore can give a clearer idea as to the size of interference effect.

The task we employed involves presentation of a single pattern on any one trial, although the pattern systematically increased in complexity over successive trial blocks. This is in contrast with the earlier studies which involved a sequence of patterns, each of which was roughly similar in complexity to other patterns in the sequence. However, the crucial aspect of Phillips's work was that the last single item in the list was the item that reflected the use of visual short-term memory. In this sense our task ought to tap the same resources.

We used a dual-task procedure in which the secondary task involved the Brooks spatial task described above. The prediction from Phillips's view would be that the Brooks spatial task ought to interfere with the matrix-span task. This result would be unsurprising and is in line with the working-memory model. However, typically the Brooks control or verbal task is also used in dual-task designs of this sort. Here the two approaches differ. The Phillips view presumably would be that, since retention of a single matrix pattern appears to rely heavily on general-purpose resources, a fairly demanding secondary verbal task ought also to interfere. The working-memory view would be that if visuo-spatial processing enjoys a specialized mechanism, it is unlikely to be prone to interference from a secondary verbal task.

Even if the result came out in the way predicted by the working-memory model, it could still be argued that this simply indicates that the Brooks spatial task is considerably more difficult and therefore more demanding of general-purpose resources than is the Brooks verbal task. In order to anticipate this criticism we chose to incorporate a further primary task which might be thought equivalent to the matrix-span task, but with greater verbal load. This involved visual letter span.

Subjects were presented with a series of letters that appeared sequentially in the centre of a screen. A short retention interval was followed by the same sequence of letters, this time with one of the original letters replaced by a new letter that had not appeared in the original sequence. The subject's task was to point to the screen when the new letter appeared. A span procedure was adopted such that the early trials involved sequences of three letters, and the sequence length was gradually increased until the subject could no longer accurately identify the new letter.

This task thus had some formal similarity with the matrix task in that it involved recognition of a change between original presentation and test, in addition to the span procedure. As with the matrix task, the letter-span task was performed in conjunction with either the Brooks spatial or the Brooks verbal task. In the case of both the letter span and the matrix span, each of these tasks was performed alone in order to provide a baseline performance against which to measure any changes associated with dual-task conditions. Similarly, each of the Brooks tasks was performed alone to give a baseline of performance on the secondary tasks.

The prediction is now rather more complex. The Phillips position assumes a general-purpose system plus a specialized verbal system. This model would presumably predict that the letter-span task would be interfered with by the secondary Brooks verbal task, but not to any great extent by the Brooks spatial task. On the other hand, the matrix-span task should be affected by both the Brooks spatial and verbal tasks. The working-memory model has in addition a specialized visuo-spatial system, and would predict the same result as the Phillips model for the letter-span task, but would predict interference with the matrix task only by the secondary Brooks verbal task.

In the event the working-memory model received some support. Both the letter-span and matrix-span tasks were affected by both of the Brooks tasks, but to greatly different extents. The matrix task was substantially affected by the Brooks spatial task, while affected only minimally by the verbal secondary task. In contrast the letter-span task was substantially affected by Brooks's verbal task, but only minimally affected by the spatial version of the secondary task.

It could be argued that this is not a fair test of the Phillips hypothesis since the secondary task employed in Phillips and Christie (1977a) was mental arithmetic. However, in a further experiment we replaced the two Brooks tasks with contrasting tasks, one of which was mental arithmetic. The complementary task involved the generation of a visual image of a number shape from a series of verbal instructions. With these as secondary tasks, the result was essentially the same as that for the Brooks tasks. Mental arithmetic interfered substantially with letter-span performance, while the number-image task interfered only minimally with letter span. The converse was true for the matrix-span task.

In both experiments it was clear that the differential interference could not be attributed to the subjects paying more attention to the relevant secondary task at the expense of the primary task.

VSSP or central executive: double or triple dissociation?

The main logic underlying dual-task procedures is that of demonstrating a double dissociation: that is, in order to demonstrate that two independent processing systems are present, it is necessary to show selective interference of one with a particular secondary task, and selective interference of the other with a rather different secondary task, thus involving four experimental conditions. In the case of working memory, there is ample evidence that serial-ordered recall of verbal material is affected by concurrent articulation of irrelevant speech (for example, Murray 1965; Levy 1971; Baddeley *et al.* 1984), and by unattended speech (Salamé and Baddeley 1982). Other verbal tasks such as counting also appear to be affected by concurrent articulation (Logie and Baddeley 1987). Verbal short-term memory tasks tend to be unaffected by concurrent visuo-spatial tasks such as tracking (Baddeley *et al.* 1975) or unattended visual input (Logie 1986). In contrast, secondary visuo-spatial tasks do appear to affect retention of visuo-spatial material (Baddeley *et al.* 1975; Johnson 1982; Logie 1986), while they tend not to be affected by unattended speech (Logie 1986) or by concurrent articulation (for example, Farmer *et al.* 1986; Morris 1987). The argument is that this provides evidence for separable mechanisms, an articulatory loop, and a visuo-spatial sketch-pad.

This argument works well if only two mechanisms are involved. However, the original working-memory formulation suggested a third mechanism – the central executive. While the need for a central executive seems fairly clear, the role and characteristics of the system are somewhat less clear. The evidence in favour of a specialized system for verbal short-term storage, the articulatory loop, is fairly convincing. Is it therefore possible that the central executive is responsible for the findings that have been attributed to a visuo-spatial sketch-pad? We would thus need to postulate only two mechanisms: an articulatory loop and a central executive. In order to make a logically compelling case for three mechanisms, a *triple dissociation* is required, involving nine experimental conditions. However, most of the research has concerned itself with dissociation between just two systems. Indeed, we have already presented evidence that visuo-spatial processing may separate further into visual and spatial processing. This complicates the definitive experiment even further.

One solution to this problem of increasingly complex experimental designs is to use the procedure of converging operations – that is, to accumulate information from a number of different experimental paradigms, in the hope that they may provide a coherent picture. This approach has been successful in the study of the articulatory loop, with effects of word length, phonological similarity, articulatory suppression, and unattended speech all converging on the current view of the operation of the loop (Baddeley 1986). In one sense a review of the sort presented here involves just such convergence. However, at least some of the evidence reviewed should consider further the relationship between the central executive and the postulated visuo-spatial sketch-pad. Two fairly recent papers have attempted to do just this.

Farmer *et al.* (1986) took the suggestion from the Phillips and Christie studies that if a separate visuo-spatial system exists, then it should be possible to devise a task that places heavy demands on the slave system, without a requirement for central executive capacity. Such a task would interfere with concurrent visualization but would not interfere with the performance of tasks (such as mental arithmetic) that have a low visuo-spatial load but place a substantial demand on general-purpose resources. Farmer *et al.* identified the Baddeley (1968b) verbal-reasoning task as a candidate for heavy central-executive involvement. This task involves verification of a sentence which purports to describe the order of two letters that follow. An example item might be: A IS NOT PRECEDED BY B – AB (True). Hitch and Baddeley (1976) reported that articulatory suppression has only a minimal effect on the performance of this task, although it is substantially impaired by a concurrent memory load of six random digits.

Farmer *et al.* combined the verbal-reasoning task with either articulatory suppression or a spatial task involving tapping four metal plates placed in a square arrangement on a table in front of the display monitor that was used to display the stimulus material. The spatial task had no effect on verbal reasoning. Articulatory suppression had a small effect on the reasoning task, but the effect was largely confined to the most difficult problems.

These researchers also studied a spatial-reasoning task which would be likely to place a greater demand on visuo-spatial processing. The manikin test (Benson and Gedye 1963) involved the display of a man-ikin figure holding in one hand a circle and in the other hand a square.

One of these shapes was displayed as a target below the figure. The subject's task was to indicate in which hand the target shape was being held. The manikin figure could be in a number of orientations: facing towards or away from the subject, and upright or inverted. With this task, articulatory suppression had no effect on performance, while the tapping task had a substantial effect.

These results support the notion that the articulatory loop and the postulated visuo-spatial sketch-pad are dissociable. In this sense the result is perhaps unsurprising and in line with previous literature. What is interesting about these findings is that the verbal reasoning task appears to rely on general-purpose resources rather than the articulatory loop. A heavy demand on the articulatory loop would have resulted in substantial effects of articulatory suppression which failed to appear in either these studies or in those reported by Hitch and Baddeley (1976). The Farmer *et al.* results therefore appear to show something of a dissociation between what might be considered to be central-executive functioning and the functioning of a specialised visuo-spatial system.

One issue that has been glossed over so far is the relative importance of the various stages of the memory tasks involved, namely encoding, maintenance, and retrieval. It may be that the crucial factor in these studies is the processing stage at which the interference takes place. The Phillips and Christie studies, for example, placed their secondary task between presentation and retrieval, presumably when the visual information was to be maintained. Logie (1986) presented the secondary visual material throughout presentation, maintenance, and recall, as did Farmer *et al.* This issue was examined in a series of studies by Morris (1986, 1987).

Morris (1987) devised a task which involved presenting circles at random locations on an otherwise blank screen, and later requiring subjects to draw the circles in their appropriate positions. This task was shown to be disrupted by a concurrent, non-visual tracking task, but not by irrelevant articulation when the secondary tasks were concurrent with presentation of the circles display. However, when the secondary tasks were interpolated between presentation and recall, neither task interfered with memory for circle patterns. A further experiment examined the effect on recall of a concurrent verbal load. The results of these experiments appeared to suggest that visuo-spatial processing was relatively vulnerable to general disruption at encoding and at retrieval, but that it is relatively insensitive to disruption during maintenance. This is an interesting issue that clearly merits further study.

Non-visual imagery

We shall briefly describe a few studies that have examined the role of working memory in acoustic or auditory imagery. Baddeley and Lewis (1981) examined the role of the articulatory loop in adult reading. In particular they studied the effect on a number of reading tasks of repeating an irrelevant word (articulatory suppression). The interesting aspect of these studies for our purposes was that under suppression subjects could adequately make judgments as to whether a visually presented nonsense word sounded like a real word when pronounced (for example, KAYOSS). In addition, subjects reported 'hearing inside their heads' the material they were reading under suppression. Baddeley and Lewis concluded that there appeared to be some form of auditory image that allowed such homophone judgements and that was quite separate from the functioning of the articulatory loop. (Note that judgements as to whether two words *rhyme* is affected by suppression, but a detailed discussion of this point is beyond the scope of this chapter. See Besner (1987) for a discussion of this topic.)

This conclusion may suggest that the system responsible for representing words in the form of 'auditory imagery' might be involved in processing auditory, non-verbal material such as environmental sounds or music. Such a system would be independent of the mechanism for storage of words in short-term verbal-memory tasks. Evidence for this view was reported by Shallice and Warrington (1974), who compared memory span for spoken words with that for environmental sounds such as a creaking door or a barking dog. They found that a patient with a deficit in verbal-memory span showed no deficit in memory for the environmental sounds.

Further evidence came from a study by Logie and Edworthy (1986), in which they reported a deficit in discrimination between musical tones of different pitch when this task was combined with homophone judgements. Articulatory suppression had no effect on pitch discrimination. These results are, however, somewhat preliminary and this area leaves much scope for further investigation.

Visual working memory in learning complex tasks

One very recent development has involved studying the role of working memory in learning complex cognitive skills. In the past, working memory and visual working memory in particular have been studied

121

using laboratory tasks whose components are relatively clear, where relatively little practice is involved. There has been little attention paid to more complex tasks involving several components, and little study of how the role of working memory might change with increased expertise.

In a series of experiments, Logie, Baddeley, Mane, Donchin, and Sheptak (1988; in press) examined the role of working memory in learning a complex computer game, Space Fortress. Unlike earlier studies of working memory, Space Fortress relies on perceptuo-motor skills and accurate timing of responses as well as short- and long-term strategic decisions. These studies were part of a large-scale project concerned with training of complex skills, involving a number of research groups world-wide, all of whom used Space Fortress as the task for study. A theme underlying the general approach to the project was that performance on Space Fortress may be fruitfully subdivided into a number of subcomponent skills. Our approach was to test this directly by means of the secondary task procedures which have proved fruitful in the development of the concept of working memory. We were particularly interested in whether secondary task procedures would be appropriate in this context. We were also very keen to find out whether the working memory concept could be applied successfully to this sort of study, and if so, what new developments would be necessary.

We employed a wide range of secondary tasks, chosen to examine the role of various components of the Space Fortress task. However, of primary relevance to this chapter was the role of visuo-spatial working memory in the process of acquiring the skills necessary for the game. The first set of secondary tasks used was the Brooks (1968) matrix paradigm, chosen to contrast the role of verbal and spatial processes. However, one difficulty with these tasks is that they tend to have a fairly heavy general processing load in addition to their specifically visuo-spatial or verbal components. We were concerned that when combined with a complex primary task, the effects of general processing overload would be such as to mask any differential effects. Therefore, we devised a further pair of contrasting tasks with a lighter general processing load.

The visuo-spatial task involved subjects memorizing a map of a fictional island on which were marked six locations. The task involved answering questions concerned with the relative direction of pairs of locations – for example, 'Is Newton Swamp North-West of Curie Stables?' Subjects were to consult a visual image of the memorized map and simply answer yes or no to each question. The verbal task involved subjects memorizing a short poem in the form of a limerick. They were then asked questions concerning the relative order of pairs of words in the poem – for example, 'Does lady come before vicar?'

Results showed that during the early stages of training, important components of the game were disrupted by secondary visuo-spatial tasks more than by secondary verbal tasks. As we suspected the general processing load associated with the two Brooks tasks masked much of the differential disruption. However, there was a very clear difference between the effects of the map and limerick tasks. The map task produced a much greater impairment in performance on Space Fortress. In addition, the map task affected a cluster of game components which were concerned with visuo-spatial aspects of the game. With increased practice on the game, the differential nature of the disruption changed. The map and limerick tasks had a roughly equivalent effect on overall game performance. However, the map and the Brooks spatial tasks appeared to affect a rather different cluster of game components than did the limerick and Brooks verbal tasks.

This approach has potential for a fairly detailed mapping of the component skills involved at various stages in training. It also provides much encouragement for the applicability of secondary-task procedures in this context. The importance of these results theoretically is that a visuo-spatial component was clearly identified as one of several subcomponents in performance of the game.

Conclusions

The coverage provided by this chapter cannot be totally comprehensive, since more detailed discussion of many of these topics would run to several chapters. We have had to leave out discussion of some studies altogether for the same reasons. However, we have attempted to cover as wide a range as possible of both the history and more recent work on the role of imagery in working memory in the context of a specialized visuo-spatial system. This would be an appropriate place to summarize some of the findings. We also provided a short discussion on the role of auditory imagery. However, research on auditory imagery in this context has a long way to go and we shall leave further discussion to a later date.

Writing even a couple of years ago, it would have been safe to say that the 'visuo-spatial sketch-pad' was the poor sibling of the articulatory loop in terms of research effort, and we reiterated this view at the start of this chapter. While this is still largely true, it is clear that there has been increased effort in recent years. As such we have accumulated more information, but has this added new pieces to the jigsaw or simply added confusion by introducing pieces from other puzzles?

On the whole, we would take the more optimistic view. The evidence for some form of specialized visuo-spatial system in working memory is changing from 'being consistent with the view' to a more positive 'in favour of'. There does appear to be evidence for some form of system separate from short-term verbal storage and from general-processing resources. It would be difficult to explain all of the data that we have described without recourse to such a system. To go much beyond this view in discussing the characteristics of the mechanism may not be quite so straightforward.

What does seem to be clear is that the system is involved in temporary storage of visuo-spatial material and that this function is disrupted by performing concurrent visuo-spatial tasks. It also has some involvement in the use of visuo-spatial mnemonics (Baddeley et al. 1975; Baddeley and Lieberman 1980; Logie 1986). Its operation appears to be disrupted by presentation of irrelevant, unattended visual material (Logie 1986), and by some types of concurrent movement, including eye movements (Idzikowski et al., unpublished, cited in Baddeley 1986; Baddeley and Logie, unpublished) and arm movements (Johnson 1982; Quinn and Ralston 1986; Quinn 1988).

However, there are still many aspects that are unclear. The results of Morris (1987), for example, suggest that the effects of a secondary general-processing load appear during encoding and retrieval, but not during maintenance of the material. Broadbent and Broadbent (1981) and Phillips and Christie (1977b) suggest that there is also an effect when the secondary task (for example, arithmetic) is interpolated between presentation and recall.

The other aspect which requires further exploration is the possible separation of function between spatial and visual processing of material. The results of several studies suggest that this may be the case (Baddeley and Lieberman 1980; Logie 1986). In addition, concurrent spatial tracking does not appear to affect the memorial advantage for highly imageable words (Baddeley et al. 1975), while concurrent shape-matching does appear to undermine this effect (Matthews 1983).

Thus, some progress has been made, although the area is ripe for further exploration. The effects of similarity and complexity of patterns, for example, have received very little attention (Broadbent and Broadbent 1981), as has the study of the stages of encoding, maintenance, and retrieval (Morris 1986, 1987). The study of the role of the visuo-spatial sketch-pad in complex tasks seems to have a great deal of potential for further development. We have said nothing of individual differences. We suspect that many of the psychometric tests of spatial visualization are in fact tapping this aspect of working memory, and would be well worth exploring using dual tasks or even factor-analytic techniques. Morra and Scopesi (in preparation) have made an encouraging start using factor analysis with a battery of standardized tests to measure working memory in children. Their results suggest that three factors are present, and these appear to map onto general processing resources, short-term verbal ability, and visuo-spatial ability as separate factors. However, this work is fairly preliminary.

Finally, one area of research that is already beginning to yield important findings, but which is beyond the scope of the present chapter, concerns the neuropsychology of visual imagery (see Farah, 1988). Neuropsychological evidence has made substantial contributions to our understanding of long-term memory and of the articulatory loop. We expect a similar contribution in the next few years to our understanding of visual working memory.

References

Allport, D. A. (1977) 'On knowing the meaning of words we are unable to report: the effects of visual masking', in S. Dornic (ed.) *Attention and Performance VI*, Hillsdale, NJ: Erlbaum.

Atkinson, R. C., and Shiffrin, R. M. (1968) 'Human memory: a proposed system and its control processes', in K. W. Spence and J. T. Spence (eds) *The Psychology of Learning and Motivation: Advances in Research and Theory*, vol. 2, New York: Academic Press.

Atwood, G. E. (1971) 'An experimental study of visual imagination and memory', *Cognitive Psychology* 2: 290–9.

Baddeley, A. D. (1968a) 'How does acoustic similarity influence short-term memory?', *Quarterly Journal of Experimental Psychology* 20: 249–69.

(1968b) 'A three minute reasoning test based on grammatical transformation', *Psychonomic Science* 10: 341–2.

(1986) *Working Memory*, London: Oxford University Press.

and Hitch, G. J. (1974) 'Working memory', in G. H. Bower (ed.) *The Psychology of Learning and Motivation: Advances in Research and Theory*, vol. 8, New York: Academic Press.

(1977) 'Recency re-examined', in S. Dornic (ed.) *Attention and Performance VI*, Hillsdale, NJ: Erlbaum.

and Lewis, V. J. (1981) 'Inner active processes in reading: the inner voice, the inner ear, and the inner eye', in A. M. Lesgold and C. A. Perfetti (eds) *Interactive Processes in Reading*, Hillsdale, NJ: Erlbaum.

and Lieberman, K. (1980) 'Spatial working memory', in R. Nickerson (ed.) *Attention and Performance VIII*, Hillsdale, NJ: Erlbaum.

Lewis, V. J., and Vallar, G. (1984) 'Exploring the articulatory loop', *Quarterly Journal of Experimental Psychology* 36: 233–52.

Grant, W., Wight, E., and Thomson, N. (1975) 'Imagery and visual working memory', in P. M. A. Rabbitt and S. Dornic (eds) *Attention and Performance V*, London: Academic Press.

Benson, A. J., and Gedye, J. L. (1963) *Logical Processes in the Resolution of Orientational Conflict*, Farnborough: Report No. 259, RAF Institute of Aviation Medicine.

Besner, D. (1987) 'Phonology, lexical access in reading, and articulatory suppression: a critical review', *Quarterly Journal of Experimental Psychology* 39A: 467–78.

Broadbent, D. E., and Broadbent, M. H. P. (1981) 'Recency effect in visual memory', *Quarterly Journal of Experimental Psychology* 33A: 1–15.

Brooks, L. R. (1968) 'Spatial and verbal components in the act of recall', *Canadian Journal of Psychology* 22: 349–68.

Christie, D. F. M., and Phillips, W. A. (1979) 'Simple drawing and pattern completion techniques for studying visualization and long-term visual knowledge', *Memory and Cognition* 7: 360–7.

Farah, M. J. (1988) 'Is visual imagery really visual? Overlooked evidence from neuropsychology', *Psychological Review* 95: 307–17.

Farmer, E. W., Berman, J. V. F., and Fletcher, Y. L. (1986) 'Evidence for a visuo-spatial sketch-pad in working memory', *Quarterly Journal of Experimental Psychology* 38A: 675–88.

Hitch, G. J., and Baddeley, A. D. (1976) 'Verbal reasoning and working memory', *Quarterly Journal of Experimental Psychology* 28: 603–21.

Hyvarinen, J. (1982) 'Posterior parietal lobe of the primate brain', *Physiological Reviews* 62: 1060–129.

Johnson, P. (1982) 'The functional equivalence of imagery and movement', *Quarterly Journal of Experimental Psychology* 34A: 349–65.

Jones, G. V. (1976) 'A fragmentation hypothesis of memory: cued recall of pictures and of sequential position', *Journal of Experimental Psychology: General* 105: 277–93.

(1985) 'Deep dyslexia, imageability, and ease of predication', *Brain and Language* 24: 1–19.

(1988) 'Imageability and a performance measure of predicability', in M. Denis, J. Engelkamp, and J. T. E. Richardson (eds) *Cognitive and Neuropsychological Approaches to Mental Imagery*, Dordrecht: Martinus Nijhoff.

Levy, B. A. (1971) 'The role of articulation in auditory and visual short-term memory', *Journal of Verbal Learning and Verbal Behaviour* 10: 123–32.

Logie, R. H. (1986) 'Visuo-spatial processing in working memory', *Quarterly Journal of Experimental Psychology* 38A: 229–47.

and Baddeley, A. D. (1987) 'Cognitive processes in counting', *Journal of Experimental Psychology: Learning, Memory, and Cognition* 13: 310–26.

and Edworthy, J. (1986) 'Shared mechanisms in the processing of verbal and musical material', in D. G. Russell, D. F. Marks and J. T. E. Richardson (eds) *Imagery 2*, Dunedin: Human Performance Associates.

Zucco, G. M., and Baddeley, A. D. (in press) 'Interference with visual working memory' *Acta Psychologica*.

Baddeley, A. D., Mane, A., Donchin, E., and Sheptak, R. (1988) 'Visual working memory in the acquisition of complex cognitive skills', in M. Denis, J. Engelkamp, and J. T. E. Richardson (eds) *Cognitive and Neuropsychological Approaches to Mental Imagery*, Dordrecht: Martinus Nijhoff.

(in press) 'Working memory and the analysis of a complex skill by secondary task methodology' *Acta Psychologica*.

Marr, D. (1982) *Vision*, San Francisco: Freeman.

Matthews, W. A. (1983) 'The effects of concurrent secondary tasks on the use of imagery in a free recall task', *Acta Psychologica* 53: 231–41.

Mishkin, M. (1982) 'A memory system in the monkey', *Philosophical Transactions of the Royal Society of London* B298: 85–96.

Morra, S. and Scopesi, A. (in preparation) 'Can children's working memory be measured?'

Morris, N. (1986) 'Working memory constellations', unpublished PhD thesis, University of Durham.

(1987) 'Exploring the visuo-spatial scratch pad', *Quarterly Journal of Experimental Psychology* 39A: 409–30.

Murray, D. J. (1965) 'Vocalization-at-presentation with varying presentation rates', *Quarterly Journal of Experimental Psychology* 17: 47–56.

Paivio, A. (1971) *Imagery and Verbal Processes*, New York: Holt, Rinehart & Winston.

Phillips, W. A. (1983) 'Short-term visual memory', *Philosophical Transactions of the Royal Society of London* B302: 295–309.

and Christie, D. F. M. (1977a) 'Components of visual memory', *Quarterly Journal of Experimental Psychology* 29: 117–33.

(1977b) 'Interference with visualization', *Quarterly Journal of Experimental Psychology* 29: 637–50.

Quinn, J. G. (1988) 'Imagery and working memory', in M. Denis, J. Engelkamp, and J. T. E. Richardson (eds), *Cognitive and Neuropsychological Approaches to Mental Imagery*, Dordrecht: Martinus Nijhoff.

and Ralston, G. E. (1986) 'Movement and attention in visual working memory', *Quarterly Journal of Experimental Psychology* 38A: 689–703.

Richardson, J. T. E. (1980) *Mental Imagery and Human Memory*, London: Macmillan.

and Baddeley, A. D. (1975) 'The effect of articulatory suppression in free recall', *Journal of Verbal Learning and Verbal Behavior* 14: 623–9.

Salamé, P., and Baddeley, A. D. (1982) 'Disruption of short-term memory by unattended speech: implications for the structure of working memory', *Journal of Verbal Learning and Verbal Behavior* 21: 150–64.

Shallice, T., and Warrington, E. K. (1974) 'The dissociation between long-term retention of meaningful sounds and verbal material', *Neuropsychologia* 12: 553–5.

Steiner, G. (1980) *Visuelle Vorstellungen beim Kösen von elementaren Problemen*, Stuttgart: Klett-Cotta.

Warren, M. W. (1977) 'The effects of recall-concurrent visual-motor distraction on pictures and word recall', *Memory and Cognition* 5: 362–70.

Watkins, M. J., and Peynircioglu, Z. F. (1983) 'Three recency effects at the same time', *Journal of Verbal Learning and Verbal Behavior* 22: 375–84.

Wilson, J. T. E., Scott, J. H., and Power, K. G. (1987) 'Developmental differences in the span of visual memory for pattern', *British Journal of Developmental Psychology* 5: 249–55.

Chapter five

Imagery and blindness

Susanna Millar

For most people a mental 'image' means 'a picture in the head': something akin to seeing, albeit in the 'mind's eye' rather than for real. No one is really surprised that the 'mind's eye' does not operate in exactly the same way as visual perception; that mental 'pictures' are not necessarily accurate copies of real objects or scenes; that in contrast to visual perception you can see through and around mental pictures of solid objects (Neisser and Kerr 1973). Moreover, images are often difficult to conjure up at will, and some people deny having imagery at all. Nevertheless, the immediate association of the term 'image' is with vision or, much less often, with other modalities.

The aim of this chapter is to argue for a particular view of imagery which has arisen from evidence from the congenitally totally blind. It may seem paradoxical to suggest that we can improve our understanding of imagery by studying representation by the blind, but paradoxes of this kind are often useful. Briefly, the thesis is that imaging consists of using modality-specific information to symbolize objects, situations, and events. The important implication is that imaging can be acquired like other symbolic skills. It is assumed further that the link between imagery and vision (or other modalities) is neither fortuitous nor necessarily pre-ordained or invariable. Images, unlike arbitrary associations between words and things, 'resemble' the objects they depict. The situation is not unlike onomatopoeia, in which the sounds objects make are used to name or label them. In imagery, modality-specific qualities which are associated with objects, situations, or events are used symbolically, as memory aids in thinking. On the present view, however, imaging is an acquired strategy which, for the blind at least, has an important basis in movement plans. The nearest analogy is with drawings which often resemble the depicted object in form and mode, although the resemblance need not be accurate and can be remote. Imagery, like drawing, carries with it some modality-specific element. It will be argued that these assumptions fit in well with findings from the blind as well as from the sighted.

Models of imagery and drawing

In briefly considering theories of representation, it must be said that theoretical models are often needlessly placed in opposition to each other. It may seem more exciting, and apparently gives added credence to a model, to argue that a different model is wrong. However, this sort of dichotomy is usually stultifying in the end. In fact, models in psychology often differ not because they are necessarily incompatible, but because they are actually geared to slightly different questions. There is no real conflict, for instance, between the model of Paivio (1971) which encapsulates the reported experience of most people that thinking often seems to involve either words or imagery, and the model of Kosslyn (1983) which suggests a computer implementation of that experience, expressed in terms of analogue versus digital computation.

Furthermore, although our major concern as psychologists is happily not with the ontological status of either imagery or thought, we do need to distinguish between the types of questions we are asking. Thus, for instance, answers to the question where and how past experience or memory is literally 'stored' must be in terms of brain tissue and function, whether brain loci or parallel distributed processing (for example, Rumelhart *et al.* 1986) is assumed. However, litanies of brain locations and neuronal activities are not immediately satisfactory or relevant answers if the question about 'storage' is actually about the coding and/or organization of information for memory or problem-solving tasks. Similarly, the controversy whether thought or memory should be described in terms of propositions or in terms of imagery (for example, Anderson and Bower 1973; Pylyshyn 1973) is mainly due to a confusion of levels of discourse (Millar 1982, 1986a). 'Propositions' and 'images' are not true opposites of any kind. The term 'proposition' refers to the outcome of a linguistic analysis, and not to an experience. By contrast, the term 'image' refers to an experience, that is to say, to a (reported) empirical phenomenon. An image of an object, situation, or event does not either necessitate, equal, or preclude a propositional analysis of the statement which describes the object, situation, or event. The distinction needs to be highlighted, because the two terms are often used so widely that the difference in the level of discourse is obscured. It should be quite clear, therefore, that here the term 'imagery' is used to refer to a reported empirical phenomenon. The central question is thus about the modality-specific element which seems to be an essential part of such reports.

Not all models are primarily concerned with this particular issue. The nearest is Paivio's dual-system theory (1971), which assumes that imagery is modality-specific, and describes experiments to support the assumption. Kosslyn's theory (1983) is also based on ingenious experiments to support the assumption of a modality-specific (visual) element in imagery; but the main point of the theory is to explain which type of computational model (analogue rather than digital) is best for describing imagery. The theory also assumes that imagery is spontaneous, unlearned, and arises as a matter of course from perception in different sensory modalities. However, the latter assumptions are not necessary ingredients in the model. They are assumptions which are commonly made, to the point of being almost unquestioned. The point of the present thesis is to question them.

Another means of dealing with the modality-specific element in imagery is to consider it irrelevant. Neisser (1976), for instance, assumes cognitive (modality-free) schemata (cognitive maps) as the end-products of hierarchical processes of construction and synthesis. The neglect is reasonable also for theories which are specifically concerned with computational modelling because they are concerned with cognitive skills in problem solving and representation rather than with modality-specific aspects of information-processing. Kosslyn (1983) has shown that, in principle, the latter can be modelled in computer systems.

Theories of perception also sometimes minimize the relevance of modality-specific information (for example, J. J. Gibson 1966; E. J. Gibson 1969). This is less intelligible, because, from an evolutionary point of view, it is difficult to understand why, in that case, the sense modalities are specialized. It is, no doubt, important to make the point that we perceive (phenomenologically) objects rather than a mosaic of sensory qualities, and that there are considerable similarities in structure and function between different sensory systems. However, the notion (Gibson 1966; Gibson 1969) that we perceive higher-order relations 'directly' (if this means anything different from perceiving objects in relation to each other), and that we perceive 'amodal' qualities directly, begs too many questions. The notion (Gibson 1979) that perception functions over time rather than in discrete 'moments' is important, and a good corrective to some time-honoured but useless dichotomies (innate/acquired; perceptual 'moments'). The newer theory also places more emphasis on the notion that the sense modalities provide complementary information. Gregory's (1974) theory is that perception is indirect and depends on innate (peripheral and central nervous system) structures, constancy scaling, and computations of the stimulus array which can change with experience. The interest for the present question is that Gregory's theory assumes specifically that ideas drawn from active touch are not necessarily exactly the same as those based on visual experience. This, together with the notion of complementarity, will be discussed further below.

Imaging, in the sense at least of reports and tests of imagery, is better considered in the context of memory skills. It is fair to say that in the mainstream three-box storage models of the late 1950s to early 1970s (for example, Atkinson and Shiffrin 1968), visual and modality-specific information was at best consigned to an initial, very brief and fast-decaying sensory store, or possibly to relatively unimportant intervening 'buffers', or to long-term memory from which it is retrieved via verbal labels or descriptions (Norman 1970). More recently, visual imagery has made a theoretical come-back as an aspect of temporary or working memory of the kind needed to 'hold' information temporarily during problem solving. Baddeley (1986) assumes a 'central executive' with overall control, and 'slave systems', of which the most important is the 'articulatory loop' which allows verbal rehearsal to take place. He reviews the evidence for such a subsidiary passive phonological holding system and for a visuo-spatial 'scratch-pad' as another subsidiary slave system. Evidence for tactual and kinaesthetic effects in temporary memory will be considered below.

Traditionally, the most prominent place for imagery has been in accounts of drawing. The naive assumption, certainly made by many people including the blind, and acted on in practice, is that drawing is impossible without vision and that it depends crucially on visual imagery. The assumption is not shared by art historians (for example, Gombrich 1970), who discern social, cultural, and conceptual influences in the changing art productions over the centuries. The analogy of mental representation with actual representation was made most explicitly by Arnheim (1969). His assumption that the concept and the image are interchangeable notions (thinking is embodied in imagery:

the concept 'is' the image and vice versa) is mainly geared to the question of actual representation in the visual arts, and is less illuminating about the modality-specific aspect of imagery. Clearly, the illusions intended to 'deceive' the eye, for instance in perceiving depth on flat surfaces, which art creates, are relevant to the psychology and physiology of vision and vice versa (Gregory and Gombrich 1973); but they are not a major key to what people mean when they report imagery.

The analogy of mental representation with actual representation is nevertheless useful on a number of counts. Perhaps the most important lesson to be drawn from the analogy is that drawing involves a multiplicity of subsidiary skills, and their importance and interrelations depend on tasks and aims as well as on analytical, planning, and executive proficiency. In the past, theories of drawing have tended to focus on a particular aspect or subsidiary skill. For Lowenfeld (1952), the fact that drawing can serve as a vehicle of emotional expression and meaning was the main concern. Goodnow's original view of drawing (1973) centred on executive skills. The influence of the linguistic (syntactic) analyses of Chomsky in the later 1950s and mid-1960s which guided a number of psychological enquiries at the time led Goodnow (1973) to describe drawing as a 'grammar of action' with a (finite) number of sequencing ('syntactic') rules which lawfully constrain the movement sequence. Freeman (1975) focused on the question of why the drawings of children at given ages exhibit almost universal stereotypes, and first explained the problem in terms of short-term memory which involves the retrieval of serial items so that the middle items of a drawing sequence are left out, in analogy with serial position curves. In a later version, Freeman (1980) suggested that 'canonical' views of objects as well as difficulties in co-ordinating different spatial axes are involved: houses drawn as seen from the front, dogs from the side, and spatial relations internal to the figure (for example, limb to body) are at odds with spatial relations external to the figure (for example, figure to room). Goodnow's (1973) analogy of drawing with language was taken further, and possibly too literally, by Van Somers (1984). However, he documented the multiplicity of skills involved in drawing, and this is important.

Goodnow's (1977) second model emphasized that drawing requires problem solving. The assumption is reasonable enough. Drawing sets the subject a number of different puzzles: for instance, attempts at 'realistic' pictures almost always involve translations from three to two dimensions (Millar 1975a). The solutions are far from being immediately obvious, as the history of drawing and painting shows (Richter 1970), but they are not arbitrary either. Millar (1975a) argued that marks on the page are 'translations' in which two-dimensional scribbles, and later, flat geometric shapes, stand for or symbolize three-dimensional objects and spatial relations. Typically, circles stand for heads for the blind as well as for the sighted, although no head is a circle. However, it is the simplest (to draw) two-dimensional shape which also captures the quality or feature which heads, both seen and felt, have in common. Orientating a figure on the page so that its vertical axis is parallel with the left-hand margin of the page is such a common solution for representing someone standing upright in three-dimensional space that it comes as a shock to realize that the congenitally blind do not immediately invent this solution too (Millar 1975a). They had no difficulty, of course, in understanding or using this translation of 3-D space, once it was pointed out. However, similarities in the direction of line projections in the gravitational vertical and the frontal medial planes are more easily culled from vision than from active touch. Such similarities are more easily available to the sighted, and are consequently more easily used by them as devices to 'represent' 3-D postures on the flat page. The point is that drawing involves symbolic devices which are based on and derived from modality-specific perception, and this also involves problem-solving skills. Neither purely data-driven nor purely 'top–down' explanations suffice.

Given that actual representations require as many symbolic, memory, 'translation', and cognitive skills generally as other problem-solving tasks, the analogy of imagery with drawing suggests that we should not look for a single unitary explanation for imagery either. If imagery is involved in thinking and memory, the use of remembered lines, shapes, and configurations as representations in solving mental problems is no more likely to depend on a single factor than does actual representation of objects or situations by drawing on the page.

A related reason for invoking an analogy with drawing is that in drawing there is no real contradiction between the conceptual and the modality-specific element; that is to say, the fact that visible lines on the page are used symbolically is not in the least self-contradictory. However 'abstract' a representation of an object on the page is meant to be, it owes something to the modality of perception and execution as well as to the particular notion associated with the object or event. The view that drawings are faithful reflections of people's mental representations, is no more tenable than the naïve assumption that vision is a necessary and uniquely important factor in drawing. Piaget and Inhelder (1948) proposed that children draw what they know rather than what they see. However, it is unlikely that children know, see, or remember only what they can draw. Kosslyn *et al.* (1977) were clearly correct to argue that drawings are not direct reflections of levels of thought, or knowledge, or of the level of visual analysis. Equally, however, the fact that ratings of visual imagery do not predict copying skills (Slee 1976) does not entail the assumption that proficiency in drawing owes nothing to visual analysis: it clearly does. It is contended here that the image or representation of an object, situation, or event similarly owes something to the mode in which the object or event was perceived and/or produced, even though it is used symbolically. The findings which lead to this view are discussed next.

Suggestions from empirical evidence

The literature on empirical evidence on visual imagery is far too large and varied for an overview to be feasible here. In any case, there are many well-known discussions of this (for example, Paivio 1971; Pylyshyn 1973; Kosslyn 1980, 1983; Richardson 1980), although they do not all come to the same conclusion. The point here is to focus on findings which have some bearing on perceptual modalities other than vision, because these suggest that another factor should be taken into consideration – namely, the role of executive movements in giving rise to spatial imagery.

At least three main lines of evidence have been used to attempt to establish modality-specificity for imagery. The earliest and most obvious are introspective and retrospective reports, including questionnaires. The second type of evidence is based on findings from complex spatial tasks which are assumed to require visual imagery for their solution. The third type of empirical study uses a variety of experimental paradigms to test the relation between perception and memory. The three types of study will be briefly considered below in so far as they also have some bearing on modalities other than vision. Finally, some suggestive findings from actual representations by the blind will be considered.

The most vivid introspective report of imagery which I have ever heard came from a congenitally totally blind postgraduate student whom

I had asked to describe his room at home. He talked of the textured feel of the chest of drawers near the entrance, and a feeling of 'empty space' between that and another piece of furniture across the room. The feeling of 'empty space' was particularly vividly described. It seemed to consist partly of remembered (echoing) sound and partly of a slightly cold, almost 'windy' sensation on the face as of a slight breeze when walking through the room. According to him, he clearly felt the space to be in front of him as he (mentally) stood by the chest of drawers. By contrast, a congenitally blind boy who had light and shadow (although no shape) perception reported visual imagery. He could mentally see himself as a compact shadow hanging on to something not so clear (a swing) in a much lighter surround. He insisted that this was a mental picture, not a felt sensation, because the mental shadow picture was very small, not in the least the size he knew himself to be in reality. The enormous difference which even minimal light perception can make is far too often forgotten by researchers who treat 'the blind' as an undifferentiated subject group to be compared with 'the sighted'.

Of course, the totally blind student could have merely remembered a verbal description which he covertly used at the time of experiencing the feelings when he was in his room. I only have his word for it that he could image the feelings which he was describing: this is, of course, the trouble with all forms of introspective and retrospective reports. However, such reports are accepted by many people as similar to their own experience, and the student's report is clearly not an isolated case. Schlaegel (1953), for instance, collected reports from a number of sighted, partially blind, and totally blind adolescents. The difference in the modality of reported imagery between the early blind and sighted was striking. He found that only images of sounds and feels and kinaesthetic images were reported by the congenitally or very early totally blind. By contrast, the partially sighted reported quite vivid visual imagery.

However, the second line of evidence apparently contradicts the modality-specificity of reported imagery. The argument is that the congenitally blind can perform tasks which were specifically designed to test for visual imagery in the sighted (for example, Kerr 1983). Typical are tasks involving spatial inference, mental rotation, and mental 'scanning' of spatial locations and extents. In the inference tasks, subjects are familiarized with paths leading from A to B and from B to C and are then required to indicate the path from A to C. In mental rotation tasks subjects are presented with particular locations on a spatial display and have to imagine what their own relations to the locations would be if the display were rotated, or if their own positions were rotated relative to the display. The fact that the time people take to verify the identity of shapes which are rotated with respect to each other increases with the degree of rotation (for example, Shepard and Metzler 1971) and the difference in time for imaging large versus small shapes (Kosslyn 1976) have also been used as indicators that the time course of mental scanning is similar to visual scanning. The discovery that the blind can solve these problems too (and sometimes with similar chronometric functions to those of the sighted) seems to contradict the assumption.

Kerr (1983) suggested that, because the blind can solve inference, rotation, and mental-scanning tasks, the representations which lead to successful performance must be 'abstract'. Millar (1986a) argued that this is a mistaken view on several counts. First, it must be realized that the findings in many of the most frequently quoted studies (for example Carpenter and Eisenberg 1978; Kerr 1983; Leonard and Newman 1967; Marmor and Zaback 1976) are based on group data which include blind people with at least light perception. There certainly is no reason to suppose that these blind people are incapable of remembering or using visual information from this source – quite the contrary. In fact, even very minimal visual experience, such as light perception, can be a very important source of external reference information for people who are otherwise labelled as congenitally and profoundly blind (for example, Millar 1979). Group data which include such people are therefore unreliable. Second, it should be clear that nothing can be inferred about the *means* of solving a problem simply from the fact that it was solved.

Consider mental spatial-rotation tasks. 'Ego-centric' or body-centred reference frames lead to errors in locating external objects after rotation, because the object is located by means of cues or spatial axes which remain stationary, so that the object is sought on the original (wrong) side. For this reason it is often forgotten that it is, nevertheless, perfectly possible to achieve correct mental rotation solutions with 'ego-centric' or body-centred references, provided updating rules are used. Conversely, visual experience provides more information than does experience without vision about the usefulness of external reference axes, and about updating cues. Strategies which take this visually mediated information into account are less likely to lead to rotation errors. However, this does not, by any means, guarantee perfect performance for heuristics which are derived from visual information (Millar 1976, 1979). Moreover, errors can also occur when verbal strategies are used (for example, Saddala *et al.* 1979). In principle, patterns of performance which have been predicted from differences in strategies are more useful as evidence about the heuristics subjects actually use than straight efficiency counts.

Assessing the time course of performance is also potentially a better indicator of the means by which people achieve solutions. Nevertheless, how we interpret findings must depend on a job analysis of the particular task. Kerr (1983), for instance, suggests that spatial representation must be 'abstract' because time measures are similar for blind and sighted subjects in tasks which involve mental scanning of figures which differ in size, or are rotated with respect to each other. However, it is worth remembering that actual haptic scanning as well as actual visual scanning increases in time with increased size of the objects to be scanned. Linear increases with time could thus occur whether the subjects used mental scanning heuristics derived from visual or from haptic scanning – although overall time might be greater in the latter case. Time also increases with the number of judgements a task may demand; but the basis of time increases in the latter case is different. It depends on the amount of cognitive load, and there is no reason to suppose that it has anything to do with differences in heuristics which are derived from perceptual aspects of the information. Experimental manipulations which are designed to assess modality-specific aspects of representation but actually tap memory load – and vice versa – are a potential source of apparently contradictory evidence.

The difference between 'do' and 'can' is another source of confusion. As a matter of fact, the congenitally totally blind do often have specific difficulties in tasks which demand that a location be coded relative to an imagined external configuration, while they are no worse than the sighted on tasks which can be solved in terms of distances or sequential order (for example, Revesz 1950; Millar 1975b, 1976, 1979, 1981b; Casey 1978; Colley and Colley 1981; Byrne and Salter 1983). However, to say this is not, of course, even remotely to suggest that the blind are *incapable* of using current reference information, let alone that they are *incapable* of perceiving shapes, as such statements have sometimes been interpreted (for example, Bailes and Lambert 1986).

What the evidence which shows differences between the blind and sighted in the pattern of performance does suggest is that the modality of experience tends to elicit strategies which are most directly compatible with that experience. Slator (1982) has shown this directly. Young, sighted children are better at remembering spatial locations in terms of sequential paths when the original information was given in that form, and are better at remembering locations in terms of reference information when the original input showed the locations within a prominent frame. Reliable information about external reference frames is less available in the long-term spatial experience of the blind than of the sighted, while reliable movement information is available. It is thus entirely intelligible if the blind tend to use sequential, kinaesthetically based strategies which are compatible with their long-term experience. However, the fact that long-term experience elicits strategies that are compatible with it, does not imply that this incapacitates people from using any other strategy. There is no reason to suppose that the blind are, in principle, *incapable* of using spatial mapping strategies. The evidence does suggest that they acquire such strategies in a less direct manner. It is, indeed, one of the main assumptions of the present thesis that the blind can use remembered shapes and configurations for mental mapping. Precisely how this may occur is suggested in the final part of this section.

In considering the third type of paradigm which has been used to test for modality-specific effects, it is interesting to note that this has not, on the whole, received central attention in all theories of imagery. This may be because it concerns verbal rather than visual performance. However, probably the most successful demonstration of modality-specific effects in memory is for coding by sound, using Conrad's (1964, 1971) method of assessing acoustic confusions. This compares short-term recall of a series of items which have similar sounding names with recall of items with dissimilar sounding names. Typically, recall of phonologically similar lists is considerably worse, even when the lists consist of pictures (Conrad 1971) or of tactual objects or braille letters (Millar 1975c, d). The logic of the method is that people must be assumed to have coded the sounds of the names for these to have any effect on memory.

Conrad's method has also been adapted to demonstrate tactual coding (Millar 1975c, d). Series of tactually similar objects and letters are remembered less well than dissimilar lists; but these tactual-similarity effects are associated with recall of at most three or four items, and they occur when identification by name is slow or impossible. The results on tactual-similarity effects are thus precisely the opposite of findings for phonological-similarity effects, because phonological coding is associated with fast naming and large memory spans (Conrad 1971; Millar 1975c, d). Modality-specific effects can thus be demonstrated even in memory for touch. Theories such as that of Baddeley (1986) could, in principle, incorporate the finding by adding another passive 'slave' system to the model of working memory. However, it is also of considerable interest that tactual similarity effects are associated with recall of only a few serial items, while the phonological strategy which is most clearly associated with large recall spans depends on subvocal rehearsal; that is to say, it is the active execution of (speech) movements which seems to be of major importance (ibid.). As such, the stimulus-similarity effects are as much a function of the output systems as of the input system.

The present thesis is that the executive system is of similar importance in spatial memory, both long- and short-term. The main paradigms for testing for movement coding have been interference and relocation tasks (Laabs and Simmons 1981). Evidence that the congenitally totally blind tend to code movement information in spatial tasks in terms of kinaesthetic cues or sequential movements has been reviewed previously (Millar 1981a). The strategy is not, of course, confined to the blind (for example, Laabs and Simmons 1981). Whether or not it is used depends on the task and on the informational conditions. The most important conditions are absence of visual information about relative object locations in a task, and absence or uncertainty about spatial reference frames in terms of which the test locations could, in principle, be coded (Millar 1985). There is no doubt that under blind conditions, irrelevant interpolated movements and irrelevant cues produced by changing the direction of positioning movements, generate errors in locating the target, even if the target location remains the same (Laabs and Simmons 1981; Millar 1981a,b, 1985). There is also evidence that interference from (irrelevant) changed directions of blind positioning movements is reduced by providing a reference frame for the target with instructions on how to use it (Millar 1985). This finding suggests that movement information can be used strategically.

In principle, therefore, memory for movement sequences seems to have all the ingredients needed for an active output strategy. The question is whether and how people can use movement coding, not only to remember sequential or 'route' information, but also as a means of coding the shape and configuration or 'map' which the routes produce.

So far, there is no decisive experimental evidence on the relation between movement coding and cognitive mapping under blind conditions. However, at least three types of findings on drawings by the blind are relevant to the question. The first stems from observations of the means which congenitally totally blind children of different ages use to depict the human figure (Millar 1975a). The second comes from an experiment in which blind and blindfolded sighted children were asked to draw the space around which they had walked just previously (Millar 1981a, 1986a). The last finding is from a study, as yet unpublished, which compares blind children's performance on recognizing and drawing geometric shapes and meaningful shapes.

Millar (1975a) compared the very first drawings of the human figure which congenitally totally blind subjects had ever made with drawings by blindfolded sighted children (also using raised line drawings) of the same ages. The older blind produced figures which showed essentially the same main schemas as those of their sighted peers: circles for heads, circles, oblongs, or vertical lines for the body, and lines ending in smaller protuberances for arms and hands, legs and feet, respectively, aligned to the body in more or less 'appropriate' places. By contrast, the younger blind, unlike their sighted peers, produced what seemed to be just fragmented scribbles. Fortunately, the children had been asked to label their productions as they were drawing, and this produced some clues about how scribbles progress to becoming recognizable body schemas. One eight year old, for instance, produced separate scribbles for each body part as he named it, starting with one ear. He included a separate scribble for the skin; clearly, therefore, he had as yet little idea how the human figure should be depicted. Another solution was to use separate lines for all body parts, but to angle the lines for arms and legs differently from lines for the head, chin, and tummy. Such solutions were not due simply to not having drawn before, as that also applied to the older blind. In any case, most of the younger blind were quite capable of drawing circles, or at least round squiggles, when asked to do so. However, with the exception of one little girl, the younger ones did not immediately cotton on to the possibility of using two-dimensional shapes to represent 3-D body parts. At the same time, the scribbles and lines were not intended as nonsense; they were used as tokens for the body part that the child wished to depict. The exception was a highly intelligent little girl who asked what she should do for the head, and on having the question thrown back, commented that she thought that a circle would do.

The use of two-dimensional shapes to represent 3-D objects can be seen as a first step to cognitive mapping. Berlà and Butterfield (1977)

141

have shown, for instance, that giving blind children practice in recognizing the shapes of countries on the map, greatly improved their ability to make sense of geographic maps. The point is that it is more difficult to recognize similarities between movement sequences and the geometric configurations which they make, in blind conditions than in vision. This applies even more to the movement sequences followed in walking through large-scale spaces. It is not necessary, however, to give blind children extended practice before they understand that hand movements can represent the routes followed by moving in large-scale space. It is sufficient to point out the similarity to them once. A study designed to investigate how blind children represent a square space around which they had walked repeatedly (Millar 1981a) showed that most young congenitally totally blind children simply drew a long line for the square walk, with squiggles at various intervals to show the toys at the four corners. However, they knew quite well that they had turned several times in their walk, and some said so. Simply telling the child to show the turns in the drawing was sufficient for her to realize that hand movements in drawing could be used to represent body movements and turns in large-scale space. The realization of similarities between body movements in large-scale space, hand movements, and feedback from the (raised line) configurations that had been drawn can thus, in principle, provide the blind child with an excellent entry into 'cognitive mapping'. Memory of the configurations produced by hand movements on the page, and the understanding that these can represent large-scale space, would clearly fulfil the basic requirements of 'cognitive maps'.

Finally, there is evidence that movements are an important basis of haptic shape recognition in young congenitally totally blind children. For blind children without any visual experience, for instance, discrimination of new shapes depends on using systematic exploratory movements (Davidson 1972). More surprising, perhaps, is the finding from a recent (as yet unpublished) study that the considerable lag between recognizing shapes and drawing them, which is well-known for sighted children (Maccoby and Bee 1965), is actually reversed for the congenitally totally blind. Young sighted children can recognize pictures long before they are able to reproduce them by drawing; for the blind the opposite is the case. An apparently contrary observation, that the blind also recognize raised figures easily (Pring, personal communication) was obtained in conditions in which the figures had previously been named. Naming is not, of course, needed for sighted children to recognize shapes. In the current study, the figures to be recognized were not named beforehand. In these conditions, blind children had no difficulty in recognizing familiar shapes such as circles and squares, and to a lesser extent, triangles from raised line drawings. Only one out of twenty congenitally totally or near totally blind children (with no useful light perception) recognized the human figure from raised line drawings. Sighted children have no difficulty in recognizing these. At the same time, the majority of the blind children actually produced recognizable drawings of the human figure themselves, although they had not been able to recognize the figure from raised line drawings. Production in this case clearly preceded recognition.

Taken together, the findings suggest how active production of movements in small-scale space may lead to using these to represent spatial configurations in large-scale space, and thus suggest a reasonable basis for demonstrating how coding movement information may lead to 'cognitive' mapping.

Ingredients for a model of imagery

The foregoing brief review of theories of imagery and drawing, and of evidence for imagery in modalities other than vision, has produced several points that need to be taken into account in theoretical explanations. First, imagery in modalities other than vision occurs, and it cannot simply be assumed that studies of visual imagery tell the whole story. Second, it is extremely unlikely that imagery can be explained in terms of a single perceptual or cognitive factor. Perceptual inputs as well as symbolic skills, inference, and the eduction of communalities and analogies are involved. These factors are not mutually exclusive, but work together. Third, it is possible to acquire important aspects of imagery, such as map-like (cognitive map) heuristics. It is, therefore, not necessarily best described as a spontaneous, inevitable occurrence. Fourth, imagery is a form of coding which is based on, and compatible with, the modality of input; but it can also represent other forms of information. Finally, imagery should not be regarded as a purely passive register or transducer of information. Output systems can be importantly involved in the heuristics which are compatible with the principal modes of input. An attempt to outline the relation of imagery to perception, cognition, and output factors is given below.

Basic to the present description is the view that the sense modalities form neither a 'unitary' nor separate systems; they are sources of convergent and complementary information (Millar 1981a).

This means that it is unnecessary to assume a mechanism of learnt 'translations' for perceptions in different modalities in order to account for matching between modalities. It also obviates the need to assume direct perception of 'amodal' qualities. The fact that inputs from different modalities converge (often literally – for example, Sakata and Iwamura 1978) and so overlap, and usually coincide in space and time, is sufficient for matching, and provides redundancy. Redundancy of information can aid performance (for example, Millar 1986b). It is particularly useful in conditions of uncertainty and as a 'fail–safe' device. At the same time, information from different modalities is not homologous. This fact is obvious and needs no further elaboration. The point is that such differences in input are an advantage, not a disadvantage, as is often supposed in normal conditions, because they provide the organism with further information which complements inputs from any one source. Even in vision alone, for example, two eyes are better than one, not because they provide precisely the same information, but because the overlapping but slightly different inputs provide the third dimension of depth.

Before we start being mystified by the concept of space, it should be clear that what is meant by coding the location of an object spatially is that the objects can be related in terms of distance (extent) or direction (angle) to some other cue (reference), however insufficient or fragmentary. It is impossible to code any location (even one's own) spatially unless there is some reference information. Sight, sound, smell, and active touch and movement can contribute. However, the modalities must provide some reference cue or axis in relation to which positions can be coded, whether the reference is the person's own body, or external to that, if the information is to be used in spatial tasks at all. This is what is common to spatial coding. But the reference information as such is not amodal or 'abstract': it is culled from a particular modality or from several modalities which converge, and is thus potentially multi-modal. The fact that a specific characteristic or conglomerate of characteristics can be used to stand for or symbolize a class of objects, or relations between object locations, does not alter this. It is the formal (general) description of the procedures and operations involved in coding which does not necessarily need to refer to the modalities of input.

Further, information from different modalities differs in quality, type, and quantity, whether this is about reference cues, about textures, or about sequencing. The fact that in normal conditions the inputs complement each other, converge, and coincide means that features perceived in one modality can signal, signify, or symbolize the complementary qualities in a different mode. This makes for cold or loud colours, warm sounds, and other forms of synaesthesia. However, in conditions in which one sensory source is totally absent, the fact that inputs are complementary also means that qualities which are prominent in the remaining modalities may exert a disproportionate biasing influence on procedures which are compatible with them. The bias can be rectified by providing the missing information in some other form. This is usually a more roundabout process. These assumptions explain the differences and similarities in spatial tasks between the blind and sighted.

What is meant by imagery here is that modality-specific perceptual qualities can be remembered and used in the short as well as over the longer term. It entails that imagery does not belong to the class of temporary physical after-effects of actual stimulation, but to processes of recognition and recall. Furthermore, I take it as axiomatic that strict 'bottom–up' processing, from perception to thought, as well as pure 'top–down' processing, from cognition to sensation, are limiting cases. Most tasks demand a confluence of inputs from a number of external and internal sources. Thus, in principle, a remembered perception, including a quality specific to a modality, while tending to bias coding in the direction of the modality of input, can be used to signify a prototype, signal or symbolize an event, or may be used heuristically to code information in a form other than the modality of input.

Imagery, whether of sound or colour, phonological features or configurations, smell, touch, or kinaesthetic sequences, is thus explained in terms of memory for perceptual qualities, and the interactions with 'top–down' processing and knowledge. However, it has been argued throughout this chapter that to assume passive input coding is not enough. An important link must also be assumed between memory for perceptual qualities and output systems. This assumption deals with a major controversy in the literature, namely whether imagery is of any use as far as memory efficiency is concerned. In part, this problem is due to a tacit presumption that for imagery to count as a factor in thinking, it must be shown to be useful in every type of task and in all connections; that it must be shown, for instance, that rated vividness of imagery produces better drawings, when there is no *a priori* reason to assume a necessary link between ratings of 'vividness' (which could refer to clarity of colour or shape) and purely procedural skills. More importantly, the problem stems from a failure to distinguish between passive and active heuristics. Passive recall of input qualities is probably relatively inefficient in most cases (for example, Millar 1975d). It is when executive processes can be recruited that heuristics based on perceptual features seem to be most effective. This is most obvious in verbal rehearsal where articulatory processes are used in the recall of sounds. It is suggested here that executive movements can also be recruited to code spatial information in terms of configurations. Cognitive mapping in the spatial representation of the blind, based on kinaesthetic and movement information, is thus no mere figment of the imagination, but a perfectly reasonable heuristic, provided the relevant information is made available, so that configurational similarities can be inferred.

References

Anderson, J. R., and Bower, G. H. (1973) *Human Associative Memory*, New York: Wiley.

Arnheim, R. (1969) *Visual Thinking*, Berkeley, CA: University of California Press.

Atkinson, R. C., and Shiffrin, R. M. (1968) 'Human memory: a proposed system and its control processes', in K. W. Spence and J. T. Spence (eds) *The Psychology of Learning and Motivation: Advances in Research and Theory*, vol. 2, New York: Academic Press.

Baddeley, A. D. (1986) *Working Memory*, London: Oxford University Press.

Bailes, S. M. and Lambert, R. M. (1986) 'Cognitive aspects of haptic form recognition by blind and sighted subjects', *British Journal of Psychology* 77: 451–8.

Berlà, E.P. and Butterfield, I.H.J. (1977 'Tactual distinctive feature analysis: training blind students in shape recognition and in locating shapes on a map', *Journal of Special Education* 11: 336–46.

Byrne, R. W. and Salter, E. (1983) 'Distance and direction in the cognitive maps of the blind', *Canadian Journal of Psychology* 37: 293–9.

Carpenter, P. A. and Eisenberg, P. (1978) 'Mental rotation and the frame of reference in blind and sighted individuals', *Perception and Psychophysics* 23: 117–24.

Casey, S. M. (1978) 'Cognitive mapping by the blind', *Journal of Visual Impairment and Blindness* 72: 297–301.

Colley, A., and Colley, M. (1981) 'Reproduction of end location and distance of movement in early and later blind subjects', *Journal of Motor Behaviour* 13: 102–9.

Conrad, R. (1964) 'Acoustic confusions in immediate memory', *British Journal of Psychology* 55: 75–84.

—— (1971) 'The chronology of the development of convert speech in children', *Developmental Psychology* 5: 398–405.

Davidson, P. W. (1972) 'The role of exploratory activity in haptic perception: some issues, data, and hypotheses', *Research Bulletin of the American Foundation for the Blind*, 24: 21–8.

Freeman, N. H. (1975) 'Do children draw men with arms coming out of the head?' *Nature* 254: 416–17.

(1980) *Strategies of Representation in Young Children*, New York: Academic Press.

Gibson, E. J. (1969) *Principles of Perceptual Development*, New York: Appleton-Century-Crofts.

Gibson, J. J. (1966) *The Senses Considered as Perceptual Systems*, London: Allen & Unwin.

(1979) *The Ecological Approach to Visual Perception*, Boston, MA: Houghton-Mifflin.

Gombrich, E. H. (1970) *Art and Illusion*, Princeton, NJ: Princeton University Press.

Goodnow, J. J. (1973) 'The grammar of action: sequence and syntax in children's copying', *Cognitive Psychology* 4: 82–95.

(1977) *Children's Drawings*, London: Fontana.

Gregory, R. L. (1974) *Concepts and Mechanisms of Perception*, London: Duckworth.

and Gombrich, E. H. (1973) *Illusions in Nature and Art*, London: Duckworth.

Kerr, N. H. (1983) 'The role of vision in visual imagery experiments: evidence from the congenitally blind', *Journal of Experimental Psychology: General* 112: 265–77.

Kosslyn, S. M. (1976) 'Can imagery be distinguished from other forms of internal representation? Evidence from studies of information retrieval times', *Memory and Cognition* 4: 291–7.

(1980) *Image and Mind*, Cambridge, MA: Harvard University Press.

(1983) *Ghosts in the Mind's Machine: Creating and Using Images in the Brain*, New York: Norton.

Helmeyer, K. H., and Lockyear, E. P. (1977) 'Children's drawings as data about internal representations', *Journal of Experimental Child Psychology* 23: 191–211.

Laabs, G. J., and Simmons, R. W. (1981) 'Motor memory', in D. Holding (ed.) *Human Skills*, New York: Wiley.

Leonard, J. A., and Newman, R. C. (1967) 'Spatial orientation in the blind', *Nature*, 215: 1413–14.

Lowenfeld, V. (1952) *The Nature of Creativity*, London: Routledge & Kegan Paul.

Maccoby, E. E., and Bee, H. L. (1965) 'Some speculations concerning the lag between perceiving and performing', *Child Development* 36: 367–77.

Marmor, P. S., and Zaback, L. A. (1976) 'Mental rotation by the blind: does mental rotation depend on visual imagery?' *Journal of Experimental Psychology: Human Perception and Performance* 2: 515–21.

Millar, S. (1975a) 'Visual experience or translation rules? Drawing the human figure by blind and sighted children', *Perception* 4: 363–71.

(1975b) 'Spatial memory by blind and sighted children', *British Journal of Psychology* 66: 449–59.

(1975c) 'Effects of phonological and tactual similarity on serial object recall by blind and sighted children', *Cortex* 11: 170–80.

(1975d) 'Effects of tactual and phonological similarity on the recall of Braille letters by blind children', *British Journal of Psychology* 66: 193–201.

(1976) 'Spatial representation by blind and sighted children', *Journal of Experimental Child Psychology* 21: 460–79.

(1979) 'The utilization of external and movement cues by blind and sighted children', *Perception* 8: 11–20.

(1981a) 'Crossmodal and intersensory perception and the blind', in R. D. Walk and H. L. Pick, Jr. (eds) *Intersensory Perception and Sensory Integration*, New York: Pergamon.

(1981b) 'Self-referent and movement cues in coding spatial location by blind and sighted children', *Perception* 10: 255–64.

(1982) 'The problem of imagery and spatial development in the blind', in B. de Gelder (ed.) *Knowledge and Representation*, New York: Routledge & Kegan Paul.

(1985) 'Movement cues and body orientation in recall of locations of blind and sighted children', *Quarterly Journal of Experimental Psychology* 37A: 257–79.

(1986a) 'Drawing as representation and image in blind children', in D. G. Russell, D. F. Marks, and J. T. E. Richardson (eds) *Imagery 2*, Dunedin: Human Performance Associates.

(1986b) 'Aspects of size, shape, and texture in touch: redundancy and interference in children's discrimination of raised dot patterns', *Journal of Child Psychology and Psychiatry* 27: 367–81.

Neisser, U. (1976) *Cognition and Reality*, San Francisco: Freeman.

—— and Kerr, N. H. (1973) 'Spatial and mnemonic properties of visual images', *Cognitive Psychology* 5: 138–50.

Norman, D. A. (ed.) (1970) *Models of Human Memory*, New York: Academic Press.

Paivio, A. (1971) *Imagery and Verbal Processes*, New York: Holt, Rinehart & Winston.

Piaget, J., and Inhelder, B. (1948) *La Représentation de l'Espace chez l'Enfant*, Paris: Presses Universitaires de France.

Pylyshyn, Z. W. (1973) 'What the mind's eye tells the mind's brain', *Psychological Bulletin* 80: 1–24.

Revesz, G. (1950) *Psychology and Art of the Blind*, London: Longmans, Green.

Richardson, J. T. E. (1980) *Mental Imagery and Human Memory*, London: Macmillan.

Richter, J. M. A. (1970) *Perspective in Greek and Roman Art*, London: Phaidon.

Rumelhart, D. E., McClelland, J. L., and the PDP Research Group (1986) *Parallel Distributed Processing*, vols 1 and 2, Cambridge, MA: MIT Press.

Saddala, E. K., Staplin, L. J., and Burrows, W. J. (1979) 'Retrieval processes in distance cognition', *Memory and Cognition* 7: 291–6.

Sakata, H., and Iwamura, Y. (1978) 'Cortical processing of tactile information in the first somatosensory and parietal association areas in the monkey', in G. Gordon (ed.) *Active Touch: The Mechanism of Recognition of Objects by Manipulation*, Oxford: Pergamon.

Schlaegel, T. F. (1953) 'The dominant method of imagery in the blind as compared to sighted adolescents', *Journal of Genetic Psychology* 83: 265–77.

Shepard, R. N., and Metzler, J. (1971) 'Mental rotation of three-dimensional objects', *Science* 171: 701–3.

Slator, R. (1982) 'The development of spatial perception and understanding in young children', unpublished D.Phil. thesis, University of Oxford.

Slee, J. A. (1976) 'The perceptual nature of visual imagery', unpublished PhD thesis reported in Van Somers (1984).

Van Somers, P. (1984) *Drawing and Cognition*, London: Cambridge University Press.

Chapter six

Imagery and action: differential encoding of verbs and nouns

Johannes Engelkamp and Hubert D. Zimmer

The title 'Imagery and action' might evoke two expectations: first, one might expect to learn something about the imagery of actions, about what distinguishes imagining objects from imagining actions; second, one might expect to learn something about what distinguishes forming images from performing actions. In this chapter, we shall deal with both of these issues, but predominantly with the latter distinction, probing the relationship between the mental representation of objects and actions, their typical linguistic labels (nouns and verbs) and modality-specific encoding processes.

The term 'encoding' refers to the different kinds of information processing which take place during the learning phase. In other words, it refers not only to the activation of meanings or concepts but also to the automatic activation of visual features in the case of an auditory stimulus (cf. Nelson 1979) as well as to output operations such as saying a word aloud or performing a relevant action. In this sense we shall talk of 'modality-specific' encoding processes if images are formed or actions acted out. We shall also describe the formation of images as 'imaginal encoding' and the performance of actions as 'motor encoding'. In this chapter we shall be concerned with the issue of the influence of modality-specific encoding operations upon memory performance. The reason that we prefer to use the term 'encoding' in this broad sense is that all information processing produces memory traces and all such traces can potentially be used in remembering previous episodes. This incorporates the notion that both imaginal and motor processes might influence memory performance, and we are therefore interested not only in creating images to nouns (as is usually the case in imagery research), but also in acting out verbs.

In this chapter, we shall deal in turn with the following questions. First, are there differences between modality-specific encoding processes? Second, does the mental representation of nouns and verbs differ? Third, how does modality-specific encoding influence the learning of nouns and verbs? In the first section, we shall distinguish between two types of modality-specific processing, imaginal and motor encoding, which work on different representational systems specialized for different kinds of information. We shall then consider differences between the mental representations of nouns and verbs. Here we shall confine ourselves to concrete nouns referring to people and objects such as 'waiter' or 'flower' and action verbs which refer to motor actions such as 'to jump' or 'to tear off'. We assume that the differences in the types of referent are reflected in the conceptual representations of concrete nouns and action verbs, and that they have an impact upon the modality-specific encoding of such nouns and verbs. This differentiation relates to Aylwin's distinction (1988; Chapter 10 in this volume) between visual and enactive cognitive structures, the latter often having an affective component in addition to the purely cognitive content. It leads to the question of how modality-specific encoding influences the learning of concrete nouns and action verbs. Verbal learning will be discussed with regard to the constructs of item-specific and relational encoding (see, for example, Einstein and Hunt 1980; Hunt and Einstein 1981).

Imaginal versus motor encoding

Although, theoretically speaking, various kinds of imaginal encoding have been distinguished, such as acoustic, visual, and olfactory encoding (Paivio and Okovita 1971; Segal and Fusella 1971), previous studies have concentrated almost exclusively upon visual imaginal processing and for the most part upon the processing of nouns. Normally, subjects have to imagine the object denoted by a noun or, less often, the scene or event described by a phrase or a short text. The theoretical construct behind visual imaginal encoding is, however, considered to be the same, whether the referents in question are objects or events. The shift from images of objects to images of action events complicates the situation. In the case of action phrases such as 'to bend the wire' or 'to tear off a piece of paper', the person imagined to be performing the action may be oneself or somebody else. While imagining the actions of others is primarily a sensory process, we assume that imagining oneself performing an action to a considerable extent involves motor processes (cf. also Aylwin 1988; Chapter 10 in this volume). We have devoted our attention to this difference. However, instead of having our subjects imagining themselves performing actions, we required them to pantomime those actions – that is, they were required to act out the action without the real object (for instance, to pretend that they were tearing off a piece of paper). We call this experimental condition 'motor encoding' and contrast it with 'imaginal encoding'. In the latter encoding condition, the subjects are required to form images of others performing actions or to watch others performing those actions.

Our goal was to find out whether there was good reason to distinguish between imaginal and motor encoding as two kinds of modality-specific encoding, in the manner in which others have distinguished between imaginal and verbal or propositional encoding (for example, Kosslyn 1980; Paivio 1986). In a series of experiments in which the subjects had to learn identical lists of action phrases (such as 'to bend a wire') under imaginal and motor encoding and for control purposes also under a verbal encoding condition, we found consistently significant differences. First, performing actions led to better recall than seeing somebody else act out those actions or imagining those actions. The two latter conditions led to roughly equal memory performance, and were superior to verbal encoding (for reviews, see Engelkamp and Zimmer 1985; Zimmer and Engelkamp 1985b; Engelkamp 1987, 1988a). Similar results have been reported by Cohen (1983, 1985). The idea that different encoding processes are involved is further supported by the finding that introducing real objects (for instance, giving the subjects a piece of paper to act with or showing them models who tear off a real piece of paper on a television screen in the imaginal condition) has an independent effect upon recall. In other words, motor encoding and introducing real objects have additive effects on performance (Engelkamp and Zimmer 1983).

Other important findings which support the claim of two different encoding processes stem from experiments involving selective interference. Learning is worse if two concurrent tasks both involve the motor system than when one involves visual imaginal processing and the other involves motor processing (Zimmer and Engelkamp 1985a; Zimmer et al. 1984). Similar effects of selective interference have been reported by other researchers (Hulme 1979; Saltz and Donnenwerth-Nolan 1981; cf. also Logie and Baddeley, Chapter 4 in this volume).

Taken together, we interpret the results of both types of experiment as a strong argument for the distinction between imaginal and motor encoding. The next step was to investigate this difference in more detail. We tackled two aspects of the problem in a further series of experiments: the influence of motor encoding upon recognition and the effects of elaboration. With regard to recognition memory, we obtained nearly perfect discrimination between old and new items under conditions of motor encoding (Engelkamp and Krumnacker 1980). However, if we held the similarity of the verbal surface structure and the similarity of meaning constant, a changing movement pattern did not influence either the error rate or the decision time to reject distractors (Zimmer 1984, 1986). Further, we observed no effect of elaboration within the motor domain: to act more, to act longer, or to act in a different manner when the subjects had to enact the same items twice had no influence upon memory performance (Cohen 1983; Zimmer 1984). Thus, we assume that motor encoding has a particularly strong effect upon the distinctiveness of the memory traces of individual items, which cannot be easily improved by further processing, whereas detailed information about the movement pattern is not processed during the recognition of verbal items.

Recently, we commenced a further line of research which we shall describe in the remainder of this chapter. Up to this point, we have described experiments which studied imaginal and motor encoding in the case of action phrases (that is, verb–object phrases). On closer inspection, however, it becomes clear that this is not the ideal manner in which to compare imaginal and motor encoding, since action phrases consist of *both* nouns *and* verbs. Yet the referents of nouns and verbs are prototypical candidates for imaginal encoding and for motor encoding, respectively. It follows that the two components of action phrases might well foster different processing systems. A better approach would therefore be to analyse 'pure' cases and to compare the processing of concrete nouns and action verbs in isolation. This should provide a greater opportunity to learn about imaginal and motor encoding as well as about differences between nouns and verbs (see also Chapter 10 by Aylwin in this volume). In the following sections, we shall therefore consider the distinction between imaginal and motor encoding by studying the relationship between nouns and verbs.

Item-specific and modality-specific encoding and the representation of nouns and verbs

We assume with others that memory performance is mainly influenced by the amount of relational and item-specific encoding (for example, Einstein and Hunt 1980; Hunt and Einstein 1981). *Relational* information refers to the relationship among the items to be learned: that is, to the features that they share and to the amount of organization that is possible on the basis of feature overlap. This information is used by relational encoding and influences the processes of memory search and retrieval. *Item-specific* information refers to the distinctiveness of each individual item; it is therefore a function of the number of discriminative features of an individual item. This information is used by item-specific encoding. We assume that the modality-specific encoding of nouns and verbs has different effects upon the availability of item-specific and relational information and therefore upon the corresponding encoding processes. Our underlying assumption is that perceiving objects is basically different from experiencing actions: consequently, the representations of objects will be different from the representations of actions. Moreover, since different sorts of information are relevant to processing objects and actions, nouns and verbs which refer to them are assumed to reflect these differences in their conceptual structure.

At first sight, objects seem to form more natural units of perception than actions. We perceive objects as natural figures against a background and the principle of the perceptual unit seems to be an inherent quality of the stimulus. Object perception therefore tends to be relatively independent of context (cf. Gentner 1981). As a result, objects are easily represented as visual prototypes. These prototypes are associated with the conceptual representations of nouns which denote those objects. The concepts point to the visual prototypes and might even directly incorporate information about the appearances of the relevant objects. The encoding of a concrete noun is assumed to involve the activation of these prototypes. This probably always happens to some extent, but is likely to be enhanced when the subjects are instructed to construct mental images.

The situation is far more complex in the case of actions. Not only do they not take the form of natural units of perception in the way that objects do, but also actions are motor units as well as perceptual units. (Our use of the notion of a motor process is restricted to motor processes that lead to body movements, and is therefore more restricted than that of Neisser 1976.) Actions might not form natural perceptual units in the way that objects do, because the basis of such a unit lies less in the inherent quality of the stimulus event than in the conceptual system. The perception of events requires the observer to relate objects to persons. Actions can be considered to be complex units consisting of agents and objects, both changing over the course of time. When we see the action of bending, for instance, we might see at Time 1 a straight wire in the hands of a person which is then curved at Time 2. This transition in the state of the wire which is accompanied by specific arm and hand movements is the basis of the perception of bending. It is difficult to say what in this case corresponds to the visual prototype of an action: one proposal is to think of movement vectors (Cutting 1981; cf. Zimmer and Engelkamp 1985b). In any case, the conceptual representation of an action has to include information about possible agents and objects as well as information about possible transitions, no matter how abstract this information is, and there should be pointers to all three types of representation in the sensory systems. Yet it is plausible that only the movement vectors can be imagined without further processing while the agents and objects will typically include a wide variety of alternatives. In the example given above, for instance, the wire can be replaced by a stick without changing the action of bending.

Thus, the relationship between an action verb and its representation is more complicated and 'abstract' than in the case of concrete nouns. The encoding of an action verb involves the activation of a small network, which might be described as a 'proposition' (cf. Gentner 1981). The activation of the movement vectors is assumed to be optional – that is, dependent upon the specific task. The degree to which activation of the vectors implies the instantiation of a particular agent and a particular object remains an open question. We expect at least that the instruction to imagine an action would lead to some instantiation, including that of the object.

As mentioned above, actions are also motor units. It may be assumed that we also have mental representations of ourselves performing actions such as bending a wire. There are important differences between the representation of seen and performed actions. Experiences of performance are always experiences of our own movements: we ourselves are the agent. Furthermore, the action is represented as a motor movement; this representation might be called a motor 'program' (cf. Summers 1981). The instruction to perform an action has far more specific consequences for the encoding process than the instruction to form an image. First, the intended agent is clear: it is the subject to whom the instruction is given. Second, the activation of a motor program specifies the parameters necessary for the execution of that action. These are both important preconditions for creating distinctive episodes.

Hence, the fact that action verbs are more abstract than nouns and are represented as small conceptual networks or propositions should have consequences for their encoding, compared with that of concrete nouns. We assume that under standard learning instructions, item-specific encoding primarily involves the activation of conceptual information, and that this is true for both nouns and verbs. An important part of the conceptual representation of a concrete noun is the knowledge of what its referent looks like. At encoding, activation spontaneously spreads to the corresponding object representation, and this tendency can be enhanced by imagery instructions.

On the other hand, the encoding of an action verb somehow requires the activation of the propositional information mentioned above. This information is more complex than that associated with concrete nouns. This might account for the consistent finding that nouns are better recalled than verbs under standard encoding instructions (see Gentner 1981, for a review). Another reason might be the fact that in the case of action verbs there is less of a spontaneous tendency to activate imaginal or motor representations. This might be because the information at the sensory level is less specified in the case of action verbs than in the case of concrete nouns: with verbs, a specific object has to be selected or instantiated. Finally, the activation of motor programs is linked to the intention to perform, a condition which is not normally incorporated into learning experiments.

Nonetheless, if the subjects were instructed to perform an action or to imagine it being performed, some activation of the sensory and motor representations would be possible. In this case, however, imagery instructions would be less efficient than performance instructions because performing an action forces the subjects to specify the action more than imagining it: performing an act makes it necessary to specify a motor program and results in a clear, distinctive episodic representation. This would account for the fact that in the case of action phrases, performance instructions lead to better recall than imagining somebody else performing that action (see Engelkamp and Zimmer 1985, for a review). In an unpublished experiment we have observed that the latter effect holds true equally for action verbs. One might argue that the reason for the better recall of action phrases under performance instructions is not a more distinctive episodic representation but an enhanced emotional component (cf. Chapter 10 in this volume). This argument can however be refuted, because performing a non-specific motor activity does not lead to enhanced recall: Schaaf (1987) found that the performance of the actions described by action phrases led to improved recall, but that the performance of unrelated actions did not.

To sum up, learning concrete nouns is generally expected to be easier than learning action verbs because noun concepts are less complex than verb concepts. Modality-specific encoding is assumed to improve verbal learning of both classes of item by different mechanisms and to different extents. Memory for nouns would be improved with regard to item-specific encoding by activating the object representation and thereby elaborating perceptual information. The item-specific encoding of verbs would be strongly improved by performing the relevant actions because this activates motor programs. In any case, the difference in recall between nouns and verbs should be reduced by giving modality-specific encoding instructions: that is, to construct images in the case of nouns and to perform in the case of verbs.

Experiment 1

To test these hypotheses, we asked thirty-six subjects to memorize a list of twenty-four concrete nouns and another thirty-six subjects to memorize a list of twenty-four action verbs. The nouns and verbs were selected in such a way that they were unrelated to each other as far as possible; this precaution was taken to reduce relational encoding on the basis of categorical information. The subjects had five trials to memorize the corresponding list, and a test of free recall was given after each trial. The twenty-four items were presented at a rate of one every 5 sec., and their order was varied from trial to trial. Half of the subjects were given standard learning instructions, in which they were instructed simply to listen to the items as they were presented. The remaining subjects were given modality-specific instructions, in which they were instructed to memorize the items by forming images of the nouns or by enacting the verbs. This results in a 2x2x5 design.

The nouns were better recalled than the verbs (75 vs. 70 per cent correct, respectively; $p < 0.02$), and modality-specific instructions led to better recall than standard instructions (78 vs. 67 per cent respectively; $p < 0.001$). Both these findings substantiated our theoretical expectations. They also agree with other empirical results: the fact that nouns are better recalled than verbs was reported by Kintsch (1972) and Thorndyke (1975). We are not aware of any previous comparison of nouns and verbs under modality-specific instructions. Verbs were memorized much less well than nouns under standard instructions (63 vs. 72 per cent, respectively), but this difference was eliminated under modality-specific instructions (77 vs. 79 per cent, respectively). Over the first three trials, the difference between nouns and verbs was significant under standard instructions ($t = 2.53$; d.f. = 34; $p < 0.02$), but not under modality-specific instructions ($t = 0.56$; d.f. = 34; n.s.); on the fourth and fifth trials both lists showed ceiling effects. This interaction indicates that modality-specific encoding removes the difficulty of learning verbs compared with learning nouns. This may be because the episodic character of verbs is particularly enhanced by performing. Under this condition verbs may be as unitary as nouns: to act and thereby to activate a motor program seems to produce very efficient item-specific information (cf. Engelkamp 1988b; Zimmer 1984, 1987).

In order to compare the effects of item specificity with those of relational encoding, we counted the PF (pair frequency) score according to Sternberg and Tulving (1977) to test for subjective organization. The PF score was found to be better in the case of nouns than in the case of verbs (2.1 vs. 1.5; $p < 0.05$). There was no effect of instructions and no interaction between the effects of word class and instructions. This result suggests that it is in fact item-specific information and not relational encoding which enhances memory performance. This assumption is also supported by the following results. Under the different experimental conditions, we correlated the PF scores between the nth and the (n+1)th trial with the number of items recalled on the (n+1)th trial. Under the standard instructions, all such correlation coefficients were around 0.40 or greater (with $r = 0.40$ being the critical value for $p < 0.05$). The same was true under imaginal instructions, except for the first PF score. Under performance instructions, however, no correlation coefficient was significant (the highest value was less than 0.30). For further details, see Zimmer and Mohr (1986).

We can summarize by saying that nouns are better recalled and better organized than verbs when they are learned under standard instructions. Furthermore, subjective organization correlates positively with recall for both item classes. When nouns are learned by imagining and verbs by performing, the nouns are still better organized than the verbs, but there is no longer any difference in recall performance: subjective organization still correlates with recall in the case of the nouns, but not in the case of the verbs. We interpret this to mean that performing brings about an item-specific elaboration for individual items. This strong effect is linked to the performance condition: in that case, the verbs become as distinctive as nouns and are therefore recalled as well as nouns. The results of recognition experiments support this interpretation: after performing, barely 3 per cent of errors (misses and false alarms) were made (Engelkamp and Krumnacker 1980; Zimmer 1984). In the case of verbs, imaginal encoding is not sufficient to yield this item-specific elaboration. The distinctiveness of verbs is only achieved by performing, and this is apparently independent of relational encoding. It is this interesting finding which we shall consider in the next section.

Modality-specific encoding and the organizational structure of nouns and verbs

The best interpretation of the finding that recall performance is not correlated with the degree of subjective organization under motor encoding is that organization is independent of item-specific encoding and that it is predominantly the latter which determines recall performance under conditions of motor encoding. To test this hypothesis we attempted to influence relational encoding more directly through the list structure.

The sort of structure to which most attention has been paid in the past is the taxonomic structure of lists of nouns. Recall performance is much better when nouns are presented categorized according to taxonomies than when they are presented in random order (Bower et al. 1969). Yet randomly ordered lists of nouns which can be organized into categories show a categorical organization in free recall. This 'clustering' effect, first reported by Bousfield (1953), has been repeatedly observed, as has the fact that the degree of clustering tends to correlate with recall performance (cf. Puff 1979).

These findings have been attributed to the central role played by taxonomic organization in semantic memory. Class inclusion has been taken to be one of the most important relationships among concepts in semantic memory (for example, Collins and Quillian 1969; Lindsay and Norman 1981; Rosch 1978). Yet the question arises as to whether this organizational principle also holds true in the case of verbs. The answer seems to be 'no'. Indeed, although it is easy to organize nouns into hierarchical categories, such as 'robin', 'bird', 'animal', 'living being', it is far more difficult in the case of verbs, such as 'to eat', 'to take in food'. This has occasionally been noted in the literature (Kintsch 1972; Huttenlocher and Lui 1979).

Huttenlocher and Lui (1979) contrast the hierarchical organization of noun concepts with a matrix-like organization of verbs. By 'matrix-like' they mean that the actions to which verbs may refer may be grouped according to semantically independent properties. Thus, for instance, actions can be grouped according to the limbs that take part in the movement, according to the duration or stress of the action, according to their purpose, and so on. In our opinion, however, the important point is not that verbs can be organized according to semantically independent properties. This is possible in the case of nouns, too: you can, for instance, group objects according to their size, colour, location, and so on. What *is* important is that verbs cannot be organized to the same degree as nouns according to semantically dependent properties. How is the hierarchical organization of nouns achieved? One important organizing principle seems to be how we behave towards objects; and this organizational principle, of course, cannot be applied to motor behaviour itself. In conclusion, since hierarchical organization is typical for noun concepts but not for verb concepts, a taxonomic list structure is not appropriate to our purpose.

What other type of list structure or conceptual organization might serve our purpose better? Spatio-temporal structure might be an apt candidate. Spatial and temporal contiguity has always been considered to be the basis of associative connections (cf. Strube 1984). Although it is difficult to establish this in any specific case, the assumption is plausible as a general principle. We experience objects in spatial and spatio-temporal neighbourhoods: for instance, if we look at a breakfast table, we see a certain arrangement of objects (cups, plates, knives, butter, bread, and so on); if we have breakfast, we experience these objects again, yet now in spatial and temporal contiguity. In the case of verbs, the situation is more complex: they happen within a series of actions which takes place in a temporal vicinity and often in a fixed order. Thus, we set out the coffee, pour it out, drink it, and so on. These contiguities may be used to organize verb concepts in memory.

Objects should be organized in static scenes. The psychological reality of scenes is generally recognized and demonstrated by experiments on scene organization (for example, Biederman et al. 1982; Mandler and Johnson 1976) or priming by scene context (for example,

Palmer 1975). Furthermore, objects may be organized by, or at least connected to, 'scripts', since they appear in scripts as instruments, objects, or locations. On the other hand, scripts also appear to be a typical organizational structure in the case of action verbs. Both scenes and scripts are partonomies, organized by a part-of relation. This relation, however, is qualified in the case of scenes as a spatial part-of relation specifying locations and in the case of scripts as a temporal part-of relation specifying the consecutive order of actions (cf. Barsalou and Sewell 1985). Both structures are derived from episodes: the episodic structure of noun concepts is derived from scenes and scripts, while that of verb concepts is derived only from scripts. An episodic list structure therefore seems a suitable means for inducing relational encoding of nouns and verbs which can be measured by clustering indices. The critical question is the extent to which modality-specific encoding influences relational encoding on the one hand, and item-specific encoding on the other, in episodically structured lists.

Under standard learning instructions, nouns and verbs presented in episodically structured lists should be organized in terms of scripts, and nouns should also be organized in terms of spatial scenes. We should thus observe moderate clustering effects for both word classes, perhaps more so in the case of nouns. Under modality-specific instructions, the situation should be different for nouns and verbs. In the case of nouns, the degree of clustering as well as the amount recalled should be improved by forming images, if (as the results of Experiment 1 suggest) forming images to noun lists influences both item-specific and relational encoding. As was found in Experiment 1, enacting verbs should strongly improve item-specific encoding, and this effect should be independent of relational encoding. As a result, there should be better recall performance under conditions of motor encoding, while clustering should show little change. Moreover, under conditions of motor encoding, the correlation with recall performance is once again expected to break down in the case of verbs.

Experiment 2

In order to test these hypotheses, we constructed two episodically structured lists, one containing verbs and the other containing nouns. Each list contained four items in each of six categories. In the case of the nouns, the episode categories were 'in the restaurant', 'at school', 'at the bank', 'on camping grounds', 'in a train', and 'on a building site'; in the case of the verbs, they were 'to do carpentry', 'to drive a car', 'to wash', 'to garden', 'to work in an office', and 'to cook'. English translations of some of the original German items are as follows. Nouns: waiter, tip, wine, menu (in the restaurant); teacher, blackboard, chalk, exercise-book (at school). Verbs: to send, to saw, to varnish, to screw on (to do carpentry) to water, to weed, to rake, to sow (to garden). The nouns and verbs were assigned to two separate lists. The order of the elements in each list was randomized, with the constraint that no two consecutive items were from the same category. Both lists were presented for two trials to each of thirty-six subjects. Half of the subjects were given standard instructions, and the other half were given modality-specific instructions (once again, imagining nouns and performing verbs). Independent of this manipulation, half of the subjects learned the nouns and then the verbs, while the other half learned the two lists in the reverse order. Thus, there were four factors (word class, trials, instructions, and order of word class), where word class and trials were within-subjects factors.

Clustering was measured by adjusted ratio of clustering (ARC) scores following Roenker et al. (1971). As expected, both word classes showed clear organization, although the nouns showed more clustering than the verbs (0.68 vs. 0.51, respectively; $p < 0.005$). In the case of nouns, the ARC scores were somewhat higher under modality-specific instructions than under standard instructions (0.75 vs. 0.60); in the case of verbs, there was no such increase (0.51 for both groups), although the interaction between word class and instructions was not statistically significant. As usual, free recall was better in the case of nouns than in the case of verbs (83 vs. 67 per cent, respectively; $p < 0.001$), but this was qualified by a significant interaction with the effect of instructions ($p < 0.01$): that is, modality-specific instructions led to a greater increase compared with standard instructions in the case of verbs (77 vs. 60 per cent) than in the case of nouns (85 vs. 79 per cent). This was not simply due to a ceiling effect because it was obtained on both the first trial and the second trial, and there was no three-way interaction with the effect of trials (see also Engelkamp 1988c). There were significant correlations between free recall and ARC scores only under standard instructions, with correlations greater than 0.40 in the case of both nouns and verbs; under modality-specific instructions, the correlations were less than 0.30 for both nouns and verbs.

The findings obtained in the case of nouns are puzzling. Apart from the well-known recall superiority of nouns over verbs, the effects were relatively slight. Clustering (that is, relational encoding) was improved by instructions to form images, but there was little concomitant increase in free recall, and there was no significant correlation between recall and clustering under imagery instructions. The relationship between forming images and the assumed underlying processes of relational and item-specific encoding remains unclear. Similar results were reported by Ritchey (1980) in the case of taxonomic lists, a situation in which other types of relational encoding were possible.

However, we were more interested in the results obtained in the case of verbs, and here the findings were clear-cut. Motor encoding produced a substantial increase in recall performance compared with non-specific encoding. On the other hand, motor encoding had no effect upon clustering at all, and there was no significant correlation between clustering and recall under motor encoding. These findings support the assumptions that motor encoding primarily influences item-specific encoding and that under motor encoding it is the item-specific information that determines the level of recall performance (cf. Engelkamp 1986a, b; Zimmer 1987). What remains unclear is how retrieval is organized in this situation. One possibility might be that with motor encoding subjects use an unstructured memory search, and that they decide whether an item was a member of the list to be remembered on the basis of familiarity or activation level. Further experiments are needed to clarify this hypothesis (cf. Zimmer 1984).

Conclusions

In this chapter we have analysed and studied experimentally the relationship between modality-specific encoding, types of semantic information, and word class. In contrast to the idea that imaginal encoding is a homogeneous process, we showed in the first section that there was good reason to distinguish between sensory and motor encoding. This becomes evident when one studies actions: the manner in which action phrases are processed is quite different when the subjects form images of somebody else performing the actions from when they symbolically perform those actions themselves, as can be concluded from differential effects under the two conditions. In a series of experiments we have obtained evidence for the distinction between imaginal and motor encoding (for reviews, see Engelkamp 1988a; Engelkamp and Zimmer 1985; Zimmer and Engelkamp 1985b).

In this chapter we have focused upon a specific implication of the distinction between the two encoding strategies. There are certain elements which are prototypical for imaginal encoding and others which are prototypical for motor encoding: these are objects and actions, respectively. While objects are often experienced without overt motor processes, actions are inherently bound to motor processes. Concrete nouns and action verbs should therefore be highly appropriate for the study of imaginal and motor-encoding processes. Studying the referents of the two sorts of item allows us not only to learn more about the specific processes that constitute the imaginal encoding of concrete nouns and the motor encoding of action verbs, but also to learn about their differential representation and organization in memory.

Our experiments have shown, first of all, that modality-specific encoding brings about an item-specific effect. The memory traces of the different items are more distinct after performing or imagining them than under standard instructions. This is true in particular in the case of the motor encoding of action verbs. Under standard instructions, action verbs are less well remembered than concrete nouns; under instructions to perform the relevant actions, action verbs were recalled as well as nouns in both experiments. In the latter case, verbs seem to receive a mental representation as unitary as that of nouns, but performing the relevant actions is necessary to bring about this effect: imagining or seeing somebody else performing those actions or planning those actions oneself is not sufficient (Zimmer and Engelkamp 1984).

The effects of modality-specific instructions upon relational encoding are more complicated. It is evident that motor encoding influences item-specific information, independent of any effect upon relational encoding: indeed, there is no effect of performing the actions upon clustering scores and no correlation between clustering scores and recall under such instructions. Nevertheless, recall tends to be improved by performing the relevant actions. What is the basis for this improved recall if there is no improvement in relational encoding? We argue that the subjects may use unstructured memory search, and that in so doing they may decide whether an item has been presented before on the basis of familiarity or activation level. The high level of item-specific information following motor encoding would provide an accurate basis for this decision. Further research is clearly necessary to clarify these processes.

The situation in the case of imaginal encoding is not so clear-cut. Imaginal encoding produces rather weak effects upon the recall of action verbs, and its effects have not been consistently observed for nouns, either (cf. Paivio 1976). There is a small improvement in clustering, and sometimes there are positive correlations between organizational and recall scores. Imagining might be used in relational encoding, but this depends upon particular strategies which are not regularly used. The idea that imaginal encoding provides an opportunity for enhanced relational encoding has been demonstrated, for instance, in studies of interactive imagery in paired-associate learning experiments (for example, Begg 1978). The question is: under what conditions do these effects occur?

Acknowledgements

The research reported here was made possible by a grant from the Deutsche Forschungsgemeinschaft (En 124/6, 124/7). Our thanks are due to Margit Mohr and Gilbert Mohr for their help in preparing the experiments and in evaluating the data.

References

Aylwin, S. (1988) 'Cognitive structure in thought and personality', in M. Denis, J. Engelkamp, and J. T. E. Richardson (eds) *Cognitive and Neuropsychological Approaches to Mental Imagery*, Dordrecht: Martinus Nijhoff.

Baddeley, A. D. (1986) *Working Memory*, London: Oxford University Press.

Barsalou, L. W., and Sewell, D. R. (1985) 'Contrasting the representation of scripts and categories', *Journal of Memory and Language* 24: 646–65.

Begg, I. (1978) 'Imagery and organization in memory: instructional effects', *Memory and Cognition* 6: 174–83.

Biederman, J., Mezzanotte, R. J., and Rabinowitz, J. C. (1982) 'Scene perception: detecting and judging objects undergoing relational violations', *Cognitive Psychology* 14: 143–77.

Bousfield, W. A. (1953) 'The occurrence of clustering in the recall of randomly arranged associates', *Journal of General Psychology* 49: 229–40.

Bower, G. H., Clark, M. C., Lesgold, A. M., and Winzenz, D. (1969) 'Hierarchical retrieval schemes in recall of categorized word lists', *Journal of Verbal Learning and Verbal Behavior* 8: 323–43.

Cohen, R. L. (1983) 'The effect of encoding variables on the free recall of words and action events', *Memory and Cognition* 11: 575–82.

—— (1985) 'On the generality of the laws of memory', in L. G. Nilsson and T. Archer (eds) *Animal Learning and Human Memory*, Hillsdale, NJ: Erlbaum.

Collins, A. M., and Quillian, M. R. (1969) 'Retrieval time from semantic memory', *Journal of Verbal Learning and Verbal Behavior* 8: 240–7.

Cutting, J. E. (1981) 'Coding theory adapted to gate perception', *Journal of Experimental Psychology: Human Perception and Performance* 7: 81–7.

Einstein, G. O., and Hunt, R. R. (1980) 'Levels of processing and organization: additive effects of individual item and relational processing', *Journal of Experimental Psychology: Human Learning and Memory* 6: 588–98.

Engelkamp, J. (1986a) 'Differences between imaginal and motor encoding', in F. Klix and H. Hagendorf (eds) *Human Memory and Cognitive Capabilities*, Amsterdam: North Holland.

—— (1986b) 'Nouns and verbs in paired-associate learning: instructional effects', *Psychological Research* 48: 153–9.

—— (1987) 'Modalitätsspezifische Gedächtnissysteme im Kontext sprachlicher Informationsverarbeitung', *Zeitschrift für Psychologie* 195: 1–28.

—— (1988a) 'Images and actions in verbal learning', in M. Denis, J. Engelkamp, and J. T. E. Richardson (eds) *Cognitive and Neuropsychological Approaches to Mental Imagery*, Dordrecht: Martinus Nijhoff.

—— (1988b) 'Modality-specific encoding and word class in verbal learning', in M. M. Gruneberg, P. E. Morris, and R. N. Sykes (eds) *Practical Aspects of Memory: Current Research and Issues*, vol. 1, Chichester: Wiley.

—— (1988c) 'Nouns and verbs in the mental lexicon', in W. Hullen and R. Schulz (eds) *Understanding the Lexicon: Meaning, Sense and World Knowledge in Lexical Semantics*, Tübingen: Niemeyer.

—— and Krumnacker, H. (1980) 'Imaginale und motorische Prozesse beim Behalten verbalen Materials', *Zeitschrift für experimentelle und angewandte Psychologie* 27: 511–33.

—— and Zimmer, H. D. (1983) 'Der Einfluss von Wahrnehmen und Tun auf das Behalten von Verb-Objekt-Phrasen', *Sprache und Kognition* 2: 117–27.

—— (1985) 'Motor programs and their relation to semantic memory', *German Journal of Psychology* 9: 239–54.

Gentner, D. (1981) 'Verb semantic structures in memory for sentences: evidence for componential representation', *Cognitive Psychology* 13: 56–84.

Hulme, C. (1979) 'The interaction of visual and motor memory for graphic forms following tracing', *Quarterly Journal of Experimental Psychology* 31: 249–61.

Hunt, R. R., and Einstein, G. O. (1981) 'Relational and item-specific information in memory', *Journal of Verbal Learning and Verbal Behavior* 20: 497–514.

Huttenlocher, J., and Lui, F. (1979) 'The semantic organization of some simple nouns and verbs', *Journal of Verbal Learning and Verbal Behavior* 18: 141–62.

Kintsch, W. (1972) 'Notes on the structure of semantic memory', in E. Tulving and W. Donaldson (eds) *Organization of Memory*, New York: Academic Press.

Kosslyn, S. M. (1980) *Image and Mind*, Cambridge, MA: Harvard University Press.

Lindsay, P. H., and Norman, D. A. (1981) *Einführung in die Psychologie*, Berlin: Springer.

Mandler, J. M., and Johnson, N. S. (1976) 'Some of the thousand words a picture is worth', *Journal of Experimental Psychology: Human Learning and Memory* 2: 529–40.

Neisser, U. (1976) *Cognition and Reality*, San Francisco: Freeman.

Nelson, D. (1979) 'Remembering pictures and words: appearances, significance, and names', in L. S. Cermak and F. I. M. Craik (eds) *Levels of Processing in Human Memory*, Hillsdale, NJ: Erlbaum.

Paivio, A. (1976) 'Imagery in recall and recognition', in J. Brown (ed.) *Recall and Recognition*, London: Wiley.

—— (1986) *Mental Representations: A Dual Coding Approach*, New York: Oxford University Press.

—— and Okovita, H. W. (1971) 'Word imagery modalities and associative learning in blind and sighted subjects', *Journal of Verbal Learning and Verbal Behavior* 10: 506–10.

Palmer, S. E. (1975) 'The effects of contextual scenes on the identification of objects', *Memory and Cognition* 3: 519–26.

Puff, C. R. (ed.) (1979) *Memory Organization and Structure*, New York: Academic Press.

Ritchey, G. H. (1980) 'Picture superiority in free recall: the effects of organization and elaboration', *Journal of Experimental Psychology: Learning, Memory, and Cognition* 8: 139–41.

Roenker, D. L., Thompson, C. P., and Brown, S. C. (1971) 'Comparison of measures for the estimation of clustering in free recall', *Psychological Bulletin* 76: 45–8.

Rosch, E. H. (1978) 'Principles of categorization', in E. H. Rosch and B. B. Lloyd (eds) *Cognition and Categorization*, Hillsdale, NJ: Erlbaum.

Saltz, E. and Donnenwerth-Nolan, S. (1981) 'Does motoric imagery facilitate memory for sentences? A selective interference test', *Journal of Verbal Learning and Verbal Behavior* 20: 322–32.

Schaaf, M. (1987) 'Motorische Aktivität und verbale Lernleistung: Leistungssteigerung durch Simultanität?' unpublished manuscript, Psychologisches Institut der Universität Heidelberg.

Segal, S. J., and Fusella, V. (1971) 'Effect of images in six sense modalities on detection of visual signal from noise', *Psychonomic Science* 24: 55–6.

Sternberg, R. J., and Tulving, E. (1977) 'The measurement of subjective organization in free recall', *Psychological Bulletin* 84: 539–56.

Strube, G. (1984) *Assoziation: Der Prozess des Erinnerns und die Struktur des Gedächtnisses*, Berlin: Springer.

Summers, J. J. (1981) 'Motor programs', in D. H. Holding (ed.) *Human Skills*, Chichester: Wiley.

Thorndyke, P. W. (1975) 'Conceptual complexity and imagery in comprehension and memory', *Journal of Verbal Learning and Verbal Behavior* 14: 359–69.

Zimmer, H. D. (1984) *Enkodierung, Rekodierung, Retrieval und die Aktivation motorischer Programme*, Report No. 91, Department of Psychology, Universität des Saarlandes, Saarbrücken.

(1985) 'Die Differenzierung sprachlicher Bedeutung durch die Aktivation motorischer Komponenten', in D. Albert (ed.) *Bericht über den 34. Kongress der Deutschen Gesellschaft für Psychologie in Wien 1984*, Göttingen: Hogrefe.

(1986) 'The memory trace of semantic or motor processing', in F. Klix and H.Hagendorf (eds) *Human Memory and Cognitive Capabilities*, Amsterdam: North Holland.

(1987) 'Argumente für ein motorisches Gedächtnissystem', in J. Engelkamp, K. Lorenz, and B. Sandig (eds) *Wissenrepräsentation und Wissensaustausch*, St Ingbert: Röhrig.

and Engelkamp, J. (1984) 'Planungs- und Ausführungsanteile motorischer Gedächtniskomponenten und ihre Wirkung auf das Behalten ihrer verbalen Bezeichnungen', *Zeischrift für Psychologie* 192: 379–402.

(1985a) 'An attempt to distinguish between kinematic and motor memory components', *Acta Psychologica* 58: 81–106.

(1985b) 'Modality-specific representation systems and inference: task-dependent activation processes in motor memory', in G. Rickheit and H. Strohner (eds) *Inferences in Text Processing*, Amsterdam: North Holland.

Zimmer, H. D., and Mohr, M. (1986) *Organisation und Organisierbarkeit von Verben und Substantiven bei einer verbal semantischen bzw. 'modalitätsspezifischen' Lernweise*, Report No. 100, Department of Psychology, Universität des Saarlands, Saarbrücken.

Zimmer, H. D., Engelkamp, J., and Sieloff, U. (1984) 'Motorische Gedächtniskomponenten als partiell unabhängige Komponenten des Engramms verbaler Handlungsbeschreibungen', *Sprache und Kognition* 3: 70–85.

Chapter seven

Imagery effects on problem solving

Geir Kaufmann

Our knowledge about the role of imagery in thinking and problem solving clearly falls short of the level reached in the areas of learning and memory. Although no negligible amount of research has been addressed to the issue (cf. Kaufmann 1979, 1980, 1984; Richardson 1983; Kaufmann and Helstrup 1985), the field clearly suffers from a lack of explicit theoretical formulations that could assimilate the presently available evidence and give direction to future research. The major aim of this chapter is, accordingly, to clarify alternative theoretical positions in this domain and tentatively to assess their respective validity *vis-à-vis* existing data. In so doing I hope to lay the foundation for more systematic and fine-grained enquiries into the possible effects of imagery on problem-solving performance.

Taxonomies of problems

A framework for describing alternative theories of imagery effects on problem solving may be found in the different ways of classifying problems. Greeno (1978) has developed a taxonomy of problems based on the general *information-processing functions* assumed to be relevant to different task demands. Greeno distinguishes between three basic types of problems (more complex problems can be regarded as combinations of these):

(1) In *problems of inducing structure*, some elements are given, and the task of the subject is to identify the pattern of relations among the elements. An example is the analogy problem, in which some elements are given and the subject has to decide whether they are related in some way that fits a structure (for example, A:B::C:D). The main

cognitive ability required for handling problems in this category is, according to Greeno, that of *understanding*, which involves the processes of apprehending relations and constructing integrated representations. (For research aimed at elucidating the process of understanding at a more detailed level, see Simon and Kotovsky 1963; Reitman 1965; Kotovsky and Simon 1973; Rumelhart and Abrahamsen 1973; Sternberg 1977).

(2) *Problems of transformation* involve an initial situation, a goal, and a set of operations that produce changes in the situation at hand. The major source of difficulty in this type of task is to find a sequence of operations that could transform the initial situation into the required goal situation. Many puzzles belong to this category, as well as mathematical problems, such as proofs of theorems and algebra tasks. According to Greeno, the main process involved here is *planning* based on the general method of *means-end analysis*: that is, systematically handling the problem by way of a continuous analysis of what is given, what is required, and what means can be used to obtain the required from the givens (cf. Newell and Simon 1972; Atwood and Polson 1976; Simon 1977; and Greeno and Simon 1985 for reviews of research on problems of transformation).

(3) Finally, there is the *arrangement problem*, in which the subject is given some elements and asked to fit them together in a way that satisfies some criterion. An example is the anagram problem, where the subject is to arrange a set of scrambled letters into a meaningful word (ierldos – soldier). According to Greeno, the major cognitive ability relevant to this type of problem is *skill in composition*, which depends on *constructive search processes*, i.e. finding the solution by generating the possibilities that constitute the search space (cf. Greeno and Simon 1985 and Kaufmann 1987a for reviews of research on such problems).

As Greeno points out, the kinds of problems described above are *ideal types*. Most problems probably involve strong components of different types. However, classification on the basis of this taxonomy allows us to describe available research on imagery and problem solving in a systematic way and naturally occasions the question of whether imagery is more important in some information-processing functions than in others. A specific imagery-process relationship was posited by Berlyne (1965), who claimed that imagery was particularly suited for performing transformational operations in thinking. Paivio (1971, 1975, 1986) emphasized the particular adeptness of imagery for a simultaneous representation of elements of information. Such a function may be particularly useful in problems of arrangements.

Imagery and level of programming

Simon (1977) conceives of problems as falling on a continuum from *programmed*, where the problem solver has a definite procedure to handle the task, to *non-programmed*, where the task facing the subject is novel, unstructured, or unusually complicated for the individual.

In several theoretical formulations, mainly inspired by psycho-analytic conceptions of primary/secondary process thinking (cf. Suler 1980 and Horowitz 1983), the relevance of imagery is linked to the less programmed aspect of problem solving by assigning a special role to imagery processes in creative thinking.

Rugg (1963) assumes that imagery is predominant in the *discovery* phase of problem solving, whereas verification processes are assumed primarily to involve the more logical and directed verbal symbolic system. Similar views have been suggested by McKellar (1957, 1963, 1972), who distinguishes between 'A' (autistic) thinking and 'R' (realistic) thinking and assumes a central role for imagery in the former category.

Such theoretical formulations are, however, essentially descriptive and do not adequately answer the question of *why* imagery has such a credit role in this domain of problem solving. More recently, Shepard (1978a, b) also postulated a central role for imagery in creativity functions. Shepard suggests the following characteristics of imagery to be important in this respect:

(1) imagery is less constrained by tradition than language;
(2) the richness of imagery makes it possible to note significant details and relationships that are not adequately contained in purely verbal representations;
(3) the spatial character of images makes them directly accessible to potent competencies for spatial intuition and manipulation; and
(4) vivid images may constitute more effective substitutes for corresponding external objects and events than it is possible to achieve with a purely verbal representation; Thus, images have a stronger tendency to engage the affective and motivational system.

While interesting, Shepard's conjectures essentially constitute a loosely formulated *ad hoc* rationale, based on informal evidence, rather than theoretical statements that can be operationally distinguished and more precisely brought to bear on the posited role of imagery in creative thinking.

Morris and Hampson (1983; see also Chapter 3 in this volume) argue for a special role of imagery in non-practised, novel tasks. The theoretical rationale for this assumption is given in their BOSS model. Here the function of consciousness is held to be that of monitoring and controlling processing which does not proceed in an automatic way. Since imagery is a form of conscious representation, the assumption is made that imagery is particularly useful in the top–down processing required under novel task conditions. However, the model does not distinguish between the role of imagery and other forms of conscious representations, like verbalization, in regard to task novelty. Thus, Hampson and Morris seem committed to the rather unconstrained position that imagery is relevant under all conditions where processing does not run automatically. After all, 'non-automatic cognitive processing' is close to a definition of thinking.

The present author has developed a theory that prescribes a division of labour between linguistic-propositional and imagery representations along the task-novelty dimension (Kaufmann 1975, 1979, 1980, 1986). It is argued that imagery is an auxiliary representational system under superordinate control of linguistic-propositional representations. Thus, imagery is held to be particularly useful where the need for processing is high, as is generally the case under high task-novelty conditions. Recently (Kaufmann 1987b), I have expanded the theory to take account of the view on the function of consciousness advocated by Hampson and Morris. Also, the theory is brought to bear on the more general level of programming, which includes task complexity and ambiguity as well as task novelty. A rather firmly established conclusion reached in contemporary research on problem solving is that the individual has to resort to *weak* methods when the task at hand is low in programming (for example, Newell 1969; Simon 1977). Weak methods may be applied over a wide range of problems. They are 'weak' in the sense of lacking precision, and do not guarantee success, in contrast with 'strong' methods, which are precise, tailor-made to the situation, and a safe and fast way to solving the task.

With reference to the general theory of strong and weak methods in problem solving, I have suggested that imagery is a back-up system that

Table 7.1 Elements and structure of the theory

CONSCIOUS REPRESENTATIONS:	*VERBAL*		*IMAGINAL*	
MODE OF OPERATION:	COMPUTATIONAL Transformations (Rule-governed inferences)		PERCEPTUAL Simulations (Mental modelling)	
Main information processing categories:	Deductive reasoning	Inductive reasoning	Perceptual comparisons	Perceptual anticipations
UNDERLYING REPRESENTATIONS:	*PROPOSITIONAL*		*ANALOGUE*	

gives access to a set of simpler cognitive processes of a perceptual kind. Such simpler processes may be needed in an ill-structured problem, where computational processes in the form of rule-governed inferences are difficult or impossible to perform. The essentials of the theory are presented in Table 7.1. Its basic theses are as follows. Conscious representations are invoked when processing does not run automatically. A linguistic-propositional format is a strong one in the sense that great precision may be achieved in the form of explicit descriptions. It is easily and quickly manipulated and contains the full range of computational operations within its potential. In contrast, imagery is more ambiguous and less easily manipulated, and only realizes simple cognitive operations of a perceptual kind, like anticipations and comparisons. These may, however, be useful and even necessary in ill-structured task environments, characterized by lack of experience with the task at hand (either factual or strategic), where computational processes break down due to lack of rule-based information on which to operate (novelty). Limitations of computational operations may also result from strain on working memory due to high information load (complexity). Finally, uncertainty as to which rule or procedure should be applied may lead to computational dysfunctions (ambiguity). Images may thus be best described as perceptual-like *mental models* (cf. Johnson-Laird 1983; Sanford 1985). Such models allow translation from computational to perceptual operations. More specifically, we suggest that deductive operations may be translated into simple, quasi-perceptual comparisons, where certainty of judgement may be reached. The imagery parallel to inductive operations may be quasi-perceptual anticipations, where a future state of affairs may be imagined on the basis of a previous sequence of events.

173

Imagery and the concrete-abstract dimension

Another way of classifying problems is along the *concrete-abstract* dimension. The concept of concreteness-abstractness is defined in different ways in the psychological literature (cf. Paivio 1971: 16–18). Stimulus-response definitions are most commonly employed in the imagery literature. Here, concreteness refers to how directly the stimulus denotes particular objects and events or to task characteristics on the response side (for example, drawing vs. writing).

The view that imagery is intimately related to concreteness is widespread in the psychological literature (for example, Galton 1883; Bruner *et al.* 1966; Paivio 1971, 1986). There are two somewhat different contentions behind this suggestion. First, image cognition is a primitive form of thinking which is concrete and may disrupt more powerful, abstract ways of thinking. This view is found in the early literature (for example, Galton 1883) as well as in more recent writings (for example, Humphrey 1959; Bruner *et al.* 1966). Second, use of imagery is most appropriate for concrete tasks. This view is advocated by Hebb (1968) and Paivio (1971, 1986).

Contemporary empirical research on the functional role of imagery in problem solving

It should be noted that it may be somewhat arbitrary to decide whether a task is a *problem*, or whether it more naturally belongs to another category of information processing (detection, judgement, or even memory, learning, and perception). Some authors (for example, Reitman 1965; Helstrup 1976; Kaufmann 1980) employ very wide limits in their definitions of problem solving, and argue that it may be seen as a superordinate framework for studying cognitive processes. However, the present discussion will be confined to tasks traditionally defined as problems in the experimental psychology literature (for example, Woodworth and Schlosberg 1955; Greeno 1978), where a problem situation always includes a barrier between start and goal, preventing the first and immediate responses from solving the task. For this reason, mental rotation and mental-comparison tasks are not included in the present discussion (cf. Corballis 1982 and Paivio 1986 for reviews of literature and theoretical discussions of research on such tasks).

Problems of structure

Syllogisms

In imagery research on problem solving, the most carefully studied task is the three-term series problem, a type of linear syllogism. An example would be the following one: *Anne is taller than Jean; Mary is shorter than Jean; Who is tallest?* This task requires the subject to discover the correct structure of relations, and then infer the solution. Thus, the task qualifies as a structure problem.

De Soto *et al.* (1965) claim that subjects often attack this problem by combining the premisses into a unitary image representation. This procedure will allow the subject to 'read off' the correct answer directly. The image theory has been further developed by Huttenlocher (1968). According to the imagery interpretation it is, for instance, easier to place a premiss in a representational array if its first item is an 'end-anchor', i.e. occurring at one end of the final array, rather than in the middle position. However, this interpretation has been challenged by Clark (1969a, b), who claims that the required transitive inference is based upon linguistic representations of the premisses. Task performance is, accordingly, explained with reference to basic psycholinguistic principles only. Thus, for instance, subjects are assumed to search for information that is congruent with the format of information given in the premisses.

Support for the imagery theory rests on five kinds of evidence (cf. Johnson-Laird 1972; Kaufmann 1980, 1984; and Richardson 1983 for reviews). These are:

(1) Introspective reports which suggest that mental imagery is often used in this task.
(2) Correspondence in task difficulty between adults solving the task in writing and children arranging physical objects in an actual spatial array (placement tasks). The interpretation is that inferences made by adults are based on an internal analogue (image) of the physical task relations.
(3) Visual interference disrupts performance to a stronger degree than does auditory interference.
(4) Spatial ability predicts task performance.
(5) Asked to describe the task elements in terms of a spatial array, the arrangements agree with predictions from the image theory.

However, reaction times and error rates reflecting variations in task difficulty fit more precisely with the pattern predicted by Clark's linguistic theory (Clark 1969a, b, 1971, 1972; see also Eley 1979 and Jones 1970). Nonetheless, French (1979) was able to show that the affective value of adjectives was an even better predictor of task performance than Clark's psycholinguistic principles, and argues that adjectives of high affective value are probably more easily imaged than their low-affective counterparts.

Williams (1977) suggests that the two theories may be reconciled. He found that syllogisms rated high in imageability were most easy to solve. In conflicting cases, the linguistic theory gained support when latency was used as a measure of task difficulty, whereas the image model was supported by measurements of error rate. Williams concluded that the image model is more relevant to the problem-solving dimension, whereas the linguistic model applies better to the sentence processing of the task. These findings may explain why Richardson (1987) found no support for the imagery theory in a recently performed experiment. All of the subjects first learned a four-term linear ordering and were then asked to make comparative judgements on all possible pairs of items. Performance was measured through latency of responding. No effect was found for imagery operationalized through proximity of pairs of stimuli, concreteness of the property defining the linear ordering, concreteness of the stimuli to which the relevant property was ascribed, modality of responding, and spatial ability. However, Richardson's procedure clearly minimizes the problem-solving aspect of the task, and his conclusion that mental imagery is not involved in tasks of transitive inference does not, therefore, seem warranted.

Potts and Scholz (1975) isolated the time required to encode the two premises of a three-term series problem from the time required to generate an answer to the test question. Their results indicated that the subjects tend to integrate the two premises into a unified representation as posited by the image theory. However, Potts points out that such an integrated representation may not require imagery for its generation.

Given the somewhat *ad hoc* assumptions made by both parties, the accumulated research has made it difficult to distinguish between the opposing theories (for example, Johnson-Laird 1972). Like Williams (1977), Wood has also tried to solve the conflict between the two theories (Wood 1969; Wood *et al.* 1974). Wood employed tasks involving up to six premises, which made it possible to study different

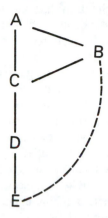

Figure 7.1 A Haas diagram of a five-term series problem.

arrangements of premisses. All the premisses involved the comparative term 'taller', and the subjects were always asked 'Who is taller, X or Y?' An example of a typical problem is the following one: (1) D is taller than E; (2) C is taller than D; (3) A is taller than C; (4) A is taller than B; (5) B is taller than C – 'Who is taller, B or E?'

The structure of such a problem can be visualized in the form of a Haas diagram, as shown in Figure 7.1. The items in the array are here seen to be represented according to their relative heights. The question posed at the end is represented by the dotted line. Being interested in possible developmental sequences of problem-solving strategies, Wood proceeded in the following way. First, the subject was given a number of conventional problems to solve. Then a special test was administered, where the subject was asked an *unexpected question*, such as 'Who is taller, A or D?' These questions were all formulated in such a way as to be easily answered only by subjects who had constructed an image representation of the premisses. It seems, then, that the subjects relied heavily on imagery representations in the initial phase of problem solving. With increasing familiarity, the subjects switched to more economical, linguistic representations. A similar strategy shift has been observed by Quinton and Fellows (1975). They recorded reports of strategies used by their subjects, and, subsequently, gave instructions and training in the use of those strategies found to be most efficient. However, in a later study, Sternberg (1980) failed to observe this strategy shift. His findings indicated that a combined spatial-linguistic strategy was used throughout. Still, it should be noted that Sternberg used only two premisses, in contrast with the six employed by Wood. Even more important is the fact that Sternberg operationalized the imagery construct solely through scores on a spatial test, which affords only a very rough indicator of imagery effects (cf. Paivio 1971; Richardson 1978). Newstead *et al.* (1982) employed a selective interference procedure, but did not find a clear effect of visual interference on task performance presumed to involve imagery. However, their experiments were not systematically designed to check the posited role of imagery in the initial phase of the problem-solving process. When a rough, *post hoc* examination of interference effects on the first trial was made, a trend in the expected direction was found, and they therefore conclude that it remains an interesting possibility that the subjects start with an imaginal strategy.

In a series of recently performed experiments, Clement and Falmagne (1986) report findings clearly in line with the level of programming theory proposed above. The tasks used were syllogisms requiring deductive reasoning, where two yield determinate solutions and two are indeterminate. In indeterminate problems, the subjects must realize that the conditional relation between connected propositions (p,q) is asymmetrical, i.e. the antecedent implies the consequent, but the converse is not necessarily the case. Thus, it may be argued that a computational procedure may be used straightforwardly in determinate, but not in indeterminate, problems. This proposition is in accord with Clement and Falmagne's reasoning, when they argue that 'a well mastered, formal mode of representation was unavailable in indeterminate problems' (ibid.: 300). Thus, it is explicitly entailed by my theory that imagery should be most effective in indeterminate tasks. With imagery indexed through variations in imagery value of the task material, this is exactly what Clement and Falmagne find in their experiments. Subjects' reports of strategies suggest that imagery is helpful in generating counter-examples to invalid inferences.

Kinship problems

Another kind of structure problem is the task of inferring kinship relations from specifically stated problems, such as 'what relationship to her is her mother's mother?' Wood and Shotter (1973) obtained evidence for the same effect of imagery in relation to task novelty as observed in the syllogism problem. The evidence indicates again that imagery strategies are used in the initial phase of the task, followed by a switch to more economical, linguistic short-cut strategies (for example, 'up, across, down' in the image means 'cousin').

Problems of transformation

In problems of transformation, the burden on understanding processes is normally much smaller. Ideally, in transformation tasks both start and goal condition are clear and well understood by the subject. The difficulty of the task lies in finding efficient ways of transforming the initial situation to the required goal situation. Three tasks in this category have been studied with explicit reference to the relevance of imagery processing.

The spy problem

This task was introduced by Hayes (1965). A list of word pairs, said to represent a spy network, are given to the subject. The word pairs denote those, and only those, spies who are able to communicate jointly. Cox (1976, 1978) has performed a series of experiments aimed at uncovering the possible role of imagery in the solution of this task. The main finding reported by Cox is that *concrete* word lists were more easily solved and better memorized than abstract ones. Cox claims that this is due to imagery coding, which is held to aid problem solving and memory performance. However, this conclusion is not compelled by the evidence obtained. As Richardson (1975a, b; 1976) has argued, imageability and concreteness may not be strictly commensurate dimensions. Clearly, a more direct measure of imageability would have been preferable.

Water-jar tasks

This kind of task involves volume-measuring problems. Each jar has a specified volume, and the task is to figure out how to obtain a stipulated amount of fluid. Start conditions as well as goal conditions are clearly stated. A particularly interesting feature of this task is the opportunity it gives for studying developmental sequences of problem-solving strategies.

Kaufmann (1987c) has examined the potential role of imagery in this task. Imagery was operationalized through (a) variations in stimulus presentation (with or without a graph); (b) subjects' report of strategies used; and (c) scores on a spatial visualization test. There was no effect on problem solving of variations in stimulus presentation. However, both reported strategies and scores on the visualization test indicated that imagery was used in the initial phase of the task. Subsequently, the subjects tended to switch to rule-based, linguistic strategies. These findings fall nicely in line with the strategy shifts observed in linear syllogisms and kinship problems, cited above.

Mathematical problems

Many mathematical problems belong in the category of transformation problems. Often, the task is to find efficient computational procedures for calculating a specified answer using some precisely specified information. Unfortunately, in most of the relevant research, only differential methods have been used, where scores on tests of spatial visualization have been related to task performance. Thus, safe conclusions are difficult to draw. A further complication concerns the measurement of task performance. The grading procedures usually employed are crude, making it difficult to tell exactly whether the tasks in question represent clear-cut transformation problems. With these reservations in mind, some of the most pertinent research on the potential relationship between visualization and mathematical problem-solving will be reviewed.

Largely from testimonial evidence, Skemp (1971) has suggested that visual imagery has an important function in mathematical problem-solving – not only in geometric problems, but in algebraic ones as well. Tests on mathematical ability have been found to load substantially on the g-factor of intelligence (Smith 1964). The question thus arises if spatial imagery makes for an independent contribution. The available evidence is affirmative. Barakat (reported in ibid.) obtained interesting findings from a comprehensive investigation of mathematical aptitude with grammar-school children. After the effect of g was eliminated, a *negative* effect was obtained for verbal ability. The geometry tests had a substantial loading on the spatial factor. This finding has been replicated in several other investigations (ibid.). On the algebra test there was a significant loading on the spatial factor for girls, but not for boys. Earlier, Wrigley (1958) found a negative loading on the mathematical group factor for verbal tests, but a positive one for spatial visualization tests. This pattern was obtained with algebra tasks as well as with geometry tasks. In a large-scale investigation, where Guilford tests were used to predict mathematical achievement, Hills (1957, reported in Smith 1964) found a positive relationship between scores on visualization tests and general mathematical aptitude. A low and non-significant correlation was obtained for verbal ability. Of considerable interest is the conclusion drawn by Vernon (1950) from a study of the mathematical abilities of college students and army cadets. Vernon found the effect of spatial ability to be particularly pronounced at high grade levels. More recent research points in the same direction. Spatial ability thus seems to be important in mathematical thinking (see also Poole and Stanley 1972; Maccoby and Jacklin 1974; Sherman 1979, 1980). Burnett *et al.* (1979) conducted an experiment in which they demonstrated that with general level of intelligence controlled, a clearly significant correlation was found between scores on a spatial visualization test and mathematical-quantitative ability at an advanced level. With the spatial visualization factor statistically controlled, they failed to observe sex differences in high-level mathematical ability. Taken together, these findings indicate that visualization plays an important role in abstract problem-solving, particularly at the advanced level.

With the above reservations in mind, it is interesting to note that the findings with mathematical problems stand in sharp contrast with what is entailed by Paivio's theory, in which the functional significance of imagery is linked to task concreteness, and verbal processes are held to be the most important mediators of abstract thinking. The results are, however, clearly in line with my own theory as presented above, where the utility of imagery is held to increase systematically with decrementing level of programming in the task to be solved.

Problems of arrangement

The anagram task is a prototype of arrangement problems, and is the only task in this category that has been systematically examined with respect to the possible involvement of imagery. Anagram tasks require a set of letters (for example, albet) to be transformed into a meaningful word (table). Gavurin (1967) found a significant positive correlation between time to solve ten six-letter anagrams and scores on a test of spatial aptitude, when the subjects were instructed to perform the anagram task 'in their heads'. This correlation disappeared when overt arrangement of the letters was permitted. Gavurin concluded that spatial representation is used to perform the required transformations in the 'covert' condition. Furby (1971) found a significant predictor-effect for spatial ability on the task of rearranging from nonsense to word conditions, but not on word to word rearrangements. Wallace (1977) conducted a factorial experiment with two levels of spatial aptitude, two levels of anagram difficulty, and overt vs. covert rearrangement conditions. Spatial aptitude and anagram difficulty both revealed significant main effects. However, the absence of interaction effects contradicted Gavurin's findings of the special utility of spatial aptitude in the covert condition. Since these experiments failed to control for general level of intellectual ability, the findings are difficult to interpret. Frandsen and Holder (1969) found both verbal reasoning and spatial ability to be significantly related to success in solving complex anagram tasks. A partial correlation analysis revealed that both tests made independent contributions, and it was furthermore shown that a diagrammatic presentation of the tasks significantly influenced problem-solving performance for subjects low in general aptitude.

Using another approach, Jablonski and Mueller (1972) found that high-imagery items (Paivio's I) were solved somewhat faster than low-imagery items. Dewing and Hetherington (1974) found high-I words to be solved significantly more quickly than low-I words. In this study, the subjects were provided with structural cues (initial and final letters of the solution word) and semantic cues (superordinate concepts). The results showed that the structural cues affected performance on the low-I words, whereas the solution time of high-I words was facilitated by semantic cues. With word frequency controlled, Stratton and Jacobus (1975) found a significant effect on anagram solution performance for high-I words also. However, the results from these studies are not easy to interpret. Whereas a visual image interpretation of the I variable is plausible in contexts of learning and memory, it is difficult to conceive of a similar mediational function for imagery in anagram-solving performance, since it seems logically required that a word must first be recognized for imagery to be released. The effect of the I variable may therefore be confounded with other variables not controlled for.

Problems of structure and transformation

Many problems that require transformation of a situation also make heavy demands on understanding processes. Greeno (1978) has identified two loci for understanding in transformation tasks: first, comprehension of the information given in the initial conditions, which requires a representation of the problem in a problem space; and secondly, understanding of the goal conditions and the procedures necessary to reach it. The first aspect of understanding, which involves the construction of a representation, is most directly related to the question of the role of imagery in problem solving. Unfortunately, the available research evidence is rather scant. Among the few systematic studies, Paige and Simon (1966) have examined the strategies used in the solution of algebra word-problems. The following one is a representative example:

If the number of customers Tom gets is twice the square of 20 per cent of the number of advertisements he runs, and the number of advertisements he runs is 45, what is the number of customers Tom gets?

It is clear that such a problem requires both understanding of the initial conditions and a subsequent discovery of computational transformations for reaching the goal.

As regards imagery, interesting findings are reported in the case of preferences for *verbal* vs. *physical* strategies. In the verbal strategy the problem is represented mainly as sets of equations. The physical strategy, on the other hand, was based on spatial representations (in the form of diagrams, graphs, or physical models). With spatial representations, the subjects were, in fact, more able to detect contradictions and impossible combinations of information. The results reported by Paige and Simon indicate that such spatial representations may help in reducing ambiguity, and in this way lead to better understanding of the information. However, the non-experimental set-up of this study makes it difficult to assess this interpretation. Moreover, it is difficult to decide whether the spatial representations really are imagery-based, or if they reflect the operation of more abstract cognitive processes. A more direct experimental approach in which the imagery variable is systematically manipulated, is clearly needed. Also, there is the need to distinguish more sharply between the understanding and the transformation aspect of the problem to pinpoint a potential imagery effect more accurately.

Problems involving transformation of arrangements

This kind of problem contains tasks which require both the arrangement of specified elements, and a transformation of the arrangement. A representative example is the 'matchstick problem' used by Katona in his classic studies of problem solving (Katona 1940). Chess represents another task in this category. Imagery-relevant observations are available for both of these kinds of tasks.

Matchstick problems

Here, the subject is presented with a configuration made up of matches, and the task is to rearrange the initial configuration according to certain specified requirements. In a series of experiments, Katona (ibid.) investigated the usefulness of different methods for solving such tasks. Of particular interest in the present context is the comparison of effect on performance between *verbal rule instruction* and *visual demonstration* of a relevant problem-solving procedure. The results generally showed visual information to have the strongest positive impact on performance. Corman (1957) has made similar observations, and noted that the effect of visual information was greatest in the *initial phase* of problem solving. These results could mean that imagery processes facilitate performance in this kind of task, particularly in the initial phase. However, these experiments are not explicitly conducted in the context of the imagery issue, and the imagery interpretation thus clearly needs further, and more direct confirmation.

Chess problems

According to Greeno (1978), the chess game represents a problem situation which requires transformation of arrangements. The initial position is a particular arrangement of the pieces, and the task is to transform this into a desired arrangement (goal condition). Several studies have examined the cognitive processes involved in chess (cf. De Groot 1965; Newell and Simon 1972; Chase and Simon 1973a, b).

Although imagery has often been considered an important cognitive operation in chess playing, the evidence to this effect is largely anecdotal. However, recently Milojkovic (1982) has carried out some interesting experiments, in which he compared the chess performance of *novices* with that of *masters*. All subjects were first taught a colour code for different chess moves. A problem situation was then created by tachistoscopically presenting a display of three different pieces, followed by a colour display. The subjects were then to perform the capturing move mentally. When a third display was presented immediately afterwards, the task was to decide as quickly as possible whether the display presented was a correct move or not. Distances between pieces varied from one to five separating squares, and each triangle so formed was displayed in four orientations (0, 90, 180, and 270 degrees). With reference to experiments on mental rotation and mental travel (cf. Shepard 1978a; Kosslyn 1980), Milojkovic argued that images under transformation often behave like spatial analogs of the represented objects. The test of the involvement of images is then to be answered by examining the relationship between decision times and distance between the pieces on the board displays. A major finding was that of a systematic relationship between decision time and distance between chess pieces for novices, but not for masters. Milojkovic interprets this finding as indicating that novices use imagery, whereas masters base their judgement on more abstract representations of the board positions. These findings fall nicely in line with evidence suggesting that *task novelty* is a major determinant of the functional use of imagery in problem solving.

Structure-arrangement problems

The final problem category to be examined contains arrangement problems where solution requires an improved understanding of the problem, often entailing a novel perspective. In this category we find the traditional *insight problems* (for example, Duncker 1945; Szekely 1950; Ray 1955, 1967; Raaheim 1961, 1974; Weisberg 1980), *design* and *invention tasks* (for example, Gordon 1961), and *composition problems* (for example, Getzels and Csikszentmihalyi 1975). These tasks are strongly related to the *creativity* aspect of problem solving. Basic processes involve understanding and constructive search processes, such as flexibility in the generation of trial partial solutions.

Idea production tasks

Ideational fluency tasks (cf. Guilford 1967) have been regarded as a valid measure of cognitive flexibility (Wallach 1970), and may be regarded as a component process in the generation of trial partial solution. Since imagery is often linked to creativity in problem solving, several investigators have examined the role of imagery in idea production tasks. Significant, albeit low, correlations between scores on an imagery questionnaire and performance on the Unusual Uses and Alternate Uses tests have been found (Ernest 1977). Rhodes (1981) found a weak, but significant, effect for vividness of imagery in relation to ideational fluency production, particularly to the elaboration category. Durndell and Wetherick (1976) found imagery control to be significantly related to ideational fluency. No relation was obtained between imagery vividness and performance on ideational fluency tasks. Forisha (1978) found a significant relationship between vividness of imagery and ideational fluency performance for females, but not for males. However, there was no relationship between vividness of imagery scores and performance on the Remote Associates Test developed by Mednick and Mednick (1967) as a measure of cognitive creativity.

Such weak and inconsistent findings may be due to methodological flaws inherent in the imagery questionnaire technique, for example differences in subjective conceptions of the rating scale employed (Kaufmann 1976, 1981a, 1983; Richardson 1979). In line with this argument, when Hargreaves and Bolton (1972) used a paired-associate technique to assess individual differences in imagery ability, they obtained quite strong correlations with measures of ideational fluency performance. A similar finding has been noted by Schmidt (1973), who used a spatial visualization test in his study.

However, correlational data of the kind reported above are, of course, difficult to interpret. In an experimental approach, Davis and Manske (1966) observed a significant increase in ideational fluency production under instructions to visualize the critical object in a particular setting, compared with a control condition with standard instructions. With a selective interference technique, Kaufmann (1974) examined the potential role of visual imagery in ideational fluency. The experimental procedure aimed at disrupting visual and verbal processes by presenting irrelevant visual and auditory stimuli during task performance. The results showed a significant interaction between sex and type of interference. Males were most disrupted by visual interference, whereas females responded in the opposite direction. Males and females thus seemed to rely on different representational strategies, with the males being more prone to visualize than females.

A series of studies on response patterns in ideational-fluency tasks consistently shows the ideas given early in the production sequence to be conventional, whereas novel and original ideas appear at a later stage (Christensen et al. 1957; Meadow and Parnes 1959; Parnes 1961). Given this relationship between time and frequency of conventional versus original ideas, the imagery-creativity theories predict that the utility of imagery will increase with production time. In an experiment designed to test this hypothesis (Kaufmann 1981b), the imagery construct was operationalized through scores on a spatial visualization test. When the predictor effect for the spatial visualization test was calculated in relation to ideational fluency performance at different time intervals, the results showed a systematic increase in predictor efficiency with increasing production time from non-significance at 1 minute to strong significance in the final, 4 minute interval. There was no relationship between ideational fluency performance and scores on a verbal control test. Using the Barron Independence of Judgement Scale as a measure of creativity, Schmeidler (1965) found a small, but significant relationship with scores on an imagery questionnaire. The scatter-plot of scores showed the quadrant which contained low-creativity and high-imagery scores to be sparsely populated. This observation indicates that imagery is a useful but not a necessary ingredient in creative thinking, and may explain why blind subjects have been found equal to their sighted peers in ideational fluency performance (Tisdall *et al.* 1971; Halpin *et al.* 1973). In an earlier study, however, Singer and Streiner (1966) found blind subjects to be inferior to their sighted peers in tasks involving imagination and cognitive flexibility.

Insight problems

In many of these tasks, an invention of a workable practical construction that meets certain specified requirements is demanded of the subject. Since novel task-arrangements are necessary, it has been argued that imagery processes are likely to be induced (Kaufmann 1979, 1980). In line with this hypothesis, a comparison between a visual and a verbal presentation of insight problems proved the visual mode to be the most efficient (Kaufmann 1979). These findings are in line with previous observations (Katona 1940; Szekely 1950; Anderson and Johnson 1966; Fitzpatrick 1978). Further, scores on spatial visualization tests were found to be significantly related to success in solving insight problems, in contrast to non-significant predictor effects for verbal-ability tests. It may, of course, be argued that the insight problems studied in these experiments are highly concrete tasks, and that concreteness, rather than novelty, is therefore responsible for the imagery effect. However, no difference between verbal and visual presentation was obtained in an experiment by Kaufmann and Bengtsson (1980), where the task could be solved by use of a rather well-known physical principle, thus indicating that novelty requirements may be important for imagery manipulations to be effective in the case of insight problems. As regards the concreteness factor, Fitzpatrick (1978), in accord with Paivio's theory, predicted verbal-ability test scores to relate to performance on a verbally presented task, and that spatial-ability scores would correlate with task performance under visual presentation. However, the results failed to support the hypotheses. Similar negative results have been reported by Ernest (1980). In line with the novelty interpretation of imagery effects in insight problems are several findings converging in the conclusion that visual rather than verbal information is particularly important in the initial exploratory phases of solving insight problems (for example, Hendrix 1950; Haslerud and Meyers 1958). Actually, emphasis on verbalization in the initial phase has been found to *inhibit* subsequent performance (for example, Hendrix 1950).

Some negative findings concerning the role of imagery in insight problems have also been reported. When Wicker *et al.* (1978) asked their subjects to form a clear and detailed visual image of the problem components, no positive effects of the visualization instructions were obtained. In the study by Durndell and Wetherick (1976), subjects were asked to report use of imagery during the solution of insight problems. No relationship between reported imagery and ability to solve the task was found. Indeed, the time taken to reach solution correlated positively with rated use of imagery during attempted solution. The results may be taken to mean that the solution processes were actually hindered by the use of imagery. Alternatively, the results might indicate that those subjects who experienced most difficulty with the tasks resorted to the use of imagery, and the imagery thus employed may actually have been useful. Examination of the effect of inducing imagery on performance of subjects high and low in solving this kind of task may resolve the issue.

Search tasks

Zinchenko *et al.* (1973) examined the functional usefulness of imagery in performance on complex search tasks. Imagery and verbal processes were indexed by various physiological registrations during problem solving (eye movements, EEG, electromyogram [EMG]). Their results indicated that the incidence of visualizing increased with incrementing task complexity, whereas verbal processes seemed to dominate in the culminating phase of problem solving. The observations were taken to mean that imagery was particularly useful in the search phase of problem solving.

Conclusions

Does imagery play a functional role in problem solving?

It has been argued that imagery is an irrelevant byplay of more abstract cognitive processes and, thus, has a purely epiphenomenal status in cognition (for example, Neisser 1967; Pylyshyn 1973). In contrast to the anti-imagery thesis, the evidence reviewed above strongly suggests that imagery is indeed of functional importance in problem solving. There is also a trend in the evidence which suggests that the functional utility of imagery increases with incrementing task difficulty. It may be argued that this is the condition where the individual is least likely to engage in irrelevant luxury activities, but rather has to draw upon all relevant resources.

Is imagery related to the type of processes used in problem solving, to the level of programming, or to the concreteness of a task?

With reference to Greeno's (1978) grouping of problem-solving tasks, the evidence shows imagery not to be specifically tied to particular information-processing functions as defined by Greeno. Indeed, imagery is seen to be functional across the full process spectrum determined by Greeno's model. Although more evidence is required for definite conclusions to be drawn, available findings do not support the theories of Berlyne (1965) and Paivio (1971, 1986), in which the functional utility of imagery is tied to specific modes of processing.

There are, however, clear indications to the effect that *level of programming* is a major determinant of the usefulness of imagery. In particular, the evidence linking imagery to task novelty replicates over a broad spectrum of tasks. Task complexity may also be an important determinant of the appropriateness of using imagery, as indicated by the evidence which shows that visualization may have a special role in high-level quantitative thinking (see also Baylor 1971, for evidence linking imagery processing more specifically to complexity in a spatial task). A few studies also point to imagery strategies as particularly relevant in resolving ambiguity and inconsistency. It should be emphasized, however, that the available research evidence is still scarce, and that the conclusions drawn should be treated as reasonable working hypotheses.

The results pertaining to the concreteness-abstractness dimension are intriguing, and indicate that imagery may not always be antagonistic to abstract thinking. Neither is the function of imagery limited by task concreteness. Several independent lines of evidence converge in the conclusion that imagery may have important functions in highly *abstract* tasks, particularly under conditions of low programming. This may seem paradoxical, but to understand the functions of imagery it is

189

important to make a distinction between two kinds of imagery effects. In the first place, imagery may be used as a representational instrument when it is easily *available* and particularly appropriate for the *type* of information to be handled. This is often the case with highly concrete task material. Still, the use of imagery may be most highly *needed* when the *amount* of processing required is high due to low programming in the task, regardless of the type of information to be processed. This dual functional role of imagery has been emphasized in the theory developed by the present author (Kaufmann 1986, 1987b). The results from investigations on the role of imagery in problem solving, then, make it reasonable to expand the scope of imagery research to take account also of the theoretically significant and practically important role that imagery may have under task conditions characterized by a low degree of programming.

References

Anderson, B. and Johnson, W. (1966) 'Two methods of presenting information and the effects of problem solving', *Perceptual and Motor Skills* 23: 851–6.
Atwood, M. E., and Polson, P. G. (1976) 'A process model for water jug problems', *Cognitive Psychology* 8: 191–216.
Baylor, G. W. (1971) 'A treatise on the mind's eye: an empirical investigation of visual mental imagery', unpublished doctoral dissertation, Carnegie-Mellon University, Pittsburgh (Ann Arbor, MI: University Microfilms no. 72–12).
Begg, I. (1972) 'Recall of meaningful phrases', *Journal of Verbal Learning and Verbal Behavior* 11: 431–9.
Berlyne, D. E. (1965) *Structure and Direction in Thinking*, New York: Wiley.
Bruner, J. S., Oliver, R. R., and Greenfield, P. M. (1966) *Studies in Cognitive Growth*, New York: Wiley.
Burnett, S. A., McLane, D. M., and Dratt, L. M. (1979) 'Spatial visualization and sex differences in quantitative ability', *Intelligence* 3: 345–54.
Chase, W. G., and Simon, H. A. (1973a) 'The mind's eye in chess', in W. G. Chase (ed.) *Visual Information Processing*, New York: Academic Press.
—— (1973b) 'Perception in chess', *Cognitive Psychology* 4: 55–81.
Christensen, P. R., Guilford, J. P., and Wilson, R. C. (1957) 'Relation of creative responses to working time and instructions', *Journal of Experimental Psychology* 53: 82–8.
Clark, H. H. (1969a) 'Linguistic processes in deductive reasoning', *Psychological Review* 76: 387–404.
—— (1969b) 'The influence of language in solving three-term series problems', *Journal of Experimental Psychology* 82: 205–15.

(1971) 'More about "Adjectives, comparatives, and syllogisms": a reply to Huttenlocher and Higgins', *Psychological Review* 78: 505–14.

(1972) 'On the evidence concerning J. Huttenlocher and E. T. Higgins' theory of reasoning: a second reply', *Psychological Review* 79: 428–32.

Clement, C. A., and Falmagne, R. J. (1986) 'Logical reasoning, world knowledge, and mental imagery: interconnections in cognitive process', *Memory and Cognition* 14: 299–307.

Corballis, M. (1982) 'Mental rotation: anatomy of a paradigm', in M. Potegal (ed.) *Spatial Abilities: Development and Psychological Foundations*, New York: Academic Press.

Corman, B. R. (1957) 'The effect of varying amounts of information as guidance in problem solving', *Psychological Monographs* 71 (Whole No. 431).

Cox, W. F. (1976) 'Problem solving as influenced by stimulus abstractness-concreteness', *Psychology* 13: 37–44.

(1978) 'Problem solving as a function of abstract or concrete words', *Contemporary Educational Psychology* 3: 95–101.

Davis, G. A., and Manske, M. E. (1966) 'An instructional method of increasing originality', *Psychonomic Science* 6: 73–4.

De Groot, A. (1965) *Thought and Choice in Chess*, The Hague: Mouton.

De Soto, C.B., London, M., and Handel, S. (1965) 'Social reasoning and spatial paralogic', *Journal of Personality and Social Psychology* 2: 513–21.

Dewing, K., and Hetherington, P. (1974) 'Anagram solving as a function of word imagery', *Journal of Experimental Psychology* 102: 764–7.

Duncker, K. (1945) 'On problem solving', *Psychological Monographs* 58: (Whole No. 270).

Durndell, A. J., and Wetherick, N. E. (1976) 'The relation of reported imagery to cognitive performance', *British Journal of Psychology* 67: 501–6.

Eley, M. G. (1979) 'The suitability of placement tasks as analogues for syllogistic reasoning', *British Journal of Psychology* 70: 541–6.

Ernest, C. H . (1977) 'Imagery ability and cognition: a critical review', *Journal of Mental Imagery* 2: 181–216.

(1980) 'Imagery ability and the identification of fragmented pictures and words', *Acta Psychologica* 44: 51–7.

Fitzpatrick, T. J. (1978) 'The relation of imagery and word association abilities to various problem solving tasks', unpublished PhD dissertation, New York University.

Forisha, B. L. (1978) 'Creativity and imagery in men and women', *Perceptual and Motor Skills* 47: 1255–64.

Frandsen, A. N., and Holder, J. R. (1969) 'Spatial visualization in solving complex verbal problems', *Journal of Psychology* 73: 229–33.

French, P. L. (1979) 'Linguistic marking, strategy, and affect in syllogistic reasoning', *Journal of Psycholinguistic Research* 8: 425–49.

Furby, L. (1971) 'The role of spatial visualization in verbal problem solving', *Journal of General Psychology* 85: 149–52.

Galton, F. (1883) *Inquiries into Human Faculty and its Development*, London: Macmillan.

Gavurin, E. I. (1967) 'Anagram solving and spatial aptitude', *Journal of Psychology* 65: 65–8.

Getzels, J. W., and Csikszentmihalyi, M. (1975) 'From problem solving to problem finding', in I. A. Taylor (ed.) *Perspectives in Creativity*, Chicago, IL: Aldine Publishing.

Gordon, W. J. (1961) *Synetics: The Development of Creative Capacity*, New York: Harper & Row.

Greeno, J. G. (1978) 'Nature of problem-solving abilities', in W. K. Estes (ed.) *Handbook of Learning and Cognitive Processes*, vol. 5, *Human Information Processing*, Hillsdale, NJ: Erlbaum.

— and Simon, H. A. (1985) 'Problem solving and reasoning', in R. C. Atkinson, R. Herrnstein, Q. Lindzey, and R. D. Luce (eds) *Stevens' Handbook of Experimental Psychology*, New York: Wiley.

Guilford, J. P. (1967) *The Nature of Human Intelligence*, New York: McGraw-Hill.

Halpin, G., Halpin, G., and Torrance, E. P. (1973) 'Effects of blindness on creative thinking abilities of children', *Developmental Psychology* 9: 268–74.

Hargreaves, D. J. and Bolton, N. (1972) 'Selecting creativity tests for use in research', *British Journal of Psychology* 63: 451–62.

Haslerud, G. M., and Meyers, S. (1958) 'The transfer value of given and individually derived principles', *Journal of Educational Psychology* 49: 293–8.

Hayes, J. R. (1965) 'Problem typology and the solution process', *Journal of Verbal Learning and Verbal Behavior* 4: 371–9.

Hebb, D. O. (1968) 'Concerning imagery', *Psychological Review* 75: 466–77.

Helstrup, T. (1976) *Hva er Kognitiv Psykologi?*, Oslo/Bergen/Tromsø: Universitetsforlaget.

Hendrix, G. (1950) 'Prerequisite for meaning', *Mathematics Teacher* 43: 334–9.

Horowitz, M. J. (1983) *Image Formation and Psychotherapy*, New York: Aronson.

Humphrey, G. (1959) *Thinking*, London: Methuen.

Huttenlocher, J. (1968) 'Constructing spatial images: a strategy in reasoning'. *Psychological Review* 75: 550–60.

Jablonski, E. M., and Mueller, J.H. (1972) 'Anagram solution as a function of instructions, priming, and imagery', *Journal of Experimental Psychology* 94: 84–9.

Johnson-Laird, P. N. (1972) 'The three-term series problem', *Cognition* 1: 57–82.

— (1983) *Mental Models*, London: Cambridge University Press.

Jones, S. (1970) 'Visual and verbal processes in problem solving', *Cognitive Psychology* 1: 201–14.

Katona, G. (1940) *Organizing and Memorizing*, New York: Columbia University Press.

Kaufmann, G. (1974) 'Visual imagery and problem solving: II. Effect of visual and auditory interference on ideational fluency performance', *Reports from the Institute of Psychology, University of Bergen*, No. 4.

(1975) 'Visual imagery and its relation to problem solving: a theoretical and experimental inquiry', unpublished doctoral thesis, University of Bergen.

(1976) 'Is imagery a cognitive appendix?' *Reports from the Institute of Psychology, University of Bergen*, No. 1.

(1979) *Visual Imagery and its Relation to Problem Solving: A Theoretical and Experimental Inquiry*, Oslo/Bergen/Tromsø: Universitetsforlaget.

(1980) *Imagery, Language, and Cognition*, Oslo/Bergen/Tromsø: Universitetsforlaget.

(1981a) 'What is wrong with imagery questionnaires?' *Scandinavian Journal of Psychology* 22: 59–64.

(1981b) 'The functional significance of visual imagery in ideational fluency performance', *Journal of Mental Imagery* 5: 115–20.

(1983) 'How good are imagery questionnaires?', *Scandinavian Journal of Psychology* 24: 247–9.

(1984) 'Mental imagery and problem solving', in A. Sheikh (ed.) *International Review of Mental Imagery*, vol. 1, New York: Human Sciences Press.

(1986) 'The conceptual basis of cognitive imagery models: a critique and a theory', in D. F. Marks (eds.) *Theories of Image Formation*, New York: Brandon House.

(1987a) 'Problem solving and reasoning', in K. Grønhaug and G. Kaufmann (eds) *Innovation: A Crossdisciplinary Perspective*, Oslo/Bergen/Tromsø: Norwegian Universities Press.

(1987b) 'Mental imagery and problem solving', in M. Denis, J. Engelkamp, and J. T. E. Richardson (eds) *Cognitive and Neuropsychological Approaches to Mental Imagery*, Dordrecht: Martinus Nijhoff.

(1987c) 'Imagery and the discovery of a rule', *Reports from the Institute of Psychology, University of Bergen*.

and Bengtsson, G. (1980) 'Effect of mode of presentation on performance in a familiar task', *Scandinavian Journal of Psychology* 21: 61–3.

Kaufmann, G., and Helstrup, T. (1985) 'Mental imagery and problem solving: implications for the educational process', in A. Sheikh (ed.) *Imagery and Education*, New York: Baywood Press.

Kosslyn, S. M. (1980) *Image and Mind*, Cambridge, MA: Harvard University Press.

Kotovsky, K., and Simon, H. A. (1973) 'Empirical tests of a theory of human acquision of concepts for sequential events', *Cognitive Psychology* 4: 399–424.

Maccoby, E., and Jacklin, D. (1974) *The Psychology of Sex Differences*, Stanford, CA: Stanford University Press.

McKellar, P. (1957) *Imagination and Thinking*, New York: Basic Books.

(1963) 'Three aspects of the psychology of originality in human thinking', *British Journal of Aesthetics* 3: 129–47.

(1972) 'Imagery from the standpoint of introspection', in P. W. Sheehan (ed.) *The Function and Nature of Imagery*, New York: Academic Press.

Meadow, A., and Parnes, S. J. (1959) 'Evaluation of training in creative problem solving', *Journal of Applied Psychology* 43: 189–94.

193

Mednick, S., and Mednick, M. (1967) *Remote Associates Test*, New York: Houghton Mifflin.

Milojkovic, J. D. (1982) 'Chess imagery in novice and master', *Journal of Mental Imagery* 6: 125–44.

Morris, P. E., and Hampson, P. J. (1983) *Imagery and Consciousness*, London: Academic Press.

Neisser, U. (1967) *Cognitive Psychology*, New York: Appleton-Century-Crofts.

Newell, A. (1969) 'Heuristic programming: ill-structured problems', in J. Aronsky (ed.) *Progress in Operations Research*, vol. 3, New York: Wiley.

—— and Simon, H. A. (1972) *Human Problem Solving*, Englewood Cliffs, NJ: Prentice-Hall.

Newstead, S. E., Manktelow, K. I., and Evans, J. St. B. T. (1982) 'The role of imagery in the representation of linear orderings', *Current Psychological Research* 2: 21–32.

Paige, J. M., and Simon, H. A. (1966) 'Cognitive processes in solving algebra problems', in B. Kleinmuntz (ed.) *Problem Solving: Research, Method, and Theory*, New York: Wiley.

Paivio, A. (1971) *Imagery and Verbal Processes*, New York: Holt, Rinehart & Winston.

—— (1975) 'Imagery and synchronic thinking' *Canadian Psychological Review* 16: 147–63.

—— (1986) *Mental Representations: A Dual Coding Approach*, New York: Oxford University Press.

Parnes, S. J. (1961) 'Effects of extended effort in creative problem solving', *Journal of Educational Psychology*, 3: 117–22.

Poole, C., and Stanley, G. A. (1972) 'Factorial and predictive study of spatial abilities', *Australian Journal of Psychology* 24: 317–20.

Potts, G. R., and Scholz, K. W. (1975) 'The internal representation of a three-term series problem', *Journal of Verbal Learning and Verbal Behavior* 14: 439–52.

Pylyshyn, Z. W. (1973) 'What the mind's eye tells the mind's brain: a critique of mental imagery', *Psychological Bulletin* 80: 1–23.

Quinton, G., and Fellows, B. J. (1975) '"Perceptual" strategies in the solving of three-term series problems', *British Journal of Psychology* 66: 69–78.

Raaheim, K. (1961) *Problem Solving: A New Approach*, Oslo/Bergen/Tromsø: Universitetsforlaget.

—— (1974) *Problem Solving and Intelligence*, Oslo/Bergen/Tromsø: Universitetsforlaget.

Ray, W. S. (1955) 'Complex tasks for use in human problem solving research', *Psychological Bulletin* 52: 134–49.

—— (1967) *The Experimental Psychology of Original Thinking*, New York: Macmillan.

Reitman, W. R. (1965) *Cognition and Thought: An Information Processing Approach*, New York: Wiley.

Rhodes, J. W. (1981) 'Relationship between vividness of mental imagery and creative thinking', *Journal of Creative Behavior* 15(2): 90–8.

Richardson, J. T. E. (1975a) 'Imagery, concreteness, and lexical complexity', *Quarterly Journal of Experimental Psychology* 27: 235–49.

(1975b) 'Concreteness and imageability', *Quarterly Journal of Experimental Psychology* 27: 211–23.

(1976) 'Imageability and concreteness', *Bulletin of the Psychonomic Society* 7: 429–31.

(1978) 'Reported mediators and individual differences in mental imagery', *Memory and Cognition* 6: 376–8.

(1979) 'Correlations between imagery and memory across stimuli and across subjects', *Bulletin of the Psychonomic Society* 14: 368–70.

(1983) 'Mental imagery in thinking and problem solving', in J. St B. T. Evans (ed.) *Thinking and Reasoning: Psychological Approaches*, London: Routledge & Kegan Paul.

(1987) 'The role of mental imagery in models of transitive inference', *British Journal of Psychology* 78: 189–203.

Rugg, H. (1963) *Imagination*, New York: Harper & Row.

Rumelhart, D. E., and Abrahamsen, A. S. (1973) 'A model for analogical reasoning', *Cognitive Psychology* 5: 1–28.

Sanford, A. J. (1985) *Cognition and Cognitive Psychology*, London: Weidenfeld & Nicholson.

Schmeidler, G. R. (1965) 'Visual imagery correlated to a measure of creativity', *Journal of Consulting Psychology* 29: 78–80.

Schmidt, H. E. (1973) 'The identification of high and low creativity in architecture students', *Psychologica Africana* 15: 15–40.

Shepard, R. N. (1978a) 'The mental image', *American Psychologist* 33: 125–7.

(1978b) 'Externalization of the image and the act of creation', in B. S. Randhawa (ed.) *Visual Learning, Thinking, and Communication*, New York: Academic Pres.

Sherman, J. A. (1979) 'Predicting mathematics performance in high school girls and boys', *Journal of Educational Psychology* 71: 242–9.

(1980) 'Predicting mathematics grades of high school girls: a further study', *Contemporary Educational Psychology* 5: 249–55.

Simon, H. A. (1977) *The New Science of Management Decision*, Englewood Cliffs, NJ: Prentice-Hall.

(1978) 'Information processing theory of human problem solving', in W. K. Estes (ed.) *Handbook of Learning and Cognitive Processes*, New York: Wiley.

and Kotovsky, K. (1963) 'Human acquisition of concepts for sequential patterns', *Psychological Review* 70: 534–46.

Singer, J. L., and Streiner, B. F. (1966) 'Imaginative content in the dreams and fantasy play of blind and sighted children', *Perceptual and Motor Skills* 22: 475–82.

Skemp, R. R. (1971) *The Psychology of Learning Mathematics*, Harmondsworth: Penguin.

Smith, I. M. (1984) *Spatial Ability*, London: University of London Press.

Sternberg, R. J. (1977) *Intelligence, Information Processing, and Analogical Reasoning: The Componential Analysis of Human Abilities*, Hillsdale, NJ: Erlbaum.

(1980) 'Representation and process in linear syllogistic reasoning', *Journal of Experimental Psychology: General* 109: 119–59.

Stratton, R. P., and Jacobus, K. A. (1975) 'Solving anagrams as a function of word frequency, imagery, and distribution of practice', *Canadian Journal of Psychology* 29: 22–31.

Suler, J. R. (1980) 'Primary process thinking and creativity', *Psychological Bulletin* 88: 144–65.

Szekely, L. (1950) 'Productive processes in learning and thinking', *Acta Psychologica* 7: 388–407.

Tisdall, W. J., Blackhurst, E. A., and Marks, C. H. (1971) 'Divergent thinking in blind children', *Journal of Educational Psychology* 63: 468–73.

Vernon, P. E. (1950) *The Structure of Human Abilities*, London: Methuen.

Wallace, I. G. (1977) 'The role of overt rearrangement in anagram solving in subjects of high and low spatial ability and anagrams of two levels of difficulty', *Journal of General Psychology* 96: 117–24.

Wallach, M. A. (1970) 'Creativity', in P. Mussen (ed.) *Carmichael's Manual of Child Psychology*, vol. 1, New York: Wiley.

Weisberg, R. W. (1980) *Memory, Thought, and Behavior*, New York: Oxford University Press.

Wicker, F. W., Weinstein, C. A., and Brooks J. D. (1978) 'Problem-reformulation training and visualization training with insight problems', *Journal of Educational Psychology* 70: 372–7.

Williams, R. L. (1977) 'Imagery and linguistic factors affecting the solution of linear syllogisms', *Journal of Psycholinguistic Research* 8: 123–40.

Wood, D. (1969) 'Approach to the study of human reasoning', *Nature* 223: 101–2.

—— and Shotter, J. (1973) 'A preliminary study of distinctive features in problem solving', *Quarterly Journal of Experimental Psychology* 25: 504–10.

Wood, D., Shotter, J., and Godden, D. (1974) 'An investigation of the relationship between problem solving strategies, representation and memory', *Quarterly Journal of Experimental Psychology* 26: 252–7.

Woodworth, R. S., and Schlosberg, H. (1955) *Experimental Psychology*, London: Methuen.

Wrigley, J. (1958) 'The factorial nature of ability in elementary mathematics', *British Journal of Educational Psychology* 28: 61–78.

Zinchenko, U. P., Munipov, U. M., and Gordon, V. M. (1973) 'The study of visual thinking', *Voprosy Psikhologii* 2: 3–14.

Chapter eight

Enhancing people's knowledge about images

Michel Denis and Maryvonne Carfantan

The last two decades have undoubtedly been the richest period in terms of the gain in our knowledge about mental imagery, a field of research which has benefited from the development of both the conceptual apparatus and the methodology of modern cognitive psychology. It should however be stressed that, while imagery is now approached with modern, increasingly sophisticated technologies, its study is one of humankind's oldest concerns, as is testified by the writings of Greek and Roman philosophers and rhetoricians (cf. Meyerson 1932; Yates 1966). In addition, in current times the notion of mental imagery is present in many areas of human intellectual activity that are far removed from the preoccupations of scientific psychology. This is illustrated, for instance, in such domains as education, mnemonic training, psychotherapeutic treatment, literature, and artistic creativity. The notion of mental imagery is also a familiar one to the layperson, who generally acknowledges the idea that the human mind is able to give some sort of mental presence to the objects that are outside of ongoing perceptual experience and to retrieve in these representations some of the information that was originally available in those objects. While this notion may be rather vague and based upon intuitions that vary across individuals, it is a matter of fact that people have at least some insight into their own mental processes, especially those which are usually accompanied by conscious experience.

What can be said about this knowledge? Could it be the case that people's nonscientific notions about images have some validity and have something in common with the notions and the facts that have been established by the scientific approach? It was our purpose to provide some answer to this question through a research programme devoted to the characterization of people's informal knowledge about images, their functions and properties. This chapter begins with an overview of our approach to this topic. Following this, data are presented from further research with investigated the possibility of enriching such knowledge through an appropriate informative text. The last section of the chapter reports on a conversational version of this instructional device.

People's knowledge about images

Undergraduates' responses to questionnaires designed to capture some aspects of their knowledge of mental images were collected over a series of successive experiments (Denis and Carfantan 1985, 1986; Denis in press). The procedure which was judged to be the most operational entailed presenting the subjects with short descriptions of typical imagery experiments, and asking them to predict what the outcome of these experiments would be. In other words, subjects were invited to consider a situation in which a person has to process an image in some specified way, and to make a conjecture about the result recorded by the experimenter.

Data analysis on these questionnaires revealed a clear-cut differentiation between two sets of questions. On the one hand, there were questions to which respondents overall furnished a relatively high rate of correct predictions. These items were considered to tap some aspects of imagery for which people apparently possess knowledge which is very similar to current scientific knowledge. On the other hand, there were questions in which subjects were rather poor predictors: that is, they either produced predictions which were not congruent with scientific results or they were simply unable to make any sort of prediction. These items were considered to reflect aspects of imagery which, although attested to by research, are contrary to the intuitions that people have of the corresponding phenomena. Upon examination, this differentiation in fact practically overlapped with another distinction, this time between questions dealing with the *effects of imagery* in cognitive activities, and questions relating to *processing characteristics* of visual images.

On the whole, the highest rates of correct responses were given to the questions regarding imagery effects in cognitive functioning. Subjects' responses show, for instance, that most of them have a clear and accurate idea of the efficiency of visual imagery in verbal learning, spatial reasoning, or problem solving. They predict higher performance for people using visual images to memorize verbal information, or for people spontaneously inclined to converting verbal information into images. The only domain in which our subjects were reluctant to predict any positive effect of imagery was the acquisition of motor skills. Only a small number of respondents entertained the possibility that visualization can efficiently serve motor learning.

The questions regarding the processing of images reveal that subjects have no clear insight into phenomena such as mental rotation or mental scanning, as these phenomena have been demonstrated in typical Shepard and Kosslyn paradigms (see Kosslyn 1980a; Shepard and Cooper 1982). Thus, for instance, only a small number of subjects (less than 15 per cent) can conceive of the fact that more time is required to perform rotation through larger angles. A similar low percentage of subjects (less than 10 per cent) is ready to believe that more time is required to scan longer distances in imagery.

The differential predictability of both sets of questions is not surprising: while many subjects may have experienced the usefulness of imaging in daily cognitive tasks, fine mechanics of visual imagery are not typically introspected by individuals. However, it should be pointed out that at the same time, these low percentages of correct predictions reflect a great unwillingness on the part of subjects to project on to mental images the knowledge they have derived from the physical world regarding the relationships between time, speed, and physical distance. If such knowledge were so highly available, as is argued by 'tacit knowledge' accounts of mental imagery phenomena (for example, Pylyshyn 1981), one should expect high percentages of people to give rather accurate accounts of imaginal processes on the basis of this knowledge. If subjects actually only mapped their knowledge of the relationships between speed, time, and physical distance on to their imaginal representations of objects when performing mental-rotation or mental-scanning tasks, they would be likely to do so steadily when required to reason about image-processing, and their rate of correct predictions would be more substantial than is the case. In brief, the fact that so few people are able to predict time-distance relationships in mental rotation or mental scanning is in line with the notion that people do not make much use of their knowledge of the physical world when required to reason about imagery processes.

The opacity of imagery phenomena reveals itself to be highly resistant. In subsequent experiments, for instance, we introduced additional instructions or provided subjects with information expected to increase the attainability of correct predictions. Requiring subjects to simulate the processes described in the question before responding did not increase the rate of correct predictions. Similarly, when subjects were provided with detailed descriptions of mental-rotation or mental-scanning experiments, the rate of their correct predictions still remained at best at a chance level or clearly below this level. On the other hand, prediction patterns were apparently unaffected by subjects' individual imagery characteristics, as assessed by standard imagery questionnaires or tests. People reporting more vivid visual imagery, for instance, were not better at predicting results from imagery experiments than people less prone to imaging. Thus, greater inclination to vivid imagery experiences does not entail having more accurate knowledge about these experiences. In addition, subjects obtaining high scores on a mental rotation test did not perform better than others in predicting mental rotation phenomena. Thus, higher performance on a task requiring rather complex image processing does not entail having more accurate knowledge about such processing.

The main question which arose at this state of the investigation was whether a lack of knowledge about imagery should be viewed as a permanent cognitive state or whether this state was amenable to some modification via an instructional device. Thus, for instance, would the exposure of subjects to descriptions of imagery experiments and their actual results lead them to modify their beliefs in the case of questions that did not receive correct answers? Issues of this type are at the core of current research programmes whose purpose is to elaborate procedures in which individualized instructional texts are constructed as a function of students' initial states of knowledge (cf. Le Ny and Denhière 1982; Le Ny 1983). The experiments presented below represent the initial steps of a programme designed to produce instructional texts providing scientific knowledge on imagery to uninformed subjects, for instance in scholastic settings.

The effects of an instructional text on people's knowledge about images

The procedure used in this research first entailed presenting people with short descriptions of classic imagery experiments and asking them to state what the typical outcome of these experiments would be. Then, the procedure consisted in exposing the subjects to a description of the actual results of imagery experiments, and in having them once more give answers to the same series of questions. The text we used was devised to bring pertinent information clearly to readers, and to enable them to integrate fragments of information which the initial test would have shown to be lacking. As regards questions correctly answered by subjects on the test, the information presented in the text would simply confirm readers' previous knowledge. However, for questions that had not received correct answers initially, it was of interest to observe whether exposure of subjects to true statements sufficed to correct their initial (erroneous) beliefs as concerns images.

The questionnaire we used comprised fifteen items (see Appendix 1). The first question explored subjects' beliefs as to the ability of psychology to investigate mental images scientifically. Ten of the questions which followed consisted of short descriptions of typical procedures used in imagery experiments (or experiments closely related to the issue of imagery, such as picture-word memory experiments). The questions entailed predicting the outcome of the experiments described. In some cases (Questions 3–7 and 12), subjects had to decide which out of two possible outcomes was correct; in other cases (Questions 2, 9, 14, and 15), subjects had to choose one out of three possible outcomes. One question (8) had to do with people's ability to visualize rotating objects. The three remaining questions (10, 11, and 13) were of yet another kind, in the sense that they investigated subjects' agreement with theoretical interpretations of some experimental results.

A text of four and a half pages entitled 'Mental Imagery' was composed (see Appendix 2). It consisted of a report written in a non-academic style, describing typical imagery experiments and their results. The text was prepared, partly from passages in texts available in French (Denis 1979; Kosslyn 1980b), but the document as a whole was new to the subjects involved in this investigation. A foreword indicated that all results described had been found for a great many subjects and repeatedly confirmed in several studies, so that they could be considered as highly susceptible to generalization.

The first part of the text described experiments demonstrating the effects of mental imagery on learning and reasoning. It comprised short descriptions of experiments demonstrating:

(a) the superiority of pictures over words in memory experiments (for example, Paivio et al. 1968; Denis 1975);
(b) positive effects of instructions to image in learning word lists (for example, Paivio and Yuille 1967; Denis 1975);

(c) positive effects of imagery ability on verbal learning (for example, Ernest and Paivio 1969; Di Vesta and Ross 1971);
(d) positive effects of mental practice in learning motor skills (for example, Mendoza and Wichman 1978);
(e) effects of visualization on spatial reasoning (for example, Frandsen and Holder 1969);
(f) effects of visualization on deductive reasoning (for example, Shaver *et al.* 1975).

The descriptions in this part of the text paralleled the order of the corresponding items in the questionnaire (Questions 2–7). Finally, the general assumption that imagery may be functionally similar to perception in several kinds of cognitive activity was stated in this part of the text.

The second part of the text reported several imagery experiments whose results have been frequently put forward as reflecting intrinsic properties of visual images. It described experiments investigating: (a) the rate of mental rotation for a stimulus as a function of the angle of rotation (for example, Cooper and Shepard 1973); (b) duration of mental scanning as a function of the distance to be scanned (for example, Kosslyn *et al.* 1978); (c) and (d) time to check properties of objects as a function of the size of images (for example, Kosslyn 1975). Descriptions of the experiments again paralleled the order of the corresponding items in the questionnaire (Questions 8–15). The hypothesis of equivalence of images to perception, in terms of structure and processing, was suggested at several times in this passage as a likely interpretation for reported results.

Subjects participating in the experiment were first given printed instructions on how to complete the questionnaire they were about to receive. The instructions indicated that questions should be read one at a time, in order, and that subjects should check the appropriate answers. They were also instructed to rate the degree of certainty for each of their responses on a five-point scale (by circling the appropriate number, from 1 to 5). In order to avoid guessing, subjects were required to check the 'Don't know' response if they could not decide. Subjects received question forms, which consisted of booklets with one question per page. In the second stage, after completing the questionnaire, subjects received copies of the text, with instructions to read it at their own rate, as carefully as possible. Third, after reading the text, subjects were requested to complete the initial questionnaire again. At the end of the experiment, the experimenter answered subjects' questions and described the exact purpose of the experiment. A total of 148 subjects (34 male, 114 female) participated in the experiment. They were students in psychology, enrolled as first-year students, and native speakers of French.

Appendix 1 shows the response patterns for the fifteen items of the questionnaire, resulting from the first completion (before studying the text) and the second completion of the questionnaire (after the text). We will concentrate here on the analysis of items which consisted in predictions of experimental outcomes. Overall, responses following the text show higher percentages of correct predictions than those given before reading. Not surprisingly, the subjects revealed their capacity to process new information and to incorporate it into previous knowledge, in some cases substantially revising their representations of the phenomena under discussion. However, our point here is not so much to evaluate the overall efficiency of the text in enriching people's knowledge on the subject of mental imagery, but to compare the response patterns for items on which subjects initially possessed valid knowledge, on the one hand, and for items on which subjects were not aware of actual phenomena. More specifically, on these latter items, we wanted to detect the efficiency of the text as a function of individuals' initial state of knowledge and degree of certainty, as reflected by the first completion of the questionnaire.

As expected, questions correctly answered by large numbers of subjects on the first completion of the questionnaire received high, close-to-maximal rates of correct responses on the second completion, with only slight increases of the initial rates (Questions 2, 3, 4, 6, and 7). In all these cases, rates of incorrect responses and of abstentions were negligible on the second completion of the questionnaire. In addition, the subjects who responded correctly to these items on both completions of the questionnaire exhibited a significant increase in degree of certainty as regards their responses. If we look, for example, at Question 3, which concerns the effects of imaging on learning word-lists (see Table 8.1), not only did the vast majority of subjects respond positively on both completions of the questionnaire – that is, for these subjects, the text provided confirmation of their available initial knowledge – but the average certainty ratings of these subjects increased significantly (from 3.94 to 4.43; $t(127) = 6.13$, $p < 0.001$). The same pattern emerged for all four other items. Thus the text, in these cases, while essentially providing readers with information they had available before reading, nevertheless demonstrates actual effects.

Table 8.1 Response patterns for Question 3 (effects of imaging on learning word lists)

| | | Second Completion | | | |
		Yes	No	Don't Know	Totals
	Yes	128	0	5	133
First	No	7	2	0	9
	Don't know	6	0	0	6
completion					
	Totals	141	2	5	148

More interesting in our view were the response patterns to the questions which initially elicited low rates of correct prediction. In this case, the effect of the text is the most apparent, although, on the whole, final rates of prediction still remain lower than those corresponding to the above-mentioned questions. This is the case for Question 5 (effects of imaging on learning motor skills), which is the question that received the lowest rate of correct predictions after reading the text (see Table 8.2). Similar to the effect previously observed, among the few subjects who answered affirmatively on both completions of the questionnaire, certainty increased significantly (from 3.18 to 3.91; $t(21) = 2.81$, $p < 0.02$). Another result of interest is that, among subjects who answered negatively on both completions – that is, who rejected the information provided to them by the text – certainty of their negative responses nevertheless demonstrates a significant decrease (from 4.08 to 3.33; $t(39) = 4.17$, $p < 0.001$). In other words, they showed that they had taken into consideration the information provided by the text, but they did not go one step further and appropriate this information.

Similar patterns are observed for the four items dealing with image-processing (Questions 9, 12, 14, and 15). First, all show that even for those mostly counterintuitive imagery phenomena, it is possible, with an appropriate text, to modify the initial state of belief of subjects substantially, although slight signs of resistance to modification may still be observed for some individuals, reflected, for example, in a relatively stable abstention rate on certain questions. Table 8.3 gives, as an example, the response patterns for Question 12 (mental scanning). The effect of the text was particularly evident here, in that the proportion of the correct predictions increased from 9.5 to 80.4 per cent. As previously observed, subjects who made correct predictions on both completions

Table 8.2 Response patterns for Question 5 (effects of imaging on learning motor skills)

| | | Second Completion | | | |
		Yes	No	Don't Know	Totals
	Yes	22	1	1	24
First	No	66	40	8	114
completion	Don't know	6	2	2	10
	Totals	94	43	11	148

showed increased certainty (from 2.77 to 4.38; $t(12) = 2.61$, $p < 0.05$). On the other hand, subjects who gave initially incorrect predictions and persisted in the same responses after reading the text nevertheless exhibited a significant lowering of their certainty ratings at the second completion (from 4.05 to 3.10; $t(20) = 2.71$, $p < 0.02$). This latter finding shows that even those subjects who reject counterintuitive information regarding imagery phenomena show that their certainty nevertheless wavers when they have to process corresponding information.

Further analyses concerned the certainty of positive responses on the second completion as a function of the nature of the response given on the first completion. Subjects who responded affirmatively right from the start produced higher certainty ratings on the second completion than subjects who first answered negatively (4.38 vs. 3.73; $t(75) = 1.86$, $p < 0.08$). Thus, people who changed their opinions in accordance with facts provided by the text still reflected doubt through the moderate degrees of certainty expressed for their final responses. Another result of interest was finding certainty of negative responses on the first

Table 8.3 Response patterns for Question 12 (mental scanning)

| | | Second Completion | | | |
		Yes	No	Don't Know	Totals
	Yes	13	1	0	14
First	No	64	21	2	87
completion	Don't know	42	0	5	47
	Totals	119	22	7	148

completion of the questionnaire to be a function of the nature of responses on the second completion. Subjects who first responded negatively and who maintained their negative response on the second completion initially produced higher certainty ratings than subjects who later gave affirmative responses (4.05 vs. 3.17; $t(83) = 2.44$, $p < 0.02$). Thus, higher certainty ratings for incorrect responses on the first completion of the questionnaire indicate lower probabilities for subjects to accept new (correct) information conveyed by the text, whereas lower degrees of certainty facilitated acceptance of such new information. These findings suggest that in a learning procedure, people having erroneous belief or representation of a given notion and who express high certainty as to this belief should receive more active guidance from an instructor than people with wrong beliefs and low certainty.

The comparative analysis of both questionnaires demonstrated that people differ not only in their initial beliefs concerning images, but also in their ability to accept modifications of initial beliefs, when given new information contradicting these beliefs. Such cognitive flexibility may well be dependent on various factors. Our questionnaire provided us with information regarding one of these potential factors, namely, subjects' responses reflecting their conviction that psychology can investigate mental images scientifically (Question 1). Would it be the case that people expressing this opinion demonstrate better acceptance of information which contradicts their initial beliefs than people who are dubious with respect to this idea?

We compared two subpopulations – that is, one group of subjects who responded to Question 1 positively on the first completion of the questionnaire (here briefly characterized as 'confident' subjects) and another group, composed of those who responded negatively ('non-confident'). Within these two subpopulations, we looked more particularly at performances of subjects who had initially made erroneous predictions for the outcomes of the five most counterintuitive experimental situations (Questions 5, 9, 12, 14, and 15), and we computed the probability of these subjects changing their responses for correct ones, once they had read the text.

On the question concerned with the possible effects of imagery on motor learning (Question 5), this probability was 67.2 per cent for 'confident' subjects, and 31.3 per cent for 'non-confident' ones. The corresponding figures were 72.5 and 40.0 per cent, respectively, for the question concerned with duration of mental scanning as a function of the distance to be scanned (Question 12). They were 69.4 and 22.2 per cent, respectively, for the second question concerned with the time necessary for verifying properties of objects as a function of image size (Question 15). All these differences produced significant chi-square values ($p <$ 0.05 or less). For Question 9 (mental rotation) and 14 (verification of properties), the differences were not significant.

These results are illustrative of a highly general phenomenon: simple exposure of subjects to facts that contradict their beliefs does not entail their automatically making up their minds to adopt new beliefs. More general beliefs that make more or less likely the acceptance of new information must also be taken into account. Confidence in the scientific approach to psychological phenomena is one such 'general belief'. In a sense, it is equated here with confidence in the authors of the text presented. For any kind of text, it is probably true that some kind of 'contract' has to be reached between reader and writer in order for maximal information to be transmitted. This is certainly truer for domains like imagery where knowledge is contaminated with intuitions and ill-founded beliefs.

The conclusions as to the effectiveness of the text used here, for modifying beliefs about images, should be supplemented with the following considerations. First, the second completion of the questionnaire took place only a short time after subjects read the text – that is, when the text's effectiveness is likely to have been maximal. It would be interesting to investigate long-term effects of such a text, especially as regards questions dealing with topics on which the text provided readers with new, counterintuitive information. There is scant, but nevertheless suggestive, evidence that people can use what they have learned about imagery processes – and, more generally, about elaborative processes – provided they have already actually practised strategies relying on such processes in previous situations (cf. Paivio and Yuille 1969; Pressley 1982; Pressley *et al.* 1984).

Second, the text used here was considered as a first step in the elaboration of a computer-assisted procedure by which specific, individualized texts are constructed as a function of the initial state of knowledge of specific individuals. The text is now part of a conversational system containing interspersed questions, which presents only those passages of the text giving subjects the information they lack, and which skips passages corresponding to information that subjects already possess or may infer, with on-line computation of the text to be presented, as a function of subjects' current states of knowledge.

A conversational version of the text on mental imagery

The conversational version used the previously constructed text, with questions interspersed throughout the text and the entire material being presented on a computer screen. The questions were those questionnaire items which required prediction of experimental outcomes. For each question, the computer program was designed to evaluate the response given by the subject as well as the rate of certainty expressed by the subject, this resulting in a step-by-step evaluation of the subject's knowledge. Immediately after the evaluation of the response given to a specific question, the computer delivers a piece of text adjusted to the current knowledge of the subject. When knowledge revealed by a given question is evaluated as satisfactory, the reader receives a correct-answer message, and the program proceeds to the next question. When knowledge is evaluated as unsatisfactory, the program delivers the piece of information judged to be missing on the basis of the subject's response.

What are the advantages of such a conversational version of the text? The first advantage of this system is the individualization of the information provided to readers, with exact adjustment of this provision of information to each individual reader. The obvious interest here is that readers who possess given information will not have to devote time to the processing of that information. Most of the reader's cognitive activity will thus be devoted to the processing of new information. The other expected advantage of such a system relies on the fact that it is not necessary to conduct an exhaustive evaluation of reader's knowledge before the instructional phase begins. At every step of evaluation, the reader receives appropriate new information (or confirmation of information already possessed by the reader), which is expected to facilitate the use of just-processed information in the understanding of further questions. The consequence would then be that readers are in a position to transfer rapidly newly processed information to upcoming steps of text processing.

In the case of our questionnaire, we observed that overall, knowledge was better for the first part of the questionnaire (items concerning the effects of imagery) than for the second part (items concerning image-processing). In addition, in the standard condition of questionnaire completion, when responding to a given question, subjects did not receive any feedback as to the correctness of their response. In the conversational version, subjects' responses to questions were immediately followed by an appropriate piece of information. Furthermore, several passages emphasized the similarity of imagery processes to perceptual processes. One would thus expect that this information would be used, during the processing of the conversational version, as a basis for making adequate predictions for the most counterintuitive imagery phenomena. We could thus expect that subjects from the same population as those used in the previous experiments would exhibit better ability to predict the actual outcomes of imagery experiments, relying on their earlier integration of correct information provided through the conversational version, and appropriate transfer of this information to the new experimental situations they have to examine and to reason about.

In the conversational version, the evaluation of a response to a given question leads to one of the following two cases:

(1) The response is considered as acceptable by the program if (a) it corresponds to the actual outcome of the experiment described, and (b) the reader expresses a high rate of certainty (≥ 4 on the 5-point scale). In this case, the subject only receives a short message confirming his or her response, and the program moves to the next question.

(2) The response is evaluated as non-acceptable in all other cases (correct response with certainty rating lower than 4; wrong response; abstention). In this case, the subject receives a piece of text describing the actual experimental outcome in detail; only then does the program proceed to the next question.

This procedure thus produces a large variety of 'pathways' through the text, with a large number of different, individualized texts generated for each reader. Thirty subjects were presented with the conversational version. Their responses to the ten questions requiring predictions were compared with those of a control group of thirty subjects who completed the standard version of the questionnaire. The response patterns of these control subjects were quite similar to those of the larger sample investigated earlier (Appendix 1).

In the first part of the questionnaire (Questions 2–7), few differences were observed between the rate of correct predictions to items presented in the conversational version and in the standard questionnaire (see Figure 8.1). Percentages of correct predictions are highly comparable. They only tend to be slightly higher, although non-significantly, in the Conversational Version group than in the Standard Version group for Questions 4, 5, and 7. Chi-square tests revealed a significant difference

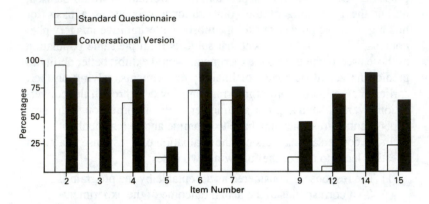

Figure 8.1 Rate of correct predictions in the conversational version and in the standard questionnaire.

only in the case of Question 6 ($p < 0.01$). Later on in the series of questions concerned with image-processing, there is a more pronounced advantage for the group using the conversational version. Percentages of correct predictions are markedly higher for Questions 9 ($p < 0.01$), 12, 14, and 15 (in all three cases, $p < 0.001$). The clear superiority of the Conversational Version group over the control group, as readers go through the questionnaire (whereas the two groups were equivalent at the initial items of the questionnaire), should be taken as resulting from the readers' use of information provided during the conversational version, and from transfer of this information to initiate the appropriate reasoning about the most counterintuitive questions.

In short, the conversational version of the text seems to be especially appropriate for instructing readers about mental imagery. First, it allows for a close adjustment of a text to the specific cognitive needs of each reader, as computed by the program which controls version-sequencing. Second, it creates favourable cognitive conditions for the use of information provided in order better to understand unusual experimental situations and to make appropriate conjectures about them. This version thus seems more appropriate to enhancing readers' knowledge about imagery phenomena than the standard questionnaire–text–questionnaire procedure initially used.

Conclusion

Why develop efforts to investigate people's knowledge about images? And why develop efforts to enhance such knowledge? As to the first question, there are arguments for the informational value of meta-cognitive research on imagery. One draws on researchers' current interest in individual imagery differences and more specifically in the analysis of imagery ability into specific components (for example, Kosslyn *et al.* 1984; Poltrock and Brown 1984; see also Chapter 2 of this volume). In addition, the 'analytical approach' to imagery abilities is orientated towards identifying the different levels on which a person can be qualified as being a 'high imager' (cf. Katz 1982, 1987). First, people differ in terms of basic imagery *skills*, such as those postulated in Kosslyn's modular theory (see Kosslyn *et al.* 1984; Chapter 2 in this volume). On the second level, people may also differ in their proficiency to *use* and to control their use of these capacities. On a higher level, people differ in their *preference* for using these skills rather than others (regardless of the appropriateness of calling upon mental imagery in a given context). On a still higher level, people differ in their *beliefs* as to the effectiveness of imagery in cognitive processing. Clearly, this 'level' analysis takes into account people's metacognitive knowledge about imagery, which is considered to be an intrinsic component of individuals' imaginal-processing capacities (cf. Denis, in press). Furthermore, the relevance of a metacognitive approach to imagery with respect to the 'tacit knowledge' account of imagery phenomena has been discussed earlier in this chapter (see also Denis and Carfantan 1985, 1986).

With regard to the valid reasons for developing people's knowledge of images, it is likely that simply enhancing knowledge would be sufficient as an objective (for example, in academic curricula: see Keenan and Keller 1980). However, we believe that enhancing people's awareness of mental imagery should encourage its actual use, even in situations in which its effectiveness has not yet been widely recognized. This is the case, for instance, in domains as diverse as second-language learning (Paivio and Desrochers 1981; Desrochers 1982), acquisition of motor skills (Feltz and Landers 1983; Denis 1985), and behaviour modification (Cautela 1977). While it is far from our intention to promote the notion of some universal 'magical' power of mental imagery, it is our contention that people can benefit from considering images as useful cognitive tools, but must also learn to identify those situations to which imagery processes are suited and those in which other modes of thinking are more efficient.

Appendix 1

Questions 1–15 and their response patterns (in percentages) on the first and second completions of the questionnaire

	1	2
Question 1.		
Do you think psychology can investigate mental images scientifically?		
(a) Yes:	54.1	83.8
(b) No:	13.5	10.1
(c) Don't know:	32.4	6.1

Imagery and learning (Questions 2–5)

Question 2.

When you ask a group of people to learn a list of concrete objects (or pictures of such objects) and another group to learn a list of the names of these objects, which of the following results would you generally expect?*

(a) Learning is better for individuals who have been shown the objects:	85.1	86.5
(b) Learning is better for individuals who have been shown the words:	2.7	0.7
(c) Learning is the same in both conditions:	8.8	10.1
(d) Don't know:	3.4	2.7

Question 3.

Does forming visual images of the objects named in a list generally facilitate the learning of the list?*

(a) Yes:	89.9	95.3
(b) No:	6.1	1.4
(c) Don't know:	4.1	3.4

Question 4.

Do people with special aptitude for forming mental images generally have better scores in word memory tests than people with poor aptitude for imagery?*

(a) Yes:	62.8	91.9
(b) No:	18.2	4.7
(c) Don't know:	18.9	3.4

Question 5.

Are there cases in which simply imagining oneself carrying out a new motor skill is enough to be capable of executing this skill correctly later?*

(a) Yes:	16.2	63.5
(b) No:	77.0	29.1
(c) Don't know:	6.8	7.4

Imagery and reasoning (Questions 6–7)

Question 6.

In general, when people have visualized the spatial relationships among objects described to them, are they more capable of answering questions about the relative positions of these objects later?*

(a) Yes:	71.6	95.3
(b) No:	7.4	2.0
(c) Don't know:	20.9	2.7

Question 7.

Is it generally the case that forming mental images helps in solving logical problems?*

(a) Yes:	66.2	93.2
(b) No:	13.5	4.1
(c) Don't know:	20.3	2.7

Mental rotation (Questions 8–11)

Question 8.

Generally, is it possible to visualize the rotation of
an object in space?

(a) Yes:	76.4	95.3
(b) No:	9.5	2.0
(c) Don't know:	14.2	2.7

Question 9.

When people are asked to imagine an object rotating
through 60° or the same object rotating through
120°, which of the following is generally observed?*
If it takes a given time to imagine a 60° rotation for
one object,

(a) it takes longer to imagine a 120° rotation:	14.9	76.4
(b) it takes less time to imagine a 120° rotation:	21.6	4.7
(c) it takes the same time to imagine a 120° rotation:	40.5	14.9
(d) Don't know:	23.0	4.1

Question 10.

When people imagine the rotation of an object in
space, is it generally the case that the object is
visualized as passing through all the intermediate
positions?

(a) Yes:	24.3	75.7
(b) No:	54.1	19.6
(c) Don't know:	21.6	4.7

Question 11.

Can mental images be said to occur and to undergo
transformations in a mental medium possessing the
same properties as physical space?

(a) Yes:	13.5	65.5
(b) No:	33.8	17.6
(c) Don't know:	52.7	16.9

Mental scanning (Questions 12–13)

Question 12.

When people are asked to inspect a mental image, is it generally the case that the time it takes to scan between any two points is proportional to the distance to be scanned?*

(a) Yes:	9.5	80.4
(b) No:	58.8	14.9
(c) Don't know:	31.8	4.7

Question 13.

Can the structure of mental images be said to reflect the spatial organization of the objects they refer to?

(a) Yes:	32.4	82.4
(b) No:	33.8	10.1
(c) Don't know:	33.8	7.4

Verification of properties of objects in visual imagery (Questions 14–15)

Question 14.

When people are asked to visualize a given object either in very large-sized or very small-sized images, and to verify whether a specific detail is present in each image, which of the following is generally observed?*

(a) It takes longer to verify the presence of a detail in a very small-sized image:	23.0	84.5
(b) It takes longer to verify the presence of a detail in a very large-sized image:	10.8	4.7
(c) It takes the same time in both cases:	52.7	8.1
(d) Don't know:	13.5	2.7

Question 15.

Suppose people are asked to visualize an object X beside a much larger-sized object Y. Or suppose these same people are asked to visualize the same object X beside a much smaller-sized object Z. In each case the subjects are asked to verify whether some specific detail is present in the image of the object X. Which of the following is generally observed?*

(a) It takes longer to verify the presence of a detail in the image of X when X is beside Y:	18.9	68.9
(b) It takes longer to verify the presence of a detail in the image of X when X is beside Z:	13.5	14.9
(c) It takes the same time in both cases:	45.3	11.5
(d) Don't know:	22.3	4.7

Note: The original version was presented in French. No headings appeared on the questionnaire administered to the subjects. Those items requiring prediction of experimental findings are marked with an asterisk.

Appendix 2

English version of the text used

Mental imagery

Mental life is peopled with images, which occur not only in dreams and memories, but also in many forms of thought and reasoning. Early in this century, the study of mental images was central to psychology. When imagery later became a controversial issue, the major trend was to reject all study of mental phenomena, and concentrate instead on behaviour, the sole objectively observable aspect of human activity. Over the last decade, however, experimentation has been carried out which makes indirect observation of mental images possible. Two main orientations have developed in research, the first concerned above all with the function of imagery in human thought processes, the second, more particularly with the nature and internal organization of mental images.

All the experimental data presented in the sections below are based on large-scale samples, and the results have been consistently confirmed in works by a number of psychologists. They may, therefore, be considered as highly susceptible to generalization.

Illustrating the first line of research are experiments comparing imagery and perception, that is, situations in which concrete objects are simply called to mind by individual subjects, and situations in which these objects are physically present and visible to the individuals. The question is the following: Can visualizing an object possibly affect a person in the same way as directly perceiving that same object?

Studies bearing on this question were first carried out in the field of learning, since it is well established that direct perceptual contact with concrete objects is highly conducive to their memorization. In particular, many experiments have shown that retention is better for lists of real objects (or their photographs) presented to individuals, than for lists of names of the same objects. What would happen if subjects were told to learn a list of words by visualizing each of the objects included in it? Results show that in this situation, people who have imagined the objects attain levels of memorization equal to those of people who have actually seen the objects (or their photographs). These findings suggest that in this particular task, images have a function equivalent to that of perception. In addition, in this type of word memory test, subjects with very high aptitudes for forming mental images (according to their responses on specialized tests) perform better than subjects with low aptitudes for mental imagery.

Another type of research demonstrates, for another aspect of learning, how images can substitute for a person's direct contact with objects. Subjects were asked to practise gymnastics on horizonal bars mentally. Five minutes a day, six days in a row, they were to 'see themselves' performing each of the movements described to them. None of these subjects had any prior training on horizontal bars. Immediately subsequent to this period of mental rehearsal, subjects were tested for the quality of their physical performance. Subjects with the highest aptitudes for forming mental images proved to be better than subjects with low aptitudes for mental imagery. Other studies, in which subjects were instructed to imagine themselves playing basketball, or throwing darts, indicate that in some circumstances, mental practice gives results almost equal to those obtained through physical practice.

Still another field of activity in which mental imagery is put to use is reasoning. When the spatial relationships of several objects are described to an individual (for example: 'The mirror is to the right of the picture, above the shelves'), and when this person is later asked to indicate the location of each object on a drawing, or judge the accuracy of a statement (such as : '... so the shelves are to the right of the picture'), subjects who formed mental images during the initial presentation do better on the tests than subjects who had no recourse to mental imagery. Advantages due to mental images are not confined to spatial reasoning; these latter can also play a part in deductive reasoning. Take, for example, the following problem: Jack is richer than Peter; Peter is not as poor as Alan; which of the three is the richest? Wealth can be visualized as a vertical axis, along which the three protagonists are located, as their relative status is described in the problem. Experiments have shown that subjects told to form such mental representations for the data involved in the problem, and those who construct this type of representations spontaneously, all solve problems more rapidly and with fewer error than other subjects.

From these examples it is clear that each of us can make efficient use of mental images in many sorts of situations. Now let us examine the nature and organization of mental images. Here too, studies show that properties inherent to images are highly similar to those of perceived objects.

One means of studying these properties of images consists in observing their characteristics during performance of a task which involves bringing about some change in mental imagery. If subjects are presented with tilted capital letters (as, for example, the letter R tilted to the left at an angle of 30° – or 60°, 90°, or 120°), these subjects can then be required to decide as quickly as possible whether the letter can be set upright by simple rotation, and superimposed on an upright letter R (indeed, in some cases the letter not only is slanted sideways, initially, but also mirrors its normal counterpart, and so cannot be directly matched over it). Most subjects state that they are able to visualize the rotation of the letter.

The most interesting finding in this experiment is that the greater the initial slant – and thus the greater the angle of rotation required to make it coincide with the upright figure – the longer the response time. This seems to indicate that subjects indeed turn the letter sideways in their imaginations, causing it to pass through all intermediate positions, exactly as if they were rectifying the position of the page on which it was printed. Just as is the case in making a concrete object rotate physically, the larger the movement of rotation required to set the image of the tilted letter straight, the more time it takes to accomplish the mental rotation. Thus, in our minds, images apparently behave like 'models' of objects around us, and we handle these 'models' as though they were the objects themselves. This probably does not imply that the space in which images appear in our minds is real physical space, but rather indicates that they occur in a mental medium which shares certain functional properties with physical space.

Some researchers have also attempted to identify the properties of images by examining the nature of characteristics which these 'mental pictures' have in common, for example, with real pictures or photographs. If mental images resemble pictures or photographs, not only must they contain information, but also they must preserve ratios of distances between different parts of the depicted object. Several experiments have shown that images preserve this kind of information. The method employed here is as follows. Subjects are asked to inspect their mental images, and the time necessary for such scanning is used as a test measure. If images depict objects accurately, then the greater the span between the different parts of the object, the longer it should take to scan.

In one of these experiments, the subjects have to observe and to memorize the map of an imaginary island, which contained seven target points (a hut, a well ...), situated in such a way that all twenty-one distances separating the various objects are different. After the memorization phase, the experimenter removes the map, and asks the subjects to picture it mentally, concentrating on one particular target point. The name of another target point is then mentioned, and the subjects are asked to state whether this point is present on their 'mental maps'. Findings indicate that the time it takes subjects to answer this question is exactly proportional to the distance they have to scan on the map. This suggests that in all likelihood, subjects conduct an actual survey of their 'mental maps', and that these maps contain the same information about distances as the real map. The claim is therefore justified that mental images have a structure which reflects the internal (spatial) organization of objects.

Other experiments emphasize still other similarities between imagery and perception, both of which are subject to the same constraints, as, for example, constraints linked to the apparent size of objects. Perception studies have clearly shown that it is more difficult to distinguish details of an object in a photograph of small dimensions than in an enlargement. In one experiment on images, subjects were trained to visualize an animal – a cat, for example – in different-sized images: very large, large, medium-sized, small. Subjects were then asked to verify whether the animal in question had some particular attribute, whiskers, for example. The smaller the size of the animal visualized, the longer subjects took to 'perceive' such details.

In another experiment, certain subjects were instructed to form the mental image of a cat alongside an elephant; the cat then appeared very tiny. Other subjects were to form images of a cat beside a fly; this time, the cat appeared very large. When the subjects had to check whether the cat had whiskers (or any other attribute), it took the subjects in the first group longer to answer than those in the second group.

Distinguishing details within images is therefore more difficult when they are very small, exactly as is the case in perceiving real objects.

The studies presented here emphasize the similarity between imagery and perception. Of course, such similarity in no way entails that the experience of imagery and the experience of perception are strictly identical, nor that they would engender confusion in people's minds. Resemblances between imagery and perception attest more particularly to the fact that people's aptitudes for mental imagery are dependent on their perceptual activity. Research in neuropsychology has shown that imagery and perception follow similar pathways in the nervous system.

Acknowledgements

This research was funded by a grant from the Agence de l'Informatique to a research programme on individual regulation of comprehension and cognitive acquisition, Contract No. 81/168, Project EAO No. 257. Preparation of this chapter was supported by the Groupement Scientique CNRS No. 040660, 'Activités Cognitives et Conduites Complexes'. Thanks are due to Connie Greenbaum for assistance during the preparation of the manuscript.

References

Cautela, J. R. (1977) 'Covert conditioning: assumptions and procedures', *Journal of Mental Imagery* 1: 53–64.
Cooper, L. A., and Shepard, R. N. (1973) 'Chronometric studies of the rotation of mental images', in W. G. Chase (ed.) *Visual Information Processing*, New York: Academic Press.
Denis, M. (1975) *Représentation imagée et activité de mémorisation*, Paris: Editions du CNRS.
(1979) *Les images mentales*, Paris: Presses Universitaires de France.
(1985) 'Visual imagery and the use of mental practice in the development of motor skills', *Canadian Journal of Applied Sport Sciences*, 10: 4S–16S.

(in press) 'Cognitive and metacognitive approaches to visual imagery', *Zeitschrift für Psychologie*.
and Carfantan, M. (1985) 'People's knowledge about images', *Cognition* 20: 49–60.
(1986) 'What people know about visual images: a metacognitive approach to imagery', in D. G. Russell, D. F. Marks, and J. T. E. Richardson (eds) *Imagery 2*, Dunedin: Human Performance Associates.

Desrochers, A. (1982) 'Imagery elaboration and the recall of French article–noun pairs', *Canadian Journal of Psychology* 36: 641–54.

Di Vesta, F. J., and Ross, S. M. (1971) 'Imagery ability, abstractness, and word order as variables in recall of adjectives and nouns', *Journal of Verbal Learning and Verbal Behavior* 10: 686–93.

Ernest, C. H., and Paivio, A. (1969) 'Imagery ability in paired-associate and incidental learning', *Psychonomic Science* 15: 181–2.

Feltz, D. L., and Landers, D. M. (1983) 'The effects of mental practice on motor skill learning and performance: a meta-analysis', *Journal of Sports Psychology* 5: 25–57.

Frandsen, A. N., and Holder, J. R. (1969) 'Spatial visualization in solving complex verbal problems', *Journal of Psychology* 73: 229–33.

Katz, A. N. (1982) 'What does it mean to be a high imager?' in J. C. Yuille (ed.) *Imagery, Memory, and Cognition: Essays in Honor of Allan Paivio*, Hillsdale, NJ: Erlbaum.
(1987) 'Individual differences in the control of imagery processing: knowing how, knowing when, and knowing self', in M. A. McDaniel and M. Pressley (eds) *Imagery and Related Mnemonic Processes: Theories, Individual Differences, and Applications*, New York: Springer-Verlag.

Keenan, J. M., and Keller, R. A. (1980) 'Teaching cognitive processes: software for laboratory instruction in memory and cognition', *Behavior Research Methods and Instrumentation* 12: 103–10.

Kosslyn, S. M. (1975) 'Information represented in visual images', *Cognitive Psychology* 7: 341–70.
(1980a) *Image and Mind*, Cambridge, MA: Harvard University Press.
(1980b) 'Les images mentales', *La Recherche* 11: 156–63.
Ball, T. M., and Reiser, B. J. (1978) 'Visual images preserve metric spatial information: evidence from studies of image scanning', *Journal of Experimental Psychology: Human Perception and Performance* 4: 47–60.

Kosslyn, S. M., Brunn, J., Cave, K. R., and Wallach, R. W. (1984) 'Individual differences in mental imagery: a computational analysis', *Cognition* 18: 195–243.

Le Ny, J. -F. (1983) 'Belief and knowledge in man and machine', paper presented at a conference on 'The Man and the Machine', London.
and Denhière, G. (1982) 'Profile of CINNA: construction of individualized texts', *Text* 2: 193–210.

Mendoza, D., and Wichman, H. (1978) '"Inner" darts: effects of mental practice on performance of dart throwing', *Perceptual and Motor Skills* 47: 1195–9.

Meyerson, I. (1932) 'Les images', in G. Dumas (ed.) *Nouveau traité de psychologie*, Tome II, *Les fondements de la vie mentale*, Paris: Alcan.

Paivio, A., and Desrochers, A. (1981) 'Mnemonic techniques in second-language learning', *Journal of Educational Psychology* 73: 780–95.

Paivio, A., and Yuille, J. C. (1967) 'Mediation instructions and word attributes in paired-associate learning', *Psychonomic Science* 8: 65–6.

—— (1969) 'Changes in associative strategies and paired-associate learning over trials as a function of word imagery and type of learning set', *Journal of Experimental Psychology* 79: 458–63.

Paivio, A., Rogers, T. B., and Smythe, P. C. (1968) 'Why are pictures easier to recall than words?' *Psychonomic Science* 11: 137–8.

Poltrock, S. E., and Brown, P. (1984) 'Individual differences in visual imagery and spatial ability', *Intelligence* 8: 93–138.

Pressley, M. (1982) 'Elaboration and memory development', *Child Development* 53: 296–309.

Levin, J. R., and Ghatala, E. S. (1984) 'Memory strategy monitoring in adults and children', *Journal of Verbal Learning and Verbal Behavior* 23: 270–88.

Pylyshyn, Z. W. (1981) 'The imagery debate: analog media versus tacit knowledge', *Psychological Review* 88: 16–45.

Shaver, P., Pierson, L., and Lang, S. (1975) 'Converging evidence for the functional significance of imagery in problem solving', *Cognition* 3: 359–75.

Shepard, R. N., and Cooper L. A. (1982) *Mental Images and their Transformations*, Cambridge, MA: MIT Press.

Yates, F. A. (1966) *The Art of Memory*, London: Routledge & Kegan Paul.

Chapter nine

The photographic image

Liam Hudson

In this chapter, I am going to discuss certain photographs, and will invite you to inspect them. My aim in so doing, beyond the pursuit of pleasure, is primarily conceptual: for while it poses puzzles, the appeal of photography, I believe, is open to analysis; and this analysis, in turn, gives us a better grip on the notoriously slippery notions with which the processes of representation and imagination are surrounded, both inside and outside the arts.

Three puzzles posed by photography as a genre

There is a sense, of course, in which the photograph, like the painting, is a trick and an illusion. Amateurs discover this the moment they start to print for themselves, dodging and burning in, using soft paper and hard. However, the photograph carries us well beyond these relatively assimilable aspects of representational illusion to ones that are harder to put into words. Some seem at first sight questions of technology and of the properties of the central nervous system. Others are more matters of interpretative nuance, and seem to belong to the critic. Yet more raise issues of social behaviour: intellectually, the province of the social psychologist. However, the tendency of each of these aspects of the photographic illusion is convergent, or so I am going to argue. They lead us from quite different points of departure towards the same cluster of imaginative preoccupations. I shall discuss each in turn, and then sketch in some more general implications about the shape that the study of the photographic image might in future take.

Because the facts are reasonably accessible, let me start with three puzzles we face when we consider photography as a whole. These interlock, I want to suggest, and should be taken together, not piecemeal:

(1) movement is often conveyed more vividly in a still photograph than in a moving one;
(2) in still photography, black-and-white seems on the whole preferable to colour as a medium of serious expression; whereas
(3) in painting, the reverse is true, colour being on the whole superior to black-and-white.

The perception of movement

It scarcely needs saying that, as creatures, we are continually on the move, and the world around us too. Even when looking at something inert (a ruin, say), our gaze wanders ceaselessly across it, and our vantage point alters as we wander around it. With people, it is on every nuance and inflection of their movement that our attention concentrates. It is no surprise, therefore, that the moving images of cinema and television screen should engross us. And yet there is a paradox. Individuals differ, naturally: in their sophistication, and in their preference for visual images as opposed to the written word or to music. However, it is the case, often, that a sense of movement is more vividly present in a still image than in a moving one; and not just movement *per se*, but its attendant emotions of excitement, say, or awe.

There are, it has to be said, unresolved puzzles of a purely technical nature at issue here. A sprinter may be frozen in full stride at 1/4000th of a second, every detail clear, and yet a sense of movement may be absent. At the other extreme, a longish exposure of a man walking can create the illusion of movement in pure and abstracted form, Otto Steinert's 'Walking on One Foot' being a famous example (see Plate 9.1). Sometimes the illusion works, sometimes not. It seems in practice to depend on a curious alchemy in which sharp detail, blurring, camera angle, depth of field, composition, posture, and facial expression can all play a part. These details do not detract from the point being made, though – that, when the alchemy is right, the sense of movement conveyed by a still photograph often has more conviction than that conveyed by a moving one.

What is so remarkable about such effects is not that they are perceived by everyone but that they are perceived at all. In the realm of movement, one would expect the moving image of television and cinema to surpass the still photograph in every respect and on every occasion. This does not happen. With some viewers, the reverse is true, the effects being more marked, I would hazard, the more visually sophisticated the viewer in question. (An oddity of photography, incidentally, is the aplomb with which the visually unalert cast themselves in the role of expert witness. If the tone deaf were to do the same in music, their views would be dismissed out of hand.)

Colour versus black-and-white

There is an analogous surprise over the question of colour. As Halla Beloff (1985) remarks, while popular photography is in colour, serious photography is in black-and-white. Why? There are obvious explanations but none, I think, is entirely convincing. The most superficial exploits the notion of snobbery: the common herd enjoys colour, so the real pros resort to black-and-white. Also pertinent is the fact that colour film is brightly ameliorative, yielding an array of tints that, by the standards of the painter, are crude.

More interesting is the question of control. Colour printing is best done in a commercial laboratory, whereas black-and-white printing photographers can easily do for themselves. Even more telling is the impossibility, in the familiar technology, of manipulating a photograph's colours, one patch at a time. Within narrow limits, you can remove an orange cast from an image as a whole; you cannot leave the rest of the image as it is and turn a patch of orange into a patch of pink. There are games to be played with air brushes, and one can hand-tint black-and-white prints, but both activities are marginal, some remarkable images notwithstanding.

As with the perception of movement, there are doubts and qualifications. Colour, without question, is invaluable for certain sorts of photograph: those of flowers, for example, and those that convey subtle lighting effects (the play of early morning sunlight on a hillside, say). It is also the case that the aesthetic advantages enjoyed by black-and-white in still photography are less apparent in the cinema where, highbrow and popular alike, colour predominates.

In prospect, there is the likelihood, too, that the technologies of colour printing and computer graphics will merge. At least in principle, the photographer should soon be able to colour each cell of his digitized images at will. The extent to which this will be a genuine aesthetic liberation rather than a god-send to illustrators and designers is hard to foresee. My guess is that, despite the new-found freedom, black-and-white still photography will retain its special niche.

Again, why? In this context, photographers often invoke aesthetic ideas rather than purely technical ones. Thomas Hopker, himself a colour specialist, refers to black-and-white as the 'cleaner, more abstract medium' (Campbell 1981). Without wishing to put words into photographers' mouths, it does seem that the translation of our visual experience – coloured – into patterns of grey and black marks on white paper is one that exerts an unusual attraction. It seems to petrify that experience rather than merely recording, amplifying, or endorsing it. But, how is it that, if photographs invade our imaginations so effectively in black-and-white, paintings do so most convincingly in colour? The answer must be, I think, that photograph and painting bring quite different psychological mechanisms into play. The key lies in the photograph's curious *veridicity*. As Rosalind Krauss puts it, the photograph enjoys a 'special status with regard to the real', being a 'kind of deposit of the real itself' (Krauss and Livingston 1986).

The oil painting, in contrast, announces the intervening skill and sensibility of the artist. As spectator, you are made forcefully aware, often, of the artist's marks as paint: lumps and swirls of pigment standing out in 3-D on a canvas surface with, here and there, the odd hair trapped under the varnish. The same holds for what may seem at first sight to be an exception: the pencil drawings or etchings that we accept as perfectly satisfactory, in and of themselves, in black-and- white. We treasure these, but as members of genres that are subsidiary to the greater genre of oil painting; and we treasure them precisely because their creator's 'handwriting' is detectable in every line. These, like the oil painting's brush strokes, constitute a cryptographic language that intervenes between the spectator and the scene depicted; and, in that language, colour in an invaluable dimension.

A psychological explanation

Taking stock, then, it seems that the psychologist must come to terms with at least three categorical distinctions vis-à-vis the visual image:

Still	versus	Moving
Black-and-White	versus	Colour
Machine-made	versus	Handmade

These three pairs of categories yield eight possible cells: the image, for example, that is Still, Black-and-White and Handmade is the pencil drawing; the image that is Moving, Coloured and Handmade (at least after a fashion) is the modern cartoon film. The categories also identify anomalies: the etching that is, at one and the same time, both Handmade and Machine-made; likewise the photorealist painting, based on a photograph and executed with an air brush, or the black-and-white photograph that is hand-tinted. Similarly, there are films which have some episodes in black-and-white, some in colour; and others – Resnais's disquieting 'Night and Fog', for instance – which combine still and moving images within the same sequence. The psychological significance of an image alters radically, the evidence suggests, as we move from cell to cell; and special significances may result when familiar distinctions between cells are blurred.

Such alterations of significance demand an explanation, however, and the germ of an explanatory story is to be found, I think, in the perception of movement. For while our perception of movement, 'out there' in the everyday world, is smooth and continuous, our internal perception of movement is quite different; movement, that is to say, as it appears in reverie, hallucination, dreams, fantasies, and the imagery accompanying orderly thought. Such movement is erratic, anomalous. What we see on our private cinema screens, in 'the mind's eye', has the character, often, of *tableaux vivants*, in which a sense of movement is present, but at the same time paradoxical and odd.

Especially pertinent to photography are those reveries and fantasies that are consciously entertained but are to some extent involuntary, and are emotionally charged. Typical are erotic fantasies: one thinks, for example, of Stoller's (1979) account of his patient Belle and the images of ritual humiliation that were, for her, a concomitant of sexual excitement. The movement in such scenes has several facets. There is the sense of movement trapped, as it were, within each *tableau*. There is narrative progression from one *tableau* to the next. And there is the ebb and flow of excitement within the spectator.

As explanation of what might be meant by the notion of movement 'trapped' within a *tableau*, one resorts to analogies, none of which is entirely satisfactory. It is unclear whether the 'entrapment' is, at one extreme, a question of intelligence and construction, or, at the other, one of brain physiology. Perhaps most helpful is the sense of movement present in experimental demonstrations of the *phi* phenomenon. If two lights, side by side in the dark, are flashed on and off alternately, and if the rate is gradually increased, there comes a point when we perceive only one light, moving from side to side; and then, with a further increase, another point where we perceive both lights on continuously, but – an eerie experience – with a sense of movement trapped between them.

For the present purpose, the explanation is less important than the fact itself: that, whatever the cause, our internal perception of movement is quite unlike our external perception. One might hypothesize that what goes for movement goes for colour, too: that both are perceived internally as if they were illusions or sleights of hand. On such an argument, colour might present itself on our private cinema screens not naturalistically, but more in the manner of a black-and-white photographic print that has been stained with dyes. The *tableaux* of the inner eye thus 'contain' movement and colour, but detached from literal movement and literal colour.

If our fantasies and imaginings really are expressed in terms of *tableaux vivants*, two explanations of the appeal of the still, black-and-white photograph come immediately to hand, one much better than the other. The more obvious is that such photographs echo the mode of perception – the imaginative mode – that matters to most of us most. The photograph is a fantasy made public, its interest being not so much its content, though this too may echo our imaginings, but its *form*.

As it stands, though, this will not quite do. Its clear implication is that photographs will appeal to us most when, like our imaginative imagery, they are in significant respects indirect, elusive, or indistinct. In fact, the reverse is the case. Many of the photographs that we find most compelling are in sharp focus, sharper by far than almost all our everyday perception. However, this awkwardness provides a stepping-stone to a second, and better, explanation – namely, that still, black-and-white photographs appeal to us because, at one and the same time, they present the kind of image we would otherwise expect to see only on our private cinema screens, *and* they resolve the cardinal anxiety with which such internal imaginings are plagued: our inability to *scrutinize* what we see before us. The appeal of the photograph is thus two-fold: it creates a public iconography of the kinds of image we see otherwise only in our imaginations; and it renders such images literal, turning them into public entities that wait for us with limitless patience while we gather strength to confront whatever challenge to our sensibilities they might contain.

If this is granted, the different roles played by colour in still photography and painting cease to be so surprising. The entry of colour into the terrain explored by the still photograph is bound, if I am right, to have the character of an invasion. While such invasions are not necessarily undesirable, they are bound to be tricky, the basic traffic of that terrain being one in which both colour and movement are figments.

Photographic reality

So the still, black-and-white photograph has singular properties. As Krauss suggests (Krauss and Livingston 1986), the photographic negative is a 'take' rather than a 'representation' of the people and places to which it has momentarily been exposed. It seems to have been peeled off those people and places like an extra membrane or skin. As a 'deposit of the real itself', it has unusual powers: looking at an Atget of a Paris street, you are aware, reassuringly, of the 'thinghood' of the material world, the sense of its persistence apart from the perceptions and imaginings of human agents, an illusion heightened rather than muted by the translation from multi-colour to black-and-white.

The photograph scores, too, in its particularity. While Goya's etchings convey war's horror in a generalized way, it is Robert Capa's photograph of Omar Bradley that shows us the curiously unathletic stance of the man, the precise quality of the flesh around his eyes, and the plaster on the end of the great man's nose, covering a recently lanced boil (see Plate 9.2). Less expectedly, perhaps, the photograph's particularity also makes it an ideal vehicle for nuances of mood. Looking at Doisneau's image of a coalman sharing a bar with bride and groom, black and white counterpoised, you become sensitive to the precise quality of a visual joke, and catch something, too, of what it was like to be French in the late 1940s.

Most forcefully of all, perhaps, the photographic image, a thing-in-itself and secure in its objectivity, can serve the spectator as stimulus for fantasy and metaphor. If you stare at Heinrich Riebesehl's image of a farm trailer in an empty field, loaded with sacks of potatoes, you at first see just that: trailer, empty field, sacks of potatoes (see Plate 9.3). Gradually, though, in my case at least, the sacks, one burst open on the ground, turn into something else: 'memories' of corpses never in fact seen, the flat field of Flanders battleground, often imagined but never in fact visited. And out of such partially grasped metaphors there develop in turn further more embracing ones, about our cycles of death and regeneration.

The still photograph is thus inherently paradoxical. From the photographer and printer's point of view, it is plainly an artifice; a wilful construction dependent on any number of choices and tricks. Yet as spectators, we find that all sense of such choices and tricks drops away. With a painting, there is characteristically an interaction or exchange: we look for a part of the image's surface to 'penetrate'. With the photograph, however, we plunge straight through, relating as directly to the world the photograph reveals as we would to that world itself. Like a painting or drawing, of course, a photograph can be a good or poor likeness; but there remains a challenge in the photograph that a portrait painting lacks. If a portrait painter fails to capture the essential 'something' about a person we know well, the failure, we assume, is the artist's. If a photograph does this, we ask ourselves, on the contrary, whether that fleeting 'something' might not really be there; a trick played on our senses by our sentiments.

If the novel is the 'laboratory of the narrative', as Michael Butor claims (Bradbury 1977), the still, black-and-white photograph is the laboratory of the *veridical*. In terms of the folk philosophies by which human scientists live, it is plain that photographic reality is comfortably compatible neither with red-necked materialism ('A-table-is-a-table-is-a-table') nor with the cultural relativism that sees all truths as culturally mediated constructions and nothing more. For photography is *both* a technology *and* a vehicle of self-expression and discovery: the bonds it creates between the photograph and the photographed are both mechanically mediated *and* imagined. What are at issue here are the terms of a marriage between science and art. It is a region of our experience undergoing an unprecedented change; and we will make sense of it, one supposes in terms of the values neither of science and technology nor of the social sciences, but of a stance equidistant from each.

In passing, it is worth noting that the adjective 'veridical' is itself helpfully ambiguous. It means truthful. It also refers to those insights that first reach us in dreams and reveries and are subsequently discovered to be true. It is just this movement between the actual and the imagined on which the photograph depends. It is a dependence, what is more, that already possesses a historical basis in the work of surrealist photographers like Man Ray.

Surrealism and its recent influence

Among the seas of surreal images produced between the two World Wars, now vaguely *outré*, there is a tiny minority that remain beautiful (some Man Rays, some Brassais), and a further minority, even tinier, that retain undiminished their original power to destabilize our experience, jarring it loose from its moorings. Rightly famous among the latter are Hans Bellmer's dolls, put together out of spare parts, posed in positions of provocation or violence, photographed in black-and-white, and then, often, hand-tinted (Krauss and Livingston 1986).

Analogous affronts are to be found more recently in the work of certain fashion photographers (Hall-Duncan 1979; Devlin 1984). At one level, the fashion photographers' purpose is pragmatic: to sell frocks. At another, their role is to create in the minds of those who read fashion magazines a climate conducive to psychic adventure and risk. Deborah Turbeville has taken pictures of women in a bathhouse that look like pictures of women in a gas chamber. Helmut Newton has shown, among a great many other things, a lesbian embrace between two young women in bikinis, the active of whom proves, on closer inspection, to be a dressmaker's dummy. Guy Bourdin has taken a photograph that purports to be the aftermath of a traffic accident, with limousine, dark stains on the pavement, and the chalk outline of a body to show where the victim fell. Scattered inconspicuously, out of focus, are the objects of the advertisement, her Charles Jourdan shoes.

It is of course not only the surreal image that can provide such access. Roland Barthes (1984) demonstrates this in his memorable *Camera Lucida*. There, discussing images that seem uncontentious, he argues for the distinction between 'studium' and 'punctum': on the one hand, the appreciation that assimilates an image to the intelligent and sensitive views about the world we already possess; and, on the other, the discovery of the image's power to 'wound' us – to open a rent in the fabric of our everyday understanding and bring less governable forces into play.

In two respects at least, then, the looking we do at photographs can be dangerous. The emotions photographs release in us, should our powers of civilized appreciation be punctured, will often be disquieting. And, beyond, there is the possibility that the very process of taking photographs and looking at them will turn into a scrutiny that is indecent. As Diane Arbus once said, 'I always thought of photography as a naughty thing to do . . . and when I first did it, I felt very perverse' (Sontag 1979). Even those whose images are categorically less cruel than Arbus's may feel the same. In photographing people we care about we petrify them, turning them, like Lot's wife glancing back towards Sodom as she flees, into pillars of salt.

Plate 9.1 Otto Steinert, 'Walking on One Foot' (1950)

Plate 9.2 Robert Capa, 'General Omar Bradley' (1944)

Plate 9.3 Heinrich Riebesehl, 'Schillerslage (Hannover), October 1978'

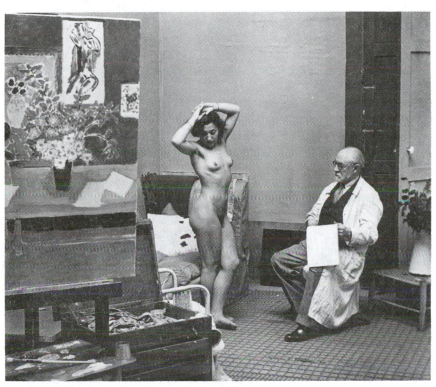

Plate 9.4 Brassai, 'Matisse with his Model' (1939)

Plate 9.5 'Bernadine, North Park – August 1986'

The point translates itself of its own accord into psychoanalytic terms. In his essay on Leonardo, Freud (1963) suggests that our curiosity about the facts of life is transformed into 'research' of a non-sexual nature, but claims that disturbing ambivalences will nonetheless continue to make themselves felt. In photography, where the focus on the body is often explicit, we return to precisely the issue from which, in Freud's view, we are all in flight: the Oedipal nexus and its incestuous reverberations.

The development of theory

If we are to make progress with phenomena as complex as these, we will have to be tidy. A number of interpretative themes or threads are evident in what has already been said:

(1) the power of the photograph to freeze or *petrify* experience (and that process's attendant gratifications and risks);
(2) the ability it gives us to *scrutinize* what is important to us, but is otherwise fleeting or indistinct;
(3) its ability not only to *contain* nuances of experience – to serve in Gass's (1976) phrase as 'containers of consciousness' – but,
(4) as Barthes stresses, to *puncture* the obscuring fabric of commonsense, and give us access to our own true feelings and needs.

At the heart of this nest of notions, and giving them their sense of family resemblance, there is yet another:

(5) that the photograph invites us to marry previously separate facets of our concern with what *is*, the imagined truth with the literal truth, veridicality in its personal and scientific forms.

In the midst of the conceptual activity surrounding the photographic image, two sorts of apperception, traditionally compartmentalized, can be seen to meet: public and private. It follows that if we approach the photographic image incautiously, expecting to use conventional bifurcations, we are bound to be nonplussed. Is movement in the *phi* phenomenon real or 'illusory'? Is Barthes's response to the photograph of his mother real or 'subjective'? Is the consciousness contained within any work of art – the spatial games being played in a Sickert, the wit in a Doisneau – real or 'ephemeral'? 'Well, yes and no', we are tempted in each case to reply. While the photograph is a convincing reference point

in distinguishing what is real from what is, variously, illusory, subjective, ephemeral, false, bogus, epiphenomenal, or what have you, it is still
a product of choice. And, as Degas liked to remind the world, all such
feats are conjuring tricks, accomplishments that demand as much 'cunning, trickery and vice as the perpetration of a crime' (Dunlop 1979).

A heuristic framework

Glancing, apprehensively perhaps, at such paradoxes, circularities, and
apparent contradictions, and at the nature of the critical literature,
decidedly flighty in tone, one might conclude that the photographic
image is not a proper topic for academic research. It seems to me, on the
contrary, that the field cries out for just those analytical skills, plain
rather than fancy, that the academy is best suited to provide. Especially
helpful at this early stage are frameworks designed to guide enquiry.
One is adumbrated in my *Bodies of Knowledge* (Hudson 1982). It
specifies the network of relationships, six in all, that spring into being
around any act of representation, and it can quickly be adapted to fit the
photographer:

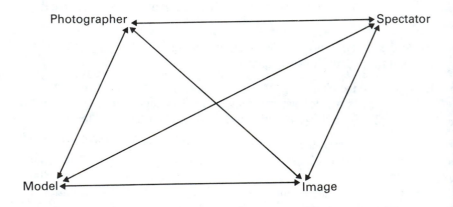

Of these six relationships, none is quite what it seems:

(1) *Photographer–Model*. Much enlightened comment about this
relationship is gloomy. Sontag (1979) says that 'to photograph people is
to violate them. . . . Just as the camera is a sublimation of the gun, to

photograph someone is a sublimated murder – a soft murder, appropriate to a sad, frightened time.' It is also widely believed that a relationship must be symmetrical, rather than reciprocal, before the parties to it can properly use it as a source of pleasure or gratification (Sontag again; and Berger 1972). The relation of any artist to any model must be asymmetric, however. Brassai's photograph of Matisse in his studio illustrates this (see Plate 9.4). Matisse turns his model into art, and then Brassai turns them both into art of another kind. To assume that such relationships are pathological, or that the pathological cannot be put to good use, is arbitrary; and it also flies in the face of the testimony of those most immediately concerned (for example, Edward Weston's conspicuously articulate model and his wife, Charis Wilson, 1977). Though often exploitative, like any other, the relationship between photographer and model can be one in which trust and affection as well as curiosity and risk-taking play parts. There are good psychoanalytic grounds, what is more, for suspecting that the relationship is imaginatively fertile precisely because – like those of the Oedipal nexus – it is asymmetric. With luck and judgement, both parties are poised (in a happy phrase that I think is Christopher Ricks's) to 'take in one another's wishing'.

(2) *Photographer–Image*. What most photographers want is not mere competence within an established genre but the ability to generate the right kind of shock or surprise; enduring rather than meretricious, and addressed to their own obsessing concerns rather than someone else's. Yet the obstacles they face are as often as not self-imposed; less grand questions of inspiration than humble habits and reflexes *vis-à-vis* camera and enlarger. It follows that they must somehow subvert their own rhythms of work, catching themselves unawares. If, in psycho-analytic terms, failures of self-expression are the product of repression, that repression seems characteristically to lodge in relatively lowly habits of eye and hand. Left undisturbed, they ensure that photographers go on producing images they do not much like, and their *oeuvre* becomes depressing: the record of an unsuccessful struggle to overcome avoidable and at times quite trivial constraints.

(3) *Model–Image*. In dealings with other people, we use their outward appearance as the format within which to lodge whatever we think or feel about them. We are well placed, therefore, to judge a photograph of them as a good or poor likeness, and as expressive or not of who – in our eyes – they really are. Confronted with an image of ourselves, we can only compare what we see with an unruly and shifting

mélange of impressions, some glimpsed in a mirror, some gleaned by introspection. It is perhaps for this reason that the camera is so often perceived as a threat. It is not so much that it offers unwelcome evidence; it is that the evidence it offers is so singularly non-negotiable.

(4) *Spectator–Image.* As its critics insist, this relationship can alienate, forming part of the envelope of unexperienced knowledge with which we protect ourselves from ourselves. In Sontag's (1979) words: 'Ultimately, having an experience becomes identical with taking a photograph of it, and participating in a public event comes more and more to be equivalent to looking at it in photographed form.' It is in this sense that the more we look, the less we see. For a minority, however, the 'photoerotic', visual images reveal hidden staircases and open trapdoors. Not for the first time, there seems to be a parallel of sorts between our apprehension of photographs and our apprehension of sex. While the sexual, like the visual, is a field within which familiarity often leads to boredom, there are couples, as Stoller (1976) remarks, for whom the reverse seems to be true. In both fields, one suspects, pleasure is commensurate with risk: the paradigmatically photoerotic Ruskin, it is worth remembering, succeeded in unhinging himself by gazing too long on horrors contained in Turner's painting *The Slave Ship* (Hudson 1982).

(5) *Photographer–Spectator.* Like the relationship of photographer to model, this too is asymmetric. While, idly, it is often assumed to be a question of 'communication', it is in practice more often one of take-it-or-leave-it. Even in those cases in which photographer and spectator know one another well, what passes between them usually seems potent when unacknowledged and even unacknowledgeable: a case of transaction between one unconscious and another via a public 'text' or 'sign'. Ruskin and Turner are again paradigmatic: Ruskin claimed *The Slave Ship* as the embodiment of his doctrine of Truth to Nature, whereas its special fascination for him seems more to have centred on death, madness, and revulsion from the human body.

(6) *Spectator–Model.* The strangest relationship of the six: a spectral meeting of a real person, the spectator, with another real person, the model, who has been turned into an object and turns back into a person in the mind's eye; flesh and blood that seems magically accessible, yet is out of reach. From the spectator's point of view, the model is a recruit to the cast of his or her fantasies; from the model's, the spectator is a fantasy creature, too – one of the audience who silently looks. Implausible though it may seem, it is on this bond between two people

who almost certainly know little or nothing of one another that the art of personal representation depends.

A virtue of this framework is that it invites comparison, the heart and essence, I would want to argue, of disciplined enquiry in the human sphere. We can compare the photograph with genres of representation apparently far-flung: the novel, biography. We can compare it with its more immediate neighbours: the cinema and painting. And we can make comparisons within still photography itself, not just between colour and black-and-white, but between one choice of subject matter and another. For while it is an assumption of the present framework that the model is a person, there remains a wealth of photography – of landscape, architecture, and still life – where human beings are present only by implication or absent ('still life', *nature morte*, in turn, providing photography with one of its more disquieting and psychoanalytically significant metaphors).

The framework also points us towards zones of the theory of representation ripe for further development. Two are especially inviting, apparently separate but in fact closely linked: one a question of social construction and control, the other that of the relation between what a photograph states and what it implies.

Social meanings and social roles: 'amateur' and 'pro'

Despite our astonishing laxity over what we watch on the television or cinema screen, or look at between the covers of glossy magazines, we are puritanically restrictive about the photographs we take for ourselves. Many of us want to take photographs that capture the intimacy of feeling that exists between ourselves and those we care about. Some also want to take photographs that are erotic or rude. Such images are however potent sources of unease; or more specifically – and the distinction is crucial – they are so long as we remain 'amateurs'. If we are 'professionals', the system of intuitive judgement that comes to bear is quite different. Not only are previous responses cancelled, they are in many instances reversed.

If we see, most of us, fully frontal and thoroughly sexual pictures by Edward Weston of the young and lovely Charis Wilson, what we see is a 'nude'. For a professional product, the work of a 'real' photographer, there already exists a niche in our minds, and no excuse or extenuating argument is required. Such images can perfectly well shock, but this shock is circumscribed. They do not lead us to assume that there is something wrong either with the person photographing, or with the person photographed. If anything, the ability to produce shocking images adds to the social cachet such professional image-makers enjoy.

The same holds for Lucien Clergue's images of young women in the sea. We accept these as the work of a great photographer, authenticated by the praise of Cocteau and Picasso. We may know, as a matter of fact, that his earliest works in this remarkable genre were taken, much as we ourselves might take them, in a spirit of sexual curiosity, when he was still very young and no less an amateur than the rest of us. All that is of only passing interest. The legitimating cloak of his subsequent career protects him from our censure, and protects us from our own embarrassment.

Likewise, again, if the body we look at belongs to the former Mrs David Bailey: Marie Helvin is a professional model, her former husband a professional photographer. The fact that some of his images of her seem perverse, the one, for instance, in which she appears, tied in string and newspaper, as a naked parcel in an attic, causes us only a containable ruffle of unease.

The amateur/professional distinction, plainly, is dependent on the process of publication. If a photograph of his wife taken by an amateur is published even in a context as arcane as the present one, it acquires the rudiments of legitimacy. As an image, it starts to move across the inner landscape from amateur and embarrassing towards the 'real' (see Plate 9.5).

However, while real photographers and their models enjoy liberties (and we enjoy liberties with regard to them) from which ordinary mortals are banned, there is also a sense in which such professionals are depersonalized in our imaginations, and in which we treat them not so much as real people but as 'personalities'. Yet ordinary people, *real* people, distrust the legitimacy – the 'realness' – of their own experience and greedily borrow the experience of professionals as their own. We behave, in other words, as though we are in the grip of a radical antithesis between two sorts of reality: our realness as people and the realness of our experience. The result is, again, a paradox. Ordinary people treat as real the experience of someone (the professional) whom they assume to be unreal; and they treat as unreal the experience of people like themselves (amateurs) whom they assume to be real in just the ways that they are.

The linguistic philosopher can rush in at this point and explain to us what we already know: that the adjective 'real' is being used here in quite different senses, and that we are threatening to turn semantic complexity into semantic porridge. Conversely, we might reply, reasonably enough, that ambiguities in the use of centrally placed adjectives and nouns – 'real', 'truth', 'illusion' – are valuable to us in as much as they serve as signposts, pointing to powerful ambivalences at work: dangerous games being played, elusive syntheses sought.

The given and the implied

The photographic image has a social context, then, the semantics of which invite close inspection. Its significance lies not in what is stated but in what is implied, the stock-in-trade of the social psychologist.

The distinction between implied and given also expresses itself more formally, however, within the frame of the photographic image itself. In Renaissance painting, and even in the art of the nineteenth century, it was usual for artists to present their audiences with an array of visually arresting and symbolically significant elements. They did this with more or less cunning: see, for example, Quentin Skinner's (1986) analysis of the political propositions implicit in Ambrogio Lorenzetti's famous Sienese frescoes, and my own account of Titian's *Venus and the Organ Player* (Hudson 1982). In our own time, however, visual images are offered to the spectator more minimally, their force being dependent not so much on the quasi-literary meaning of what is given as on the relation of what is given to what is implied or absent. This tendency plays upon an answering appetite in the spectator for what is hidden: as Lacan puts it, 'what I look at is never what I wish to see' (Wright 1984).

In shorthand, the representational work of art, of which the still photograph is, for analytic purposes, an especially helpful instance, poses for the spectator relationships of three basic kinds:

(1) Given : Given
(2) Given : Implied or Absent
(3) Implied or Absent : Implied or Absent

The nature of this distinction between the given and the implied or absent becomes clearer if one compares a conventionally composed image with a more minimal one: Brassai's photograph of Matisse and his model with, say, a Ralph Gibson nude – little more than a glimpse of arms, thighs, breast, and stomach, viewed at close quarters and foreshortened by means of a portrait lens. In the Brassai, to take a telling detail, the *gaze* is given: Matisse stares fixedly at his model, just as the organ player stares fixedly at the naked Venus in Titian's painting. In the Gibson, no one is shown to be looking or staring. But we become aware, nonetheless, of the fixity of the gaze that must have played on this naked body through the camera's lens; and, empathetically, as we look at the image, that gaze becomes our own. In the Gibson, in other words, the gaze is implicit. It is not just a nude, but a nude as the object of obsessive observation.

The special interest of photography in the context of such relationships and distinctions is that what it asserts it asserts so non-negotiably, forcing us to concentrate all the more carefully on what is missing. What is it that lies just outside the photograph's frame? What happened just before the shutter clicked – and what will happen just afterwards? The very act of framing and freezing automatically creates in the spectator's mind, antithetically, an awareness of what the image omits. And, more and more, it is in these areas of implied knowledge that the modern photographer invites the audience to operate, never quite seeing what they want to see nor quite grasping what fascinates them most.

Borrowed theory

While recent developments in psychoanalytic theory help create a context for the discussion of the implications and absences in images like Gibson's (Lacan's commentary, for example, on *The Purloined Letter*: Wright 1984; and, especially, Bowie 1987), the reliance in such theorizing on linguistic models of the unconscious is inapposite. The idea that the signified is submerged irretrievably beneath the signifier, for instance, which makes good sense in literary contexts, serves to obscure just those aspects of the photographic image that require a particular delicacy of touch: the notion of the photograph as a 'deposit of the real', and the sense it can give of 'the thing itself'.

That there exist 'syntactical' – that is to say, formal but largely non-verbal – relationships not just within photographic images, but between them, is neatly demonstrated in Gibson's (1983) recent collection of juxtapositions. Images of light falling across the corner of a building and across a face; the soft shadow of a man cast against sharply defined architectural details and a nude, out of focus, against sharply focused waves; a portrait in which eyes and mouth are dark details in an otherwise white expanse of face and a wall of black tiles, their interstices catching the light: each pairing adumbrates the formal 'language' of the photographer, but it is one that can only with effort and ingenuity be translated into words and which remains at root visual.

Especially difficult for borrowed theory is the 'objectification' that the camera's gaze so effortlessly achieves (witness leaden-footed comments about photographs made by the otherwise preternaturally attentive William Gass, 1976). While the effects of objectification are sometimes reprehensible, as in the more sordid sorts of pin-up, the fact remains that this skill is at the heart of the visual artist's discipline, painter and photographer alike. It is just this quality of 'thinghood', what is more, optically and chemically mediated, that makes the photograph so potent. Images like Riebesehl's potato cart and Bourdin's traffic accident make claims on us that are unconscious, certainly, their reverberations running far and wide, but the unconscious they point to, stocked with 'thing-representations' as well as 'word-representations', seems nearer to Freud's or Jung's than to Lacan's. (Just as Lacan sought to rescue what Freud really meant from what his followers said he meant, there is now the task, as Bowie reminds us, of rescuing what Lacan said and meant from the gentle brooks of Lacanobabble.)

In sum, borrowed models of the mind should be examined not swallowed. The visual, and more specifically the photographic, far from being an outlying and backward colony of the Great Empire of the Word, is a thriving kingdom in its own right, with lessons to teach. In place of pre-emptive similes and metaphors – 'the unconscious is structured as a language' – we need taxonomy: the patient discrimination of one genre of imaginative expression from the next, and the clarification of the principles on which these discriminations depend. For while there are respects in which taking and printing photographs is like writing a paragraph, there are also respects in which it is like pursuits apparently quite distant: jazz improvisation, say; even cooking a meal.

References

Barthes, R. (1984) *Camera Lucida*, London: Fontana.
Beloff, H. (1985) *Camera Culture*, Oxford: Blackwell.
Berger, J. (1972) *Ways of Seeing*, Harmondsworth: Penguin.
Bowie, M. (1987) *Freud, Proust and Lacan*, London: Cambridge University Press.
Bradbury, M. (ed.) (1977) *The Novel Today*, London: Fontana.

Campbell, B. (ed.) (1981) *World Photography*, London: Hamlyn.
Devlin, P. (1984) *'Vogue' Book of Fashion Photography*, London: Thames & Hudson.
Dunlop, I. (1979) *Degas*, London: Thames & Hudson.
Freud, S. (1963) *Leonardo da Vinci*, Harmondsworth: Penguin.
Gass, W. H. (1976) *On Being Blue: A Philosophical Inquiry*, Boston, MA: Godine.
Gibson, R. (1983) *Syntax*, New York: Lustrum.
Hall-Duncan, N. (1979) *The History of Fashion Photography*, New York: Alpine.
Hudson, L. (1982) *Bodies of Knowledge*, London: Weidenfield & Nicolson.
Krauss, R., and Livingston, J. (1986) *L'Amour Fou*, London: Arts Council.
Skinner, Q. (1986) 'Ambrogio Lorenzetti: the artist as political philosopher', *Proceedings of the British Academy* 72: 1.
Sontag, S. (1979) *On Photography*, Harmondsworth: Penguin.
Stoller, R. J. (1976) *Perversion*, London: Harvester.
—— (1979) *Sexual Excitement*, New York: Pantheon.
Wilson, C. (1977) *Edward Weston Nudes*, New York: Aperture.
Wright, E. (1984) *Psychoanalytic Criticism*, London: Methuen.

Chapter ten

Imagery and affect: big questions, little answers

Susan Aylwin

Discussion of the relationship between imagery and affect is likely to lead one into a morass trodden around the approach to Big Questions. Big Questions enchant. They present themselves as specifiable scientific questions, but they tend to be permeated with (usually unspecified) human and philosophical questions.

The current most salient Big Question on the relationship between imagery and affect, or more generally on the relationship between cognition and affect, is the question of which comes first. Some theorists hold that cognitive processing has priority and that we must conduct at least some 'cognitive appraisal' before affect is possible (Arnold 1960; Lazarus 1982). Others (especially Zajonc 1980) hold that affective processes have priority and may operate in almost total independence of cognition. The vigour with which the ground around this question has been trodden suggests that it is not scientific knowledge alone that is at stake, but something more fundamental: who we are. Within the debate about which comes first, cognition or affect, lurks an avatar of the nineteenth-century debate provoked by Darwin's evolutionary theory, about whether we are the offspring of the angels or the beasts. If cognition comes first, we are capable of rationality and self-control; if affect comes first, we are the victims of our bodily inheritance and have a degraded moral worth.

When so much is at stake it is difficult to keep one's feet on the narrow empirical path. Compounding the problem is the enchantment of the heavyweight terms, 'cognition' and 'affect', which encourages some direct and cover-all formulation of the relationship between them, and which tends to blind one to the fact that cognition and affect are both generic terms, denoting species rather than individuals. Cognition utilizes representations which are themselves complex, using a variety

247

of different cognitive structures and occurring in different modalities. Affect is also complex, ranging from simple evaluations to a wide range of emotions, each of which consists of a number of components.

This chapter breaks down the question of the relationship between cognition and affect by looking first at some of the different kinds of mental representations and their characteristic cognitive structures, and by then looking at how different kinds of affects and emotions map on to these.

Levels of representation

Empirical work on representations has tended to take one of two alternative directions: either concentrating on phenomenal representations and on surface properties such as vividness; or focusing on structural properties of representations without regard to surface manifestation, as in many studies of semantic memory.

Zajonc and Markus (1984) suggest that work on affects shows a related divergence between research on the *experience* of affects and emotions, which requires conscious representations; and research on the *expression* of affect, which may in at least some circumstances occur without conscious processing.

It seems likely that a full account of the relationship between cognition and affect will require not only integration of research traditions between the two areas, but also an integration between the two levels within each area.

On the cognitive side, integration of the two aspects of representations into a full theory has not been encouraged by Pylyshyn's (1973) argument that imagery and other surface representations are in fact epiphenomenal, mere by-products of processing which takes place at a deeper structural level. Pylyshyn thus raises a second big question – namely, 'Does imagery have a functional role?' – which he answers by saying that in his opinion it does not. This question is in turn an aspect of an even bigger question – namely, 'Does consciousness of any kind have a functional role?' While the question of the function of images or other conscious representations arises in the cognitive domain, it is clearly also a question of importance in the affective realm. Techniques of cognitive behaviour-modification assume that manipulating conscious cognitions can alter affective processes (for example, Bandura 1977; Beck *et al.* 1979). Critics of such approaches (for example, Wolpe 1978) assume that no such cognitive mediation is necessary.

Pylyshyn's argument that imagery does not have a functional role rests on the assumption that all real cognitive business is transacted in terms of abstract and *amodal* propositions at a level inaccessible to consciousness. In other words, cognitive processing takes place in terms of structures which have no intrinsic connection to any particular surface form of representation.

There is some empirical evidence which casts considerable doubt on the validity of this assumption, as it shows that different surface forms of representation are in fact specialized for representing particular kinds of cognitive structures.

Structures in verbal, visual, and enactive representations

Evidence from developmental psychology suggests that there are three main forms of representation – enactive, visual, and verbal, each originating in a different period of childhood:

At first the child's world is known to him principally by the habitual actions he uses for coping with it. In time there is added a technique of representation through imagery that is relatively free of action. Gradually there is added a new and powerful method of translating action and image into language, providing still a third system of representation.

(Bruner 1966:1)

The three systems of representation begin as ways of interacting with the real world, and gradually become internalized, so that as adults we have three different though interconnected forms of representation available to us: *verbal representation,* or inner speech; *visual imagery,* or 'pictures in the mind's eye'; and *enactive imagery,* a kind of imagined action or role play.

All three forms are available for a wide variety of tasks. When reading a novel, some people will mutter the words to themselves under their breath and rely mainly on inner speech; some will follow the plot through pictures in their mind's eye; and some will identify with hero or heroine and follow the plot through imagined identification and action. Most people can switch their strategy depending on what they are reading: verbal representation for abstract and technical matters, visual and enactive representations for good escapist fiction.

The characteristic structures of verbal, visual, and enactive representations have been elucidated in a series of association studies by

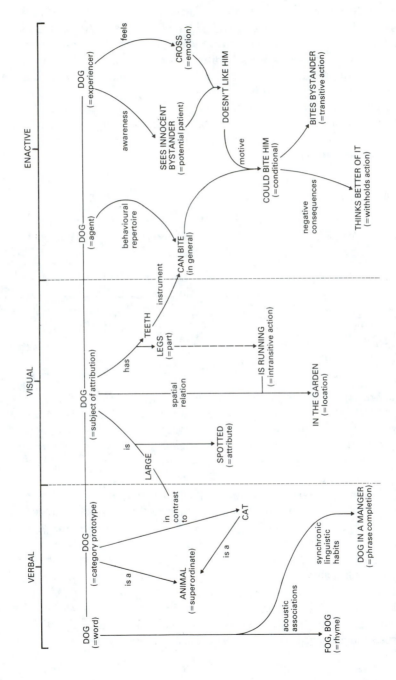

Figure 10.1 Cognitive structures in verbal, visual, and enactive representations

Aylwin (1977, 1981, 1985). In these studies people were given a stimulus word or sentence, and asked to represent it in one of three ways: using verbal representation (repeating the stimulus subvocally), using visual imagery (conjuring up a mental picture), or using enactive imagery (imagining themselves to be identified with the object or situation referred to). They were then asked to free associate to the stimulus as represented. Content analysis of the associations showed that each form of representation is characterized by a particular set of cognitive structures, as shown in Figure 10.1.

Verbal representation yields associations which indicate that it is specialized for representing hierarchical conceptual structures. Thus, the stimulus 'dog' may give rise to the superordinate 'animal', and also to the oppositional or contrast response 'cat'. These two structures are enough to define a taxonomy in which two concepts differentiated at one level in the taxonomy (dog and cat) are seen as related at the superordinate level (both are animals). Taxonomies deal with generic concepts and typical examples and do not allow much scope for imaginative departures from the constraints of the conventional. Subjects using verbal representation draw on conventional and typical knowledge in producing their associations, unlike visual and enactive subjects who show much greater imaginative freedom.

Verbal representation also shows signs that in it words rather easily become detached from their referents, with associations being generated either on the basis of well-established linguistic habits, as when the stimulus 'April' gives rise to the phrase-completion response of 'showers'; or on the basis of rhymes, as when 'weasel' elicits the association 'easel'.

Visual imagery shows a static spatial organization. It is particularly specialized for articulating objects in terms of the relationship between whole and part (as when the stimulus 'squirrel' gives rise to the response 'tail'), and the relationship between object and attribute (as when the stimulus 'gorilla' elicits the response 'brown'). Furthermore, visual imagery fills in the background of these articulated entities, using object-environment structures, as when 'boat' evokes 'harbour'. The most basic version of the object-environment relationship is expressed in terms of a simple spatial relationship ('the dog is in the garden'), with additional specification being possible in terms of intransitive action ('the dog is running in the garden'). The tense of the intransitive verbs used in such cases is almost invariably the present continuous, which has the *is* verb*ing* form. This suggests that visual images tend not to depict actual movement but rather capture static snapshots of movement.

Enactive imagery is, like visual imagery, a nonverbal form of representation. Its characteristic structures are however quite different. Enactive imagery is specialized for representing the temporal and affective aspects of the stimulus. In it actions are frequent, expressed in the use of transitive verbs (as in 'the dog bites the postman'). This transitivity gives the enactive image a spatial structure, but one quite different from that found in visual imagery. In the visual image the space is absolute, defined by a framework, the environment, within which objects are suspended and through which the spatial relationships between objects are mediated. Enactive space is relative, there is no environment, and spatial relationships are direct, through the action which links agent with patient.

In enactive imagery there appears to be a much more dynamic representation of action than is found in visual imagery (see Chapter 6 by Engelkamp and Zimmer in this volume). This is indicated by the predominant verb tenses, which include the ordinary present (as in 'the dog bites the postman') and the use of future and conditional modes ('the dog will or could bite the postman'). In enactive imagery there is a temporal perspective which allows a foresight absent from the static and spatialized time-perspective of visual imagery. This temporal perspective of enactive imagery extends to include the possible consequences of action. These consequences may be either physical, as when the stimulus 'dropping something' elicits the response 'broken'; or affective, as when 'slicing' elicits 'ouch!' Occasionally, action is withheld because its consequences are foreseen as being undesirable.

Enactive imagery provides an insider's perspective on situations, and allows access to subjective aspects opaque to subjects using verbal or visual representations. Enactive subjects frequently give associations referring to feelings and emotions, and these are sometimes used as reasons for and justifications of action, as in the 'the dog feels cross, so he bites the postman'.

Cognitive structures as features of internal attention

The association studies show that verbal, visual, and enactive representations are characterized by particular sets of cognitive structures: verbal representation is characterized by superordinate and oppositional structures; visual imagery by whole-part, object-attribute, and object-environment structures; and enactive imagery by affective and transitive action structures. The existence of these non-arbitrary relationships between surface representations and cognitive structures indicates that structures are not neutral with regard to surface represent-ation, and are not therefore as amodal as Pylyshyn (1973) claimed.

Particular surface forms of representation afford the associative use of particular cognitive structures, and to that extent the surface representations are not mere epiphenomena, but have a functional role in cognition. This role has to do with the direction of attention, for the cognitive structures characteristic of each form of representation act to direct attention in the associative process.

Attention is normally studied in its external version, in terms of attention to the real world. William James (1890/1950) emphasized that attention may also be directed internally, and focused on the contents of the stream of consciousness. One neglected feature of both versions of attention is its dynamic nature. The attentional spotlight apparently cannot rest on any static focus, external or internal, for longer than the duration of the specious present (not longer than about half a second). Attention needs change. Externally this can be supplied either by a changing stimulus (as is provided by television, films, or speech) or by the saccades which shift the eyes and attention to a new aspect of the stimulus.

The movements of external attention are at least partially stimulus-driven. The movements of internal attention, however, must be internally driven. The association experiments can be considered as tapping the movements of internal attention, and showing that these movements follow the paths dictated by the cognitive structures characteristic of the form of representation being used. If someone first represents the word 'dog' to themselves in inner speech and then associates 'animal', that person's internal attention has moved along a pathway specified by the relationship of superordinacy. Similarly, if a person has a visual image of a dog and then gives the response 'brown', their attention has moved from object to attribute, exemplifying an object-attribute structure.

The structures characteristic of the three forms of representation are thus essentially descriptions of the moves that attention may make. Figure 10.1 becomes a map of the possible cognitive pathways down which attention may travel in each of the three modes of thought.

One of the advantages of interpreting cognitive structures in attentional terms is that recent work on attention can supply some leverage on the differences between the kind of processing that takes place at a conscious level, the level of mental representations, and the kind of processing that may take place outside of awareness. As Marcel (1983) points out, much thinking on this matter is contaminated with the 'Identity Assumption', the assumption that conscious processing is just preconscious processing writ larger, which is to say at a more highly activated level. This assumption is false. The difference between conscious and preconscious processing is not quantitative but qualitative.

One of the critical features of conscious processing is that it allows integration between different aspects of a representation, and thus the apprehension of unitary objects. Marcel claims that in preconscious processing the different aspects of a representation (for example, the form, the colour, and the name) are processed separately. Only in consciousness do they all come together in the representation of the object which possesses them.

Treisman's work (Treisman and Gelade 1980; Treisman and Schmidt 1982) points in the same direction. Features of the same object, such as colour and shape, are not processed conjointly outside the attentional focus, and may come apart to form 'illusory conjunctions'. Only within attention are features correctly conjoined in unitary objects. Attention integrates, preattentive processes do not.

Extrapolating this to the different cognitive structures found in verbal, visual, and enactive representations suggests that different representational instructions prime the integration of different aspects of the stimulus into the representation, and delineate the different paths that attention may take in the association process.

Imagery and affect in day-dreams, fantasies, and other idle thoughts

The association task is useful for characterizing verbal, visual, and enactive representations in terms of cognitive structures, but it is not ideal for elucidating the relationships between the different forms of representation and affect. One thing does emerge, however, and this is the fact that affective and other subjective constructs are most frequent in enactive imagery. This is in line with Lang's (1979) work, which shows that representations involving active participation are accompanied by more affective arousal (as indexed by physiological indices such as heart rate) than purely visual representations.

254

A more appropriate topic for revealing representation-affect relationships is that of day-dreams. Day-dreams are generally assumed to have an affective origin, yet to issue into consciousness wearing some palpable representational garb. Here, then, it might be possible to look at whether there are important relationships between the kind of affect expressed, and the form of representation that it is expressed in.

Toward this end a diary study was undertaken (Aylwin 1985) in which twenty-one people kept a 'Journal of Idle Thoughts' in which they recorded their 'day-dreams, fantasies, and other idle thoughts' for a period of ten days.

The idle thoughts were analysed into representational types using structural criteria arising from the association studies, the affective and other themes were extracted by content analysis, and the significant relationships between type of representation and affective theme were analysed using combined S tests (Leach 1979).

Verbal idle thoughts: criticism of misfits

A large proportion (68 per cent) of verbal idle thoughts were critical or belittling in tone, and of these many were critical of taxonomic misfits. One writer, for example, heard the phrase 'He's a darkie' on seeing a black student crossing the university campus. Another heard the phrase 'Hitler was right!' being repeated in his head on visiting a unit for handicapped children (implying that Hitler was right to want to kill all the handicapped people in Nazi Germany). A third heard the following while walking behind an odd-sized couple walking hand in hand: 'If she was only two feet smaller, and he was about four stone lighter, there may be some hope!!!!'

To be oversized for one's sex, or overweight, or black in a white community, or handicapped, is to be peculiar; and, as if that were not enough to cope with, it is evidently also to be the butt of rude remarks inside the heads of local strangers.

Verbal idle thoughts often shocked their recipient by expressing levels of prejudice to which the person him- or herself would in no way subscribe. This may be part of the reason for a second important feature of these idle thoughts, which is that the voice speaking them is frequently experienced as alien, as belonging to someone else, as if in an attempt to distance oneself from the prejudice expressed.

It may however be that the voices are in some real sense alien, and that they emanate from a conventionalized part of the psyche for which the individual cannot really be held responsible.

In the association studies, verbal representation emerged as characteristically conceptual in nature, exhibiting a hierarchical organization based on typical instances of categories. The focus of criticism in these verbal idle thoughts appears to be precisely those entities which do not fit within this conventional order, and which therefore constitute a threat to it. Criticism is a way of coping with those objects that would unwittingly subvert the foundations of the conceptual edifice.

That we do have difficulties in coping with ambiguous stimuli has long been known. Bruner and Postman (1949) showed that perception may break down when people are tachistoscopically presented with such unexpected things as playing cards showing red spades or black hearts. Pavlov's (1927) work on experimental neurosis in dogs goes further, in showing how under some circumstances behaviour may also disintegrate.

In anthropology also there is evidence that anomalous objects get special treatment. Edmund Leach (1964, 1969) claims that objects which are marginal with respect to major category boundaries tend to become taboo. Blood, urine, spittle, and nail and hair clippings all start out as *me* but end up as *not me*. They are thus ambiguous with respect to the major category boundary between self and world.

It may be that in order to make any sense of the world at all we must draw conceptual lines across it, yet because of the nature of that world there will always be some entities that are marginal with respect to the lines we have drawn. Criticism is one among a number of strategies for coping with these marginal cases.

There are typically no emotions as such manifest in the verbal idle thoughts, and affect is found only in the form of the negative evaluations implicit in the criticisms they express. The data suggest that verbal representation has a value system which favours order and conceptual tidiness (the prototypical), and has a distaste for (and hence shows criticism of) taxonomic misfits. What fits the conventional order is good; what departs from it is bad.

Visual day-dreams: social emotions and the importance of being seen

Visual idle thoughts correspond to most people's idea of a good day-dream, especially in their detail and in their frequently rosy tinted view of the world and of the self.

Like the images in the association studies, visual day-dreams frequently involve a detailed environment. This usually takes the form of a social environment, manifest in the group of friends or the sea of faces who constitute the audience before whom one appears, and through whose eyes one sees oneself. The affective emphasis is on social emotions. Thus, for example, someone just about to become a student teacher wrote:

> I began on my way home to imagine myself teaching in the school. I could feel the tension and nervousness beforehand and the embarrassment at certain things that could go wrong in the class. I could experience the relief at being regarded as a teacher and the fun it would be to have someone I knew in the class (the latter being quite possible).

Or someone imagines his own marriage ceremony: '. . . a feast of music and friends. I am particularly pleased with my cream linen suit. Now my rule begins and will be wise and carefree. Comment. Help!'

In visual day-dreams there are no strong emotions such as fear or anger, only social feelings such as pride, embarrassment, and the self-esteem that comes from being seen by others as good, competent, or beautiful. Not surprisingly, romance is a visual theme:

> I was simply listening to some songs by Olivia Newton-John and I began to imagine myself singing those songs dressed in a pure white dress and to a huge audience (as well as being televised). I was very well received and afterwards the agents were fighting to sign me but I already had an agent who was also madly in love with me . . . . The feelings are naturally pleasurable and make me feel comfortable.

In these day-dreams people see themselves as others see them, or especially as they would like others to see them. The feelings the day-dreamer experiences are the complement of the feelings or attitudes the audience is construed as experiencing: being admired as a teacher evokes pride; doing something stupid evokes embarrassment; being loved evokes pleasure and comfort.

These essentially social feelings arise out of some complex dialogue between two aspects of the self, both of which are present in many of the visual day-dreams: the *I* who experiences, and the *me* who is experienced by others.

Theorists such as Lacan (1977) and Mead (1934) see the existence of these two aspects of the self, and of the relationship between them, as fundamental to our sociability. There is some experimental evidence which supports their contention. This is the work on objective self-awareness initiated by Duval and Wicklund (1972) in an attempt to test some of Mead's ideas. People can be precipitated into a state of objective self-awareness in a number of ways – for example, by seating them in front of a mirror, or by having them perform in front of an audience. Once aware of themselves from the outside, people become acutely conscious of social evaluations, and tend to modify their behaviour in socially desirable directions. Visual day-dreams function in a similar manner, also endowing people with an objective self-awareness in which social desirability is important.

In the association studies visual imagery was shown to be characterized by object-environment, object-attribute, and whole-part relationships. In visual day-dreams these remain important, and become translated into a social form which engenders social emotions. The environment becomes a social environment, and the day-dreamer sees him- or herself through the eyes of the audience, as a social object with an appearance (parts and attributes). The feelings evoked depend on whether or not that appearance is deemed socially desirable.

Enactive fantasies: metamorphoses of being and feeling

Enactive fantasies are the most emotional of the three types, and display a full emotional range from joy to fear and sadness. Many of the negative emotions occur in conjunction with rather morbid themes, where people find themselves suddenly identifying with people seen, heard of, or read about who were in trouble of some kind – for example, reading about a woman dying of cancer and suddenly knowing what it would be like to be her; or seeing a destitute man on a night street and identifying with how he felt; or this:

> Blindness. We have a lecturer in the French department who is going – has nearly gone – blind. I frequently see him (I don't really know him) at lunch time . . . .

One day I was at lunch when he walked into the corner of a table and nearly dropped his tray – suddenly I found myself in the position of a blind man . . . .

Emotions – intrinsic – fear, I think, and helplessness. Evoked [by the fantasy] – envy of the sighted, anger, sadness at memories of past times of sightedness.

These compassionate identifications are not limited to the human realm. The following is an example from a zoologist showing equivalent empathy for a unicellular organism:

Death of a *Paramecium*. Cells die if they get too much calcium inside them. I have done experiments in which I have let too much calcium in *Paramecium*, a ciliated protozoan, and I have watched their death-throes under the microscope. Suddenly I found myself in their position, feeling 'discomfort' and 'anguish' of a condemned *Paramecium* moving in an uncontrolled way around the bottom of a petri dish.

The slightly bizarre and fantastic nature of this *Paramecium* example is typical of enactive fantasies. They are peculiar in that people experience themselves as metamorphosing into some quite other physical form, and of experiencing the emotions appropriate to that form. Thus, for one subject, being a dying *Paramecium* evoked anguish; for another, being a fish evoked joy in swimming; and for a third, imaginatively taking on the physical form of a bottle of Southern Comfort was conducive to drunkenness!

In addition to these enactive fantasies of metamorphosis, there was a second group which involved impulses to act:

Last night when I was watching TV I suddenly got this feeling I was going to grab the chair I was sitting on and throw it through the TV. A split second thought. For a brief second I felt like doing it.

These fantasies of action sometimes took on a mythological dimension, as in one subject's fantasy of becoming pregnant by eating roundworms.

Enactive fantasies in general reiterate the themes that emerged as characteristic of enactive imagery in the association studies. In both situations action is important and strong emotions are experienced. In the fantasy situation these themes are often translated into a highly imaginative form which may take on mythological dimensions.

Verbal, visual, and enactive representations as cognitive styles

Verbal, visual, and enactive idle thoughts show quite different affective concerns. Verbal idle thoughts are concerned with taxonomic order, and express criticism (showing tacit negative evaluation) as a way of coping with the misfits within that order. Visual day-dreams are concerned with social feelings, such as embarrassment, pride, or being loved, which derive from the opinion of others and the requirements of social desirability. Enactive fantasies are concerned with impulsive action and often involve imagined identification with people or objects in extreme situations. Strong emotions, positive or negative, frequently accompany such fantasies.

If different affective themes show up *within* individuals, depending on the mode of representation being used, it is tempting to hypothesize that they would also show up *between* individuals if one looked at the personality characteristics of individuals with a strong verbal, visual, or enactive bias.

This line of argument presupposes that verbal, visual, and enactive representations are cognitive style variables, an idea that has had a long history. Cognitive styles are usually seen as having both cognitive and affective aspects. Klein (1958), for example, working within the psychoanalytic tradition, describes cognitive styles as involving patterns of cognitive structures, with these structures being responsible both for making sense of reality and for channelling instinctual energy into it. A cognitive style thus has associated with it a particular way of channelling affect and hence a characteristic style of personality.

To test out the idea that there may be personality correlates of verbal, visual, and enactive styles of thinking requires an instrument. To this end I have developed the Modes of Thought Questionnaire (Aylwin 1985). The MOTQ is a 170-item questionnaire which assesses the extent to which people use thirteen types of cognitive structure, each of which was shown by the association studies to be characteristic of one of the three forms of representation. Thus, a person's propensity for using verbal representation is assessed through their use of rhyme, phrase completion, opposite, and superordinate structures; visual imagery is assessed through the use of environment, intransitive action, part, and attribute structures; and enactive imagery is assessed through the use of transitive action, conditional action, affective, physical consequence, and affective consequence structures.

To examine the personality and affective aspects of the three representational styles, three studies were undertaken (ibid.). The first used an adjective rating-scale with the MOTQ to give a general overview of personality; the second used the MOTQ with a battery of personality tests; and the third looked at representational biases in students in different faculties.

The data indicated that each form of representation is associated with a particular set of what Markus (1977) called self-schemata, and with a particular set of personality characteristics.

Those who make strong use of verbal representation in their thinking show a preoccupation with power: on the adjective rating-scale they describe themselves as *liking power*, as being *ambitious*, and, on the negative side, as having a *fear of failure*. The hierarchical order important at a conceptual level in the association studies and the idle thoughts study is important here in the form of the bureaucratic hierarchy in which verbalizers appear to feel most at home. The identity of the verbalizer appears to be tied up with status within the bureaucratic hierarchy, just as the nature of an object is tied to its location in a conceptual taxonomy. Power, ambition, and fear of failure are concomitants of this way of defining identity.

Generally, this way of defining identity seems to work well, giving people *high self-regard* on the Personal Orientation Inventory (Shostrom 1974), and (for men) an *internal locus of control* (Rotter 1966). One of the dangers of this form of self-definition is suggested by the finding that those who particularly enjoy using verbal representation show a significant correlation with *conservatism* on the Wilson and Patterson Attitude Inventory (Wilson 1975).

The study on representational biases between students in different faculties showed that commerce students tend to show a verbal bias, and this fits with the fact that careers in commerce, more than in many other professions, provide the hierarchical business framework in which verbalizers are at their best.

The social environment that was important in the visual day-dreams emerges here as also being an important feature of the visualizer's personality. Visualizers seem to get their sense of identity through being sensitive to others. They claim to be *sympathetic* and *protective*, and score highly on *social desirability* (Crowne and Marlow 1964). They also claim a *self-awareness* which, because it correlates specifically with the MOTQ environment subscale, suggests the external perspective on the self seen in the visual day-dreams.

Every way of defining identity has its own strengths and drawbacks. The advantage of defining identity in interpersonal terms is that the social sensitivity it fosters can give one a genuine role to play in the lives of others. The idea that visualizers possess considerable social skills is supported by work by Swann and Miller (1982), who found that people with vivid imagery possess the great social skill of actually remembering social information. The disadvantage of defining identity in terms of sensitivity to others is that visualizers are apparently also sensitive enough to worry that the identity may be largely external, a persona beautifully constructed but with little inside. This dark side of the visualizer is shown in such self-descriptions as *apathetic, insecure,* and *defensive* on the adjective rating-scale.

Interestingly it is social work and psychology students who tend to show a visual bias, and it seems entirely appropriate that a visualizer should find his or her best way of capitalizing on cognitive skills and affective needs within the helping professions. Furthermore, there is an unsurprising sex difference, with women scoring higher on visual imagery than men.

Enactive imagery, as might be expected from the enactive day-dreams, shows the most strongly emotional characteristics. These are shown positively in the enactive imager's *intensity* and *liking for risks,* and on the negative side by *aggression, inhibition,* and *suicidal thoughts.* The affective life of the enactive imager is bound up with a strong need for action and a distinct *solitary* streak. One gets the impression that these are strongly inner-directed individuals, *patient* and *inventive* when they have the freedom to do what they want, and *stubborn* and *aggressive* or *suicidal* when frustrated.

In general, men show a stronger tendency to use enactive imagery than do women, and in terms of personality correlates men tend to show the more positive and action-based aspects of the enactive personality portrait, with women faring less well. In terms of career choice, engineers (both sexes) tend to show an enactive bias, again showing an intuitive concordance between what a particular career may offer, and the cognitive capacities and affective needs the individual can bring to it.

Cognition, affect, and attention

The idle thoughts study and the personality work both show that different forms of representation are associated with different kinds of affects. Furthermore, in at least some cases the different affects can be associated with particular cognitive structures. Thus, there are positive and negative values associated with the hierarchical order specified by the superordinate and oppositional structures of verbal representation. In the case of conceptual hierarchies, atypical cases have low value and are criticized, and prototypical cases are (tacitly) evaluated more positively. In terms of the bureaucratic hierarchy the superordinate receives positive value. One is ambitious to climb to superordinate positions and fears the failure that would topple one from them.

In the visual domain social emotions are important. These occur in the context of the relationship to the social environment which acts as a mirror in which one sees one's appearance (parts and attributes) reflected. Positive feelings, such as pride or the sense of being loved, arise from the approbation of the audience; and negative ones, such as embarrassment, arise from behaviour or appearance which evokes the disapproval of the audience.

The enactive domain shows a strong relationship between action and emotion. The complexity of this relationship is elaborated further in phenomenological work on emotions (Aylwin 1985), which suggests that emotions are features of temporal perspective, and are particularly concerned with possibilities for the future. Negative emotions tend to be associated with threats to the future. When the future has been cut off, as in the sadness of bereavement, or as in depression, arousal and the need for action tend to be low. When the future is under threat but there is still some hope, as in fear or anxiety, arousal is high and there is a strong need for action. Positive emotions tend to be associated with the opening of the future. Love projects an endless and rosy future of happy-ever-after; and joy, for example at passing important exams, indicates that a future to which one had aspired is now within grasp. One can become who one wanted to be.

Each form of representation thus embodies both a set of cognitive structures and the affects which are their intrinsic complements. The three cognitive-affective perspectives can be encapsulated by saying that verbal representation is primarily concerned with conceptual order. Whatever fits that order is positively evaluated, and misfits are negatively evaluated. Visual imagery is primarily concerned with belonging, or social affiliation. Approval by others yields positive social emotions such as pride, and disapproval yields negative ones such as embarrassment. Enactive imagery stresses what Allport (1955) called 'becoming', the urge to aim towards some future self. Threats to these aspirations yield negative emotions, and their achievement yields positive ones.

The cognitive structures characteristic of each form of representation were earlier interpreted as having implications for attention. In each form of representation attention integrates different kinds of features into conscious representations and these differences affect the direction in which attention subsequently moves. A particular cognitive bias can be hypothesized to have a general priming effect on the kinds of features integrated within the attentional spotlight. A cognitive style can then be seen as a way of attending to objects and events, both internal and external, with each cognitive style emphasizing different features of situations and different kinds of affects.

A bias toward a particular representational style is not of course the only factor influencing attention. Attention is also called by stimulus-driven processes that are themselves preattentive. In at least some cases these preattentive processes are concerned with features of situations that happen also to have affective significance. Thus, novel features of the environment (which can be construed at some level to be misfits in the conventional order) call attention through the orientating response. Threats to one's continuing existence cause rapid arousal and avoidance reactions, a response which occurs even in young infants who show complex avoidance behaviour to looming stimuli (Bower 1974).

Zajonc and Markus (1984) see these physiological and motor responses as themselves having representational significance, representing affect without cognitive mediation. Such affective expressions may also attain a cognitive representation, and thus become part of the subjective experience of the affect, if they become the explicit focus of attention. Thus, Wegner and Giuliano (1980) have shown that arousal can induce self-focused attention, and Scheier and Carver (1977) have shown that self-focused attention can intensify the subjective experience of emotion.

The fluctuations of attention between situation and self can have important consequences for performance, as if the experience of affect and active coping were alternative and mutually interfering responses to affective situations. Early work on test anxiety by Alpert and Haber (1960) suggests that if attention is paid to the task, the arousal is integrated into performance and has a facilitative effect. However, if attention is paid to the arousal itself, it becomes a debilitating anxiety and performance suffers.

The different forms that affect takes in verbal, visual, and enactive representations may relate not only to the different cognitive structures involved, but also to the strength of the bodily or motor component, and whether or not it is sufficient to induce attention to focus explicitly on it. In the criticisms seen in the verbal idle thoughts, attention is called by some taxonomically odd feature of the environment, but the best way of coping with this is through a conceptual and verbal route (criticism) rather than through overt behavioural coping. The evaluation tends to remain a tacit part of the cognitive representation. In contrast, in enactive imagery there is a strong bodily involvement and attention may fluctuate between the behavioural expression of affect, when attention is focused on coping with the situation, and the subjective experience of emotion, when attention is focused inwardly. The social emotions of visual imagery occupy a middle ground, since in some cases of social emotions, for example, embarrassment, there is physiological arousal (blushing) which may call attention to itself, and may do so the more easily because embarrassing situations so rarely offer scope for the coping actions that would deflect attention (one's own and that of others) away from the self.

Conclusion

Verbal, visual, and enactive representations may not be the most obvious starting-points for elucidating the relationship between cognition and affect. However, the study of their cognitive structures and affective complements does serve to illustrate some of the complexity involved on both sides of the relationship. Interpreting cognitive structures in the light of recent work on attention and preconscious processes may help in further unraveling the complexity on both sides, so that one day there may be some answers to Big Questions. These may look remarkably like a lot of little answers to a lot of little questions on the multifaceted relationship between cognition and affect.

References

Allport, G. W. (1955) *Becoming: Basic Considerations for a Psychology of Personality*, New Haven, CT: Yale University Press.

Alpert, R., and Haber, R. N. (1960) 'Anxiety in academic achievement situations', *Journal of Abnormal and Social Psychology* 61: 207–15.

Arnold, M. B. (1960) *Emotion and Personality*, vol. 1, *Psychological Aspects*, New York: Columbia University Press.

Aylwin, S. (1977) 'The structure of visual and kinaesthetic imagery: a free association study', *British Journal of Psychology* 68: 353–60.

(1981) 'Types of relationship instantiated in verbal, visual and enactive imagery', *Journal of Mental Imagery* 5 (1): 67–84.

(1985) *Structure in Thought and Feeling*, London: Methuen.

Bandura, A. (1977) 'Self-efficacy: toward a unifying theory of behavioral change', *Psychological Review* 84: 191–215.

Beck, A. T., Rush, A. J., Shaw, B. F., and Emery, G. (1979) *Cognitive Therapy of Depression*, Chichester: Wiley.

Bower, T. G. R. (1974) *Development in Infancy*, San Francisco: Freeman.

Bruner, J. S. (1966) 'On cognitive growth', in J. S. Bruner, R. R. Olver, P. M. Greenfield *et al.*, *Studies in Cognitive Growth*, New York: Wiley.

and Postman, L. (1949) 'On the perception of incongruity: a paradigm', *Journal of Personality* 18: 206–23.

Crowne, D. P., and Marlowe, D. (1964) *The Approval Motive: Studies in Evaluative Dependency*, New York: Wiley.

Duval, S., and Wicklund, R. (1972) *A Theory of Objective Self-Awareness*, New York: Academic Press.

James, W. (1890/1950) *The Principles of Psychology*, New York: Dover.

Klein, G. S. (1958) 'Cognitive control and motivation', in G. Lindzey (ed.) *Assessment of Human Motives*, New York: Rinehart.

Lacan, J. (1977) 'The mirror stage as formative of the functions of the I', in *Écrits: A Selection* (Trans. A. Sheridan), London: Tavistock.

Lang, P. (1979) 'A bio-informational theory of emotional imagery', *Psychophysiology* 16: 495–512.

Lazarus, R. S. (1982) 'Thoughts on the relation between emotion and cognition', *American Psychologist* 37: 1019–24.

Leach, C. (1979) *Introduction to Statistics: A Nonparametric Approach for the Social Sciences*, Chichester: Wiley.

Leach, E. (1964) 'Anthropological aspects of language: animal categories and verbal abuse', in E. H. Lenneberg (ed.) *New Directions in the Study of Language*, Cambridge, MA: MIT Press.

(1969) *Genesis as Myth and Other Essays*, London: Cape.

Marcel, A. J. (1983) 'Conscious and preconscious perception: an approach to the relations between phenomenal experience and perceptual processes', *Cognitive Psychology*, 15: 238–300.

Markus, H. (1977) 'Self-schemata and processing information about the self', *Journal of Personality and Social Psychology* 35: 63–78.

Mead, G. H. (1934) *Mind, Self and Society*, Chicago: Chicago University Press.

Pavlov, I. P. (1927) *Conditioned Reflexes: An Investigation of the Physiological Activity of the Cerebral Cortex* (Trans. G. V. Anrep), Oxford: Oxford University Press.

Pylyshyn, Z. W. (1973) 'What the mind's eye tells the mind's brain: a critique of mental imagery', *Psychological Bulletin* 80: 1–24.

Rotter, J. B. (1966) 'Generalized expectancies for internal versus external control of reinforcement', *Psychological Monographs* 80: 1–28.

Scheier, M. F., and Carver, C. S. (1977) 'Self-focused attention and the experience of emotion: attraction, repulsion, elation, and depression', *Journal of Personality and Social Psychology* 35: 625–36.

Shostrom, E. L. (1974) *Manual for the Personal Orientation Inventory*, San Diego, CA: Educational and Industrial Testing Service.

Swann, W.B., and Miller, L. C. (1982) 'Why never forgetting a face matters: visual imagery and social memory', *Journal of Personality* 43: 475–80.

Treisman, A., and Gelade, G. (1980) 'A feature–integration theory of attention', *Cognitive Psychology* 12: 97–136.

Treisman, A., and Schmidt, H. (1982) 'Illusory conjunctions in the perception of objects', *Cognitive Psychology* 14: 107–41.

Wegner, D. M., and Giuliano, T (1980) 'Arousal-induced attention to the self', *Journal of Personality and Social Psychology* 38: 719–26.

Wilson, G. D. (1975) *Manual for the Wilson-Patterson Attitude Inventory*, Windsor: National Foundation for Educational Research.

Wolpe, J. (1978) 'Self-efficacy and psychotherapeutic change: a square peg for a round hole', *Advances in Behavior Research and Therapy* 1: 231–6.

Zajonc, R. B. (1980) 'Feeling and thinking: preferences need no inferences', *American Psychologist* 35: 151–75.

and Markus, H. (1984) 'Affect and cognition: the hard interface', in C. E. Izard, J. Kagan, and R. B. Zajonc (eds) *Emotions, Cognition, and Behaviour*, London: Cambridge University Press.

Chapter eleven

Imagery and emotion: clinical and experimental approaches

Maryanne Martin and Rachel Williams

Clinical experience has long recognized the important role of visual imagery in emotional disorders, particularly anxiety. Few people now doubt that there is a close link between cognition and emotion, although there is considerable debate about the exact nature of the causal relation between them. However, there has been a paucity, first, of empirical evidence demonstrating that emotion (for example, anxiety or depression) and imagery are related; and second, of explanations of why this should be so. In this chapter, we propose to establish such a link and to account for it in terms of a cognitive propagational theory of emotions (Martin 1988b).

There is little disagreement that imagery itself plays an important role in human cognition, resembling perception and influencing memory. Imagery shares much in common with perception, having a sensory nature pertaining to all modalities, although in the clinical literature it is most commonly used to refer to the visual modality. Imagery refers to a continuum from the near veridical reconstruction in the mind of a real event to the construction of an entirely hypothetical situation. A person imaging differs from a person hallucinating in that the former has a greater awareness that the image is the product of mental processes rather than a perception of reality. It is the relation between imagery and perception, at least in terms of subjective experience, and possibly in terms of functional representation, which may be the key. Furthermore, imageability is one of the major influences upon ease of recall from memory. The more imageable the material, the better the recall (Paivio 1971, 1986; Rubin 1980). Some of the best-known mnemonic techniques advocate the use of imagery to improve memory (for example, in the method of loci and the peg-word technique: Yates 1966).

Cognitive propagation of emotion

Martin (1988b) has suggested that depressed mood tends to bias memory processes whereas anxious mood tends to bias perceptual processes. Why should perceptual and memory processes differ in this way? An explanation may be offered in terms of the differing cognitive processes that are appropriate for propagating different emotions. Martin (ibid.: 328–9) writes:

Propagational theory proposes that the likelihood of a particular domain of cognitive processing being affected by an emotion is a positive function of the likelihood that the resulting change in that domain will itself serve to propagate the emotion in question. That is, it is hypothesised that the cognitive changes that accompany emotional change are generally of a nature that leads to either the preseveration or the intensification (or both) of the original emotional change. In the case of anxiety, it can be argued that centrally involved in its propagation is the discovery of threatening aspects of the environment. Thus on a propagational account one expects, conversely, that a major effect of anxiety will be to itself bias perception in the direction of selectively attending to negative material. In the case of depression, on the other hand, centrally involved in its propagation appears to be the continued working over mentally of unhappy memories. Thus here a propagational account leads one to expect that a major effect of depression will be to bias memory in the direction of selectively retrieving negative material.

Why should anxiety and depression exert self-propagating effects upon cognitive processing? This may occur because their cognitive effects can be highly adaptive in certain situations, and thus confer an evolutionary advantage. If one has reason to be anxious about a physical threat in the immediate environment, it is advantageous to be perceptually biased in favour of detecting such a threat. If, however, one has reason to be depressed about a particular event, then it is advantageous to be biased towards the retrieval from memory of relevant information that may assist one in working out how to deal with a similar event in the future. It may also be noted that the degree to which any individual is subject to these biases seems likely to vary considerably (e.g., to be normally distributed) over the population. Thus it may be that excessive susceptibility to these biases results in certain individuals being particularly prone to becoming anxious or depressed patients.

Empirical evidence so far is consistent with the theory that anxiety interacts primarily with cognitive processes at a perceptual level (for example, MacLeod *et al.* 1986; Mathews and MacLeod 1986), whereas depression interacts primarily with memory processes (for example, Teasdale and Fogarty 1979; Bower 1981; Teasdale and Taylor 1981; Clark and Teasdale 1982, 1985; Fogarty and Hemsley 1983).

On the basis of the similarities between imagery and perception it might be expected on theoretical grounds that anxiety may influence imagery as well as perception. To a lesser extent imagery may play a role in depression, because imagery could influence ease of retrieval of memories relevant to depression. This chapter will examine whether anxiety and depression are linked with imagery, first, from a clinical perspective and, second, from an experimental perspective.

Clinical disorders in which imagery plays an important role

Imagery has long been recognized to be an important factor in some mental disorders (Horowitz 1983). Despite the longstanding use of imagery in therapy, there has been little experimental research explaining how, if at all, imagery is working in these therapies. Since imagery is sometimes only one factor in such a therapy, it may not be a necessary condition for the success of that therapy. Experimental work is needed to isolate this factor and determine the mechanisms through which imagery might be functioning in order, first, to facilitate the onset and persistence of a clinical disorder and, second, to modify the symptoms in therapy. The beginnings of this experimental work will be the focus of this chapter.

Since mental imagery can be described as one type of cognition, we will concentrate on emotional disorders which have more obvious cognitive components.

Anxiety disorders

These include post-traumatic stress disorders, simple phobias, agoraphobia, panic disorders, generalized anxiety disorder, and obsessive compulsive disorder. Clinical observation has suggested that those suffering from disabling levels of anxiety often experience enhanced levels of imagery. The threatening image feeds into the individual's concern and leads to an increase in symptoms. The types of imagery occurring in four of the disorders listed will be discussed.

Post-traumatic stress disorders

The development of symptoms follows a traumatic event generally outside the range of usual human experience. Symptoms involve re-experiencing the traumatic event, numbing of response to, or reduced involvement with, the external world, and a variety of autonomic, dysphoric, or cognitive symptoms (DSM-III: American Psychiatric Association [APA] 1980). A vivid visual image can be triggered by any stimulus that has some resemblance to one involved in the traumatic event (Beck *et al.* 1985: 32). The original stress may be relived through the visual image. At the time of the attack, the image may be so vivid the patient cannot distinguish it from reality. Thus, the visual image in this case may be thought of as a 'flashback' to an experienced situation.

Simple phobias

According to DSM-III (APA 1980: 229), the essential features of this disorder are

a persistent, irrational fear of, and compelling desire to avoid, an object or a situation other than being alone or in a public place away from home (Agoraphobia), or of humiliation or embarrassment in certain social situations (Social Phobia). Phobic objects are often animals, and phobic situations frequently involve heights or closed spaces.

Many phobic patients have highly specific visual images when exposed to the phobic situation. Through imagery they transform the innocuous stimulus into a highly threatening one by imagining a catastrophic situation. An example cited by Beck *et al.* (1985: 129) illustrates this. A woman who had a water phobia avoided any stimulus that reminded her of being in water, because such a stimulus evoked vivid visual images of her drowning.

Generalized anxiety disorder (GAD)

The DSM-III diagnostic criteria of this disorder are a generalized, persistent anxiety manifested by symptoms of three of four categories: (a) motor tension, (b) autonomic hyperactivity, (c) apprehensive expectation, and (d) vigilance and scanning. These must be present for at least one month. The disorder may be characterized by what appears initially to be free-floating anxiety. The anxiety has been described as a response to identifiable but largely internal stimuli, that is, negative thoughts and images (Clark and Beck, in press). Beck *et al.* (1974) found that their GAD patients reported images and automatic thoughts which expressed fear of at least one of the following: physical injury, illness or death, mental illness, psychological impairment, failure to cope, and rejection. Many patients report experiencing conscious images of an unpleasant or a disastrous experience. An individual's imagery can often reveal a more specific underlying fear. A common fear is of dying, but the feared cause of death will depend on the individual's past history. The exact content of the image may help to clarify a more specific fear (Beck *et al.* 1985: 99).

Obsessive compulsive disorder

Obsessions and compulsions can occur on their own although they usually co-exist. According to the DSM-III, obsessions are recurrent, persistent ideas, thoughts, images, or impulses that are ego-dystomic – that is, they are not experienced as voluntarily produced, but rather as thoughts that invade consciousness and are experienced as senseless or repugnant. Attempts are made to ignore or suppress them. Compulsions are repetitive and seemingly purposeful behaviours that are performed according to certain rules or in a stereotyped fashion. Either the activity is not connected in a realistic way with what it is designed to produce or prevent, or it may be clearly excessive. The commonest presentation is for the obsession to be followed by the compulsion, mediated by anxiety (DeSilva 1986). An image can be a component of either the obsession or compulsion, or both. They are usually related to violence, religion, harm and danger, disease, death, and decay, together with a small proportion of order-related and nonsensical ones (Rachman and Hodgson 1980). Images in obsessions and compulsions are almost always visual. One patient, for example, suffered from obsessive imaging of people lying dead in a grave accompanied by a compulsion to image those people alive again. In obsessions the images are usually static, whereas in compulsion they often have movement or flow (DeSilva 1986).

Discussion of the imagery involved in the anxiety disorders

Distressing images of, for example, lying in hospital after an accident, collapsing in a street, or being attacked, will often occur prior to entering the feared situations. In a sense, the image is acting as a warning signal of the perceived risks involved, however distorted this perception may be. Anxiety has been described as an attention-getter, forcing the individual to focus on possible sources of danger (Clark and Beck, in press). Imagery is one mechanism involved in this hyperactive system that forces the individual to appraise the degree of danger and their ability to cope. An anxiety disorder may arise when these appraisals are bypassed and a vulnerability set is in play automatically (Beck 1985).

In all disorders described autonomous images can be characterized as follows:

(1) They may often follow an upsetting event even if the patient was not directly involved in it.
(2) Usually the image is in some way triggered by an external stimulus.
(3) Images often cannot be controlled by patients, they come autonomously, and are very persistent; the image feeds the anxiety and the anxiety, in turn, prolongs and intensifies the image.
(4) The imaged situation is often experienced as reality.

Imagery is often accompanied by specific thoughts – for example, an image of lying in hospital on a respirator may be accompanied by the thought 'I am having a heart attack'. The content of the image and the thought can be identical, which raises the question of whether they have the same impact on emotion or serve the same function in mediating anxiety?

Having described the occurrence and nature of imagery in anxiety disorders, we may ask why there is this relationship between imagery and anxiety states. It has been suggested (Beck *et al.* 1985; Beck 1985; Martin 1988b; Clark and Beck, in press) that such imagery and automatic thoughts are a sort of warning system that may have some evolutionary advantage. It allows the individual to keep one step ahead of threatening situations. The function of imagery may be to intensity this signal by representing a possible reality. Although this is a reasonable explanation, it begs the question of whether we should then try to cure this system in therapy; we do not want to make the patient oblivious to risks. Beck points out that it is the perception of danger that is faulty and so therapy must work on appraising real danger and ability to cope. The sum of these will determine vulnerability to a given danger. We still need to decide at what point the system's advantages have been outweighed by its disabling effects and why this happens. A tentative explanation will be put forward in the experimental section below.

From an examination of the type of imagery involved in the disorders discussed so far we might propose to order this imagery on a continuum, starting from near veridical imagery to non-veridical imagery, depending on the degree of construction involved in producing the image (Horowitz 1983). The imagery involved in each of the three anxiety disorders discussed would be placed at different points along the continuum. Post-traumatic stress disorders would be on the veridical end since images are of an experienced, actual event. The visual image has a flashback nature (this disorder would not be placed at the very extreme of the continuum, totally veridical, as we know from research on eye-witness testimony that the memory of the event will be subject to modification and interpretation to some extent (for example, Loftus 1975; Bekerian and Bowers 1983)). Simple phobias would come next since the image is based on a stimulus (for example, water, spider, blood), but this is then used in the construction of a catastrophic event. This disorder would be midway on the veridical/ non-veridical dimension in terms of the imagery involved. Finally, we could place Generalized Anxiety Disorder at the other, non-veridical end as the imaged event is mostly pure construction. An external stimulus will sometimes trigger off the automatic image and anxious thoughts but this stimulus may not obviously be directly involved in the image. As mentioned earlier, the anxiety has been described as a response to identifiable but largely *internal* stimuli (Clark and Beck, in press).

The continuum provides a useful way of classifying the visual imagery involved in the different disorders. It also introduces a possible distinction between imaging and imagining. A visual image may be only one part of the whole process of imagining a threatening stimulus. Thus, these disorders can be distinguished on the degree of imagination involved in constructing the threatening situation. Post-traumatic stress disorder would involve little imagination but rather vivid recall of an actual event. In contrast, GAD involves a strong imagination component. Individual differences in strength of imagination may therefore be one factor in determining to which disorder an individual is susceptible. It is interesting to note that using his 'Method of Repeated Reproduction', Bartlett (1932) observed that invention and importation could be traced to the play of visual imagery. This would help explain why imagery is such a salient feature of the invented scenarios of patients with GAD.

Depression

According to cognitive theories of affective disorders, depression is mediated by a negatively distorting set of schemata or a negative cognitive style (for example, Beck *et al*. 1979). Taking imagery to be one type of cognition and having found distorted imagery in anxiety disorders, we may expect to find enhanced levels of negative imagery in depressive thinking. However, imagery does not play a significant role in the clinical understanding of depression. Clinically, depression is characterized as a verbal thought disorder involving, for example, rumination on unhappy past events (for example, Fogarty and Hemsley 1983), negative self-evaluation (for example, Bradley and Mathews 1983), and self-penalizing attributions (Abramson *et al*. 1978).

Perhaps the reason why clinicians emphasize the relevance of imagery to anxiety and not depression lies in the specificity of focus for anxiety versus depression. Depressives usually have a *global* negative thinking style. Thus, no one event or single experience is likely to be the focus of their thoughts, and this makes the imaging of a particular scene less likely. Although reactive depression does occur in response to a distressing event or series of life events (for example, Brown and Harris 1979), the negative thinking around these rapidly becomes generalized. An example of this is the internal, stable, and global attributions characteristically made by depressives in explaining the causes of negative events (Abramson *et al*. 1978). Thus, the content of depressive thought is likely to be rather too abstract to be readily imageable. If we maintain that anxiety is more to do with events whilst depression is more to do with evaluation, the difference in the likelihood of occurrence of relevant images is readily understandable. The distinction between the anxious and depressed thoughts may be drawn in terms of concreteness. Empirical data suggest that imaginal mediators produce better recall from memory than verbal mediators when retrieval is for concrete versus abstract material (Richardson 1978). Interestingly, no relationship was found between verbal mediators and recall of abstract material (a relation would be predicted on the assumption that depressive rumination serves as a mnemonic to depressive material). Thus, the differential occurrence of imagery in depression and anxiety may be due to the latter being more specifically event-focused and thereby associated with more concrete (and therefore more easily imaged) material. A study comparing the imageability of the contents of depressive and anxious thoughts will be reported in the Discussion towards the end of the chapter.

If this does explain the observed differences, we should predict that a case of depression that *is* caused by a specific set of experiences that do stay the focus for thoughts will be accompanied by relevant imagery. Beck *et al.* (1979) cite the example of a woman who had an overriding sense of incompetence. She visualized scenes in which she would disappoint her family. Such examples should warn against too strict a distinction being drawn between the role of imagery versus verbal processes in the emotional disorders.

Furthermore, if depressive thinking is centred largely around mnemonic processes (for example, rumination), we might expect imagery to be functioning in this capacity. As discussed earlier, the extent to which imagery aids recall will depend on the concreteness of the material to be recalled. Empirical work discussed later is consistent with both these points.

Finally, whatever the role of imagery in depression, we cannot claim imagery has features peculiar only to mediating anxiety. Successful techniques, which will be discussed in more detail later, have been used to induce a depressed mood in the laboratory, and have included both a verbal method (Velten 1968) and the imaging of an unpleasant event (Bower 1981). Imagery does then interact with depressive feelings, and we might therefore reasonably expect a role for imagery in depression. Some work relevant to this will be discussed in the Experimental section.

Eating disorders

Direct exploration of mental imagery in the eating disorders has not been carried out. However, it is very clear that many anorexics (and perhaps bulimics) suffer from very distorted body image (Bruch 1961, 1973, 1978; see Garner and Garfinkel 1981 for a review). There is no single definition of this, but it has been described as the mental image that one has of one's body (Traub and Orbach 1964). From the literature on body perception/image in anorexics, it seems highly likely that eating-disorder patients do experience specific imagery distortion relevant to their eating problem.

One test for measuring body image involves the subject standing before a sheet of paper on a wall and imagining this is a mirror. The subject is asked where she sees the points corresponding to widths of parts of her own body. Anorexics often grossly overestimate their size. This could be interpreted as their visual image of themselves being so vivid that it cannot be distinguished from reality.

Although there has been no direct work on imagery in anorexia/ bulimia, a therapy described below uses images of being fat or thin with eating-disorder sufferers and explores the feelings these images incur. The fact that this reveals some powerful feelings suggests specific content of imagery might be worth investigating in relation to eating disorders.

Schizophrenia

Although a schizophrenic may experience powerful visual images they are more commonly auditory (Horowitz 1983). This type of imagery is not within the scope of this chapter as it will usually come under the classification of hallucination – that is, the patient believes in, or believes in for part of the time, the reality of the image, even in the face of contrary evidence.

Uses of imagery in therapy

In this section we shall briefly review the uses of imagery in psychoanalysis and diagnosis, and in cognitive therapy, systematic desensitization, relaxation therapy, eidetic therapy, and guided affective-imagery.

Freud and psychoanalysis

Imagery is used to evoke past memories. Once an event or experience has been vividly regained, the problems incurred at that time can be dealt with. Thus, for example, Freud used imagery in analysis to evoke past memories, as illustrated in the following passage about the treatment of a patient with hysteria:

> Throughout this whole analysis I made use of the method of evoking pictures and ideas by pressing her head, a method, therefore, which would be inapplicable without the full cooperation and voluntary attention of a patient. At times her behaviour left nothing to be desired, and at such periods it was really surprising how promptly and how infallibly the individual scenes belonging to one theme

succeeded each other in chronological order. It was as if she read from a large picture book, the pages of which passed in review before her eyes.

(Breuer and Freud 1895/1936: 109)

Similarly, in hypnotherapy, a patient is brought to a past event through regression (Wolberg 1948: 167). The scene is imaged until it is so vivid the patient can relive the experience, repairing the destructive parts.

Imagery as a diagnostic tool

The evocation of images in patients has been used as a diagnostic procedure by many different approaches. Lazarus (1981), for example, has developed a 'deserted island fantasy technique', in which this setting is described and free imagery elaboration is solicited. Ahsen (1972) has developed the Eidetic Parents Test for eliciting images about the relationship between oneself and one's parents. Orbach (1978, 1982) gives her eating-disorder sufferers certain situations to image. Once they have a clear mental picture they are asked to manipulate the image of themselves in that situation, seeing themselves at one time fat, and at another time thin. The subject describes her feelings and thoughts in this situation under both conditions (i.e. fat and thin). This may help reveal the underlying psychological problems relevant to the disorder. An overweight compulsive eater, for example, might describe feelings of power, confidence, and control when imaging herself as fat in a given situation, compared with feelings of weakness and vulnerability when imaging herself as thin. Thus, therapy would include work on attitudes towards, and feelings of, power and control.

Cognitive therapy

Anxiety

Beck *et al.* (1985) also describe uses of imagery in gaining insight into the particular nature of the anxiety disorder. As mentioned earlier, a general fear of dying may be imaged more specifically as dying of cancer. Therapy can thus be tailored for each patient's needs. An essential feature of cognitive therapy is the changing of the content of cognition, which includes thoughts and images: this will lead to a reduction in anxiety. A number of techniques have been defined (ibid.: Chapter 12), such as:

(1) Turn-off Technique – The patient is trained to turn off autonomous fantasies by increasing sensory input (for example, blowing a whistle, clapping hands, ringing a bell).

(2) Repetition – By forcing repetitions of the image, the content of the image often spontaneously becomes more realistic and anxiety may be reduced.

(3) Time Projection – By imaging a scene in the future, when the troublesome event is past, the patient may be able to distance the self from the current anxiety about the event.

(4) Symbolic Images – Symbols may be used to modify old images. An image of being attacked, for example, might be modified by imaging a shield that protects you.

(5) Facilitating Change in Induced Images – An anxious fantasy may be gradually shaped into a neutral or positive image through imagery induction: for example, patients may imagine themselves painting an image of their own choice.

(6) Substituting a Positive Image – The most comforting scene for a patient is imaged in potentially anxiety-inducing situations. The patient focuses on all sensory modalities involved in that image.

(7) Exaggeration – The patient images a consequence worse than their own fears so as to put them in perspective.

(8) Coping Models – The patient images someone whom they consider capable coping with the feared situation and follows suit.

(9) Imagery to Reduce Threat – The feared stimulus is made less threatening through imagery (for example, imagining your examiner in a tennis skirt).

(10) Goal Rehearsal – The patient images a new, frightening situation, and then images ways to cope with it.

The efficacy of therapy will depend on changing the content of the thoughts and images whilst working on false appraisals of the danger. If imagery and automatic thoughts are said to be warning signals, removing the warning system would not diminish the fear and the perceived risks of a situation. We must assume that in learning and accepting that the warning system is overactive and distorted, the patient gains mastery over it, which in turn provides both confidence for appraising more realistically the feared situation and possible coping strategies.

Depression

As discussed earlier, cognitive therapy for depression has focused on the role of verbal processes in depression. However, some use of the imagery has been described. Beck *et al.* (1979) use imagery to demonstrate to patients how changing the content of thought can change feelings (thus introducing the essence of cognitive therapy) by asking patients to describe their feelings when imagining a pleasant versus unhappy event. Furthermore, patients may use imagery to counter negative thoughts. Imaging a pleasant past event at a time in the future when they are happy can be used as a distraction from depressive thinking. In cases in which a specific event or experience is central to the depression, imagery techniques may be used to reinterpret or cope with the situation.

Systematic desensitization

This well-established therapy rests on the assumption that the imagined stimulus resembles the real stimulus to such an extent that equivalent anxiety is induced. As Lazarus (1966) states, 'a prerequisite for effective application of desensitization is the ability to conjure up reasonably vivid images'. Having been trained to relax, the patient is exposed to the first feared stimulus from their hierarchical list. Exposure is either *in vivo* or imagined, and lasts as long as relaxation can be maintained. The patient systematically works up the hierarchy until relaxation has been achieved to all feared stimuli. The theory states that relaxation and anxiety are incompatible states so relaxation will inhibit the anxiety incurred by exposure to the stimuli. Wolpe (1969) points out that approximately 5 per cent of his patients do not experience the emotion when imagining a stimulus and find it more appropriate to verbalize the stimuli. This suggests that individual differences in imagery may be important in determining the type of therapy suitable for a patient.

Since the widespread use of this therapy, a debate has arisen over the necessity of exposure to a stimulus in therapy. Learning theory defines anxiety as a conditioned fear response (Miller 1948), in which case the conditioned (feared) stimulus must be presented and a new response pattern learnt. However, DeSilva and Rachman (1981) have argued that exposure to a stimulus is a sufficient but not a necessary condition for anxiety reduction. Imagining the stimulus can be as powerful as *in vivo* exposure. This fact also makes more understandable why exposure to the feared stimulus is not a necessary prerequisite to acquiring a phobic response. Murray and Foote (1979), for example, found the majority of snake phobics in an American student population had never had a frightening snake experience. The assumption can be made that imagery can produce as powerful representations as the real stimulus.

How effective, therefore, is the imaginal exposure to the feared stimuli in terms of therapy success? The evidence so far is equivocal. Several studies have compared the differential effects of exposure in imagination and exposure *in vivo* with agoraphobic patients. Some have found no difference between *in vivo* alone and combined *in vivo* and imaginal (for example, Emmelkamp 1974), while others have found *in vivo* superior to imaginal (for example, Emmelkamp and Wessels 1975), despite the fact that imaginal exposure by itself has been demonstrated to be effective (for example, Boulougouris *et al.* 1971). One reason for this equivocal evidence, put forward by Foa *et al.* (1980), is that the imagined scene must match the patient's own internal-fear model: that is, tangible, environmental cues must be accompanied with thoughts and images of possible disaster. They compared one group given imaginal exposure plus *in vivo* to another which received *in vivo* exposure alone. Initial improvement and a short-term follow-up showed the two treatments to be equally effective, but one year later the *in vivo* alone group had not maintained recovery and showed greater relapse. The conclusion drawn was that imaginal exposure allows long-term habituation. This suggests that there are perhaps two components to the feared stimuli - first, the tangible form of specific stimuli, and second, a cognitive component containing imagined feared consequences involving those stimuli. Both must be dealt with to produce a long-lasting therapeutic effect.

In support of this two-component hypothesis, a study with snake phobics by Davis *et al.* (1970) found that a high visual-imagery score correlated positively with how close a patient would approach a live snake at the pretreatment stage. There was no relationship between visual imagery and treatment success. They suggested that for a high visual imager, fear is based on imagination and not reinforced by external events, whilst for poor visual imagers, phobic imagining is based on sensory experience. For imaginary exposure, therefore, there should be a positive correlation between image ability and fear. Consistent with this, Rimm and Bottrell (1969) found that two measures of visual imagery were positively related to respiratory changes during imaging of fearful scenes.

If imagery does have a distinctive role in maintaining the anxiety disorder, we might expect individual differences in imagery ability to be important in determining which type of exposure should be experienced in therapy. Do high-imagers benefit from imagery-exposure? A study by Dyckman and Cowan (1978), also using snake phobics, found that imagery ability as measured by the Betts Questionnaire of Mental Imagery, did not predict therapeutic success, but in-therapy imagery assessment was significantly correlated with successful therapy. Thus, the ability to image scenes from the desensitization hierarchy did predict the outcome of treatment. This suggests two points: first, that low in-therapy imagers may benefit from *in vivo* treatment, and second, that imagery of neutral material does not predict imagery ability relevant to therapy. Thus, imagery ability during therapy must be assessed. It is worth noting that in this study *in vivo* exposure produced greater reduction in fear but was also experienced as more stressful and more presentations of the hierarchy were necessary. Hence, it is worth determining first, for whom imaginal exposure works to save unnecessary stress, and second, those cases in which *in vivo* exposure is not practical – such as in obsessive compulsive disorders where a major catastrophe is feared.

It seems that the relationship between *in vivo* and imaginal stimuli is more complex than first thought, depending on both the person and the type of stimuli (emotional versus neutral). There is some evidence that, first, they may have functionally distinct components (for example, Foa *et al.* 1980), and second, that these components may have differing importance in fear-arousal for different people (for example, Davis *et al.* 1970).

Relaxation therapy

Classical techniques require the patient to relax her or his muscles and then imagine a pleasant and peaceful scene. The therapist takes the patient through the scene, pointing out details to make the imagery as vivid as possible. It is interesting to note that experimental work has shown that highly anxious subjects have relatively weaker imagery for positive than negative material (see below, and Martin 1988). This suggests that the therapy is requiring anxious patients to do something they find difficult. Care should be taken, then, not to *increase* anxiety over the task.

Eidetic therapy

Ahsen (1977, 1982) proposed a Triple-Code Model (ISM) of imagery. The eidectic is a tripartite entity comprising three clear dimensions: I, the image or the picture; S, the somatic or physiological response; and M, the meaning, the lexical or verbal aspect. According to Ahsen (1984: 37), 'Most mental illnesses can be understood as a repression of one or more aspects of the ISM.' Conflict may cause the eclipse or partial presentation of unpleasant objects in the eidectic. In order to resolve conflict in the eidectic setting, new visual effects must be introduced into the picture (Ahsen 1977: 15). It was found, for example, that when a patient with an inability to concentrate or relax imaged her relaxed body it was mostly her favourite colour, blue, except for the tense shoulders, neck, and eye regions which were an angry red. In therapy, the patient achieved more complete body relaxation by using the suggestion that her body progressively became blue all over (Marks and McKellar 1982).

Guided affective-imagery

This is a psychoanalytically oriented method. Its uncovering method begins with symbolic imaginal contents, and only at a later point in the therapeutic process transcends the threshold from experiencing symbols to verbalizing the conflicts. The use of imagery here differs from that in cognitive therapy in that the topics chosen for imagery are standard and bear no immediately obvious relation to the disorder. Patients are encouraged to relax and image a related series of standard motifs (meadow, brook, mountain, house, and edge of woods) over the course of their treatment. Each motif has its own symbolic meaning: for example, one aspect of the brook can be interpreted as the expression of the unfolding of psychic energy. With the brook, patients are requested to follow it upstream to the source in their image. 'Signs of disorder indicating conflicts are situations in which the water trickles out of the sand very inconspicuously and thinly or the spring barely flows or wells up from several small individual sills in the meadow' (Leuner 1984: 59).

Experimental studies

The recognition of a role for imagery in the emotional disorders and the successful therapies employing imagery techniques throws open many questions, such as: how does imagery interact with emotions to modify them? How do individual differences in imagery affect susceptibility to the different disorders and determine the prognosis for the disorder? What is the relation between the imaged stimulus and the real stimulus? Is the distinction between anxiety and depression in terms of imagery and verbal processes supported empirically? It is in attempting to answer some of these questions that cognitive psychologists may have something to offer clinicians. Understanding the nature of imagery and its relation to emotional states may help to clarify the mechanisms at work in therapy.

Vivid-autonomous versus weak-unstable imagery

Early work on individual differences in imagery proposed differences along two dimensions: vividness (Betts 1909) and controllability (Gordon 1950). Vivid-autonomous imagers experience strong visual images but have little control over their appearance/disappearance. Weak-unstable imagers also exercise little control over their visual images, which are faint and highly fluctuating. Costello (1957) found more vivid-autonomous imagers amongst a clinical dysthymic group compared with a clinical hysteric group and a normal control. Measures were taken on the Gordon Test of Imageability and/or the rate of reversals on the Necker cube (which had been correlated with imagery scores). In the Gordon test, subjects are asked to attempt to form visual images of scenes involving a car, most of which are emotionally neutral, but others may not be, for example, the car getting out of control and crashing through a house, the car crossing a bridge and falling into the stream below, the same car old and dismantled, standing in a car cemetery.

Dysthymics, who are defined as introverted, prone to anxiety disorders and reactive depression, have strong visual images which they cannot manipulate. Unfortunately, for our purposes of differentiating between anxiety and depression, patients with manifest anxiety, reactive depression, or obsessive compulsive features are grouped together in this study. Later, Eysenck (1960) explained these and other phenomena in terms of an excitable nervous system. A labile system has strong reaction to a stimulus and since inhibitory processes are weak, so the reaction (the visual image or perception of the Necker cube in one plane) persists. This picture fits with the clinical reports of imagery in anxious patients discussed earlier: that is, imagery is vivid, hard to control, and persistent.

This dysthymic group was compared with a hysteric group defined as extroverted and prone to psychopathic symptoms. Strong inhibitory and weak excitatory processes (ibid.) make imagery weak and unstable and reversals on the Necker cube high. Costello (1957) concludes that these types of imagery are not a defining feature of either the dysthymic or hysteric group (as both types of imagery were found in the normal control group), but individual differences in imagery may be one factor in determining the type of disorder to which a person is prone. We have already discussed this in relation to anxiety disorders. Since no explanation is given as to why weak-unstable imagery should facilitate psychopathic symptoms, we are free to speculate that (in contrast with the anxious group) weak-unstable imagery may result in the failure to imagine the negative consequences of a risky or anti-social act either to self or as a victim.

A study by Euse and Haney (1975) sought to clarify these personality differences. Using the Gordon test for controllability and clarity, and a measure of emotional intensity of the image, they correlated these measures with extraversion and neuroticism (EPI: Eysenck and Eysenck 1968) and state and trait anxiety (STAI: Spielberger et al. 1970). They found that both high state and trait anxiety scores and high neuroticism were significantly correlated with low controllability (this is consistent with Costello 1957) and low clarity. In contrast, high extraverts showed high control scores and high clarity (this is inconsistent with Costello's findings and Eysenck's interpretation).

The important finding relevant to a clinical approach is that an anxiety component was associated with low controllability. This fits the reports of anxious patients. The fact that imagery was also low in clarity is probably due to the averaging of imagery scores over materials which, when rated, produce an average rating midway on a scale running from displeasure, through no emotion, to pleasure. Moreover, in this study no correlations were found between average emotional intensity of the image and any other measure, further suggesting that the images had, on average, little emotional impact. The questions left to be asked are whether therapy should work primarily on increasing control or on decreasing vividness (or both). This invites the question of whether a

285

person can be trained to control their imagery in general and whether control of imagery *per se* would help relieve the fear-ridden autonomous images. Since the work discussed earlier on desensitization suggests that neutral and emotional imagery ability are not necessarily associated, the answer to the latter is likely to be 'No'. Therapy should work specifically on the emotional imagery, first, by attempting to reduce specifically the emotional impact of the image and, second, by teaching voluntary control of imagery.

Selective-enhancement hypothesis

Anxious patients may, then, be vivid-autonomous imagers but this does not explain the specific anxiety-inducing content of their imagery. Martin (1988) has suggested three possible ways in which this might occur. First, anxiety-related experiences in general may be accompanied by more imagery than are other types of experiences (and anxious people will have more of these experiences). Second, anxious people in general may experience more imagery than non-anxious people. Third, anxious people may have enhanced imagery specifically for anxiety-related experiences. In a series of experiments, Martin (1986, 1988) provides support for the third of these hypotheses, that is, the selective-enhancement hypothesis.

Experiment 1 (Martin 1986)

Each subject was asked to bring to mind a time when she or he had felt either anxious, depressed, angry, or happy. Subjects were then asked to answer a number of questions about that memory – for example, emotionality at the time of the event and at present, control over the event, the nature and vividness of the image of the event. The most striking result was that happy memories produced response values for the imagery questions that were greater than for any of the other emotions, for every imagery question. Conversely, the response values for the verbal components (self-comment and self-instruction) were significantly lower for the happy memories versus the negative memories (anxious, angry, depressed). For none of the questions did the imagery for the anxious memories significantly exceed the values for the others. Thus, evidence is therefore inconsistent with the idea that experiences which are anxious are associated with higher levels of imagery. However, higher levels of imagery were reported for anxious experiences for high compared with low Neuroticism scorers. It is

Table 11.1 Mean scores on the Vividness of Visual Imagery Questionnaire (VVIQ) for differing levels of trait anxiety according to Spielberger's State-Trait Anxiety Inventory

Subject group	Trait anxiety	VVIQ score
Normal sample		
Low anxiety (n=12)	20–38	56.1
Medium anxiety (n=12)	39–50	56.0
High anxiety (n=12)	51–70	55.0
Overall range (n=36)	20–70	32–80
Anxious patients sample (n=14)	55.5	55.5
Range (n=14)	42–79	28–76

worth pointing out that the depressed memories compared with other negative memories did not produce significantly higher response values for the verbal components (silent self-comment and self-instruction).

Experiment 2 (Martin 1988)

To test the hypothesis that anxious people in general have enhanced levels of imagery, three groups of subjects were selected on the basis of their trait anxiety scores (Spielberger 1966) to include a high-, medium-, and low-anxiety group. The means of the Spielberger trait score of the high group all exceeded the sample mean of the anxious patients and the low group were all below the control group used in the Mathews and MacLeod Stroop experiment (1985). Each subject completed the Vividness of Visual Imagery Questionnaire (VVIQ: Marks 1973). In this procedure, subjects judge how vivid is their mental picture of each of four components of a given scene which is emotionally neutral. The mean vividness scores shown in Table 11.1 did not differ significantly among the anxiety groups. Furthermore, Martin (1988a) found that anxious patients had a mean VVIQ indistinguishable from that of the normal sample (see Table 11.1). These experiments did not support the hypothesis that anxiety is associated with generally higher levels of imagery.

Experiment 3 (Martin 1988)

The same three groups of subjects as for Experiment 2 judged the imageability of two groups of words. The words were those used in a Stroop task by Mathews and MacLeod (1985), consisting of twenty-four potentially anxiety-provoking words (for example, 'disease', 'foolish') and twenty-four non-threatening words (for

Imagery

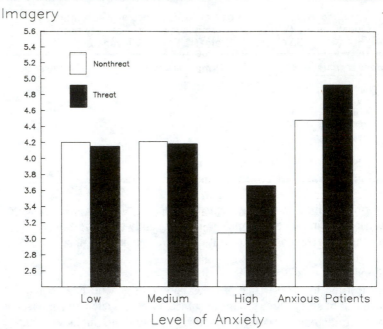

Level of Anxiety

Figure 11.1 Mean imagery scores for threat and non-threat material as a function of level of anxiety.

example, 'confident', 'holiday'). Imageability was assessed using the imagery procedure of Paivio *et al.* (1968), in which the ease of forming an image was rated on a 7-point scale. Highly anxious subjects reported very low imagery for non-threatening words, as can be seen in Figure 11.1. They revealed a higher value of imagery for threatening words relative to non-threatening words (although overall imageability was reduced compared with the other two groups). Furthermore, anxious patients also show much higher values for the ratio between imagery associated with threatening words and that associated with non-threatening words (Martin 1988a). It therefore appears to be the balance of imagery between anxious and non-anxious stimuli which is changed by high levels of anxiety (see Figure 11.1). Thus, the selective-enhancement hypothesis is supported.

In the light of these findings and those of Costello (1957), we may attempt to answer the question posed earlier as to what determines whether the warning system becomes disabling? We might speculate that this may depend on what type of imagery the individual experiences. If anxiety selectively biases imagery to anxiety-related stimuli *and* you are also a vivid-autonomous imager, this type of anxiety-inducing imagery may become overwhelming. Weak-unstable imagery (albeit anxiety-related) may not be strong enough to produce a full-blown anxiety disorder.

Imagery induction of emotional states

What are the consequences of forming images of happy, sad, or neutral topics even for short periods of time – for example, up to ten minutes? Are there emotional, cognitive, and physiological effects which can be detected in the normal population?

In one study on the emotional and cognitive effects of imagery, Wright and Mischel (1982) instructed subjects to imagine situations that would leave them feeling either sad, happy, or neutral. They were told that they can either imagine hypothetical situations or real events in their past, and are then requested to generate vivid images of the events. Imaging happy events led to positive feelings and sad events led to negative feelings as assessed by a modified version of the Mood Adjective Checklist (Nowlis 1970). Furthermore, imaging happy events led subjects to form higher expectancies about future performance on a mental-rotation task, to recall more positive outcomes from a set of mental-rotation tasks which they had completed, and to make more favourable global descriptions of themselves, whereas the converse pattern was obtained for those imaging sad events. However, it is not clear whether these changes in mood and cognition are attributable to the imagery alone since although there was an emphasis on imagery, subjects were also instructed to reconstruct both the thoughts and the feelings of the events.

A major review of the influence of imaging emotional topics on physiological responses (for example, heart rate, electrodermal activity, activation of voluntary muscles, blood flow, blood chemistry, ocular changes) has recently been published by Sheikh and Kunzendorf (1984). Our current discussion will be limited to a few illustrative studies. Haney and Euse (1976) found heightened heart rate and skin conductance reactivity while normal subjects were imaging positive and negative events compared with neutral, but there was no detectable difference between the effects of positive and negative imagery. Similarly, Schwartz *et al.* (1981) found that imaging situations that evoke happiness, sadness, anger, and fear produced cardiovascular changes.

However, change in heart rate, diastolic, and systolic blood pressure did not differentiate among happiness, sadness, and fear, although a greater change in diastolic blood pressure occurred with imagery of anger situations. Acosta *et al.* (1988) found that when students who were afraid of rats imaged rat scenes, a greater change in heart rate and skin conductance compared with base-rate responding was observed than when they imaged neutral scenes. As no imaging of positive scenes was included in this study it remains possible that the autonomic response measures do not differ for positive and negative imaging, but are showing only an effect of emotionality. In addition, Lang (1979: 15) reports that there is considerable variation in cardiovascular response among individuals, and some subjects do not respond physiologically even to imagery instructions highly salient to their own personal concerns. Recently, Miller *et al.* (1987) found among good imagers, but not poor imagers, differences in change in heart rate and skin conductance from a baseline as a function of the emotional content (fear, action, anger, neutral) of the scene being imaged. Thus, for example, greater heart-rate change was observed for anger imagery compared with fear, action, or neutral imagery. In contrast, a study conducted by Molteno (cited in Marks 1985) indicated that, while heart-rate changes from a neutral baseline were equally high for pleasant and unpleasant images in vivid imagers, unpleasant images compared with pleasant images produced relatively small heart-rate changes in a group of non-vivid imagers. These studies suggest that individual differences in imagery ability also play a role in the mediation of emotional states.

In conclusion, it appears that imaging emotional material compared with neutral material does lead to an increase in autonomic arousal level.

Individual differences, personality, and depressed mood

As discussed above, imagery may be used in the induction of depressed mood; so might imagery be playing a part in clinical depression or temporary depressed mood that has hitherto been overlooked? Thus, for example, imagery may serve as a mnemonic aid in depression where specific events are the focus of attention. If imagery is selectively biased towards the negative (as with anxious subjects), it will serve to bias the depressive's memory in such a way so as to prolong the depression. Alternatively, selective imagery in certain personality types may increase vulnerability to depression. A study of these issues may help us to move towards an explanation of how and why emotion and imagery are linked.

As part of a larger study, the effects of personality and mood on imagery were simultaneously investigated (Williams *et al.*, in preparation). Three questions are of particular interest. First, are there individual differences in emotional imageability related to personality? Second, is there an imagery 'mood-congruency effect' with depressed mood – that is, does depressed mood enhance the imagery of a negative event whilst reducing the imagery of a positive event? Third, are there individual differences in susceptibility to an imagery mood-congruency effect?

The experiment involved two sessions, four weeks apart. Having completed the Beck Depression Inventory (BDI: Beck *et al.* 1961) and the Eysenck Personality Questionnaire (EPQ: Eysenck and Eysenck 1975), the subjects' task was to recall specific autobiographical memories in response to cue-words presented on a computer screen. The words were a set of ten neutral cues (for example, a house, a school, a meeting) and ten emotional cues; five positive (for example, glad, relaxed) and five negative (for example, despairing, angry). The subject performed this task on both sessions but on one occasion in a neutral mood and on the other in an induced depressed mood (two sets of comparable word lists were used, matched for emotionality, frequency of usage, and word length). On each occasion, subjects were returned to their natural mood before rating their memories on a number of scales. Subjects were asked to rate each memory on a scale from 0 to 100 for (1) vividness in general, (2) vividness of the feelings, and (3) vividness of the visual image of the event.

Since the cue-word is used to access the memory, it would be reasonable to predict that overall, the neutral cues (all concrete nouns) would elicit memories with more vivid visual imagery than the emotional cues (abstract nouns), as the strong association between concreteness and imageability is well established. Thus, a more imageable cue may be expected to access a more imageable memory. However, overall, subjects reported stronger imagery for positively-cued memories, fitting well with the results of Martin (1986) already discussed. This result cannot be attributed to generally better memories for good events since questions about 'memory in general' and 'memory for feelings' both produced greater vividness scores for the negatively cued memories. Thus, happy memories contain more vivid imagery than negative memories, even though negative memories may in other ways be better remembered.

Table 11.2 Mean imagery scores in neutral mood for groups differentiated by scores on neuroticism and on the Beck Depression Inventory (BDI)

| | Low neuroticism | | High neuroticism | |
Cue type	Low BDI	High BDI	Low BDI	High BDI
Positive	66.8	73.5	68.4	63.0
Negative	63.7	67.5	61.0	64.9
Neutral	70.2	66.1	60.6	63.8

In addition, in the light of evidence from the Miller *et al.* (1987) and Molteno (cited in Marks 1985) studies, which reported that vivid and non-vivid imagers responded differently physiologically to pleasant and unpleasant images, the subjects in our study were assigned to two groups on the basis of the vividness of their imagery in response to the neutral cues in neutral mood. Although the vivid imagers also experienced more vivid imagery in response to affective cues than non-vivid imagers, both vivid and non-vivid imagers experienced more imagery in response to positive than to negative cues. Thus, there is at present no evidence that good and poor imagers respond differentially to positive and negative images at a subjective level.

Individual differences in emotional imageability

Although overall imagery was relatively stronger for positive compared with negative events, one group of subjects did not show this bias. A high score on Eysenck's Neuroticism scale (above a median cutpoint) accompanied by a high score on the BDI (above a median cutpoint) dislodged this positive enhancement, as can be seen in Table 11.2.

Although a causal role for imagery in depression cannot be directly inferred from this, both neuroticism and mild depression are predictors of subsequent clinical depression and negatively biased imagery is characteristic of these two factors when they occur together. It is interesting to note that only one group shows stronger imagery to neutral-cued memories: this is the group low on both vulnerability factors. This result suggests, perhaps, that these people just do not enter the emotional domain as readily as the other groups. Thus, in responding to the neutral cues, they may be responding more to the object than the emotional content of the memory.

Mood congruency

It is well documented in the literature that laboratory-induced depressed

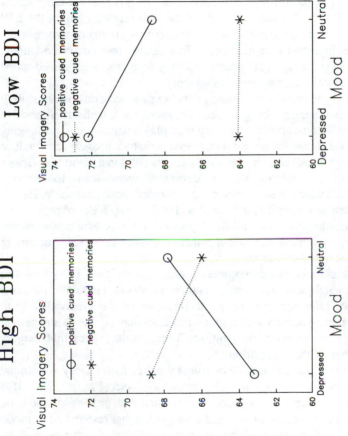

Figure 11.2 Mean visual imagery scores for positively and negatively cued memories as a function of mood induction and Beck Depression Inventory (BDI) score.

or happy mood enhances recall of material congruent with that mood. Overall, it was not the case that imagery of events congruent with mood was made more vivid compared with that incongruent with mood. Thus, although induced depressed-mood made it more likely that unhappy memories would be recalled, the imagery associated with these memories was not made more vivid.

Individual differences in mood congruency

Certain groups did, however, show an imagery mood-congruency effect. Figure 11.2 shows that those subjects scoring high on the BDI (above a median cutpoint) reported weaker imagery to positive cues and stronger imagery to negative cues when induced into a depressed mood. Low BDI subjects, on the other hand, may counteract a depressed-mood effect by strengthening positive imagery.

Thus, when mildly depressed people experience a downward shift in mood, their negative imagery becomes more vivid, whilst their positive imagery becomes less so. Imagery may play a part, then, in prolonging depressed mood (since we know that negative imagery can induce depressed mood) and may be one factor involved in activating a vicious circle of depression – that is, depressed mood leads to negative cognitions which in turn worsen the depressed mood, and so on. Hence, mild depression predicts the likelihood of future episodes of depression. It is not the case that mildly depressed subjects experience biased imagery in general, but that a selective change in imagery occurs in response to mood change.

This imagery mood-congruency effect (see Figure 11.3) was also found in high-neuroticism subjects (above a median cutpoint). The same tentative inferences can be made that part of the predisposition to depression associated with high neuroticism may be due to a negative-biasing effect of mood on cognitions. These results suggest that imagery forms part of these cognitions.

Finally, a reverse mood-congruency effect for imagery was found with subjects scoring high on extraversion (see Figure 11.4). If a negative-biasing effect of mood is associated with prolonged mood and vulnerability to depression, we should predict that responding to mood in the opposite way may protect against clinical depression and depressed mood. Although there is no direct evidence as yet on this, extraversion has been shown to antedate and predict differences in subjective well-being and happiness over a ten-year period, extraversion being associated with greater happiness and well-being, whilst

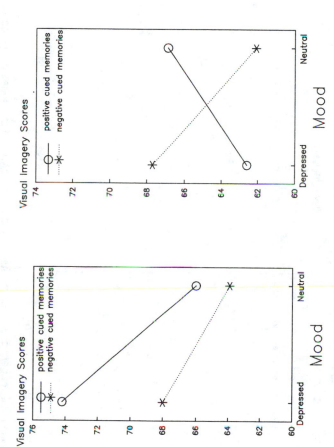

Figure 11.3 Mean visual imagery scores for positively and negatively cued memories as a function of mood induction and neuroticism.

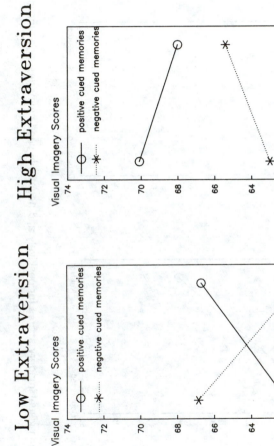

Figure 11.4 Mean visual imagery scores for positively and negatively cued memories as a function of mood induction and extraversion.

neuroticism predicted negative affect (Costa and McCrae 1980). The biasing effects of mood on imagery and memory may be part of the mechanism that will explain what it is about being high on neuroticism or extraversion that predicts mental and emotional health.

Two main points emerge from this study of visual imagery and its role in depression. First, depressive thinking is often characterized as rumination of the past, and selectively enhanced imagery for negative events may serve as mnemonic for this. The evidence for this comes from the group which was high on both neuroticism and on the BDI. In neutral mood this group showed reduced imagery for positive memories and greater imagery for negative memories. This cannot tell us directly about a clinical population (this was a student sample). However, this group did score significantly higher on depression than the high-BDI, low-neuroticism group. Since neither high BDI nor high neuroticism alone produced this bias, it is reasonable to suppose that it is due to the greater degree of depression of the high-neuroticism, high-BDI group, unless it is the result of the co-occurrence of high neuroticism and high BDI. Second, negative imagery is selectively enhanced by depressed mood in certain people (high BDI, high neuroticism, or low extraversion scorers). This mood-congruency effect for imagery may be one component of the mechanism which makes these people more prone to the vicious circle of depression. A mechanism which responds to mood in the reverse fashion may protect others from entering this cycle.

The question arises, then, as to why imagery has not previously been linked with depression. The answer perhaps lies in the very generalized content of depressive thinking. Depressives may find it hard to home in on specific relevant incidents. Williams (1984) suggests that when asked to recall personal, specific memories to cues, depressed patients were not slower to respond initially, but would often not find a specific memory, instead making a general response (for example, 'it was always like that at school'). Beck *et al.* (1985) and Clark and Beck (in press) have reported the need to probe anxiety-disorder patients about their imagery. Patients do not often report it spontaneously. Perhaps depressives must be pressed further as they have the added problem of first finding a specific experience (i.e. something concrete) that is imageable.

The next question is to look directly at how biased imagery affects people of different personality types. Are mildly depressed and high Neuroticism scorers more prone to the mood-inducing effects of negative imagery? To explore the nature of the relation between mood and imagery it would be useful to determine whether individual differences in the effect of mood on imagery are paralleled by individual differences in the effect of imagery on mood: that is, to what extent is the relationship reciprocal?

Discussion

Having shown a functional role of imagery in clinical disorders, the important question is whether this is a primary or secondary role. Is there something distinctive about imagery which contributes to the onset and/or maintenance of clinical disorders, or is it just one part of the package of distorted cognitions which characterize the emotional disorders? Is there a contribution of imagery independent of associated thoughts? Since imagery and thoughts occur very much in tandem, it is difficult to tease apart these two factors to resolve this question. There is consequently no clear evidence suggesting that imagery alone can account for the onset or severity of a disorder.

However, there are two sources of evidence which suggest that this question may be worth pursuing. First, the work on individual differences in emotional imagery, which suggests, first, that biased imagery and lack of imagery control are associated with certain personality types known to be vulnerable to emotional disorders, and second, that differences among individuals in the level of imageability of emotional stimuli may determine therapeutic success. Second, there are three studies that suggest imagery may play a particular role in emotional memory: the work by Foa *et al.* (1980) on imagery-exposure leading to long-term habituation to the feared stimulus; the study by Williams *et al.* (in preparation) showing selective mood-biasing effects for imagery of emotional memories; and a study by Turner and Layton (1976) looking at imagery as a memory-induced mediator of aggressive behaviour.

The latter work stems from the proposal by Berkowitz (1974) that memory mechanisms can influence the delayed effects of aggressive material on aggressive behaviour. The delay was thought important in order to allow the dissipation of the inhibitions that we have in our culture over displaying aggressive behaviour. Turner and Layton attempted to vary the availability from memory of words with an aggressive or neutral meaning by manipulating the imagery property of words. The question addressed was whether high-imagery aggressive material influences aggression more after delay than low-imagery aggressive material, as the former should be more accessible in memory.

Four categories of words were used, varying in high/low imageability and high/low aggressive content. Subjects were asked to learn word-pairs which contained one of these four categories of words using an imagery-coding mnemonic. Subjects were then exposed to an arousal-producing, non-noxious white noise. Subjects were asked to deliver punishing shocks to another subject (in fact a stooge) when wrong answers were given on a problem-solving task. Those subjects previously exposed to high-imagery, high-aggressive content material administered more intense shocks than the other three subject-groups. They concluded that the behavioural effect (i.e. giving shocks) of immediate aggressive material may be determined in part by the material it stimulates in memory and how retrievable that is. Imagery plays a crucial role in determining the latter. Unfortunately, no direct measure of the emotion experienced by the different groups was taken, so we do not know if imagery fed into the feeling of aggression or directly mediated aggressive behaviour.

This work is consistent with the hypothesis that stored emotional imagery, first, is long-lasting, and second, can have specific effects in determining how current material is processed and acted upon. This may provide an explanation of why imagery exposure was necessary to produce long-term therapeutic effects (Foa *et al.* 1980). *In vivo* exposure may not deal directly with the stored emotional imagery which may be retrieved when the patient is faced with an environmental feared stimulus. Although *in vivo* exposure may reduce the anxiety effects of the latter, if the retrieved emotional imagery is revived, it may, with time, start to influence behaviour. Further research is required on the emotional imagery stored by anxious patients to determine directly the relevance of this explanation to anxiety disorders. One possibility is that anxious thoughts themselves are particularly imageable. To investigate this we carried out a small-scale study. Please try to conjure up an image in your mind, making the image as vivid and full of detail as possible, of first a number of spiders crawling over your face, and second yourself as a worthless person. The first is a prototypical anxious thought and the second a prototypical depressive thought. In a study of forty normal adults (twenty female, twenty male) the majority of people (88 per cent) found it easier to image a prototypical anxious thought than an prototypical depressive thought. As can be seen from Table 11.3, this remains the case even for those individuals who are not afraid of the anxious stimulus. Further, among those individuals who find that the depressive thought produces more emotional feelings than the anxious

Table 11.3 Percentage of individuals who found it easier to image a prototypical anxious or depressive thought

	Easier to image	
	Anxious thought	Depressive thought
Afraid of spiders (n=16)	100	0
Not afraid of spiders (n=24)	79	21
Thoughts of being a worthless person (n=29)	90	10
No thoughts of being a worthless person (n=11)	91	9
Spider image produced more emotional feelings (n=21)	100	0
Worthless person image produced more emotional feelings (n=15)	73	27
No emotional feelings to either image (n=4)	75	25

thought, the majority still find it easier to image the anxious thought. If these results are replicated with a broader range of material, they may be used to explain why imagery has been so strongly implicated in anxiety disorders.

The question remains as to whether certain people are more prone to the effects of imagery in the emotional disorders. The study by Dyckman and Cowan (1978) suggests that an overall measure of imagery ability for neutral material does not predict clinical outcome, but ability to image relevant emotional material does. The question then arises as to whether differences in emotional-imagery ability are state- or trait-determined. In a recent study, Strosahl et al. (1986) propose that 'as imagery becomes more complex and emotively charged, performance is increasingly state-determined and trait level assessments may lose precision and relevance'. They took three different imagery processes – sensory modality, emotive-abstract imagery, and imagery control – arguing that emotive-abstract imagery should be state-determined and functionally distinct from sensory modality and image control. Principal components analysis did provide some evidence for the latter. Emotive-abstract imagery and imagery control were both found to be good predictors of in-therapy image clarity whereas sensory modality was not. Hence, the conclusion was drawn that in-therapy imagery is state-determined and is not associated with trait-like measures of imagery. These conclusions are consistent with experimental findings of Martin

(1988a, b), that emotional state interacts with emotional content of material to produce selective bias.

The study by Williams *et al.* (in preparation) suggests that the interaction can be taken one step further. The interaction of type-of-material with emotional state on imagery depends on certain stable personality characteristics. Only one group (low Neuroticism, low BDI) produced more vivid images to neutrally cued memories in neutral mood. This might be explained with recourse to the emotional-image retrieval hypothesis discussed earlier. Perhaps these people are less likely to store images in the emotional domain and therefore imagery scores reflect the concreteness of the cues. The fact that this group is also the least vulnerable to depression implies again a role of emotional-imagery retrieval in onset or maintenance of a disorder.

The mood-congruency imagery effects found with high neuroticism and high BDI illustrate the interaction of personality with the mood state by material-type interaction. For certain people (those who are vulnerable to depression), therefore, a depressed mood stimulates the retrieval of emotionally charged negative images. It would be informative to test directly the emotional-imagery retrieval hypothesis put forward earlier by manipulating the negativity and imageability of remembered material to see if highly imageable negative material would later affect mood, behaviour, or both.

Conclusions

High levels of visual imagery often reported by clinicians to occur in patients suffering from emotional disorders, in particular anxiety, could play a critical role in maintaining or prolonging these disorders. What appears to be of crucial importance is the interaction between the emotional state of an individual and the emotional content of the event. It is not that anxious people have higher levels of imagery in general or that memories of anxious events are more imageable in themselves. Instead, more anxious individuals in the normal population and anxious patients experience relatively more imagery for threat compared with non-threat material, whereas for low anxious individuals non-threat material is relatively more imageable. Similarly, in groups particularly vulnerable to emotional disorders – that is, high Neuroticism and high non-clinical BDI scorers – the balance of imagery for memories of negative as opposed to positive events is enhanced. In addition, when this vulnerable group is induced into a depressed mood, subjects experience an increase in mood-congruent imagery – that is, memories of negative events compared with positive events become even more imageable. In low-risk groups there is a tendency to observe the converse of this mood-congruency effect, presumably protecting such individuals from emotional disorders. It is highly probable that enhanced imagery for the negative compared with the positive domain makes the negative events much more salient and easy to retrieve from memory, acting in such a way as to propagate an anxious or depressed mood. High-risk individuals not only already have a cognitive processing style that is similar to patients with emotional disorders, but when they suffer a downward mood-swing this becomes even more extreme, thereby making it likely that the mood will be intensified and prolonged.

References

Abramson, L. Y., Seligman, M. E. P., and Teasdale, J. D. (1978) 'Learned helplessness in humans: critique and reformulation', *Journal of Abnormal Psychology* 87: 49–74.

Acosta, A., Vila, J., and Palma, A. (1988) 'Emotional imagery and cognitive representation of emotion: an attempt to validate Lang's bio-informational model', in M. Denis, J. Engelkamp, and J. T. E. Richardson (eds) *Cognitive and Neuropsychological Approaches to Mental Imagery*, Dordrecht: Martinus Nijhoff.

Ahsen, A. (1972) *Eidetic Parents Test and Analysis*, New York, Brandon House.

—— (1977) 'Eidetics: an overview', *Journal of Mental Imagery* 1: 5–38.

—— (1982) 'Imagery in perceptual learning and clinical application', *Journal of Mental Imagery* 6: 157–86.

—— (1984) 'ISM: the triple code model for imagery and psychophysiology', *Journal of Mental Imagery* 8: 15–42.

American Psychiatric Association (1980) *Diagnostic and Statistical Manual of Mental Disorders, Third Edition*, Washington, DC: American Psychiatric Association.

Bartlett, F. C. (1932) *Remembering*, London: Cambridge University Press.

Beck, A. T. (1985) 'Cognitive approaches to anxiety disorders', in B. F. Shaw, L. V. Segal, T. M. Vallis, and F. E. Cashman (eds) *Anxiety Disorders: Psychological and Biological Perspectives*, New York: Plenum.

Emery, G., and Greenberg, R. L. (1985) *Anxiety Disorders and Phobias: A Cognitive Perspective*, New York: Basic Books.

Beck, A. T., Laude, R., and Bonhert, M. (1974) 'Ideational components of anxiety neurosis', *Archives of General Psychiatry* 31: 319–25.

Beck, A. T., Rush, A. J., Shaw, B. F., and Emery, G. (1979) *Cognitive Theory of Depression*, New York: Guilford Press.

Beck, A. T., Ward, C. H., Mendelson, M., Mock, J., and Erbaugh, J. (1961) 'An inventory for measuring depression', *Archives of General Psychiatry* 4: 561–71.

Bekerian, D. A., and Bowers, J. M. (1983) 'Eye-witness testimony: were we misled?' *Journal of Experimental Psychology: Learning, Memory, and Cognition* 9: 139–45.

Berkowitz, L. (1974) 'Some determinants of impulsive aggression: role of mediated associates with reinforcements for aggression', *Psychological Review* 81: 165–76.

Betts, G. H. (1909) *The Distribution and Functions of Mental Imagery*, New York: Teachers College.

Boulougouris, J. G., Marks, I. M., and Marset, P. (1971) 'Superiority of flooding (implosion) to desensitization for reducing pathological fear', *Behaviour Research and Therapy* 9: 7–16.

Bower, G. H. (1981) 'Mood and memory', *American Psychologist* 36: 129–48.

Bradley, B., and Mathews, A. (1983) 'Negative self-schemata in clinical depression', *British Journal of Clinical Psychology* 22: 173–81.

Breuer, J., and Freud, S. (1895/1936) *Studies in Hysteria* (Trans. A. A. Brill), New York: Avon Books.

Brown, G. W., and Harris, T. (1979) *Social Origins of Depression: A Study of Psychiatric Disorders in Women*, London: Tavistock Publications.

Bruch, H. (1961) 'Conceptual confusion in eating disorders', *Journal of Nervous and Mental Disease* 133: 46–54.

(1973) *Eating Disorders: Obesity, Anorexia Nervosa, and the Person Within*, New York: Basic Books.

(1978) *The Golden Cage*, Cambridge, MA: Harvard University Press.

Clark, D. M., and Beck, A. T. (in press) 'Cognitive approaches', in C. Last and M. Hersen (eds) *Handbook of Anxiety Disorders*, New York: Pergamon.

Clark, D. M., and Teasdale, J. D. (1982) 'Diurnal variation in clinical depression and accessibility of memories of positive and negative experiences', *Journal of Abnormal Psychology* 91: 87–95.

(1985) 'Constraints on the effects of mood on memory', *Journal of Personality and Social Psychology* 48: 1595–608.

Costa, P. T., and McCrae, R. R. (1980) 'Influence of extraversion and neuroticism on subjective well-being: happy and unhappy people', *Journal of Personality and Social Psychology* 38: 668–78.

Costello, C. G. (1957) 'The control of visual imagery in mental disorder', *Journal of Mental Science*, 103: 840–9.

Davis, D., McLemore, C. W., and London, P. (1970) 'The role of visual imagery in desensitization', *Behaviour Research and Therapy* 88: 11–13.

DeSilva, P. (1986) 'Imagery in the phenomenology and the treatment of obsessional-compulsive disorders', in D. G. Russell, D. F. Marks, and J. T. E. Richardson (eds) *Imagery 2*, Dunedin: Human Performance Associates.

and Rachman, S. (1981) 'Is exposure a necessary condition for fear-reduction?' *Behaviour Research and Therapy* 19: 227–37.

Dyckman, J. M., and Cowan, P. A. (1978) 'Imaging, vividness, and the outcome of in vivo and imagined scene desensitization', *Journal of Consulting and Clinical Psychology* 46: 155–6.

Emmelkamp, P. M. G. (1974) 'Self-observation versus flooding in the treatment of agoraphobia', *Behaviour Research and Therapy* 12: 229–37.

and Wessels, H. (1975) 'Flooding in imagination vs. flooding in vivo: a comparison with agoraphobics', *Behaviour Research and Therapy* 13: 7–15.

Euse, F. J., and Haney, J. N. (1975) 'Clarity, controllability, and emotional intensity of image: correlations with introversion, neuroticism, and subjective anxiety', *Perceptual and Motor Skills* 40: 443–7.

Eysenck, H. J. (1960) 'Levels of personality, constitutional factors and social influence: an experimental approach', *International Journal of Social Psychiatry* 4: 12–24.

and Eysenck, S. B. G. (1968) *Eysenck Personality Inventory*, San Diego, CA: Educational and Industrial Testing Service.

(1975) *Manual of the Eysenck Personality Questionnaire (Junior and Adult)*, London: Hodder & Stoughton.

Foa, E. B., Steketee, G., Turner, R. M., and Fisher, S. C. (1980) 'Effects of imaginal exposure to feared disasters in obsessive-compulsive checkers', *Behaviour Research and Therapy* 18: 449–55.

Fogarty, S. J., and Hemsley, D. R. (1983) 'Depression and the accessibility of memories', *British Journal of Psychiatry* 42: 232–7.

Garner, D. M., and Garfinkel, P. E. (1981) 'Body image in Anorexia Nervosa: measurement, theory, and clinical implications', *International Journal of Psychological Medicine* 11: 263–84.

Gordon, R. A. (1950) 'An experiment correlating the nature of imagery with performance on a test of reversal perspective', *British Journal of Psychology* 41: 63–7.

Haney, J. N., and Euse, F. J. (1976) 'Skin conductance and heart rate responses to neutral, positive, and negative imagery: implications for covert behaviour therapy procedures', *Behavior Therapy* 7: 494–503.

Horowitz, M. J. (1983) *Image Formation and Psychotherapy*, New York: Jason Aronson.

Lang, P. J. (1977) 'Imagery in therapy: an information processing analysis of fear', *Behavior Therapy* 8: 862–86.

(1979) 'Emotional imagery and visceral control', in R. J. Gatchel and K. P. Price (eds) *Clinical Applications of Biofeedback: Appraisal and Status*, New York: Pergamon.

Lazarus, A. (1981) *The Practice of Multimodal Therapy*, New York: McGraw-Hill.

Lazarus, R. S. (1966) *Psychological Stress and the Coping Process*, New York: McGraw-Hill.

Leuner, H. (1984) *Guided Affective Imagery*, New York: Thieme-Stratton.

Loftus, E. F. (1975) 'Leading questions and the eye-witness report', *Cognitive Psychology* 1: 560–72.

MacLeod, C., Mathews, A., and Tata, P. (1986) 'Attentional bias in emotional disorders', *Journal of Abnormal Psychology* 95: 15–20.

Marks, D. F. (1973) 'Visual imagery differences in the recall of pictures', *British Journal of Psychology* 64: 17–24.

—— (1985) 'Imagery paradigms and methodology', *Journal of Mental Imagery* 9: 93–106.

—— and McKellar, P. (1982) 'The nature and function of imagery', *Journal of Mental Imagery* 6: 1–124.

Martin, M. (1986) 'Imagery and emotion in episodic memory', in D. G. Russell, D. F. Marks, and J. T. E. Richardson (eds) *Imagery 2*, Dunedin: Human Performance Associates.

—— (1988a) 'Individual differences in imagery for emotional events', in C. Cornoldi (ed.) *Imagery and Cognition*, Padua: University of Padua.

—— (1988b) 'Selective enhancement of imagery in anxiety', in M. Denis, J. Engelkamp, and J.T.E. Richardson (eds) *Cognitive and Neuro-psychological Approaches to Mental Imagery*, Dordrecht: Martinus Nijhoff.

Mathews, A., and MacLeod, C. (1985) 'Selective processing of threat cues in anxiety states', *Behaviour Research and Therapy* 23: 563–9.

—— (1986) 'Discrimination of threat cues without awareness in anxiety states', *Journal of Abnormal Psychology* 95: 131–8.

Miller, G. A., Levin, D. N., Kozak, M. J., Cooke, E. W., McLean, A., and Lang, P. J. (1987) 'Individual differences in imagery and the psychophysiology of emotion', *Cognition and Emotion* 1: 367–90.

Miller, N. E. (1948) 'Studies of fear as an acquirable drive: fear as motivation and fear-reduction as reinforcement in the learning of new responses', *Journal of Experimental Psychology* 38: 89–101.

Mowrer, O. H. (1960) *Learning Theory and Behavior*, New York: Wiley.

Murray, E. J., and Foote, F. (1979) 'The origins of fear of snakes', *Behaviour Research and Therapy* 17: 489–93.

Nowlis, V. (1970) 'Mood: behaviour and experience', in M. B. Arnold (ed.) *Feelings and Emotions: The Loyola Symposium*, New York: Winston.

Orbach, S. (1978) *Fat is a Feminist Issue*, London: Paddington Press.

—— (1982) *Fat is a Feminist Issue II*, London: Hamlyn.

Paivio, A. (1971) *Imagery and Verbal Processes*, New York: Holt, Rinehart & Winston.

—— (1986) *Mental Representations: A Dual Coding Approach*, New York: Oxford University Press.

—— Yuille, J. C., and Madigan, S. A. (1968) 'Concreteness, imagery and meaningfulness values for 925 nouns', *Journal of Experimental Psychology Monograph Supplement* 76(1, Pt. 2).

Rachman, S., and Hodgson, R. (1980) *Obsessions and Compulsions*, Englewood Cliffs, NJ: Prentice-Hall.

Richardson, J. T. E. (1978) 'Reported mediators and individual differences in mental imagery', *Memory and Cognition* 6: 376–8.

Rimm, D., and Bottrell, J. (1969) 'Four measures of visual imagination', *Behaviour Research and Therapy* 7: 63–9.

Rubin, D. C. (1980) '51 properties of 125 words: a unit analysis of verbal behavior', *Journal of Verbal Learning and Verbal Behavior* 19: 736–55.

Schwartz, G. E., Weinberger, D. A., and Singer, J. A. (1981) 'Cardiovascular differentiation of happiness, sadness, anger, and fear following imagery and exercise', *Psychosomatic Medicine* 43: 343–64.

Sheikh, A. A., and Kunzendorf, R. G. (1984) 'Imagery, physiology, and psychosomatic illness', in A. A. Sheikh (ed.) *International Review of Mental Imagery*, vol. 1, New York: Human Sciences Press.

Spielberger, C. D. (1966) 'The effects of anxiety on complex learning and academic achievement', in C. D. Spielberger (ed.) *Anxiety and Behavior*, New York: Academic Press.

Gorsuch, R. L., and Lushene, R. E. (1970) *Manual for the State-Trait Anxiety Inventory (Self Evaluation Questionnaire)*, Palo Alto, CA: Consulting Psychologist Press.

Strosahl, L. D., Ascough, J., and Rojas, A. (1986) 'Imagery assessment by self report: a multidimensional analysis of clinical imagery', *Cognitive Therapy and Research* 10: 187–200.

Teasdale, J. D., and Fogarty, S. J. (1979) 'Differential effects of induced mood on retrieval of pleasant and unpleasant events from episodic memory', *Journal of Abnormal Psychology* 88: 248–57.

Teasdale, J. D., and Taylor, R. (1981) 'Induced mood and accessibility of memories: an effect of mood state or of induction procedure?', *British Journal of Clinical Psychology* 20: 39–48.

Traub, A. L., and Orbach, J. (1964) 'Psychological studies of body image: an adjustable body distorting mirror', *Archives of General Psychiatry* 11: 53–66.

Turner, C. W., and Layton, J. F. (1976) 'Verbal imagery and connotation as memory-induced mediators of aggressive behavior ', *Journal of Personality and Social Psychology* 33: 755–63.

Velten, E. (1968) 'A laboratory task for the induction of mood states', *Behaviour Research and Therapy* 6: 473–82.

Williams, J. M. G. (1984) *The Psychological Treatment of Depression: A Guide to the Theory and Practice of Cognitive-Behavioral Therapy*, London: Croom Helm.

Williams, R., Martin, M., and Clark, D. (in preparation) 'Individual differences in the effects of mood and personality on visual imagery'.

Wolberg, L. R. (1948) *Medical Hypnosis*, vol. 1, New York: Grune & Stratton.

Wolpe, J. (1958) *Psychotherapy by Reciprocal Inhibition*, Stanford, CA: Stanford University Press.

—— (1969) *The Practice of Behavior Therapy*, New York: Pergamon.

Wright, J., and Mischel, W. (1982) 'Influence of affect on cognitive social learning person variables', *Journal of Personality and Social Psychology* 5: 901–14.

Yates, F. A. (1966) *The Art of Memory*, London: Routledge & Kegan Paul.

Chapter twelve

The cerebral localization of visual imagery: evidence from emission computerized tomography of cerebral blood flow

Georg Goldenberg, Ivo Podreka, and
Margarete Steiner

It is a matter of controversy in cognitive psychology whether the introspective experience of having mental visual images corresponds to a distinct mode of cognitive processing. The controversial positions have been summed up as follows: 'Does the architecture of mind contain any structures and processes that are specific to imagery, or does imagery simply consist of the application of general cognitive structures to data structures whose content happens to be about the visual world?' (Pinker 1984: 39). These alternative views give rise to different hypotheses concerning the neurological substrate of imaging. One possible extension of the view that visual imagery is subserved by specific structures is the hypothesis that these are structures which are specialized for the processing of visual information (see Chapters 2 and 3 in this volume). The anatomical substrate of imagery is then to be sought in areas of the brain which receive their main input from visual perception. Visual areas in the occipital lobe and the occipito-temporal and occipito-parietal junctions respectively would be plausible candidates. Conversely, if imagery is only the application of general cognitive structures to knowledge about the visual world, its neurological substrate should be located in brain areas which receive information from different sources and are not restricted to processing only visual information. In this case supramodal association cortex would be most likely to be the neurological substrate of visual imagery.

The assumption that imagery differs from other modes of thinking in that it employs the activity of processes that are genuinely used in visual perception is only one of several possibilities to contradict the view that the same general cognitive structure subserves visual imagery and non-imagistic thinking. Dual-coding theory (Paivio 1979, 1986), for example, assumes that there are two symbolic systems, one responsible for verbal, the other for nonverbal information-processing. Visual imagery is a domain of the nonverbal system. The division between the symbolic systems does not extend to the perceptual stage in which sensory experience is converted to a symbolic representation. Therefore, this theory would not predict an involvement of modality-specific visual areas in visual imagery. However, it would be strongly supported if within supramodal association cortex an anatomically distinct system could be found, which was responsible for nonverbal information processing as well as for visual imagery. Since there is a left-hemisphere dominance for language, the right hemisphere offers itself for being the site of the nonverbal system. A right-hemisphere dominance for visual imagery has been postulated and widely accepted (Paivio 1979; Denis 1979; Ley 1983), although empirical support is scarce and equivocal (Ehrlichman and Barrett 1983).

When we started blood-flow research with single photon emission computer tomography (SPECT) in 1983, we too believed that visual imagery would activate the right hemisphere. In our very first study we wanted to see whether our SPECT would be sensitive enough to detect any changes in blood-flow patterns caused by cognitive activities. We compared flow patterns in subjects who listened to lists of either meaningless syllables or concrete words and had to detect repetitions (Goldenberg, Podreka and Hoell, unpublished). There were only four subjects in each group and the SPECT was evaluated by mere visual inspection. However, there was a clear-cut result: concrete words caused a shift of cerebral activity to the right hemisphere where it concerned mainly the right temporal and parietal lobes. Error rates were higher with syllables and subjects reported that the distinction of syllables was a difficult task, whereas they found it easy to detect repetitions in the list of concrete words. We will come back to this aspect later. At the time of the experiment we thought that the emergence of visual images in subjects who listened to concrete words could have caused the right-brain activation, and this hypothesis motivated our first experiment.

Experimental method

SPECT offers the possibility of visualizing the distribution of an iso-tope over the whole brain (Podreka *et al.* 1984, 1987). The isotopes we used were 123-I-isopropylamphetamine (IMP) in the pilot study and in the first experiment, and Tc-99-hexamethylpropylenamineoxime

(HMPAO) in the following ones. Both isotopes are injected intravenously and trapped in brain tissue, where they remain in a steady state without further changing their distribution for several hours. Their cerebral distribution is then proportional to regional cerebral blood-flow (rCBF) during the time when the steady state was achieved. The steady state is reached within 2 minutes after injection of HMPAO but only after 20 minutes with IMP. In both cases the final distribution that is measured by SPECT represents a cumulation of all rCBF patterns during that time.

Acquisition of data is performed by a dual head rotating gamma camera (SIEMENS ZLC37) with a linear sampling distance of 3.125 mm. The spatial resolution of the measurement is 14 mm full width half maximum (FWHM) for IMP and 12 mm FWHM for HMPAO. The distribution of the isotope and hence of rCBF is reconstructed in horizontal brain cuts of 3.125 mm but for further evaluation seven adjacent slices are cumulated. Regions of interest are delineated in four adjacent cumulated slices, and the volume and mean count rate of each region of interest registered. Each regional count-rate is divided by the mean count-rate of all regions taken together. The resulting index reflects the distribution but not the size of rCBF. An index of hemispheric asymmetry is obtained by dividing the mean count-rate of all left-hemispheric regions taken together by that of all right-hemispheric regions taken together. The cerebellum is not considered for this index. The index of hemispheric asymmetry is expressed as a percentage, 100 per cent corresponding to perfect symmetry and higher values indicating a bias in favour of the left hemisphere. Generally, this procedure for normalization of data eliminates the influence of interindividual variations in global blood-flow and thus favours the detection of event slight focal changes induced by cognitive tasks, but it prohibits conclusions concerning the absolute size of blood flow.

It should be emphasized that the distribution of the isotope is influenced by rCBF variations during the whole time when the injected isotope gets trapped. With respect to stimulation studies this means that the SPECT studies reflect a summing up of all cognitive activities during 2 minutes (HMPAO) or 20 minutes (IMP) immediately following intravenous injection.

Subjects and general experimental design

The experimental subjects were healthy volunteers with an age range from 21 to 37 years who had given information consent and were paid. All were right-handed as assessed by a revised version of the Edinburgh inventory.

During the experiments subjects were in a supine position. They were blindfolded and were advised to close their eyes under the blindfold. They wore earphones which were connected to a tape recorder. Before the start of the experiment, instructions were repeated from the tape, and loudness was regulated individually for comfortable and distinct comprehension. In one hand the subject held a lamp which could be flashed by an easy touch. In the first experiment all subjects held the lamp in the left hand, while in the remaining experiments half of the subjects held the lamp in the right hand and the other half in the left. In the first experiment the right hand was placed in hot water (this was done to obtain samples of arterialized venous blood for a calculation of absolute blood-flow values which, however, were not evaluated for this research), and 5 minutes after the start of the experiment a puncture of a left cubital vein was made and the isotope was injected. In the remaining experiments an intravenous line was laid to a cubital vein of the hand that did not hold the lamp before the experiment, and the isotope was injected 1 minute after the start of the experiment.

Experiment 1

The experimental design of the first experiment (Goldenberg *et al.* 1987), was planned to disentangle the possible effects of meaningfulness of stimuli, concreteness of words, and visual imagery which had evidently been confounded in the pilot study. There were five experimental conditions:

Resting state: In this condition subjects had neither lamp nor earphones. They were only advised to lie quietly.

In the stimulation studies subjects listened to a list of words spoken with an interval of 5 seconds between them. Then, after a further interval of 30 seconds, they heard another word and had to flash the lamp if they thought that this word had been present in the preceding list. There were twice as many incorrect as correct repetitions, and the incorrect ones were either phonetically or semantically similar to a word in the list. There were four variations of this task:

Meaningless words: Phonotactically correct meaningless words were derived by reversing and exchanging syllables and letters within real German words (for example, Riroff, Schramsol, Tressebust, Popnos, Gatilu). Thirty-six lists of eight stimuli were given.

Abstract nouns had a rating of no more than 3 on a 7-point scale of imageability of German nouns (Mitterndorfer 1978). Twenty-four lists of twelve nouns were given.

Concrete nouns had been rated no less than 6 on the 7-point scale of imageability. Again, twenty-four lists of twelve nouns were given.

The frequencies of both abstract and concrete nouns showed a normal distribution when plotted on a logarithmic scale of word frequency (Meier 1978). The proportion of high-frequency words appeared to be somewhat higher in the case of abstract nouns, probably because the scale is based exclusively on written language.

In memorizing the concrete words, subjects followed one of two different instructions:

No explicit imagery: Subjects first memorized a pilot list of concrete nouns and were then asked how they had proceeded. One subject who reported having used an imagery strategy was excluded. The other subjects had either tried to rehearse the words silently or reported no particular strategy at all. They were instructed to carry on the same way as they had done with the pilot list. Subjects were questioned again after the task. One of them had changed to an imagery strategy after the first word and was consequently included in the imagery group.

Imagery: Subjects were instructed not to rehearse the words but to try to visualize the objects named and to concentrate upon the mental images. They were told that consecutively created images might happen to mingle into a composite image and that this would be rather advantageous.

Results

Without imagery instructions, the numbers of correct and false positive responses given to concrete and abstract nouns in the recognition task were virtually identical. By contrast, the imagery instructions led to a significant improvement and indeed to virtually perfect performance. With meaningless words the number of false positive responses was higher than in the other conditions.

Table 12.1 shows the indices of hemispheric asymmetry for each condition. Memorizing the same list of concrete nouns gave rise to

Table 12.1 Experiment 1: means and standard deviations (SD) of indices of hemispheric asymmetry (left-hemisphere regions divided by right-hemisphere regions)

Condition	n	Mean	SD
Resting state	18	98.6	1.6
Meaningless words	7	100.2	1.4
Abstract nouns	8	99.6	2.0
Concrete nouns, no explicit imagery	7	98.4	2.2
Concrete nouns, imagery instructions	11	100.8	1.7
Visual day-dream	1	101.2	–

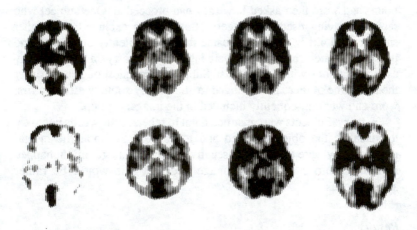

Figure 12.1 Typical results from Experiments 1, 2, and 3.
The horizontal cuts that contain the inferior occipital regions are shown. They are seen from above, and so the left-hand side of the image corresponds to the left-hand side of the brain. The frontal-occipital axis is aligned vertically with the frontal pole at the top. The darker a region, the higher its flow rate. Each image is scaled to its individual maximum which appears black. Where there is a large difference between the flow rate of the local maximum and the flow rates of other regions, the latter appear particularly pale (as in the first two panels of the bottom row). If, on the other hand, the distribution of isotope is rather uniform, all regions are dark (as in the third panel of the bottom row). (Continued opposite)

distinctly different asymmetries depending on the strategy used. Whereas the imagery instructions led to the largest leftward shift of blood flow of all stimulated conditions, the same concrete nouns given without the imagery instruction gave rise to the largest bias in favour of the right hemisphere.

When variations of single regional count-rates across conditions were evaluated, however, the results were less revealing. Compared with the resting state the stimulated conditions led to increases of local-flow indices in the left inferior frontal and left superior temporal lobe. Since these regions contain the language centres of Broca and Wernicke, their activation could be easily explained by the verbal task demands. In both superior frontal lobes and the left middle frontal lobe the flow rates were significantly higher than at rest only in the imagery condition, but no difference between any two stimulated conditions reached an appropriate significance level (Goldenberg *et al.* 1987).

On visual inspection of the SPECT images, however, we noted a salient, asymmetric maximum of activation in the left inferior occipital lobe of several subjects who had used imagery to memorize the words (see left-hand side of Figure 12.1).

The patterns of correlations between regional flow indices were studied by smallest space analysis (SSA), a non-metric multi-

---

Left-hand panels. These show results from Experiment 1. The top panel shows a subject who memorized concrete nouns without being instructed to use imagery. The bottom panel shows a subject who used visual imagery to memorize the same nouns. Note the outstanding maximum in the left frontal and left occipital region.

Middle panels. These show results from Experiment 2. The top-left panel shows a subject in the yes-no condition; the top-right panel shows a subject judging low-imagery sentences. The leftward shift from the former to the latter affected mainly the parietal lobes which are not shown in these cuts. The bottom-left panel shows a subject judging visual-imagery sentences; the bottom-right panel shows a subject judging motor-imagery sentences. Note the asymmetric occipital maximum in the visual-imagery condition. It may be observed that the asymmetry in favour of the left hemisphere is mainly confined to the anterior portion of the inferior occipital region, whereas on the posterior tip (which contains the primary visual-cortex), the maximum spreads across the midline.

Right-hand panels. These show results from the 'corners' condition of Experiment 3. The top panel shows a subject who rated his visual images as 'vague and dim'; the bottom panel shows a subject who rated his images as 'perfectly clear and vivid, as in normal vision'. Note the higher frontal flow rate in the top panel and the higher occipital flow rate in the bottom panel. There is, however, no distinct asymmetry of occipital flow in the subject who rated his images as being more vivid.

dimensional scaling-procedure (Guttman 1967; Lingoes 1979). This was done for each experimental condition separately. We reasoned that if a system of correlations were present in one condition but absent in another, this could indicate the formation of a functional link between the regions concerned in the condition that showed the relevant correlations.

The most salient correlational structure was a tight relationship between homologous regions of both hemispheres. Only in the resting state and when concrete words had been memorized without imagery was there a rather clear-cut division between right- and left-hemispheric regions. These were also the conditions with the largest asymmetry in favour of the right hemisphere (see Table 12.1). This division may have indicated a restriction of task-specific activity to only one hemisphere, so that the task was experienced as 'easy'.

SSA showed a close association between inferior temporal and occipital regions in both concrete-nouns conditions but not in the remainder of the conditions. The association concerned the lateral and medial inferior temporal regions and the inferior and superior occipital regions of both hemispheres with the imagery instructions, but spared the right lateral inferior temporal and superior occipital region without such instructions. These regions appeared to co-operate with the remainder of the right-hemisphere regions rather than with their own left-hemisphere counterparts. The inferior temporal lobe is known to play a crucial role in memory but contains also secondary visual cortex. The occipital area is where the primary and secondary visual cortex is located (Creutzfeld 1983). The association between these regions was hence interpreted as indicating an involvement of visual cortex in the memorizing of imaginable words. This interpretation appeared quite straightforward with respect to those subjects who intentionally used imagery to memorize the words. With respect to those who were not instructed to use imagery, one may well speculate that listening to concrete nouns elicited visual mental images in them also, but that they did not benefit from them for task performance. Perhaps the subjects received some benefit from visual imagery in this condition, but the benefit was used to release the right hemisphere from co-operation in the task, allowing it to attend to background stimuli. The task was solved only by the left hemisphere and the few right-hemispheric regions functionally associated to it, and the net result was the same as that obtained by both hemispheres together when memorizing abstract nouns without being supported by visual imagery.

This interpretation could be supported by a perusal of the literature concerning the influence of attention to background stimuli upon hemispheric asymmetries of cerebral blood-flow and metabolism. In subjects whose cerebral metabolism was investigated during a resting state, a progressive leftward shift of hemispheric asymmetry has been observed with progressing sensory deprivation (Mazziotta *et al.* 1982). On the other hand, increases of right-hemispheric blood flow have been found in subjects who attended to a touch of a finger regardless of whether they received the touch on their right or their left hand (Risberg and Prohovnick 1983). Most probably, there is a general dominance of the right hemisphere for a widely tuned attention to external stimuli (Tucker and Williamson 1984). It will be remembered that during the experiments the right hand was placed in hot water and the left one received an intravenous injection. Attention to this and other background stimuli may have enhanced right-hemisphere blood flow. At the same time the left hemisphere was probably engaged in internally driven cognitive activities: the solution of the memory task in the concrete-nouns conditions and perhaps pleasant thoughts in the resting state (unfortunately we did not ask subjects what had been going on in their minds during rest). The absence of a division between hemispheres in the SSA of the other stimulated conditions would then indicate that in them both hemispheres collaborated to solve the task, whereas in memorizing concrete nouns without imagery instruction the right hemisphere may have been engaged in attending to background stimuli.

Before turning to the second experiment, we want to report a rather informal single case study done with the isotope IMP. The subject of this study was the first author, and its original aim was to get an idea of what would happen when imagery was used without a concomitant memory task. A tape had been prepared with a list of concrete nouns and the subject was to form a corresponding image to each word. As can happen when the experimenter is a subject in an experiment, the tape-recorder broke down immediately after the isotope had been injected. It will be recalled that it takes about 20 minutes until IMP is completely trapped in brain tissue, and that the final distribution represents a summing of all cognitive activities during that time. To interrupt the experiment and report that the tape had broken down (nobody else had noticed it) would have spoiled the whole experiment. So the subject decided to image visually whatever happened to come into his mind but to avoid inner verbalizations. He entered into a pleasant and vivid day-dream which

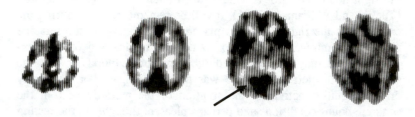

Figure 12.2 Single case study of a visual day-dream.
The orientation of the images is the same as in Figure 12.1, but all four cuts are shown. The first panel shows the superior frontal and superior parietal regions; the second panel shows the anterior and middle frontal, the inferior parietal and the superior occipital regions; the third panel shows the anterior and inferior frontal, the superior temporal and the inferior occipital regions, the anterior basal ganglia, and the thalamus; and the fourth panel shows the orbitofrontal and the inferior temporal regions and the cerebellum. The arrow points to the asymmetric maximum in the left inferior occipital region. As in the processing of visual-imagery sentences, the asymmetry is mainly confined to the anterior portion of that region.

had a distinct emotional flavour: he imagined a walk through Paris, visited apartments where he had previously lived, and met a girlfriend of long ago. When SPECT was evaluated (Figure 12.2), the most salient finding was a maximum regional flow in the occipital regions. Flow there was between 116 and 121 per cent of the global mean, the latter value being reached in the left inferior occipital region. When compared with the flow rates of the subjects examined in a resting state there were increases of 1.4 standard deviations (SD) in the right and 2.5 SD in the left superior occipital region, and of 3.6 SD in the right and 5.1 SD in the left inferior occipital region. In both hippocampal regions flow was about 1.5 SD higher than in the resting state and in the left inferior

Table 12.2 Examples of sentences used in Experiment 2

Low-imagery sentences
Lazarus was one of the twelve apostles of Jesus Christ. (w)
Aristophanes was a Greek writer of comedy. (c)
The Vatican is in Rome, but is a state on its own and not part of Italy. (c)
The categorical imperative is an ancient grammatical form which is only
   rarely used in modern language. (w)
Istanbul is the capital of Turkey. (w)

Visual-imagery sentences
The forelegs of a cat are longer than its hindlegs. (w)
A grapefruit is bigger than an orange. (c)
The roof of St Stephen's cathedral has green stripes. (w)
The cogwheel and the chain are on the right-hand side of a bicycle. (c)
If one is standing in the Town Hall Park (of Vienna) and looks towards the
   Town Hall, the University is on the right. (c)

Motor-imagery sentences
A pencil is held between one's thumb, index finger, and ring finger. (w)
If a screw is turned with a screwdriver, the whole forearm rotates. (c)
When clicking loudly with the tongue, the mouth is held shut. (w)
One can at the same time touch the left ear with the right index finger
   and the nose with the right thumb. (c)
Press buttons are usually pressed with the ring finger. (w)

Note: The original sentences were presented in German. Correct items are
denoted by 'c' and incorrect items by 'w'.

temporal region 2.2 SD. As in subjects who had been advised to use
imagery to memorize concrete nouns, the index of hemispheric
asymmetry was biased in favour of the left side (see Table 12.1). Flow
rates of frontal regions, however, were even somewhat lower than those
of the resting state.

Experiment 2

The second experiment (Goldenberg *et al.*, in press) was aimed at
exploring the use of imagery in a semantic-memory task, namely
judging the correctness of the predications of high-imagery sentences
(Eddy and Glass 1981; Glass *et al.* 1985). Introspectively, the
judgement of high-imagery sentences leads to the experience of visual
imagery regardless of whether imagery instructions are given or not. It
appears as if the knowledge concerned is stored in a pictorial
representation and can be verbally described only after the visual mental
image has been inspected. For the construction of high-imagery
sentences it was assumed that a sentence would require visual imagery
if its predication concerned aspects of the visual appearance or spatial

relations of objects which are not usually referred to in everyday verbal communication (see Table 12.2).

A second type of high-imagery sentence was assumed to demand imagery of motor actions. Research into the facilitating effects of imagery on episodic memory has suggested that motor imagery selectively enhances verbal memory for items that refer to motor actions, and that this effect is independent of and additive to the effects of visual imagery (Engelkamp and Zimmer 1986; see Chapter 6 in this volume). On the other hand it has been shown that memory for movements is interfered with by interpolated motor imagery, but that the deleterious effect of the interpolated motor-imagery task is attenuated by secondary interference from a simultaneous visual perceptual task and not by the simultaneous performance of an actual movement (Johnson 1982). This led to the conclusion that the interference is caused by the visuospatial rather than by the motor aspects of motor imagery, and that both memory for movement and motor imagery are based on spatial rather than motor codes (see also Smyth 1984). From this point of view a difference between motor and visual imagery might emerge only from the fact that the former deals exclusively with spatial relations whereas the latter might also concern other properties of visual perception like colours and local patterns. With respect to the neurological basis of mental imagery, this could lead to the expectation that motor imagery involves the dorsal visual system, which extends into the parietal lobes, rather than the basal one, which stretches into the inferior temporal lobes (Mishkin *et al.* 1983; Levine *et al.* 1985).

Twenty-eight subjects took part in the second experiment. All were residents of Vienna and had at least 12 years of schooling. They were randomly divided into two experimental groups:

Low-imagery group

'Yes-No'

From the tape subjects heard the words 'yes' or 'no' in a random order with an interval of 5 seconds between them. A beep announced the end of the interval. They were instructed to flash the light each time they heard 'no' but not to react to 'yes'.

'Low-imagery sentences'

Subjects heard fifty low-imagery sentences (see Table 12.2) spoken with an interval of 5 seconds between them. Again, a beep announced the end of the interval. Their task was to flash the light each time they considered the predication of a sentence to be wrong (that is, 'not conforming with reality'). They were instructed to behave in the manner of an academic examination; that is to say, that if they did not know whether the sentence was right or wrong they should try to come to a plausible judgement by a consideration of relevant facts and by logical inference. They were advised to try to make themselves 'perfectly clear' what the predication of each sentence was about.

High-imagery group

'Visual-imagery sentences'

The experimental design was the same as with low-imagery sentences but subjects heard fifty visual-imagery sentences (see Table 12.2). They had the same general instructions as those who judged low-imagery sentences, which included the demand to make themselves 'perfectly clear' as to what each sentence was about. However, visual imagery was not mentioned in the instructions. No special advice was given on how to arrive at a correct solution in the case of ignorance.

'Motor-imagery sentences'

This condition differed from the visual-imagery sentences only in that motor-imagery sentences were tested (see Table 12.2).

Results

After each experiment subjects were asked which strategies they had used. In both imagery conditions all subjects reported that they had used imagery. In the motor-imagery condition subjects had fluctuated between two strategies: sometimes they imagined observing someone else who performed the movement, but more frequently they imagined that they themselves were performing the movement. Several subjects reported that imagining the movement was accompanied by a feeling 'within' the body part concerned as if the body part were 'nearly moving'. No actual movements were observed during the experiment. To check for the possibility that subjects had nonetheless produced small actual movements and had solved the problems by exploiting kinaesthetic feedback, four additional subjects were given the same task and EMG (electromyogram) was registered from several muscles of the right arm. Although all subjects in this additional experiment reported that they had imagined the movement 'within' the body, no correlated EMG activities could be observed. The first author was also examined. He was able to produce a vivid feeling of 'nearly moving' the right upper extremity but again no muscle activity was shown in the EMG.

In judging low-imagery sentences subjects committed more errors than with either visual-imagery sentences or motor-imagery sentences.

The index of hemispheric asymmetry showed a significant leftward shift from the yes-no condition to the sentence conditions but did not differ between high- and low-imagery sentences. In SSA none of the conditions showed a dissociation between right and left brain regions. This difference from the first experiment was possibly due to the absence of hot water and intravenous injections which had activated the right hemisphere in the IMP study, but it might also be that our speculations concerning the apparent independence of the right hemisphere had been too speculative.

Frontal flow-rates were higher in both low-imagery conditions than they were with visual imagery. Both low-imagery conditions might have put particular demands on the voluntary control of cognitive activity: in the yes-no condition subjects had to inhibit their spontaneous reaction when responding positively to 'no' but not to 'yes', and in answering low-imagery sentences they had been advised to use specific strategies to come to a plausible decision.

Visual-imagery sentences led to significantly higher flow-rates in the left inferior occipital region than both the yes-no condition and low-imagery sentences (see middle portion of Figure 12.1). Flow rates of inferior temporal regions were highest with visual-imagery sentences, but differed significantly only from the yes-no condition which had the lowest flow-rates in these regions. Unexpectedly, flow rates of both thalamic regions were higher with visual imagery than they were with low-imagery sentences, and in the right thalamus were also higher than they were in the yes-no condition; see Goldenberg (in press) for a thorough discussion of the statistics.

The results of the motor-imagery condition were less revealing: local flow-rates were generally intermediate between the visual-imagery and low-imagery conditions, differing significantly from neither.

In SSA, the difference between high- and low-imagery conditions was much less distinct than it had appeared from the first experiment: a relationship between the inferior occipital regions and the medial inferior temporal (that is, hippocampal) region could be found in all conditions. Only in the yes-no condition did it include two inappropriate regions, the right anterior basal ganglia and the left thalamus. The lateral inferior temporal regions were represented close to the inferior-occipital/hippocampal system in all conditions except motor imagery. By contrast, the superior-occipital regions were particularly close to it in the motor-imagery condition. The superior occipital region is adjacent to the parietal lobe and is a pathway of the 'second' visual system (Mishkin *et al*. 1983). However, a covariation of superior and inferior occipital lobes had also been seen in the first experiment when subjects imagined single objects. Hence, the conclusion that the spread of activation into the superior occipital region seen with motor imagery was due to particular demands on the processing of spatial information could be drawn only with reservations.

Experiment 3

In the previous experiments imagery was used in essentially verbal tasks. We now wanted to see whether the same changes in rCBF would emerge if visual imagery were applied to the solution of a visuospatial task. We adapted an imagery task invented by Brooks (1968). In Brooks's experiment subjects had to classify the corners of an imagined capital letter as being either on top or bottom of the letter, or between top and bottom. Performance of this task was slowed down when subjects had to give their response by pointing to the letters 'Y' or 'N' dispersed on a screen rather than speaking aloud 'yes' or 'no'. An adaptation of this task very similar to the one used here has been given to patients with localized brain damage (Goldenberg, 1989): right-brain-damaged patients turned out to be impaired whereas the performance of left-brain-damaged patients did not differ from that of controls. It thus appears safe to conclude that in spite of the linguistic significance of letters, the evaluation of the number or position of their corners is essentially a visuospatial task.

We called our adaptation of the Brooks task 'corners'. Before the experiment subjects were given a sheet with the letters of the alphabet written by hand in bold capital letters of Helvetica type. Subjects were instructed to study this sheet so that they would be able either to reproduce or recognize the type of writing. During the experiment they heard from the tape twenty-three letters (G, O, and Q were omitted) followed by an interval of between 8 and 15 seconds, depending on the number of corners the letter had. A 'beep' announced the end of the interval. The subject's task was to count the number of corners of the letter and to flash the light once for each corner.

After the experiment subjects received questionnaires asking for the strategies employed. They were asked whether they had solved the task by visually imagining the letter or by an alternative strategy, whether the letter imagined was a recollection of the letter seen beforehand or a 'prototypical' letter, whether they had seen only one part of the letter at a time or the whole letter at once, and in the latter case whether the image of the letter had emerged part by part or all at once. Furthermore, the questionnaire asked whether they had had a feeling of following the contours of the letter with their eyes or head and whether they had imagined writing the letter by hand. The subjects also completed the Vividness of Visual Imagery Questionnaire (VVIQ: Marks 1973). This questionnaire describes details of four scenes from everyday life. The subject is asked to form visual images to the descriptions and to rate the vividness of the images on a 5-point scale from 'perfectly clear and vivid as normal vision' to 'no image at all, you only know that you are thinking of the object'. After completing the VVIQ they were asked to rate the vividness of the letters imagined during the experiment along the same scale.

The control condition was based on the evaluation of letters as well but was assumed to demand a consideration of the linguistic properties of letters rather than their visuospatial features. It was called 'alphabet'. From the tape, subjects heard pairs of letters, connected by the word 'to' (for example, 'A to K'), followed by an interval of between 8 and 15 seconds (depending on the distance between the letters in their alphabetical order) and a beep. Their task was to count the number of letters in the alphabet between the two letters and to flash the lamp once for each of them. The time course of the experiment was the same as in the corner condition, and when correctly performed both experiments yielded the same sequence of responses.

After this experiment the subjects received a short questionnaire concerning their strategies. They were asked whether they had internally spoken the alphabet or had used another strategy. The questionnaire also asked whether the subjects had had visual images of the letters and, if so, whether they had solved the task by counting the seen rather than the spoken letters. Unfortunately, the subjects who had experienced visual images were not asked to rate their vividness.

Eighteen subjects took part in this experiment. Each participated in both conditions with their order counterbalanced across subjects.

Results

After the 'corners' condition all of the subjects asserted that they had solved the task by mentally inspecting a visual image of the letter. However, when rating the vividness of the imagined letter, two of them chose the rating which signified 'no image at all, you only know that you are thinking of the object'. For half of the subjects, the imagined letters were concrete recollections of the letters seen before; for the other half, they were prototypical instances of the type of writing. Also, half of the subjects had created the mental images part by part and the other half all at once. Fourteen subjects felt that they had followed the contours of the letters by eye movements, seven of them had had the feeling of moving the head too, and eight had imagined writing the letters. With the exception of one subject who obviously followed the contours of the letters with the light, no actual movements could be observed during the experiment.

After the alphabet condition all of the subjects agreed that they had internally spoken the alphabet in order to solve the task. Eight subjects had experienced visual mental images of the letters, but all denied having used these images to count the seen rather than the spoken letters.

There was no marked difference in the number of errors between the two conditions, nor did they differ in the global hemispheric asymmetry of blood flow. The only significant differences in regional blood-flow rates concerned the inferior frontal regions: in both, flow was higher in the alphabet condition. The numerical differences in the inferior temporal and left inferior occipital regions were in the expected direction: flow rates were higher in the 'corners' condition and this difference was somewhat larger in those subjects who had not had visual images in the alphabet condition, but the differences were far from reaching statistical significance. Their magnitude was about 1 per cent, with standard deviations between 3 and 5 per cent. These results did not change when only those subgroups of subjects who had used the same strategy were considered, nor did any comparison between subgroups defined by the use of a strategy approach significance.

Activation of the left inferior frontal region which contains Broca's language area and of its symmetrical homologue in the alphabet condition could easily be explained by the subjects' internal speaking of the letters. (Symmetrical increases in the right-hemispheric counterparts of the left-brain language areas are a frequent finding in blood-flow studies of language tasks.) Likewise, the only salient difference between the SSA representations of correlations between regional count rates could be ascribed to the different demands on verbal processing: in the alphabet condition there was a relationship between the inferior frontal and superior temporal regions (the latter contains Wernicke's language centre on the left side) which was absent in the 'corners' condition. A relationship between the inferior occipital and hippocampal regions of both hemispheres was present in both conditions, and in both conditions the lateral inferior temporal regions could easily be included in this relational system.

At that stage of the data evaluation it seemed that visual imagery had exerted no influence at all upon cerebral blood-flow. The picture changed, however, when we looked at the rank-correlations between regional flow-rates, on the one hand, and error rate, VVIQ, and the ratings of the vividness of mental images in the 'corners' condition, on the other. The number of significant correlation coefficients did not exceed chance in the case of the VVIQ. It was somewhat higher for the error rates but the pattern of correlations could not be meaningfully interpreted. By contrast, the number of significant correlations with the vividness of the images in the 'corners' condition was definitely higher than expected by chance, and their distribution was meaningful: the vividness increased with decreasing flow-rates in regions of the frontal convexity and with increasing flow rates in the inferior temporal regions (see right-hand panel of Figure 12.1). The correlations with flow in the inferior occipital regions were positive but weaker than those in the inferior temporal regions, and the correlations in the superior occipital regions were as close to zero as those in the remaining regions. However, these correlations were not restricted to flow rates in the 'corners' condition itself, but applied also to flow rates in the alphabet condition.

The finding of significant correlations between the vividness of a mental image in the 'corners' condition and flow rates in the alphabet condition was an intriguing finding. There are, however, ways to account for this finding without dropping the assumption that the correlations are specific to imagery. One possibility is that in the alphabet condition the dichotomy between subjects who had visual images of the letters and those who did not masks a more fine-grained continuum in the vividness of the imaged letters, at least among those who reported having had visual images. If one assumes that the vividness of the images in the alphabet condition was proportional to that in the 'corners' condition (a fair assumption which is supported by a tendency of the subjects who had seen nothing in the alphabet condition to rate their images in the 'corners' condition as being less vivid), then correlations in both conditions can equally signify that the activity of the regions concerned depended on how vivid a mental visual image was being formed. A second possibility for explaining the relationship is that there are individual variations in blood flow in the regions concerned which exist independently of the cognitive task being solved, and that those subjects who have higher blood-flow in the inferior temporal and occipital regions and lower blood-flow in the prefrontal regions are inclined to form more vivid visual images when confronted with an appropriate stimulus.

The two explanations suggested are not mutually exclusive: subjects who are inclined to form vivid visual images will spontaneously 'see' letters when rehearsing the alphabet and will form vivid images of them when asked to count the number of corners they have. If, however, the subjects did form more or less vivid mental images in both the 'corners' and the alphabet condition, then our experiment did not really compare an imagery condition with a control condition but tested two different imagery conditions. Still, there remains an essential difference in the functional significance of visual imagery for both tasks. In the alphabet condition, imagining the letters was an accompanying phenomenon which did not contribute to the solution of the task. By contrast, in the 'corners' task, the visual mental image of the letters was presumed to be necessary for counting the corners of those letters. Thus, on the one hand a task analysis implies the creation of a visual representation of the letter to enable it to be visuospatially explored, and on the other hand the subjects reported the occurrence of more or less vivid visual mental images of that letter. The lack of any systematic differences between the two conditions seems to indicate that only that aspect which is tapped by the subjects' introspections depends on activity in the inferior temporal and occipital regions, a suggestion which concurs with the conclusion reached by Marks (1986).

Discussion

Before trying to answer the questions posed in the introduction to this chapter, we will summarize our results on the contributions of different brain regions to visual imagery.

Left vs. right hemisphere

In the first experiment, the voluntary use of imagery led to a leftward shift of hemispheric activity; in the second and third experiments, imagery had no influence on the global asymmetry of cerebral blood flow. The use of imagery never led to an activation of the right hemisphere, and it seems doubtful whether imagery *per se* led to any shift of hemispheric asymmetry at all. One could, however, interpret our data as indicating that imagery activates the left hemisphere (Marks *et al.* 1985; Farah 1986; see also Chapter 14 by Richardson in this volume). In the second experiment, a leftward shift caused by imagery could have been masked by an equal leftward shift caused by the judgement about the correctness of low-imagery sentences; in the third experiment, there were no differences between conditions related to imagery at all, so one would not expect any change in hemispheric asymmetry due to imagery. We feel that differences in either the complexity or the difficulty of tasks are more pertinent to explaining variations in hemispheric asymmetry, but generally the study of hemispheric asymmetry does not seem to benefit much from the results of cerebral activation studies.

When studying the pattern of cerebral activation one cannot avoid observing non-specific activities such as attention to background stimuli, in addition to those brain activities that are specifically related to task solution, and such non-specific accompanying activities may activate regions that are not engaged in task solution. Furthermore, tight correlations between flow rates of homologous regions of both hemispheres appear to be the rule rather than the exception in stimulation studies and may lead to symmetric increases of blood flow even during tasks which are safely known to depend on the integrity of only one hemisphere (Larsen *et al.* 1978). The finding of a distinct asymmetry in the activation of the inferior occipital lobes, however, gains even more relevance from these considerations.

Frontal lobes

Activation of the frontal lobes was seen in the first experiment in subjects who were advised to use imagery as a strategy for memorizing. By contrast, there was no frontal activation in the single case-study of a visual day-dream. In the second experiment frontal flow-rates were lower with visual imagery than they were in low-imagery conditions, and in the third experiment there was even a negative correlation between frontal activity and the experienced vividness of visual mental images. A similar finding was reported by Marks (1986) in a study of EEG mapping in visual imagery: frontal activation occurred only in subjects whose images were low in vividness, whereas only vivid imagery was associated with left occipital activation. Evidently, activation of the frontal lobes does not contribute to imagery *per se*. Most probably, it rather reflects to what degree voluntary control of cognitive processes was being exerted (Norman and Shallice 1986). This would suggest that in most conditions visual images emerged spontaneously rather than being evoked by an additional wilful effort. To explain the frontal activation in the first experiment, one could argue that it was due to the voluntary application of a strategy which just happened to be that of imagery and would have been observed as well in subjects using a non-imagistic mnemonic strategy of similar complexity. (Rote learning was used by several subjects who had not been advised to use imagery, and this did not lead to a comparable frontal hyperperfusion.)

Inferior temporal and occipital regions

Our experiments yielded converging evidence that visual imagery is linked to activity of the inferior temporal and occipital regions, but the activation of these regions was different in different imagery conditions. When imagery was used for memorizing concrete nouns, the activation was confined to the left inferior occipital lobe. In the single case-study of a visual day-dream, it affected the whole occipital lobe and both the hippocampal and the left lateral inferior temporal region, and was greatest in the left inferior occipital region. In the second experiment, visual-imagery sentences led to increased blood flow in the left inferior occipital region and in the inferior temporal regions of both hemispheres, but flow in the inferior temporal regions differed significantly only from the yes-no condition and was not much larger than with low-imagery sentences. In the third experiment, however, the correlations with the vividness of the visual mental images were stronger in the inferior temporal regions than they were in the inferior occipital regions, and there was no difference in the strength of correlations between the left and right inferior occipital regions. SSA suggested that a functional system unified the inferior occipital and hippocampal regions of both hemispheres in all imagery conditions. In the first experiment, the superior occipital regions appeared to belong to this system too. With motor-imagery sentences, the superior occipital regions appeared to be related to the system and the lateral inferior temporal regions were separated from it, whereas in all other conditions the lateral inferior temporal regions could easily be linked and the superior occipital regions were separated.

In sum, it seems that visual imagery activates a whole functional system, the exact boundaries of which change from task to task. Indeed, no single region was activated consistently across all imagery conditions. Although the left inferior occipital region appears to have an outstanding role within the system, its correlation with the vividness of the image in the third experiment was less strong than those of inferior temporal regions.

A consideration of the anatomical substrate of the proposed 'imagery system' leads us directly to the question as to whether visual imagery is subserved by the visual cortex. The inferior occipital lobe contains primary and secondary visual cortex. In the superior occipital regions there is secondary visual cortex. The medial (hippocampal) inferior temporal region contains secondary visual cortex in its posterior portion, but its anterior part consists of supramodal association cortex which is known to play a crucial role in memory. The hippocampus itself acts as a link between neocortex and the limbic system and on its anterior pole the region covers the amygdala which is part of the limbic system. The lateral inferior temporal region is mainly composed of supramodal association cortex (Creutzfeld 1983). Hence, visual cortex is involved in the system but it seems to work only in conjunction with the supramodal association cortex and possibly also with the limbic system. From our results we cannot say which factors determine the extension of the imagery system nor which are the specific contributions of each of its parts to visual imagery. Particularly, we have no clues as to what might be the specific role of the left inferior occipital region. However, the importance of this region for visual imagery is confirmed by studies of event-related brain potentials as well as by clinical observations of imagery deficits following brain lesions (Farah 1984, 1988; Goldenberg 1987, 1989).

Returning to our initial question of whether visual imagery corresponds to a distinct mode of cognitive processing and hence to a distinct pattern of cerebral activation, the answer now seems to be affirmative. However, until now we have neglected the negative results of our experiments. In motor imagery the evidence for a specific pattern

328

of brain activity was at best equivocal, and in the third experiment the necessity to form mental images for the purpose of visuospatial exploration did not lead to any significant changes of cerebral blood-flow patterns. Thus, it appears that one has to specify what kinds of visual mental images do correspond to a distinct mode of cognitive processing and hence to a distinct pattern of brain activity.

The difference between conditions that led to an activation of the presumed imagery system and those that did not might be one between visual and motor imagery. Although most subjects experienced some visual imagery when responding to motor-imagery sentences, motor imagery was the prevailing type of imagery in this condition. The majority of subjects in the imagery condition of the third experiment experienced motor imagery too, since they imagined following the contours of the letters with either their eyes, or their head, or even a hand. We did not record their actual eye movements, and so we cannot rule out the possibility that they solved the task by exploiting kinaesthetic feedback from actual eye movements. In any case, the information they were asked for (the form of letters) is used not only in reading but also in writing: that is, in a motor action of the hand. If they solved the task mainly by retrieving information from motor imagery, this would not lead to a systematic activation of a system specialized for visual imagery. The visual images of the letters would then be regarded as an accompanying phenomenon, not essentially different from the visual images accompanying verbal rehearsal of the alphabet. The vividness of this non-functional visual imagery did correspond to activity of the inferior temporal and occipital regions. Since motor memory most likely consists of supramodal spatial information rather than of reminiscences of motor actions (Johnson 1982; Smyth 1984), the difference between the two kinds of imagery could be reformulated as being a difference between a kind of supramodal spatial imagery and truly visual imagery (Farah, in press).

However, a further difference between the visual and motor-imagery sentences could be found in the richness of the visual information they convey. In the second experiment the visual-imagery sentences described numerous objects and scenes, whereas the motor-imagery sentences were nearly exclusively concerned with the position of body parts. The subjects were instructed to make themselves perfectly clear what the sentence was about. Once engaged in visual imagery, they might have imagined features that were not necessary for judging the correctness of the sentence but were suggested by the evocation of the objects and scenes the sentence referred to. Thus, for example, when judging whether a grapefruit was bigger than an orange, a subject might also have imagined the colours and surface structures of both fruits even though knowledge of these features does not contribute to task solution. Motor-imagery sentences referred mainly to the position of body parts. This uniform and restricted section of visible objects may give less stimulation for adding additional features to the mental images than the diversity of objects and scenes of everyday life alluded to by the visual-imagery sentences. Possibly, it is the amount and accuracy of such additional features that is experienced as vividness of a mental visual image. Thus, in the third experiment, the subjects who had vivid images of the letters might have been those whose images depicted concrete features of the letters (such as their colour, their surface structure, and the exact boundaries of the bars, in addition to the position and number of the corners). If, on the other hand, the images experienced as non-vivid did not show anything other than those features of the letters that were really necessary for a solution of the task, then their informational content was rather poor, consisting only of the limited number of systematic variations of a limited set of straight and curved lines that makes up the alphabet.

Further experiments will be necessary to find out which aspects of visual imagery are important for the degree and extent of activation of inferior temporal and occipital regions. Consider, for example, the imagination of colours. If activation of the inferior temporal and occipital regions depends on the visual as opposed to the spatial properties of the stimulus, then imagination of a colour filling the whole visual field should lead to a strong activation since the image conveys exclusively visual information (that is, information that cannot be properly apprehended by any other than the visual sense). If, on the other hand, activation depends on the amount of visuospatial information depicted by the image, imagination of a complex spatial array should lead to a stronger activation than that of a single colour filling the whole visual field.

Acknowledgements

Experiments 2 and 3 were conducted with support from the Fonds zur Förderung der wissenschaftlichen Forschung. The EMG studies were performed by Dr Wilfried Lang and Dr Frank Uhl. Technical assistance was provided by Kurt Hoell in the first experiment and by Dr Erhard

Suess in the second and third one. We wish to thank Professor Lüder Deecke for having encouraged and supported our research.

References

Brooks, L. R. (1968) 'Spatial and verbal components in the act of recall', *Canadian Journal of Psychology* 22: 349–68.

Creutzfeld, O. D. (1983) *Cortex Cerebri: Leistung, strukturelle und funktionelle Organisation der Hirnrinde*, Berlin: Springer-Verlag.

Denis, M. (1979) *Les images mentales*, Paris: Presse Universitaire de France.

Eddy, J. K., and Glass, A. L. (1981) 'Reading and listening to high and low imagery sentences', *Journal of Verbal Learning and Verbal Behavior* 20: 333–45.

Ehrlichman, H., and Barrett, J. (1983) 'Right hemisphere specialization for mental imagery: a review of the evidence', *Brain and Cognition* 2: 55–76.

Engelkamp, J., and Zimmer, H.D. (1986) 'Motor programs and their relation to semantic memory', *German Journal of Psychology* 9: 239–54.

Farah, M. J. (1984) 'The neurological basis of mental imagery: a componential analysis', *Cognition* 18: 245–72.

—— (1986) 'The laterality of mental image generation: a test with normal subjects', *Neuropsychologia* 24: 541–52.

—— (1988) 'Is visual imagery really visual? Overlooked evidence from neuropsychology', *Psychological Review* 95: 307–17.

—— (1989) 'Visual and spatial mental imagery: dissociable systems of representation', *Cognitive Psychology*.

Glass, A. L., Millen, D. R., Beck, L. G., and Eddy, J. K. (1985) 'Representation of images in sentence verification', *Journal of Memory and Language* 24: 442–65.

Goldenberg, G. (1987) *Neurologische Grundlagen bildlicher Vorstellungen*, Vienna: Springer.

—— (1989) 'The ability of patients with brain damage to generate mental visual images', *Brain* 112: 305–25.

Podreka, I., Steiner, M., and Willems, D. (1987) 'Patterns of regional cerebral blood flow related to meaningfulness and imaginability of words: an emission computer tomography study', *Neuropsychologia* 25: 473–86.

Goldenberg, G., Podreka, I., Steiner, M., Willems, E., Suess, E., and Deeck, L. (in press) 'Regional cerebral blood flow in visual imagery', *Neuropsychologia*.

Guttman, L. (1967) 'The development of nonmetric space analysis: a letter to Professor John Ross', *Multivariate Behavioral Research* 2: 71–82.

Johnson, P. (1982) 'The functional equivalence of imagery and movement', *Quarterly Journal of Experimental Psychology* 34A: 349–65.

Larsen, B., Skinhoj, E., and Lassen, N. A. (1978) 'Variations in regional cerebral blood flow in the right and left hemisphere during automatic speech', *Brain* 101: 193–209.

Levine, D.N., Warach, J., and Farah, M. J. (1985) 'Two visual systems in mental imagery: dissociation of "what" and "where" in imagery disorders due to bilateral posterior cerebral lesions', *Neurology* 35: 1010–18.

Ley, R. G. (1983) 'Cerebral laterality and imagery', in A. A. Sheikh (ed.) *Imagery: Current Theory, Research, and Application*, New York: Wiley.

Lingoes, J. C. (1979) *The Guttman-Lingoes Nonmetric Program Series*, Ann Arbor, MI: Mathesis Press.

Marks, D. F. (1973) 'Visual imagery differences in the recall of pictures', *British Journal of Psychology* 64: 17–24.

—— (1986) 'Imagery, consciousness, and the brain', in D. G. Russell, D. F. Marks, and J. T. E. Richardson (eds) *Imagery 2*, Dunedin: Human Performance Associates.

Uemura, K., Tatsuno, I., and Imamura, Y. (1985) 'EEG topographical analysis of imagery', in I. L. McGaugh (ed.) *Contemporary Psychology: Biological Processes and Theoretical Issues*, Amsterdam: North-Holland.

Mazziotta, J. C., Phelps, M. E., Carson, R. E., and Kuhl, D. E. (1982) 'Tomographic mapping of human cerebral metabolism: sensory deprivation', *Annals of Neurology* 12: 435–44.

Meier, H. (1978) *Deutsche Sprachstatistik*, Hildesheim: Georg Olms Verlag.

Mishkin, M., Ungerleider, L. G., and Macko, K. A. (1983) 'Object vision and spatial vision: two visual pathways', *Trends in Neuroscience* 6: 414–17.

Mitterndorfer, F. (1978) *'Imagery und Konkretheits–Abstraktheitswerte für 1003 Hauptwörter'* unpublished PhD thesis, Philosophische Fakultät der Universität Wien.

Norman, D. A., and Shallice, T. (1986) 'Attention to action: willed and automatic control of behavior', in R. J. Davidson, G. E. Schwartz, and D. Shapiro (eds) *Consciousness and Self Regulation: Advances in Research*, vol. 4, New York: Plenum Press.

Paivio, A. (1979) *Imagery and Verbal Processes*, 2nd edn, Hillsdale, NJ: Erlbaum.

—— (1986) *Mental Representations: A Dual Coding Approach*, New York: Oxford University Press.

Pinker, S. (1984) 'Visual cognition: an introduction', *Cognition* 18: 1–64.

Podreka, I., Hoell, K., DalBianco, P., and Goldenberg, G. (1984) 'Clinical and technical aspects of brain-SPECT with 123-I-isopropyl-amphetamine' *Nuclear Compact* 15: 305–14.

Podreka, I., Suess, E., Goldenberg, G., Steiner, M., Bruecke, T., Mueller, C., Lang, W., Neirinckx, R. D., and Deecke, L. (1987) 'Initial experience with Tc-99m-hexamethylpropyleneamineoxime (Tc-99m-HM-PAO) brain SPECT', *Journal of Nuclear Medicine* 28: 1657–66.

Risberg, J., and Prohovnik, I. (1983) 'Cortical processing of visual and tactile stimuli studied by non-invasive rCBF measurements', *Human Neurobiology* 2: 5–10.

Smyth, M. M. (1984) 'Memory for movements', in M. M. Smyth and A. M. Wing (eds) *The Psychology of Human Movement*, London: Academic Press.

Tucker, D. M., and Williamson, P. A. (1984) 'Asymmetric neural control systems in human self-regulation', *Psychological Review* 91: 185–215.

Chapter thirteen

The bisected image? Visual memory in patients with visual neglect

Alan Sunderland

In one of the most intriguing papers in contemporary neuropsychology, Bisiach and Luzzatti (1978) reported that patients with right-sided brain damage may fail to recall the left half of an imagined visual scene. Two patients who had suffered recent strokes affecting the posterior parts of the right cerebral hemisphere were asked to describe a scene familiar to them from before their illness. They were told to imagine that they were standing facing the cathedral in the Piazza del Duomo in Milan, and to describe what they would see. They described features which would be to their right from this imagined perspective, but not those to their left. However, when asked to imagine the piazza as seen from the other side, they named features they had originally omitted but not those now to the imagined left. This result was replicated in a later study in which a large group of patients with right-hemisphere damage were compared with normal controls (Bisiach *et al.* 1981), and in an unpublished study (Sunderland 1984) a similar trend was found when stroke patients from Cambridge were asked to describe the Market Square.

How are these findings to be interpreted, and are there implications for our understanding of normal visual memory? Bisiach and his colleagues have argued that these results, together with those from subsequent investigations (Bisiach and Berti 1988), provide evidence of a degree of isomorphism between the actual visual scene and its representation in visual memory, so that the left side of the mental image is generated in the right hemisphere, and the right side in the left hemisphere of the brain. This correspondence arises, they argue, because brain mechanisms used in the perception of the actual scene are also brought into play in a 'top–down' fashion in the operation of visual working memory.

To allow a critical evaluation of this interpretation, it is necessary to place the scene-description phenomenon in context. Bisiach *et al.* (1981) found that the effect only occurred in patients who also showed visual neglect – a tendency to ignore visual features to one side of the immediate environment. This was demonstrated by presenting subjects with a symmetrical array of small circles and asking them to put a mark through each circle. The scene-description effect was only seen in the subgroup of patients who showed visual neglect in this task and ignored circles on the left of the array. This chapter will provide an overview of visual neglect and the explanations which have been proposed for this syndrome. The scene description effect will be viewed from this perspective and an alternative explanation will be considered which suggests that neglect in the description of an imagined scene may not indicate unilateral mutilation of visual images.

Characteristics of visual neglect

Visual neglect occurs most frequently and in its most severe form after damage involving the right parietal lobe. Patients with severe neglect may fail to read the beginnings of lines of text, bump into obstacles on their left side, and when asked to draw objects from memory, may leave the left side incomplete (for a review, see Friedland and Weinstein 1977). Patients with damage to the left parietal lobe may show a neglect for the right, but severe right neglect is rarely demonstrated. This does not appear to be due to difficulties in assessing patients with such large left-sided lesions who often have dysphasia, as studies which have been careful to include dysphasics have still shown that left neglect tends to be more common and severe (Gainotti *et al.* 1972; Colombo *et al.* 1976).

Visual neglect is often accompanied by a visual-field defect (usually homonymous hemianopia), but the two appear to be dissociable (see, for example, Albert 1973). The validity of this apparent dissociation has been questioned as it is very difficult to assess rigorously the sensory abilities of patients with visual neglect (see Battersby *et al.* 1956). What is certain is that visual neglect can occur when there is no complete hemianopia but only a reduced ability to maintain visual attention in the visual half-field towards the neglected side ('visual extinction': see Posner *et al.* 1982). It is important to have clear the distinction between hemianopia or visual extinction, which are deficits affecting one visual hemifield, and visual neglect which is a deficit in visual scanning. Many patients with hemianopia compensate for the field defect by making head or eye movements to the blind side, but patients with neglect fail to make such compensatory movements and do not scan the neglected side of the environment.

Theories of visual neglect

There has been a long and lively debate over the primary cause of visual neglect. The theories which have been put forward can be placed under three general headings. The first, 'hemifield deficit' theory, suggests that neglect occurs when patients with impaired learning ability are unable to learn to adapt to hemianopia or visual extinction (Battersby *et al.* 1956; Sunderland 1984). The other two types of theory maintain that neglect is not caused by visual hemifield deficit but arises from a higher-level, cognitive disorder. The 'attentional' theory of neglect (Heilman and Watson 1977) proposes that this is a deficit in the control of spatial orientation, whereas the 'representational' theory (Bisiach and Berti 1988) proposes an inability to form a mental representation of the environment on the neglected side. These three theories will be discussed in turn.

The scene-description phenomenon in itself provides evidence against the hemifield-deficit theory, and additional evidence against it emerges from experiments which will be reviewed later. However, it would be dangerous to dismiss perceptual deficits entirely from further consideration. In cases where patients with visual neglect have a complete hemianopia, this field defect will influence their ability to do any task which involves visual scanning. Chedru *et al.* (1973), for example, found that when subjects were asked to search a visual array for a target, all hemianopics tended to begin their search to the side where there was intact peripheral vision. Hemianopics without visual neglect then went on to make eye movements towards the blind side, whereas those with severe neglect did not. Thus, while hemianopia cannot explain all of visual neglect, it may contribute to a biasing of visual attention towards the side of intact vision. This means that the first step in interpreting any experiment on visual neglect must be to consider what role visual hemifield deficits may have played.

Typically, patients with visual neglect do not show a clear boundary of the neglected area to one side of body midline, but show a gradient of attention across egocentric space. Chedru *et al.* (ibid.) observed that patients with severe neglect often remained with their eyes fixed at the

Figure 13.1 A cancellation test (Albert 1973) completed by a 62-year-old hemianopic man two months after a right-hemisphere stroke. The central line was cancelled by the examiner as a demonstration, and the test was concluded when the subject said that all of the lines had been cancelled.

extreme right of the visual array which they were meant to be searching for a target. A similar effect is often observed when cancellation tests are used to measure the extent of neglect (Albert 1973). Patients with severe neglect will cancel out targets to the extreme right of the array and express themselves satisfied that no targets have been omitted (see Figure 13.1). Such observations have led to the proposal that the underlying deficit in visual neglect is an imbalance in brain mechanisms which control overt orientation or covert attention to one or other side of visual space (Heilman and Watson 1977; Kinsbourne 1977; Mesulam 1981). Each cerebral hemisphere is said to contain a centre which pulls attention and orientation to the contralateral side of space. Damage to the right hemisphere therefore leaves the rightward-orientating mechanism in the left hemisphere free to dominate behaviour.

The representational theory of visual neglect proposes that these patients are no longer able to conceive that extrapersonal space extends

Figure 13.2 A 'clock face' and a 'square' drawn from memory by patients with severe visual neglect.

into the neglected side. Brain (1941) described a patient with a large right parietal lesion who ignored all left turns when trying to find his way about, even in his own home. In a second case, a woman was asked to describe her route home and named all turnings as being to the right. These cases prompted Brain to propose that there was an 'agnosia for the one half of external space'. Critchley (1953) was struck by the fact that some hemianopic patients, when asked to draw objects from memory, would leave the left side incomplete and yet seem quite satisfied with their drawing (see Figure 13.2). In these cases, he suggested, there was a 'neglect, disregard, or forgetfulness for that half of space which subtends the hemianopic field' (ibid.: 271). Most recently Bisiach and his colleagues (Bisiach *et al.* 1979, 1981) argued that visual neglect results from an inability to form a mental representation of one side of egocentric space or one side of imagined objects. It is important to recognize that there are two potentially separable proposals here. The first is that patients with neglect may not be able to think about one side of their immediate environment, and the second is that this difficulty also extends to thinking about one side of real or imagined objects. Neglect is thus said to affect both egocentric and object-centred representations.

How does the scene-description effect fit into the competing frameworks provided by these three types of theory? Obviously, it does not arise from a defect in one visual hemifield as the scene was familiar from before the brain injury, but either an attentional or a representational account can be put forward. The attentional account would be that, in the same way that patients with visual neglect attend only to one side of their actual environment, so when asked to imagine themselves in a different environment, they will only attempt to retrieve information about one side. The scene-description effect would therefore reflect an inadequate search of memory rather than an inability to generate a visual image. Support for this account can be drawn from the second part of the experiment conducted by Bisiach *et al.* (1981). After asking their subjects to describe the piazza from the two opposite perspectives, they then repeated the procedure but provided instructions to describe the left side or right side of the scene. Under these conditions of *cued* recall, the deficit for left-sided features disappeared. This may indicate that neglect in the initial *free*-recall condition arose from a failure to consider left-sided features, but when attention was directed to these features then there was no difficulty in retrieving the relevant information.

The attentional theory of visual neglect therefore provides a strong alternative to the explanation of the scene-description effect proposed by Bisiach *et al.* which was outlined at the start of this chapter. In fact, a similar account involving defective retrieval of information from memory would also be compatible with the representational theory. If patients with visual neglect have an agnosia for the left half of actual egocentric space, then they may focus their attempts at retrieval on what would be to the right in an imagined scene. Neglect in scene description does not therefore force the conclusion that right-sided brain damage leads to a loss of the left side of visual images; it may rather be the case that a reduced awareness of the left side of egocentric space (due to an attentional or representational deficit) means that no attempt is made to retrieve the relevant information during free recall. However, if such patients are specifically cued to think about the left side (as in the cued condition of the experiment by Bisiach *et al.* 1981), then they have no difficulty in accessing this information.

This explanation is tenable for scene description because the information to be recalled is made up of a number of discrete features, and recall from memory may be a serial process as each feature in the scene is considered in turn. It therefore makes sense to suggest that features to one side might be selectively affected by a retrieval deficit. However, this explanation would lose credibility if it could be shown that neglect for one side was also present when a single coherent object was imagined. Suppose that it transpired, for example, that patients with neglect had difficulty in giving information about the left side of an imagined clock face. Unlike a visual scene such as a piazza, a clock face has a holistic quality that makes it very unlikely that information about the right half would be retrieved from memory independently of information about the left half. The experimental evidence on visual neglect when imagining such coherent objects will now be reviewed.

Neglect for one side of a single imagined object?

As was illustrated in Figure 13.2, when asked to draw an object from memory, patients with severe visual neglect may leave the left half of their drawings incomplete. Bisiach *et al.* (ibid.) interpreted this as indicating the loss of the left half of the image of the object recalled from memory. However, this bizarre behaviour is also open to interpretation in terms of the other theories of visual neglect which were discussed above. The hemifield-deficit account would be that patients with visual-field defects and a short concentration-span begin by drawing the left of the object, and then, due to their confused state and inability to compensate for the field defect, fail to complete the left. The attentional account would be that visual attention is drawn to the right side of egocentric space and this causes the incompleteness of the left of the drawing to be overlooked. Given these alternative interpretations, we must look beyond simple drawing tasks for evidence of a defect in visual memory for single objects.

An obvious first step is to ask patients to describe an imagined object, and asking about an imagined clock face has several advantages. First, there is evidence from spontaneous drawing that knowledge about the left of a clock face might be lost in cases of severe visual neglect. Second, a clock face is a common object which is universally familiar in one normal orientation. There is therefore no difficulty in defining what would constitute the left and right sides of a visual image. Finally, there is evidence from normal subjects that the mental representation of a clock face may have properties in common with the spatial characteristics of the real object. Paivio (1978) asked subjects to imagine a clock at two different times and compare the angles between the hour and minute hands. He found that responses were faster for larger differences between two imagined angles. Unfortunately this task would be too difficult for stroke patients with any reduction in their powers of concentration. A much simpler task was therefore devised in which subjects were asked to say what number the minute hand would point to at different times to or past the hour.

Method

Subjects

The initial experimental group comprised thirty-three stroke patients with symptoms of unilateral right-sided brain damage. Seventeen of them showed visual neglect on a cancellation test (Albert 1973). Twelve patients (nine of whom had visual neglect) found the experimental task impossibly difficult, so the data reported here are for the remaining twenty-one. There were nine men and twelve women with a mean age of 64.5 years (ranging from 36 to 83 years). These brain-damaged patients were compared with a group of normal subjects, eleven men and nineteen women with a mean age of 68.2 years (ranging from 50 to 83).

Procedure

Subjects were asked, 'Imagine the face of a clock with the hands pointing to half past twelve. What number on the clock would the big, minute hand point to?' Once they had produced the correct answer (six) they were given times to or past the hour with instructions to respond as rapidly as possible with the corresponding number: for example, 'What time does the minute hand point to at twenty past?'

There were six blocks of trials. Within each block there were ten trials – one attempt at each clock position but excluding 'six' and 'twelve'. Times to and past the hour were cued alternately, but the sequence of cues for each side of the clock was random. Each subject wore a blindfold on half of the blocks of trials to check on whether there was any effect of concurrent visual stimulation. Responses were tape-recorded and the tape was played back at reduced speed to allow accurate timing of response latencies. The latency measured was between the experimenter's initiation of the word 'past' or 'to', and the start of the subject's response.

Table 13.1 Mean latencies for correct responses and mean percentage errors for each hemiface of an imagined clock

| | Brain-damaged subjects | | Control subjects | |
	Left	Right	Left	Right
Latency (secs.)	1.5	1.1	1.3	1.0
Errors (%)	4.7	7.1	4.8	5.7

The results were analysed using analysis of variance with condition (blindfold or no blindfold) and side (left or right hemiface of the clock) as within-subjects factors. Sequence of conditions and subject group (brain-damaged or control) were between-subjects factors.

Results

There was no detectable effect of wearing a blindfold so the results presented here are amalgamated over the blindfold/no-blindfold conditions. Table 13.1 shows that latencies were generally longer for numbers on the left half of the clock face ($F = 21.6$; d.f. $= 1.47$: $p < 0.001$), but there was no evidence of brain-damaged subjects being disproportionately slow for left-sided responses (interaction between subject group and side: $F < 2.5$, $p > 0.1$). A similar analysis of the error rate showed no significant effects. Within the brain-damaged subject group there was no evidence of any relationship between the extent of visual neglect on the cancellation test and the difference between latency for right and left clock numbers ($r_s = -0.2$). This absence of relationship to neglect is illustrated by the performance of the subject with the most severe visual neglect (whose performance on the cancellation test is shown in Figure 13.1). She had median response latencies which were slower for right- than left-sided numbers (3.0 vs. 2.2 secs, respectively) and made six errors to the left compared with ten to the right.

There was a difference in the pattern of errors made by the two subject groups. Errors were placed in four categories: 'minute errors', giving the time in minutes rather than the hour (for example, quarter past → 'fifteen'); 'right/left errors' (for example, saying 'nine' instead of 'three'); 'proximity errors', naming an hour adjoining the target one (for example, twenty past → 'five'); and unclassifiable errors. Table 13.2 shows that the brain-damaged subjects were more likely to make right/left errors than were the controls (Mann-Whitney U test: $z = 2.16$, $p < 0.05$), whereas proximity errors were more common amongst the

Table 13.2 Mean percentage errors of different types

	Brain-damaged subjects	Control subjects
Right/left errors	2.0	0.2
Proximity errors	0.3	2.3
Minute errors	2.2	1.6
Other errors	1.1	0.8

controls (Mann-Whitney U test: $z = 2.47$, $p < 0.01$). There was no significant difference between the groups in the incidence of the other types of error.

Discussion

This experiment failed to produce evidence of neglect for one side of an imagined clock face. However, it was informative in two respects. First, it illustrated the practical constraints on cognitive experimentation with patients with visual neglect. These patients typically have quite severe generalized deficits in visuo-spatial reasoning due to damage of the right parietal lobe (De Renzi 1982) and over half of the patients with neglect who were assessed for this experiment were unable to do any part of the task. It will become increasingly apparent later in this chapter that it is very difficult indeed to design tasks which might be informative about neglect in visual memory yet which are feasible for the typical patient to attempt.

A second interesting finding was that the brain-damaged subjects showed a different pattern of errors from the normal controls, suggesting that they tended to use a different strategy in the imagined-clock task. If, as indicated by the findings of Paivio (1978), normal subjects use a mental representation which has properties analogous to the spatial layout of an actual clock face, then a common type of error might be expected to be confusing a target time with its spatial neighbour. This experiment showed that such 'proximity' errors were the most common type for normal subjects. Their low incidence for the brain-damaged subjects and the higher rate of right/left errors may indicate that right-hemisphere damage led to the use of a more verbally based strategy, drawing on direct verbal association between the minute and hour scales of a clock face. Thus, for example, 'quarter to' and 'quarter past' are verbally similar but spatially dissimilar, whereas 'quarter to' and 'twenty to' are spatially similar but verbally dissimilar. A verbal strategy might therefore lead to more right/left errors but fewer proximity errors.

The findings of Paivio (ibid.) and this speculative account of the origin of proximity errors do not, of course, provide evidence to support the isomorphic model of visual memory proposed by Bisiach and his colleagues. It has been clearly argued elsewhere (for example, Pylyshyn 1973) that demonstrating such general analogous relationships between a mental representation and the spatial characteristics of an actual object does not imply physical isomorphism. Any mental description of the spatial characteristics of a clock face is likely to use a code in which the representations of neighbouring features are more similar than the representations of spatially disparate features. The frequency of proximity errors may therefore indicate whether a spatial rather than a verbal representation is being used, but it does not indicate anything about the physical embodiment of this spatial representation.

Returning to the issue of visual neglect for imagined objects, it seems there is only one other directly relevant study. Baxter and Warrington (1983) described a case of 'neglect dysgraphia'. A left-handed man had suffered two right-hemisphere strokes leading to dysphasia and dyslexia. When asked to spell words aloud he showed a consistent tendency to make errors at the beginning of the word. He described his difficulties as being like trying to read off the image of a word in which the letters to the right side were clearer than those to the left. Baxter and Warrington suggested that this was a neglect for the left side of the mental representation of the word which was comparable to neglect in scene description. This comparison is questionable, primarily because this patient showed no sign of visual neglect other than a very occasional tendency to misread the beginnings of words. He also had a very severely reduced auditory retention-span (being able to repeat only three digits on a digit span test). This raises the question of whether his introspections were misleading in suggesting a deficit in visual imagery, and that the spelling problem may have been in some way an aspect of disordered verbal working-memory.

Controlled viewing experiments

In order to obtain a greater degree of experimental sensitivity than is possible in the scene-description or imagined-clock procedures, it is necessary to present some target object visually under controlled conditions and then to assess visual memory of that object. The difficulty lies in trying to exclude any influence of visual neglect during the viewing of the target object, as any subsequent deficit in visual memory might then be due to perceptual or attentional factors at the time of the initial viewing. One approach which has produced some interesting results has been 'aperture viewing', in which target objects pass behind a narrow vertical viewing slit. The intention here is to ensure that all parts of the object are sensed at a single central section of the visual field, and it is therefore argued that any subsequent deficit in knowledge about the left side of the object could not be due to a perceptual or attentional deficit for the left side of visual space. The difficulty with this method is that it places high demands on the ability of subjects to form a mental image of the entire object viewed in this fragmented form. Brain-damaged subjects therefore require prior practice on a related task, or else the viewing slit must be widened to allow an appreciable part of the target object to be viewed at any moment during its traverse behind the slit. These problems will be discussed in relation to the two published studies on aperture viewing.

Bisiach *et al.* (1979) tested nineteen subjects with right-sided brain damage who showed left-sided visual neglect on a cancellation test. The target objects consisted of eighteen cloud-like shapes which differed from each other in the shape of the right or left sides. In the initial 'static' condition, each shape was presented under normal viewing conditions for two seconds. After a one-second interstimulus interval a comparison shape was displayed and the subject had to indicate whether it was the same as or different from the target shape. Differences on the left side of the shape were detected on only 20 per cent of occasions, whereas differences on the right were detected on 75 per cent of the relevant trials. Compared with the performance of normal controls, this indicated a severe left-sided visual neglect. Under these static conditions this could have been due to purely perceptual difficulties as all of the brain-damaged subjects had visual field defects. The crucial part of the experiment was therefore the second 'dynamic' condition in which the target and comparison shapes were viewed as they passed behind a narrow vertical slit which spanned only one-tenth of the width of the entire shape. In this condition, differences on the left sides of the shapes were detected on 33 per cent of occasions compared with 43 per cent of differences to the right. This was a weaker but statistically significant degree of left-sided neglect compared with normal controls.

A serious problem with this experiment is that the same eighteen target shapes were used in the static and dynamic conditions, and the static condition was always given first. This was presumably to familiarize the brain-damaged subjects with the procedure and stimuli, in order to allow them to attempt the unusual and difficult aperture viewing task. Unfortunately, the initial static exposure of the shapes is likely to have influenced performance in the dynamic condition, if not through recognition of the forms seen in the initial condition, then in terms of a response bias produced by initial exposure to shapes which seemed to differ mostly on the right-hand side. It may therefore be that the weak left-sided neglect seen in the dynamic condition was indirectly due to poor performance on the left side of the shapes in the initial static condition.

The same criticism can be levelled at a similar experiment reported by Ogden (1985) which indicated unilateral neglect in nine brain-damaged patients tested under aperture viewing conditions. Identical target objects were again used in an initial normal viewing procedure. Here, however, the neglect during aperture viewing was typically as strong or stronger than that in the static condition, and was even observed in subjects who showed no neglect in that condition. This could not therefore be explained as a secondary effect of perceptual difficulties in the static condition. This contrast with the results of Bisiach et al. (1979) may be because in Ogden's experiment the viewing slit spanned a much greater part of the width of the target shapes (one-third compared with one-tenth). The strong effect observed by Ogden in patients who did not necessarily show other signs of visual neglect may therefore have been due to visual hemifield deficits. This is a very real possibility not only because of the proportion of the shapes visible at any moment, but also because, if the subjects had made eye movements in an attempt to track the shapes traversing the viewing slit, the resulting image would have been spread out across the retina. Such 'retinal painting' is recognized as a factor in aperture viewing in normal subjects (Morgan et al. 1982). It may therefore have been that the left and right sides of the target shapes were projected primarily to the contralateral sides of the retina, and that the apparent neglect was due to unilateral deficits in visual processing.

Thus, these aperture-viewing experiments have produced results which need further clarification. As yet no study has been published in which a narrow slit has been used to view target objects which have not been previously seen under normal viewing conditions. Until such an experiment is carried out, the case for unilateral deficits in visual memory does not receive unequivocal support from this quarter.

An alternative to trying to prevent visual hemifield effects when viewing a target shape is to seek to dissociate these effects from deficits in visual memory. One way of doing this is to ask the subjects to carry out a mental rotation so that the left and right sides of an internal visual image no longer coincide with the left and right of the initial perceptual field. This is not easily done in the case of subjects with right parietal damage who are poor at mental-rotation tasks (Ratcliff 1979). However, by reverting again to the highly familiar clock face, it was possible to carry out a mental-rotation experiment with one patient with very severe visual neglect. He was asked to judge the position of an hour hand on a clock face which was rotated 90 degrees from the normal orientation. If, as argued by Bisiach *et al.* (1979), patients with severe neglect cannot form a mental image of the left side of a normal clock face, then a difficulty in judging the locations of the hours 'seven' to 'eleven' should still be apparent in these unusual viewing conditions.

Method

Subject

The subject of this experiment was a 54-year-old man who had suffered a stroke three months earlier. He had a left homonymous hemianopia and left hemiplegia. No brain scan was done but these neurological symptoms indicate a lesion involving the posterior part of the right hemisphere. He showed severe left-sided neglect on cancellation and reading tasks, and omitted the left sides of objects drawn from memory (see Figure 13.2). There was no suggestion of neglect on the imagined-clock task described earlier, but he showed a trend towards naming fewer left-sided features when imagining Cambridge Market Square. In his first description he named 15 per cent of the features to the left of the imagined viewpoint and 21 per cent to the right, and when instructed to imagine the scene from an opposite viewpoint, he named none to the left and 40 per cent to the right. Comparing the results for the two viewpoints, the trend towards left-sided neglect approaches statistical significance (Fisher exact probability test: $p = 0.05$).

Procedure

The 'clock face' used in this experiment consisted of a circle 10 cm in diameter with a single 'hour hand' (a 3-cm arrow with its origin at the centre of the circle). The only number on this clock face was the '12' and

Table 13.3 Mean latencies (in secs) for responses by hemispace of subject and hemiface of clock in a single case of visual neglect

| | Position of hour hand relative to subject | | |
	Left hemispace	Midline ('3' and '9')	Right hemispace
Left hemiface	2.8	2.6	2.2
Right hemiface	3.9	3.8	2.5

the subject's task was to judge what hour the hand pointed to. The clock was viewed at a distance of 30 cm and was orientated for the first twenty trials with the '12' at the extreme right (like a clock rotated 90 degrees clockwise), and for the next twenty trials, with the '12' at the extreme left (90 degrees anti-clockwise rotation). In each of these conditions, the arrow pointed in random order twice to each clock position, but excluding '6' and '12'. The subject was encouraged to respond verbally as quickly as possible with the appropriate hour on each trial.

The analysis of the data was directed at discovering the contribution of two factors: 'hemiface', whether the arrow pointed to numbers which would be on the left or right hemiface of a normally orientated clock; and 'hemispace', whether the arrow pointed to a position in the subject's egocentric space which was to the left or right of body midline.

Results

Table 13.3 shows the mean latencies for his responses. An analysis of variance was carried out with hemiface (left or right), hemispace (left or right), and rotation (clockwise or anticlockwise), as fixed factors. Responses for the '3' and '9' positions were omitted to give a balanced factorial design. Latencies for the left hemispace were significantly greater than those for the right ($F = 6.5$; d.f. $= 1,24$; $p < 0.01$), and there was no significant interaction with direction of rotation ($F < 1$). The mean latencies were longer for numbers on the right hemiface than the left, the opposite effect to that which had been predicted, but this trend did not reach statistical significance ($F = 3.2$; d.f. $= 1,24$; $p = 0.08$). The pattern of errors did not show any significant hemispace effect (errors to the left = 7; errors to the right = 6), or hemiface effect (total for left hemiface = 10, right hemiface = 6: chi-square < 1).

Discussion

These results allow an unequivocal rejection of the experimental hypothesis. This subject showed no evidence of a selective loss of knowledge about the positions of numbers on the left side of a normal clock face, but showed a selective problem for positions which were in the left part of egocentric space. This does not of course allow a rejection of the defective-imagery hypothesis as a whole. It may be that this task was not suitable: perhaps, for example, this subject made mental comparisons with the image of a clock which was itself rotated! However, these results are compatible with the view that the primary defect in visual neglect is a difficulty in attending to one side of egocentric space; and, as we have seen from the material reviewed in these two sections, there is no compelling evidence from other studies for visual neglect of a single imagined object.

Conclusions

The experimental findings reviewed and reported in this chapter can be summarized as follows. When asked to describe a visual scene from memory, patients with left-sided visual neglect tend to omit features on the left of the imagined prospect. It is still not clear whether a similar effect can occur when these patients are asked to imagine a single object. The aperture-viewing experiments suggest that this may be the case, but the studies to date are methodologically flawed. There is one case reported of an apparent problem in imagining the left sides of single words (Baxter and Warrington 1983), but this was not in the context of visual neglect and conceivably may have been due to a deficit in verbal processing. Finally, the two experiments reported here failed to produce evidence of neglect for one side of an imagined clock face.

We gain our knowledge about familiar places such as town squares from many separate episodes, and certainly not from seeing them from only one or two viewpoints. This means that if we do rely on a visual image when attempting to describe the scene from one imagined viewpoint, then this is not likely to be a memory of an actual visual experience. It is more likely that information from many experiences of the scene will be retrieved from memory and this information will then be used to assemble the image. The important point in interpreting neglect in scene description is, therefore, that the deficit may lie in a failure to attempt to retrieve information about left-sided features, rather than an inability to form the left side of a visual image of the scene. In the absence of persuasive evidence of neglect for single imagined objects, this defective retrieval account remains a strong possibility.

Bisiach and Berti (1988) suggested that neglect during scene description indicated that there was a degree of isomorphism between the actual scene and its mental image, such that right-hemisphere damage led to the loss of the left part of the image. However, if the deficit is not the loss of the left of an image but a failure to attempt to retrieve information about the imagined left, then no such isomorphism is implied. All that is necessary is to suppose that the reduced awareness of one side of the actual egocentric environment which characterizes visual neglect also has an effect in directing retrieval of information about an imagined environment. In so far as such retrieval might be at a conscious level, patients whose attention to their present environment was focused to the right would fail to ask themselves, 'What would be to my left in that scene?' This then says nothing about the properties of the mental representation of the scene except that the concept of 'my left' is used when thinking about either real or imagined egocentric space.

Future research should be aimed at clarifying the circumstances in which neglect for imagined objects can occur. It may be possible to demonstrate convincingly neglect for one side of a single imagined object, or neglect in other circumstances where a sequential retrieval process would not seem to be involved. This would entail the conclusion that mental images could indeed be bisected by unilateral brain injury. However, until the issues raised in this chapter are resolved, the implications of neglect in scene description for the understanding of visual imagery will remain unclear.

References

Albert, M. L. (1973) 'A simple test of visual neglect', *Neurology* 23: 658–64.
Battersby, W. S., Bender, M. B., Pollack, M., and Kahn, R. L. (1956) 'Unilateral "spatial agnosia" (inattention) in patients with cerebral lesions', *Brain* 79: 68–93.
Baxter, D.M., and Warrington, E.K. (1983) 'Neglect dysgraphia', *Journal of Neurology, Neurosurgery and Psychiatry* 46: 1073–8.
Bisiach, E., and Berti, A. (1988) 'Hemineglect and mental representation', in M. Denis, J. Engelkamp, and J. T. E. Richardson (eds) *Cognitive and Neuropsychological Approaches to Mental Imagery*, Dordrecht: Martinus Nijhoff.

Alan Sunderland

Bisiach, E., and Luzzatti, C. (1978) 'Unilateral neglect of representational space', *Cortex* 14: 129–33.
Bisiach, E., Luzzatti, C., and Perani, D.(1979) 'Unilateral neglect, representational schema and consciousness', *Brain* 102: 609–18.
Bisiach, E., Capitani, E., Luzzatti, C., and Perani, D. (1981) 'Brain and conscious representation of outside reality', *Neuropsychologia* 19: 543–51.
Brain, W. R. (1941) 'Visual disorientation with special reference to lesions of the right cerebral hemisphere', *Brain* 64: 244–72.
Chedru, F., Leblanc, M. and Lhermitte, F. (1973) 'Visual searching in normal and brain-damaged subjects (contribution to the study of unilateral inattention)', *Cortex* 9: 94–111.
Colombo, A., De Renzi, E., and Faglioni, P. (1976) 'The occurrence of visual neglect in patients with unilateral cerebral disease', *Cortex* 12: 221–31.
Critchley, M. (1953) *The Parietal Lobes*, London: Edward Arnold.
De Renzi, E. (1982) *Disorders of Space Exploration and Cognition*, Chichester: Wiley.
Friedland, R. P. and Weinstein, E. A. (1977) 'Hemi-inattention and hemisphere specialization: introduction and historical review', *Advances in Neurology* 18: 1–31.
Gainotti, G., Messerlie, P., and Tissot, R. (1972) 'Qualitative analysis of unilateral spatial neglect in relation to laterality of cerebral lesion', *Journal of Neurology, Neurosurgery, and Psychiatry* 35: 545–50.
Heilman, K., and Watson, R. T. (1977) 'Mechanisms underlying the unilateral neglect syndrome', *Advances in Neurology* 18: 93–105.
Kinsbourne, K. (1977) 'Hemi-neglect and hemisphere rivalry', *Advances in Neurology* 18: 41–7.
Mesulam, M. M. (1981) 'A cortical network for directed attention and unilateral neglect', *Annals of Neurology* 10: 309–25.
Morgan, M. J., Findlay, J. M., and Watt, R. J. (1982) 'Aperture viewing: a review and a synthesis', *Quarterly Journal of Experimental Psychology* 34A: 211–33.
Ogden, J. A. (1985) 'Contralesional neglect of constructed visual images in right and left brain-damaged patients', *Neuropsychologia* 23: 273–8.
Paivio, A. (1978) 'Comparisons of mental clocks', *Journal of Experimental Psychology: Human Perception and Performance* 4: 61–71.
Posner, M. I., Cohen, Y., and Rafal, R. D. (1982) 'Neural systems control of spatial orienting', *Philosophical Transactions of the Royal Society* B298: 60–70.
Pylyshyn, Z. W. (1973) 'What the mind's eye tells the mind's brain: a critique of mental imagery', *Psychological Bulletin* 80: 1–24.
Ratcliff, G. (1979) 'Spatial thought, mental rotation and the right cerebral hemisphere', *Neuropsychologia* 17: 49–54.
Sunderland, A. (1984) 'Cognitive factors in unilateral neglect', unpublished PhD thesis, Brunel University.

Chapter fourteen

Imagery and memory in brain–damaged patients

John T. E. Richardson

This chapter adopts the approach of clinical neuropsychology: that is, the investigation of psychological functions and processes in patients who have suffered physical damage to the central nervous system. Such an approach complements attempts to understand the relationships between brain systems and psychological mechanisms by the study of normal, intact individuals; examples of the latter include Chapter 1 by Marks and Chapter 12 by Goldenberg *et al.* in this volume. Both approaches provide valuable information on the physiological structures that underlie the hypothetical mechanisms and processes which are postulated by psychological theories of normal function. In principle, such information is likely to be of great importance both in the clinical treatment of brain-damaged individuals and in the development of our understanding of normal psychological function.

However, as I have pointed out elsewhere (Richardson 1982), the application of psychological theories to the study of brain-damaged patients also generates a qualitatively different body of data with which to validate, refine, and develop those theories. It is obvious that a theory that can describe normal psychological processes across the general population is to be preferred to one based entirely upon evidence from college students. Nevertheless, a psychological theory which can in addition encompass the different patterns of impairment to be found in a wide variety of neurological patients is to be preferred to either of these. The investigation of cases of impaired psychological function can thus be regarded as an opportunity to submit to radical empirical testing hypotheses previously derived solely from the study of normal, intact individuals and, typically, solely from the study of college students.

Two particular examples can be cited from mainstream experimental research on mental imagery. Research using college students has shown unequivocally that: (a) concrete material which readily evokes mental imagery is more easily remembered than abstract material which evokes mental imagery only with difficulty; and (b) instructions to use mental imagery lead to substantial improvements in memory performance (see Richardson 1980: Chapters 6 and 7). The evidence to be reviewed in the present chapter shows that many samples of neurological patients, though not all, find concrete material easier to remember than abstract material; and that many samples of neurological patients, though not all, benefit from training and instructions in the use of imagery mnemonic techniques. On the one hand, these generalizations offer some reassurance that the results of laboratory-based research on imagery and memory are typical of human cognition and are not peculiar to college students. On the other hand, the exceptions may prove to be of considerable theoretical interest.

In this chapter I shall be largely concerned with mental imagery in so far as it contributes to human learning and remembering. One reason for this is that until quite recently by far the greatest proportion of experimental research on mental imagery in normal subjects was concerned with human memory (see Richardson 1980), and this historical bias has tended to influence the direction of neuro-psychological research on mental imagery as well. Nevertheless, other chapters in this volume provide ample evidence that the interests of imagery researchers are now broadening to include many other human faculties, and the chapter by Alan Sunderland (Chapter 13) in particular provides a neuropsychological perspective upon the relationship between imagery and perception. A second reason for the emphasis in the present chapter upon learning and remembering is that the dysfunction of episodic memory is a common outcome of brain damage and indeed is often a characteristic sign that such damage has occurred.

There are three main categories of patient in whom impairment of episodic memory is particularly salient and significant (Richardson 1982). First, it is often seen following physical injury to the brain. During wartime, traumatic damage tends to be associated with open wounds that are produced by weapons or by shrapnel. In peacetime, such damage more often takes the form of 'closed' head injuries in which the contents of the skull are not exposed; these are a frequent outcome of domestic, occupational, recreational, and traffic accidents. Second, disorders of learning and memory may also be a consequence of neurological diseases, especially of those associated with the cerebrovascular system (such as thrombosis or haemorrhage) and those of a histopathological nature (such as cerebral tumours). Finally, memory disorders may arise as the result of surgical treatment intended to alleviate the symptoms of neurological disease. Such disorders have been demonstrated particularly following surgical lesions of the subcortical structures of the temporal lobes, which may be necessary in order to relieve chronic epileptic or depressive conditions that are not amenable to other forms of treatment.

The suggestion that research on mental imagery might have practical implications for the treatment and rehabilitation of such patients was first made by Patten (1972), who taught a variety of mnemonic techniques to four patients with deficits of verbal memory that were attributed to focal lesions of the left cerebral hemisphere. All four patients were able to use these techniques to improve their memory performance, although no such benefits were obtained in three other patients with more diffuse lesions in the midline structures of the brain. Subsequent research has generated a great deal of evidence on the relevance of mental imagery to the investigation and remediation of acquired memory dysfunction. The therapeutic value of imagery mnemonics has been considered by myself and colleagues elsewhere (Richardson *et al.* 1987). This chapter will be concerned more with the theoretical implications of imagery research with brain-damaged patients.

I shall consider five particular groups of individuals: those suffering from the amnesic syndrome (from a variety of causes); those who have undergone unilateral temporal lobectomy; those who have suffered closed head injuries; those with cerebrovascular disease; and those who have undergone commissurotomy. In each case, the emphasis will be upon experimental investigations that have used groups of patients, in order to avoid the idiosyncratic results that might arise from single case-studies. Finally, I shall consider the general problem of localizing the structures and systems within the brain that are responsible for the effective use of mental imagery in remembering and in other cognitive tasks.[1]

Amnesic disorders

A pronounced impairment of learning and remembering in the absence of any general intellectual impairment is clinically described as 'amnesia'. This condition may arise from a variety of causes, but it is a central feature of Korsakoff's syndrome, which results from chronic alcoholism. Clinical amnesia is associated with lesions in two different anatomical regions within the brain, the diencephalon and the medial temporal cortex, and it is currently a matter of debate whether these define two different amnesic 'syndromes', the former arising mainly from Korsakoff's syndrome, the latter mainly from bilateral temporal lobectomy and encephalitis (see Parkin 1984, 1987: Chapter 7).

An initial investigation by Baddeley and Warrington (1973) using a heterogeneous sample of six amnesic patients found improved recall as the result of either phonemic similarity or taxonomic structure within the stimulus material, but no improvement from instructions to make up complex visual images linking groups of four items in a physical scene. A matched control group of patients with peripheral nerve lesions showed enhanced performance under all three conditions. These results suggested that the amnesic subjects were specifically impaired in the use of mental imagery as a form of coding in long-term memory. Since their patients all claimed to be able to form relevant images, Baddeley and Warrington concluded that they were not impaired in the construction of mental images *per se* but had failed to construct an interactive relationship or episode.

Jones (1974) considered two patients who had bilateral lesions of the temporal lobes: one (H.M.) had undergone bilateral temporal lobectomy for the relief of chronic epilepsy, while the other (H.B.) had a bilateral tumour and had undergone unilateral temporal lobectomy. Neither of these patients showed any retention in a paired-associate learning task even under instructions to use interactive imagery, though both were apparently able to construct vivid mental images in response to those instructions. They seemed to forget that they had previously formed a visual association linking the items to be remembered and thus were unable to utilize their images at the time of recall. Even when H.M. was reminded that he had constructed a visual association, he could not retrieve his original image and instead created an entirely new one. Similar results were reported by Signoret and Lhermitte (1976) in the case of 'one amnesic subject with hippocampal lesions'.

Cermak (1975) suggested that amnesic patients might benefit from less complex interactive images than those which had been demanded in the study by Baddeley and Warrington (1973). He found that a group of six Korsakoff patients produced improved recognition and recall of paired associates as the result of interactive imagery instructions, and concluded that amnesic patients were capable of creating and utilizing images as mnemonic aids. In a subsequent study, Cermak (1976) obtained similar results with a case of amnesia resulting from herpes simplex encephalitis. However, elsewhere (Cermak 1980) he pointed out that in both studies the subjects had been provided with specific mental images by the experimenter and had been reminded to use the relevant images at the time of recall. Cermak suggested that these were crucial aspects of his experimental procedure, and that without such prompting amnesic patients would show no benefit from the use of imagery.

Indeed, a study by Cutting (1978) of paired-associate learning in ten Korsakoff patients found no evidence of any retention, regardless of whether interactive images were generated by the subjects or provided by the experimenter. Cutting ascribed the patients' failure to utilize mental imagery to a deficit in the capacity for active mental operations, and argued that Korsakoff patients were adept only at passive cognitive tasks. Nevertheless, Kapur (1978) showed that Korsakoff patients were in fact able to construct mental images and to report emergent information contained within them. In his experiment, each patient was instructed to imagine a seven-letter word and to indicate, starting from the end of the word and working backwards, whether each of the letters was large or small in size. Korsakoff patients achieved the same level of performance as alcoholic controls in terms of both their speed and their accuracy. An unpublished investigation by Brooks and Baddeley similarly found that a heterogeneous group of amnesic patients had no difficulty in producing simple line drawings to illustrate the interactive images that they had generated to link pairs of unrelated words; however, these patients still showed no benefit from the use of such images in their subsequent recall (Baddeley 1982).

In the light of the disappointing results obtained in earlier studies Kovner *et al.* (1983) proposed that amnesics were deficient in terms of the ability to organize familiar items into context-dependent combinations, and that they would need the support of a clear mnemonic structure if the use of mental imagery were to be beneficial. In their investigation, a heterogeneous group of five amnesic patients was asked to learn lists of unrelated words presented repeatedly over successive weekly sessions. When they were provided with a bizarre story which linked the items to be remembered and which they were instructed to visualize, they demonstrated some retention, but were still impaired relative to a control group of normal volunteers. However, in the absence of an opportunity to visualize a bizarre story but with an equivalent level of feedback and correction, the amnesic patients showed no sign of any learning over eight sessions. In short, it would appear that amnesic patients are able to form interactive images but that they are unable to utilize them as effective memory representations without explicit mnemonic structure at the time of learning or prompting at the time of recall.

Unilateral temporal lobectomy

I have already mentioned that one cause of memory dysfunction is the use of temporal lobectomy for the relief of chronic epilepsy, and the case of H.M. is an example of amnesia resulting from bilateral temporal lobectomy. Patients who have undergone *unilateral* temporal lobectomy also demonstrate an impairment of learning and remembering, but this is quantitatively much less pronounced and qualitatively related to the side of the brain which has been subjected to surgical intervention. Characteristically, patients with lesions of the left temporal lobe are found to be impaired in tests of verbal memory but not in tests of nonverbal memory; in contrast, those patients with lesions of the right temporal lobe are found to be impaired in tests of nonverbal memory but not in tests of verbal memory (Milner 1971). It should be remembered, however, that patients who have undergone surgical procedures of this sort have also suffered from neurological disorders of long standing (usually intractable epileptic conditions), and that there is no guarantee that the area of diseased neural tissue will be confined to those regions which have been surgically removed.[2]

In the study already cited, Jones (1974) asked thirty-six patients who had undergone unilateral temporal lobectomy to learn three lists of concrete and abstract paired associates. The first list was to be learned under conventional instructions which did not mention any particular mnemonic technique; for the second list, the concrete pairs were accompanied by relevant drawings as interactive mediators, which the subjects were instructed to visualize; and for the third list, the subjects were asked to make up their own interactive images. In the case of the concrete pairs, the patients with lesions of the left temporal lobe showed a significant impairment compared with a group of normal controls, but the patients with lesions of the right temporal lobe did not. All three groups of subjects showed a similar improvement in recall as a result of instructions to use mental imagery. In the case of the abstract pairs, the overall level of performance was lower, and there was no improvement as a result of imagery mnemonic instructions, but the three groups showed the same relative levels of performance as in the case of the concrete pairs.

Given the results of earlier research on the effects of unilateral temporal lobectomy upon nonverbal memory, Jones had anticipated that the effective use of mental imagery should depend upon the integrity of the right temporal lobe, and hence that patients with lesions of that lobe should derive less help from the use of an imagery mnemonic. However, her findings directly contradicted such an idea in three different respects:

1. The patients with lesions of the right temporal lobe showed no overall impairment in terms of their absolute level of recall performance. A subsequent study by Jones-Gotman and Milner (1978) found that patients with lesions of the right temporal lobe were impaired in their recall of paired associates under interactive imagery instructions. In addition, Jones-Gotman (1979) found that patients with lesions of the right temporal lobe were impaired in the incidental recall of unrelated words which they had previously rated with regard to ease of visualization. However, this was true only in a delayed recall test, and both of these studies are open to a number of important methodological criticisms (Richardson *et al.* 1987). Although the use of mental imagery is widely implicated in tests of verbal learning (for example Paivio 1986: Chapter 8), it is in fact well established that damage to the right cerebral hemisphere virtually never gives rise to an impairment in such tasks (Milner 1966; Newcombe 1969: Chapter 6; Miller 1972: 57; Walsh 1978: 174).

2. Although there is still some controversy on the subject (see Richardson 1980: Chapter 7), effects of stimulus concreteness in episodic memory tasks are normally taken to be diagnostic of the use of imagery as a mental representation (for example, Paivio 1986: 159). In Jones's (1974) results, the patients with lesions of the right temporal lobe demonstrated a normal superiority in their performance on concrete material compared with their performance on abstract material. A similar pattern of results was obtained by Jones-Gotman (1979) in her incidental-learning experiment, and by Shore (1979) in the case of patients with brain damage of various aetiologies restricted to one or other hemisphere.

3. Once again, although there is controversy on the matter (see Richardson 1980: Chapter 6), effects of imagery mnemonic instructions in episodic memory tasks are taken to be equally diagnostic

of the use of imagery as a mental representation. In Jones's (1974) study, the patients with lesions of the right temporal lobe demonstrated a normal superiority in their performance under imagery mnemonic instructions compared with their performance under standard learning instructions. A similar pattern of results was obtained in the study by Shore (1979).

On each of these arguments, Jones's results imply that the efficacy of mental imagery in episodic memory tasks is not affected by lesions of the right temporal lobe. Certainly, just at an empirical level, the patients in Jones's investigation who had lesions of the right temporal lobe seemed able to employ interactive mental imagery just as efficiently as normal controls. It may be concluded that the neuroanatomical basis of mental imagery is not contained within the structures of the right temporal lobe (Richardson 1980: 140).

Closed head injuries

A blow to the head sets up shearing forces within the brain which give rise to diffuse lesions and disturbance of function (Ommaya and Gennarelli 1974). Nevertheless, virtually regardless of the site of trauma, movement of the brain within the skull gives rise to lacerations and contusions in the region of the frontal and temporal lobes (Gurdjian *et al.* 1943). It is perhaps therefore unsurprising that a closed head injury characteristically gives rise to disturbances of learning and remembering. Apart from the initial phenomena of retrograde and anterograde amnesia, most patients demonstrate a disturbance of memory function which persists beyond the immediate period of recovery (Schacter and Crovitz 1977).

A number of investigators have studied the efficacy of mnemonic aids based upon the use of mental imagery with individual cases of closed head injury (Glasgow *et al.* 1977; Crovitz *et al.* 1979; Crosson and Buenning 1984). In general, such techniques seem to be effective even in the case of patients with severe head injuries, but such patients seem to encounter great difficulty in transferring these strategies to other learning situations (Richardson *et al.* 1987). There are also considerable individual differences in the benefits gained from their use (Levin *et al.* 1982: 218).

An experimental investigation by Richardson (1979) compared forty cases of minor closed head injury with a control group of forty orthopaedic patients. The head-injured patients were found to be impaired in the free recall of lists of concrete words, but not in the free recall of lists of abstract words. The control patients demonstrated the usual pattern of superior recall in the case of concrete words than in the case of abstract words. However, the head-injured patients showed no significant advantage in the recall of concrete material. This pattern of impairment was subsequently replicated by Richardson and Snape (1984) with a sample which included both severe and minor cases of closed head injury. In other words, unlike college students tested in formal laboratory experiments, and unlike orthopaedic patients from the general population who have not received head injuries, patients with closed head injuries failed to show a significant advantage in the recall of concrete material in comparison with their recall of abstract material. It is possible that this was the outcome of diffuse cerebral damage and is not peculiar to patients with closed head injuries. A similar pattern of results was obtained by Weingartner *et al.* (1979) in the case of patients suffering from Huntington's disease, though not by Richardson (1989) in the case of patients with ruptured intracranial aneurysms.

Richardson (1979) interpreted his findings in terms of the prevalent dual-coding theory of imagery and verbal processes. The superior performance of the control subjects in their recall of concrete items was attributed to their use of mental imagery as either an additional memory code or a more effective memory code in the case of concrete material. Conversely, the failure of the head-injured patients to demonstrate any significant difference in performance between concrete and abstract items was taken to mean that mental imagery was not being effectively employed by these subjects. Richardson concluded that closed head injuries gave rise to a specific impairment in the use of mental imagery as a form of elaborative encoding in long-term memory.

Further evidence was obtained by Richardson (1984) in an analysis of the intrusion errors which had been produced by the patients in his original 1979 study. The control subjects demonstrated a strong tendency to produce intrusion errors of similar concreteness to the current list: that is, most intrusion errors produced in attempting to recall concrete lists came from earlier concrete lists, and most intrusion errors produced in attempting to recall abstract lists came from earlier abstract lists. However, the head-injured patients showed no sign of such an effect: the concreteness of their intrusion errors was quite unrelated to the concreteness of the list which they were attempting to recall. This suggested that closed head injuries might impair retention by disrupting the normal encoding of the image-evoking quality of the stimulus material.

In passing, one might note that these findings do seem to bear upon the plausibility of alternative accounts of the effects of concreteness in episodic memory based upon the linguistic properties of the items to be remembered. Anderson and Bower (1973: 458), for instance, suggested that the greater memorability of concrete words might be caused by their having fewer dictionary meanings or more semantic features than abstract words. Another possibility is that retention is more efficient when the encoded information incorporates perceptual or spatial predicates (see Richardson 1980: 87, 90). On such accounts, concrete items should be *inherently* more memorable, regardless of the subject's overall level of performance. In the absence of any evidence whatsoever that closed head injuries give rise to any radical disruption of the internal lexicon, it is difficult (not to say impossible) to explain Richardson's findings in psycholinguistic terms, and certainly more congenial to interpret them in terms of a selective impairment in the use of mental imagery.

Richardson and Barry (1985) explored the locus of this impairment within the total information-processing system. Patients with minor closed head injuries were found to produce normal performance in the recognition of unfamiliar faces and in the free recall of pictured objects, which was taken to mean that the effects of minor closed head injury were restricted to the encoding of verbal information in the form of mental images. A further experiment compared the free recall of lists of concrete and abstract words by head-injured and control patients under either standard learning instructions or imagery mnemonic instructions. Under standard instructions, the head-injured patients once again demonstrated a selective deficit in the recall of concrete material. However, under interactive imagery instructions, both the head-injured patients and the control patients produced better performance with concrete items than with abstract items, and there was no sign of any difference in performance between the two groups of subjects. Richardson and Barry concluded that the effects of minor closed head injury upon human memory should be interpreted as a functional deficit attributable to the patients' failure to employ the optional mnemonic strategy of constructing interactive images. From a theoretical point of view, the problem lies not in their use of imagery or any other mnemonic strategy, but more in their efficient and spontaneous use of such strategies (cf. Pressley *et al.* in press).

Cerebrovascular disease

Patients with diseases of the cerebrovascular system also tend to demonstrate disorders of learning and remembering. In some cases (for instance, a subarachnoid haemorrhage caused by a ruptured intracranial aneurysm), surgical intervention may be necessary to try and avoid any recurrence. A very specialized form of disorder which may result from cerebrovascular accidents or strokes is that of visual neglect, which is discussed in detail by Alan Sunderland in Chapter 13 of this volume.

Signoret and Lhermitte (1976) presented an informal account of the use of interactive imagery and other associative mediators in the case of two patients with aneurysms of the anterior communicating artery and two patients with infarction in the region of the posterior cerebral artery. All four patients showed improved performance whether the images were to be created by themselves or were provided by the experimenter, to the extent that 'the number of correct responses was close to that obtained by control subjects in a standard situation' (ibid.: 68). The first two patients also benefited from the use of verbal mediators in the form of connecting sentences, and it was concluded that their lesions 'somehow prevent them from taking the initiative in choosing the right strategy' (ibid.). This is obviously a similar account to that which was subsequently offered by Richardson and Barry (1985) to explain the effects of closed head injury, but it must be noted that Signoret and Lhermitte failed to present data from control subjects given imagery or verbal mnemonic instructions. The other two patients failed to benefit from the use of mediating sentences, and it was concluded that they suffered from 'a selective disorder in the verbal encoding process' (ibid.: 72).

A more rigorous study of the effectiveness of imagery mnemonics was described by Lewinsohn et al. (1977), using a sample of nineteen 'brain-injured' patients which included fourteen cases with vascular disorders. An extensive programme of training in the use of visual imagery produced enhanced performance to roughly the same extent in both the brain-damaged patients and a group of normal controls. However, the improvement was less pronounced in a face-name association task than in the learning of concrete paired associates, and there was no facilitation at all when the subjects were retested on and relearned the same material after a week's delay. Lewinsohn et al. concluded that visual imagery was an effective mnemonic strategy under controlled conditions but of little practical value in memory rehabilitation.

Whitehouse (1977, 1981) carried out an experimental investigation of eighteen patients who had suffered cerebrovascular accidents and in whom the resulting brain damage appeared to be confined to the anterior portion of one or other cerebral hemisphere. His first experiment found that the ability to recognize previously presented pictures was poorer following right-hemisphere lesions than following left-hemisphere lesions; however, the ability to recognize previously presented words was poorer following left-hemisphere lesions than following right-hemisphere lesions. A second experiment showed that the recognition of pictured objects by patients with left-hemisphere lesions was more disrupted by a visual interpolated task than by a verbal interpolated task and was more disrupted by visually similar distractors than by phonemically similar distractors. In both of these respects patients with right-hemisphere lesions tended to produce the reverse pattern of results. Whitehouse concluded that patients with left-hemisphere lesions had impaired verbal coding and intact imaginal coding, but that patients with right-hemisphere lesions had intact verbal coding and impaired imaginal coding.

In detail, Whitehouse's results are open to other interpretations (Ehrlichman and Barrett 1983), and those of his first experiment were not replicated in a study by Gouvier (1984) which used heterogeneous groups of patients with unilateral or bilateral cerebral pathology. In a similar manner, Richardson (1989) found that the retention of verbal material by patients with surgically treated intracranial aneurysms was unrelated either to the side of their lesions or to the site of their aneurysms within the cerebrovascular system. However, two somewhat more fundamental comments need to be made about Whitehouse's study.

The first observation is that Whitehouse's findings are totally unsurprising in the light of established neuropsychological evidence on the retention of verbal and pictorial material. As mentioned earlier, investigations of the consequences of unilateral temporal lobectomy have shown that patients with lesions of the left temporal lobe are selectively impaired in the retention of verbal material, but that those with lesions of the right temporal lobe are selectively impaired in the retention of nonverbal material (Milner 1966, 1971). Moreover, the two hemispheres appear to contribute jointly to the recognition of nameable pictures. Milner (1966) administered such a task to 123 patients who were undergoing carotid amytal tests prior to neurosurgery. (In this procedure, the functioning of one of the cerebral hemispheres is selectively interrupted by the injection of a solution of sodium amytal into the common carotid artery.) Recognition failures tended to occur only when the patient had a pre-existing unilateral temporal lesion and the injections were made into the contralateral hemisphere. As I have pointed out elsewhere (see Richardson 1980: 138–9), this suggests that information about nameable objects is normally stored in both cerebral hemispheres and can be utilized provided that at least one of the temporal lobes is still functioning. Whitehouse's results are entirely consistent with such an analysis, though they add little to it.

The second observation is that Whitehouse's findings are wholly irrelevant to an understanding of the neuroanatomical basis of mental imagery. His conclusion is premissed upon the theoretical assumption that mental imagery is the effective mental representation used to remember pictorial stimuli. There does indeed appear to be some functional overlap between visual imagery and visual perception (see Chapters 2, 3 and 4 in this volume). However, as Ehrlichman and Barrett (1983) pointed out, there is no theoretically compelling reason to suppose that the retention and recognition of a pictorial stimulus requires the occurrence of mental imagery. Moreover, although the nonverbal representation aroused by the presentation of pictures and the mnemonic code engendered by the use of mental imagery seem to have structural or functional properties in common, there is little or no direct evidence to suggest that the two are actually identical (Richardson 1980: 67–70). Indeed, the neuropsychological literature would argue very much against this. On the one hand, patients with lesions of the right temporal lobe are impaired in the retention of pictorial stimuli (Milner 1971), but not in their use of mental imagery (Jones 1974). On the other hand, patients with minor closed head injury are impaired in the use of mental imagery, but not in the retention of pictorial stimuli (Richardson and Barry 1985). This 'double dissociation' implies that pictorial stimuli are not encoded in the form of mental images, and hence that studies of pictorial memory are not relevant to theoretical issues concerning the nature and function of mental imagery (cf. Richardson 1980: 140, 144; Ehrlichman and Barrett 1983).

A more practically orientated study by Gasparrini (1978; Gasparrini and Satz 1979) involved thirty patients with verbal memory deficits caused by cerebrovascular accidents involving the left hemisphere. For the first experiment, half of the patients were taught to learn paired associates using interactive imagery, while the others were encouraged to use rote memorization. Although the former subjects produced better performance on a variety of outcome measures, there was considerable variation within each of the two groups, and the difference between them was statistically significant only in the training phase, where the learning of each paired associate had been carefully monitored: in other words, there was no statistically significant enhancement of performance on other materials or learning tasks. All of the subjects then participated in a second experiment which compared the effectiveness of interactive imagery and verbal mediation by means of a counterbalanced, within-subjects design. In this case, training in the use of the imagery mnemonic was found to produce significantly better performance.

Cerebral commissurotomy

Another surgical procedure used to alleviate chronic, intractable epilepsy is the sectioning of the corpus callosum and of the anterior and hippocampal commissures, producing the so-called 'split brain'. An early study by Van Wagenen and Herren (1940) found no suggestion of any memory impairment in a series of commissurotomies. However, more recently Zaidel and Sperry (1974) described eight cases of complete commissurotomy and two cases of partial commissurotomy, all of whom were impaired according to a battery of standardized tests of memory function. Zaidel and Sperry did acknowledge that their patients' disorders might have been attributable in part to surgical lesions of other structures or to extracommissural damage not associated with the surgery. The former certainly seems probable in other cases reported in the literature (for example, Sell 1977), although the involvement of the most likely candidate, the fornix, in memory disorders is at best questionable (Parkin 1984). The latter has also been cited as the cause of postoperative memory dysfunction in commissurotomy patients (Gazzaniga and LeDoux 1978: 122–3). Nevertheless, Zaidel and Sperry argued that the loss of the cerebral commissaries was mainly responsible for the impairments which they demonstrated, and they concluded that human memory was normally facilitated by interactions between the hemispheres.

In contrast, LeDoux *et al.* (1977) described a single case of callosal section who showed no post-operative deficits on a wide range of standardized and experimental tasks, and who indeed showed a marked improvement on many measures as a result of the operation. LeDoux *et al.* ascribed the apparent deficits shown by Zaidel and Sperry's patients to sampling error in the choice of control patients. They concluded: 'These results demonstrate that the cognitive processing of complex information is not necessarily dependent on the integrity of the corpus callosum, but rather suggest that cognitive functioning is largely an intrahemispheric process' (ibid.: 102).

There have been a number of suggestions that commissurotomy patients benefit from training and instructions in the use of imagery mnemonics. Unfortunately, the most important accounts are informal ones in which the research methods and results are not sufficiently well documented to allow adequate evaluation of the reported findings. Signoret and Lhermitte (1976), for instance, referred to an unpublished study by Milner in which the learning task devised by Jones (1974) was administered to a group of eight such patients. They commented:

> The markedly impaired performance of the callosal patients in this straightforward verbal learning task was quite unexpected because these patients could use visual imagery as a mnemonic aid. It is clear then that interhemispheric connections are necessary for efficient learning of a purely verbal task.
>
> Signoret and Lhermitte (1976: 70)

However, they did not draw the equally obvious conclusion that interhemispheric connections are apparently *not* necessary for the efficient use of mental imagery in 'a purely verbal task'.

Similarly, Gazzaniga and LeDoux (1978: 122–3) discussed the performance of a patient who underwent the surgical removal of a tumour in the left prefrontal cortex at the age of four and partial commissurotomy at the age of twenty-four. When tested before the latter operation he showed a normal benefit from the use of interactive imagery in a paired-associate learning task, but he showed no sign of any such improvement when tested after that operation. Gazzaniga and LeDoux argued that his pre-operative performance had been sustained primarily by the right frontal lobe, which as a result of the surgery had been isolated from the verbal mechanisms of the left hemisphere. However, they added without further explanation: 'Other patients with no frontal damage but complete callosal sections perform normally on the task under both the imagery and the no-imagery conditions, which indicates that the imagery effect can be accomplished within the verbal half-brain' (ibid.: 123).

Indeed, the only properly documented account of the use of imagery mnemonics with a commissurotomy patient appears to be a case study by Prigatano (1983) of a patient who underwent surgical sectioning of the posterior portion of the corpus callosum to permit the removal of an arteriovenous malformation. At a follow-up examination, he demonstrated 'a clear deficit in verbal memory', achieving a Wechsler Memory Quotient of only 83. Over a three-month period, he was given intensive training in the use of interactive imagery in the context of paired-associate learning tasks. When retested, his performance was substantially improved, and the improvement was successfully maintained without additional training over a further period of six months. Although he did not attain the level of performance demonstrated by a control subject (his wife), the improvement apparently generalized to other tasks, with the result that his Wechsler Memory Quotient increased to 111. On the basis of his patient's initially poor performance, Prigatano suggested that the corpus callosum served to integrate higher-order encoding strategies. However, the improvement in performance which resulted from the use of interactive imagery suggested that the surgically isolated left hemisphere was capable of some imaginal encoding in verbal-learning tasks.

Mental imagery and hemispheric asymmetry

At various points throughout this chapter the notion has been raised that differences exist between the two cerebral hemispheres with regard to the psychological functions which they support. An assumption which is to be found in many popular accounts of cognitive psychology (and indeed in more serious writing, too) is that the neuroanatomical basis of mental imagery is contained within the right cerebral hemisphere. Such an idea seems to be as old as the notion of hemispheric asymmetries itself: Ley (1983) quoted the English neurologist Hughlings Jackson as writing in 1874 that 'the posterior lobe on the right side [of the brain] . . . is the chief seat of the revival of images' (ibid.: 252). More recently, Zaidel and Sperry (1974) suggested that the deficits of commissurotomy patients in verbal-learning tasks were attributable to the 'lack of visual imagery support from the right hemisphere' (ibid.: 270). Within the field of imagery research, the functional dissociation of the two cerebral hemispheres with respect to the processing of verbal and nonverbal information used to be taken to provide direct support for the dual-coding theory of symbolic functioning (Paivio 1971: 522–3, 1978;

Sheikh 1977). However, recent accounts are more reserved on this matter (Paivio 1986: Chapter 12).

The hypothesis of right-hemisphere specialization for mental imagery did motivate early research on the therapeutic value of imagery mnemonics, since it entailed that patients with damage to the left hemisphere should be able to overcome their problems in verbal learning by exploiting the faculty of mental imagery within their intact right hemispheres. As has been pointed out elsewhere (Richardson *et al.* 1987), it is true that some studies have shown that patients with left-hemisphere damage may benefit from training or instructions in the use of mental imagery (for example, Patten 1972; Jones 1974; Jones-Gotman and Milner 1978; Jones-Gotman 1979; Shore 1979). There is also evidence that patients with more severe forms of amnesia and more medial or bilateral damage have much more difficulty in using mental imagery unless the task is highly structured and the memory load is minimal (for example, Patten 1972; Jones 1974; Cermak 1975; Cutting 1978). Nevertheless, as explained earlier in this chapter, the idea of a right-hemisphere locus for mental imagery seems to be directly contradicted by the findings of Jones (1974; see also Shore 1979) that patients with lesions of the right temporal lobe show a normal advantage in learning concrete rather than abstract material, and that they show a normal benefit from imagery mnemonic instructions.

Ehrlichman and Barrett (1983) provided an excellent critical review of the hypothesis of right-hemisphere specialization for mental imagery. They concluded: 'None of the studies, in our opinion, can be described as unequivocally supporting the hypothesis of right hemisphere specialization for mental imagery, and some appear to be inconsistent with such a formulation' (ibid.: 72). One area of research which they regarded as being of potential importance is the study of commissurotomized patients, since it should be relatively straightforward to demonstrate whether such patients are able to construct, utilize, and report mental imagery solely within the left hemisphere. As the previous section made clear, there has been relatively little systematic investigation of this question, though what evidence is available has consistently indicated that these patients are perfectly able to use mental imagery to enhance their performance in verbal-learning tasks.

More recent analyses have rejected the notion that mental imagery is a unitary function which can be localized solely within just one cerebral hemisphere. This approach was first adopted by Kosslyn *et al.* (1984), who successfully validated a computational, componential analysis of mental imagery against the performance of fifty normal subjects in a battery of experimental tasks (see also Chapter 2 in this volume). Farah (1984) used a similar analysis in order to interpret reports in the neurological literature of the loss of mental imagery following brain damage, and concluded that 'the critical area for image generation may be close to the posterior language centres of the left hemisphere' (ibid.: 268). Levine *et al.* (1985) showed that imagery for objects and colours could be dissociated from imagery for spatial relations, although both could be disrupted by bilateral posterior lesions. These studies demonstrate that mental imagery is not a general, undifferentiated ability so much as a collection of relatively independent components to be drawn upon according to the demands of the current task.

An especially interesting application of the computational approach has concerned commissurotomy patients. Farah *et al.* (1985) asked one such patient to classify individual lower-case letters of the alphabet according to their height. When the letters were presented tachistoscopically in their lower-case form to either side of the point of fixation, the subject achieved 100 per cent correct for those stimuli presented to the left hemisphere and 90 per cent correct for those presented to the right hemisphere. However, when the letters were presented in their uppercase form and the subject was instructed to generate a mental image of the lower-case form, his performance was 97 per cent correct for those stimuli presented to the left hemisphere, but only 43 per cent correct (i.e. lower than chance responding) for those presented to the right hemisphere. These results were taken to confirm Farah's (1984) idea of a left-hemisphere locus for image generation. In a more extensive investigation by Kosslyn *et al.* (1985) involving the componential analysis of a variety of experimental tasks, this was refined into the notion of a left-hemisphere module specifically responsible for arranging the parts of an imaged object into the correct configuration.

To a considerable extent, these conclusions accord with those of neuropsychological research using medical imaging techniques with normal subjects, as described earlier by Marks and by Goldenberg *et al.* in Chapters 1 and 12 of this volume, respectively. Nevertheless, as examples of theoretically motivated investigations in clinical neuropsychology, they demonstrate that the study of brain-damaged patients can be a heuristically powerful approach towards an increased understanding of human cognitive faculties in general and of mental imagery in particular.

Notes

1. Acknowledgements are due to Narinder Kapur for his comments on a previous version of this chapter, which was written while the author was visiting the Open University as Honorary Senior Research Fellow.
2. In pre-operative investigations under local anaesthesia, patients with temporal-lobe epilepsy have provided additional results which originally appeared to implicate mental imagery in long-term episodic memory. Penfield and Perot (1963) described the application of weak electrical stimulation to the brain surface in order to determine the area of focal damage. When such stimulation was applied to the cortex of the temporal lobe, patients often reported auditory and visual hallucinations, which at least in some cases seemed to take the form of 'flash-backs' of previous events. Penfield and Perot claimed that these episodes were based upon the mental record of actual past experience (see also Penfield 1968). Similar reports of 'memory-like hallucinations' were obtained by Halgren *et al.* (1978) and by Gloor *et al.* (1982) using electrodes which had been stereotactically implanted within the limbic system, especially in the amygdala and the hippocampus. However, Loftus and Loftus (1980) convincingly argued, first, that such experiences were relatively rare following brain stimulation, and second, that far from being genuine memories of past events, they 'consist merely of the thoughts and ideas that happened to exist just prior to and during the stimulation' (ibid.: 414).

References

Anderson, J. R., and Bower, G. H. (1973) *Human Associative Memory*, Washington, DC: Hemisphere Press.

Baddeley, A. D. (1982) 'Amnesia: a minimal model and an interpretation', in L. S. Cermak (ed.) *Human Memory and Amnesia*, Hillsdale, NJ: Erlbaum.

and Warrington, E. K. (1973) 'Memory coding and amnesia', *Neuropsychologia* 11: 159–65.

Cermak, L. S. (1975) 'Imagery as an aid to retrieval for Korsakoff patients', *Cortex* 11: 163–9.

(1976) 'The encoding capacity of a patient with amnesia due to encephalitis', *Neuropsychologia* 14: 311–26.

(1980) 'Comments on imagery as a therapeutic mnemonic', in L. W. Poon, J. L. Fozard, D. Arenberg, and L. W. Thompson (eds) *New Directions in Memory and Aging*, Hillsdale, NJ: Erlbaum.

Crosson, B., and Buenning, W. (1984) 'An individualized memory retraining program after closed-head injury', *Journal of Clinical Neuropsychology* 6: 287–301.

Crovitz, H. F., Harvey, M. T., and Horn, R. W. (1979) 'Problems in the acquisition of imagery mnemonics: three brain-damaged cases', *Cortex* 15: 225–34.

Cutting, J. (1978) 'A cognitive approach to Korsakoff's syndrome', *Cortex* 14: 485–95.

Ehrlichman, H., and Barrett, J. (1983) 'Right hemispheric specialization for mental imagery: a review of the evidence', *Brain and Cognition* 2: 55–76.

Farah, M. J. (1984) 'The neurological basis of mental imagery: a componential analysis', *Cognition* 18: 245–72.

Gazzaniga, M. S., Holtzman, J. D., and Kosslyn, S. M. (1985) 'A left hemisphere basis for visual mental imagery?', *Neuropsychologia* 23: 115–18.

Gasparrini, B., and Satz, P. (1979) 'A treatment for memory problems in left hemisphere CVA patients', *Journal of Clinical Neuropsychology* 1: 137–50.

Gasparrini, W. G. (1978) 'A treatment for memory problems in brain-damaged patients', *Dissertation Abstracts International* 39: 379B. (Unpublished doctoral dissertation, University of Florida, 1977.)

Gazzaniga, M. S., and LeDoux, J. E. (1978) *The Integrated Mind*, New York: Plenum Press.

Glasgow, R. E., Zeiss, R. A., Barrera, M., Jr., and Lewinsohn, P. M. (1977) 'Case studies on remediating memory deficits in brain-damaged individuals', *Journal of Clinical Psychology* 33: 1049–54.

Gloor, P., Olivier, A., Quesney, L. F., Andermann, F., and Horowitz, S. (1982) 'The role of the limbic system in experiential phenomena of temporal lobe epilepsy', *Annals of Neurology* 12: 129–44.

Gouvier, W. D. (1984) 'The effects of brain damage on recognition memory: are verbal functions really more robust?' *Dissertation Abstracts International* 44: 3932B. (Unpublished doctoral dissertation, Memphis State University, 1983.)

Gurdjian, E. S., Webster, J. E., and Arnkoff, H. (1943) 'Acute cranio-cerebral trauma: surgical and pathologic considerations based upon 151 consecutive autopsies', *Surgery* 13: 333–53.

Halgren, E., Walter, R. D., Cherlow, D. G., and Crandall, P. H. (1978) 'Mental phenomena evoked by electrical stimulation of the human hippocampal formation and amygdala', *Brain* 101: 83–117.

Jones, M. K. (1974) 'Imagery as a mnemonic aid after left temporal lobectomy: contrast between material-specific and generalized memory disorders', *Neuropsychologia* 12: 21–30.

Jones-Gotman, M. (1979) 'Incidental learning of image-mediated or pronounced words after right temporal lobectomy', *Cortex* 15: 187–97.

and Milner, B. (1978) 'Right temporal-lobe contribution to image-mediated verbal learning', *Neuropsychologia* 16: 61–71.

Kapur, N. (1978) 'Visual imagery capacity of alcoholic Korsakoff patients', *Neuropsychologia* 16: 517–19.

Kosslyn, S.M., Brunn, J., Cave, K.R., and Wallach, R.W. (1984) 'Individual differences in mental imagery ability: a computational analysis', *Cognition* 18: 195–243.

Kosslyn, S.M., Holtzman, J. D., Farah, M. J., and Gazzaniga, M. S. (1985) 'A computational analysis of mental image generation: evidence from functional dissociations in split-brain patients', *Journal of Experimental Psychology: General* 114: 311–41.

Kovner, R., Mattis, S., and Goldmeir, E. (1983) 'A technique for promoting robust free recall in chronic organic amnesia', *Journal of Clinical Neuropsychology* 5: 65–71.

LeDoux, J. E., Risse, G. L., Springer, S. P., Wilson, D. H., and Gazzaniga, M. S. (1977) 'Cognition and commissurotomy', *Brain* 100: 87–104.

Levin, H. S., Benton, A. L., and Grossman, R. G. (1982) *Neurobehavioral Consequences of Closed Head Injury*, New York: Oxford University Press.

Levine, D. N., Warach, J., and Farah, M. (1985) 'Two visual systems in mental imagery: dissociation of "what" and "where" in imagery disorders due to bilateral posterior cerebral lesions', *Neurology* 35: 1010–18.

Lewinsohn, P. M., Danaher, B. G., and Kikel, S. (1977) 'Visual imagery as a mnemonic aid for brain-injured persons', *Journal of Consulting and Clinical Psychology* 45: 717–23.

Ley, R. G. (1983) 'Cerebral laterality and imagery', in A. A. Sheikh (ed.) *Imagery: Current Theory Research and Application*, New York: Wiley.

Loftus, E. F., and Loftus, G. R. (1980) 'On the permanence of stored information in the human brain', *American Psychologist* 35: 409–20.

Miller, E. (1972) *Clinical Neuropsychology*, Harmondsworth: Penguin.

Milner, B. (1966) 'Amnesia following operation on the temporal lobes', in C. W. M. Whitty and O. L. Zangwill (eds) *Amnesia*, London: Butterworths.

—— (1971) 'Interhemispheric differences in the localization of psychological processes in man', *British Medical Bulletin* 27: 272–7.

Newcombe, F. (1969) *Missile Wounds of the Brain*, London: Oxford University Press.

Ommaya, A. K., and Gennarelli, T. A. (1974) 'Cerebral concussion and traumatic unconsciousness', *Brain* 97: 633–54.

Paivio, A. (1971) *Imagery and Verbal Processes*, New York: Holt, Rinehart & Winston.

—— (1978) 'Dual coding: theoretical issues and empirical evidence', in J. M. Scandura and C. J. Brainerd (eds) *Structural/Process Models of Complex Human Behavior*, Leiden: Nordhoff.

—— (1986) *Mental Representations: A Dual Coding Approach*, New York: Oxford University Press.

Parkin, A. J. (1984) 'Amnesic syndrome: a lesion-specific disorder?', *Cortex* 20: 479–508.

—— (1987) *Memory and Amnesia: An Introduction*, Oxford: Blackwell.

Patten, B. M. (1972) 'The ancient art of memory: usefulness in treatment', *Archives of Neurology* 26: 25–31.

Penfield, W. (1968) 'Engrams in the human brain', *Proceedings of the Royal Society of Medicine* 61: 831–40.

—— and Perot, P. (1963) 'The brain's record of auditory and visual experience: a final summary and discussion', *Brain* 86: 595–696.

Pressley, M., Borkowski, J. G., and Schneider, W. (in press) 'Good strategy users coordinate metacognition, strategy use, and knowledge', in R. Vasta and G. Whitehurst (eds) *Annals of Child Development*, vol. 4, Greenwich, CT: JAI Press.

Prigatano, G. P. (1983) 'Visual imagery and the corpus callosum: a theoretical note', *Perceptual and Motor Skills* 56: 296–8.

Richardson, J. T. E. (1979) 'Mental imagery, human memory, and the effects of closed head injury', *British Journal of Social and Clinical Psychology* 18: 319–27.

(1980) *Mental Imagery and Human Memory*, London: Macmillan.

(1982) 'Memory disorders', in A. Burton (ed.) *The Pathology and Psychology of Cognition*, London: Methuen.

(1984) 'The effects of closed head injury upon intrusions and confusions in free recall', *Cortex* 20: 413–20.

(1989) 'Performance in free recall following rupture and repair of intracranial aneurysm', *Brain and Cognition* 9: 210–26.

and Barry, C. (1985) 'The effects of minor closed head injury upon human memory: further evidence on the role of mental imagery', *Cognitive Neuropsychology* 2: 149–68.

Richardson, J. T. E., and Snape, W. (1984) 'The effects of closed head injury upon human memory: an experimental analysis', *Cognitive Neuropsychology* 1: 217–31.

Richardson, J. T. E., Cermak, L. S., Blackford, S. P., and O'Connor, M. (1987) 'The efficacy of imagery mnemonics following brain damage', in M. A. McDaniel and M. Pressley (eds) *Imagery and Related Mnemonic Processes: Theories, Individual Differences, and Applications*, New York: Springer–Verlag.

Schacter, D. L., and Crovitz, H. F. (1977) 'Memory function after closed head injury: a review of the quantitative research', *Cortex* 13: 150–76.

Sell, S. C. (1977) 'The corpus callosum, its role in memory: a presentation of a patient with an arteriovenous malformation of the corpus callosum', *Journal of Neurosurgical Nursing* 9: 141–3.

Sheikh, A. A. (1977) 'Mental images: ghosts of sensations?', *Journal of Mental Imagery* 1: 1–4.

Shore, D. L. (1979) 'The effectiveness of verbal and visual imagery mnemonics in the remediation of organically based memory deficits', *Dissertation Abstracts International* 40: 1916B. (Unpublished doctoral dissertation, Wayne State University, 1979.)

Signoret, J.-L., and Lhermitte, F. (1976) 'The amnesic syndromes and the encoding process', in M. R. Rosenzweig and E. L. Bennett (eds), *Neural Mechanisms of Learning and Memory*, Cambridge, MA: MIT Press.

Van Wagenen, W. P., and Herren, R. Y. (1940) 'Surgical division of commissural pathways in the corpus callosum: relation to spread of an epileptic attack', *Archives of Neurology* 44: 740–59.

Walsh, K. W. (1978) *Neuropsychology*, Edinburgh: Churchill Livingstone.

Weingartner, H., Caine, E.D., and Ebert, M. H. (1979) 'Imagery, encoding, and retrieval of information from memory: some specific encoding-retrieval changes in Huntington's disease', *Journal of Abnormal Psychology* 88: 52–8.

Whitehouse, P. J. (1977) 'A neuropsychological study of imaginal and verbal encoding in memory', *Dissertation Abstracts International* 38: 1932B. (Unpublished doctoral dissertation, Johns Hopkins University, 1977.)

(1981) 'Imagery and verbal encoding in left and right hemisphere damaged patients', *Brain and Language* 14: 315–32.

Zaidel, D., and Sperry, R. W. (1974) 'Memory impairment after commissurotomy in man', *Brain* 94: 263–72.

Author index

Abelson, R. 9
Abrahamsen, A.S. 170
Abramson, L.Y. 275
Acosta, A. 290
Ahsen, A. 3, 15. 19, 32, 278, 283
Albert, M.L. 334, 336, 340
Allman, J.J. 45
Allport, D.A. 94, 111
Allport, G.W. 263
Alpert, R. 264
Anderson, B. 187
Anderson, J.R. 11, 130, 360
Anderson, R.A. 43
Appelle, S. 58
Arbus, D. 234
Arnheim, R. 132–3
Arnold, M.B. 247
Atkinson, R.C. 103, 132
Atwood, G.E. 104–5
Atwood, M.E. 170
Aylwin, S. x, xiii, 7, 151–2, 247–65

Baddeley, A.D. x, xiii; amnesia
354–5; 'central executive' 103,
118, 132, 140; masking 94;
'recollection' 90, 99; working
memory 78, 83, 86, 90, 94,
103–25, 152
Bailes, S.M. 138
Bailey, D. 240–1
Baird, J. 31, 32
Bandura, A. 248
Barakat, M.K. 180

Barber, T.X. 4, 31
Barrett, J. 308, 362–3, 367
Barry, C. 360–1, 363
Barsalou, L.W. 161
Barthes, R. 234–5
Bartlett, F.C. 5, 6, 8, 274
Battersby, W.S. 334–5
Baxter, D.M. 343, 348
Baylor, G.W. 189
Beck, A.T. 248, 271–6, 278, 280,
291, 297
Bee, H.L. 142
Begg, I. 165
Bekerian, D.A. 18, 274
Beloff, H. 226
Bengtsson, G. 187
Benson, A.J. 119
Berger, J. 236
Berkowitz, L. 298
Berla, E.P. 141–2
Berlyne, D.E. 170, 189
Berti, A. 333, 335, 349
Besner, D. 121
Betts, G.H. 284
Biederman, I. 47–8
Biederman, J. 160
Bisiach, E. 333–5, 337–9, 344–6, 349
Bliss, T.V.P. 23
Bobrow, D.G. 8
Bolton, N. 186
Bottrell, J. 281
Boulougouris, J.G. 281
Bousfield, W.A. 159

373

Subject index